RESEARCHING SOCIAL LIFE

RESEARCHING SOCIAL LIFE

SECOND EDITION

edited by
NIGEL GILBERT

SAGE Publications
London • Thousand Oaks • New Delhi

Introduction, Chapter 2, Chapter 21 and editorial arrangement
© Nigel Gilbert, 2001
Chapter 1 © Geoff Cooper, 2001
Chapter 3 © Alan Clarke, 2001
Chapter 4 © Martin Bulmer, 2001
Chapter 5 and Chapter 16 © Sara Arber, 2001
Chapter 6 © Rosemarie Simmons, 2001
Chapter 7 and Chapter 15 © Mike Procter, 2001
Chapter 8 © Nigel Fielding and Hilary Thomas, 2001
Chapter 9 © Nigel Fielding, 2001
Chapter 10 © Ann Cronin, 2001
Chapter 11 © Kate Burningham and Diana Thrush, 2001
Chapter 12 © Keith Macdonald, 2001
Chapter 13 © Martin Innes, 2001
Chapter 14 © Jane Fielding, 2001
Chapter 17 © Jay Ginn, 2001
Chapter 18 © Ann Lewins, 2001
Chapter 19 © Robin Wooffitt, 2001
Chapter 20 © Victoria D. Alexander, 2001

First published 2001. Reprinted 2001, 2002

SAGE Publications Ltd
6 Bonhill Street
London EC2A 4PU

SAGE Publications Inc
2455 Teller Road
Thousand Oaks, California 91320

SAGE Publications India Pvt Ltd
32, M-Block Market
Greater Kailash – I
New Delhi 110 048

British Library Cataloguing in Publication data

A catalogue record for this book is available from
the British Library.

ISBN 0 7619 7244 7
ISBN 0 7619 7245 5 (pbk)

Library of Congress catalog card number 2001-131807

Typeset by Photoprint, Torquay, Devon
Printed in Great Britain by The Cromwell Press Ltd,
Trowbridge, Wiltshire

Contents

ACKNOWLEDGEMENTS

We are very grateful to Karen Phillips and Stephen Barr of Sage for their encouragement during the preparation of the first and the second editions of this book, and to Agnes McGill, Jon Gubbay, Geoff Payne and several anonymous reviewers who read and commented on the first edition while it was in draft.

The authors and publishers wish to thank the American Sociological Review for permission to use copyright material from J.M. McPherson and L. Smith-Lovin (1986) 'Sex segregation in voluntary associations', *American Sociological Review*, 51: 61–79.

CONTRIBUTORS

Victoria D. Alexander is lecturer in Sociology at the University of Surrey. She has studied the funding of art museums, the training of painters, governmental policy on culture, the portrayal of children in advertisements, the use of information technology by museums, the art and culture marketplace, and visual sociology. She is author of *Museums and Money: The Impact of Funding on Exhibitions, Scholarship, and Management* (Indiana University Press, 1996) and *The Sociology of Art* (Blackwell, 2002).

Sara Arber is Professor and Head of the Department of Sociology at the University of Surrey. She is Co-Director of the Centre for Research on Ageing and Gender (CRAG), and President of the British Sociological Association, 1999–2001. She is co-author with Claudine Attias-Donfut of *The Myth of Generational Conflict: Family and State in Ageing Societies* (Routledge, 2000), and co-author with Jay Ginn of *Gender and Later Life* (Sage, 1991) and *Connecting Gender and Ageing* (Open University Press, 1995). The latter won the Age Concern prize for the best book on ageing in 1996. Her current research includes studies of inequalities in health, ageing and a UK/US comparative study of doctors' decision-making about older patients.

Martin Bulmer is Professor of Sociology at the University of Surrey, and Director of the ESRC Social Survey Question Bank, a WWW resource for social scientists and social researchers (URL: http://qb.soc.surrey.ac.uk). He has been teaching social research methods since 1970. He is a director of the Institute of Social Research in the Department of Sociology, editor of the international journal *Ethnic and Racial Studies*, and a member of the editorial board of the *American Behavioral Scientist*. His most recent books are *The Directory of Social Research Organisations in the UK*, Second Edition (with W. Sykes and J. Moorhouse, Continuum, 1999) and the Oxford reader on *Racism* (edited with John Solomos, Oxford University Press, 1999).

Kate Burningham is lecturer in Sociology of the Environment in the Department of Sociology and the Centre for Environmental Strategy (CES) at the University of Surrey. Her research interests focus on the social construction of environmental problems, local environmental disputes and the relationship between social and environmental disadvantage. She is currently completing a project for the Joseph Rowntree Foundation, exploring the environmental concerns of disadvantaged groups, and is writing a textbook on Sociology of the Environment.

Alan Clarke is a senior lecturer in Sociology. His main research interests are in the field of crime and the criminal justice system. He has undertaken research into the fear of crime, drugs throughcare for offenders serving custodial sentences, crime, deprivation and unemployment, and mentoring programmes for youth at risk of offending. He has published articles in a number of academic journals and is the author of *Evaluation Research: an Introduction to Principles, Methods and Practice* (Sage, 1999) and a co-editor of *The Economic Dimensions of Crime* (Macmillan, 2000).

Geoff Cooper is a senior lecturer in Sociology at the University of Surrey. He teaches courses on theoretical and conceptual issues in social science. His main research interests are in science and technology studies and social theory, and he is currently leading a project on the social dimensions of mobile telecommunications.

Ann Cronin is a lecturer in Sociology at the University of Surrey. She teaches social theory, the sociology of work and economic life and gender studies. She also runs a day course on Focus Groups. Her main research interests are gender and the social construction of sexual identities, the sociology of story telling and sociological theory.

Jane Fielding is a lecturer in Quantitative Methods in the Department of Sociology at the University of Surrey. She teaches introductory statistics and the use of the statistical package, SPSS, to both undergraduates and post-graduates. She is co-author with Nigel Gilbert of *Understanding Social Statistics* (Sage, 2000). Her main research interest is the career pathways of female and male science and engineering graduates.

Nigel Fielding is Professor of Sociology and Co-Director of the Institute of Social Research at the University of Surrey. He has taught field methods and criminology at Surrey since 1978. His research interests are in qualitative methods, new research technologies, and criminal justice. He was editor of the *Howard Journal of Criminal Justice* from 1985 to 1998, and is co-editor of the series *New Technologies for Social Research* (Sage). He has published thirteen books and is currently working on the second edition of *Computer Programs for Qualitative Data Analysis* (with E. Weitzman and R. Lee) and a four-volume set on *Interviewing* (both for Sage).

Nigel Gilbert is Professor of Sociology at the University of Surrey. He has written and edited a number of books on research methods for sociologists, including co-authoring *Understanding Social Statistics* with Jane Fielding (Sage, 2000) and *Simulation for the Social Scientist* with Klaus G. Troitzsch (Open University Press, 1999). His main research interests are in the sociology of the environment and the sociology of science. He is co-author with Michael Mulkay of *Opening Pandora's Box: a Sociological Analysis of Scientists' Discourse* (Cambridge University Press, 1984). He is one of the pioneers of the use of computer simulation as a research method in

Sociology, and is editor of the *Journal of Artificial Societies and Social Simulation* (http://www.soc.surrey.ac.uk/JASSS).

Dr Jay Ginn is employed on an ESRC Research Fellowship in the Department of Sociology of the University of Surrey and is a Co-Director of the Centre for Research on Ageing and Gender. She has published widely on gender differences in the economic resources of older people, including international comparisons. She co-authored *Gender and Later Life* (Sage, 1991) and co-edited *Connecting Gender and Ageing* (Open University Press, 1995), both with Sara Arber, and has edited a book with Debra Street and Sara Arber, *Women, Work and Pensions: International Issues and Prospects* (Open University Press, 2001).

Martin Innes is lecturer in Sociology at the University of Surrey. He has taught courses on criminology, social policy and social theory. His research interests are in the fields of policing, crime investigation, contemporary patterns of social control and symbolic interactionist sociology.

Ann Lewins graduated in 1992 from Royal Holloway, University of London with a first in Modern History and Politics. In her role as resource officer for the CAQDAS Networking Project at the University of Surrey, she advises and teaches the use of software for qualitative data analysis. She manages the academic Internet discussion list *qual-software*, and maintains the project web site as a free resource for a worldwide research community.

Keith Macdonald is Visiting Professor in Sociology at the University of Surrey having previously been a senior lecturer there for many years. In the past, he has worked on large-scale research projects at Aston and Edinburgh Universities, but recent work has been documentary and historical studies of professions, especially accountancy and the military. He is author of *The Sociology of the Professions* (Sage, 1995).

Mike Procter was, until recently, a lecturer in the Department of Sociology at the University of Surrey. He helped to set up the MSc in Social Research in 1973 and has taught mainly in the areas of quantitative research methods. His current research is focused on cross-national comparisons of attitudes; in the past he has worked on studies of poverty and on the social psychology of adolescence.

Rosemarie Simmons runs Surrey Social and Market Research (SSMR) Ltd, a company carrying out social research that is linked to the Department of Sociology at the University of Surrey. Her main fields of research have been training, rehabilitation, becoming blind in adult life, the effects of disability on life chances, and adoption. Since setting up SSMR, Rosemarie has been involved in a diverse range of projects, mainly conducted for the public sector. She has contributed to a number of reports, books and journals on the subject of disability, housing and ageing, for example, *Assessing Older*

People's Health and Social Needs by L. Fee, A. Cronin, R. Simmons and S. Choudry, published by the Health Education Agency.

Hilary Thomas is a senior lecturer in Sociology at the University of Surrey. She teaches social research methods and the sociology of health and illness. She is co-editor of *Locating Health: Sociological and Historical Explorations* (Avebury, 1993) and *Private Risks and Public Dangers* (Avebury, 1993). Her main research interests are in the sociology of health and illness, the sociology of the body and time, and the sociology of women's health and reproduction. She is President of the European Society of Health and Medical Sociology and is a member of the QAA Sociology Subject Benchmarking Group.

Diana Thrush has been involved in numerous research projects at the University of Surrey, the most recent of which explored the environmental concerns of disadvantaged groups for the Joseph Rowntree Foundation. Her doctoral thesis evaluated interventions designed to reduce the prevalence of cigarette smoking among schoolchildren and examined the smoking behaviours of nine to thirteen year olds.

Robin Wooffitt is a senior lecturer in Sociology at the University of Surrey. He teaches courses on Conversation Analysis and Discourse Analysis. His publications include *Telling Tales of the Unexpected: the Organisation of Factual Discourse* (1992), *The Language of Youth Subcultures: Social Identity in Action* (with Sue Widdicombe, 1995), *Humans, Computers and Wizards: Conversation Analysis and Human (Simulated) Computer Interaction* (with N. Fraser, N. Gilbert and S. McGlashan, 1998) and *Conversation Analysis: Principles, Practices and Applications* (with Ian Hutchby, 1998).

INTRODUCTION

NIGEL GILBERT

Researching social life is partly about having the right knowledge: for instance, how to design samples, when to take fieldnotes and how to analyse interview data; and partly about practical skills: how to lay out questionnaires, how to get access to historical archives and how to get the cooperation of an interviewee. It is because research is such a mixture that this book includes chapters that touch on philosophy and theory as well as more down-to-earth 'exemplars' that recount the problems and false starts of real research projects.

The book is organised around the idea of the research process – roughly, deciding what you want to find out, finding a setting or a sample, collecting some data, analysing the data and writing up the results. Thus, the book is subdivided into sections, on 'Beginnings', 'Into the Field', 'Back home' and 'Endings'. But as the stories of actual research projects in the three 'exemplar' chapters make clear, the process can be a lot messier than is implied by this image of a steady progression through clear stages.

As a first step, however, it is important to clarify what counts as social research, and, in particular, how it differs from 'fact gathering'. In the first chapter, it is argued that social research has to be embedded within a **theoretical framework** that offers perspectives, methods and a 'tradition'. The final chapter, Chapter 21, returns to these concerns.

Chapter 2 introduces some of the **conceptual tools** that a researcher will need. It is concerned with the link between theory and data – a link that continues to trouble philosophers as well as sociologists. Do data exist 'out there', waiting to be collected by the researcher? Or is what we find influenced or even determined by the theories and the methods we employ to understand the social world? This chapter and most of the following chapters conclude with a project that can be carried out with minimal resources and in a reasonably short time. These projects are important because it is difficult to become a good researcher simply by reading about research; you need to have a go yourself. Every chapter also includes a list of 'Further Reading' which suggests where to look for a deeper or more extended treatment of the issues it covers.

Most social research is relevant to policy, but the relationship between research and **policy** is far from a straightforward one. Researchers need to be aware that their work, no matter how revelatory and thoroughly grounded it may be, will often not be taken up by policy-makers as they might hope. Chapter 3 deals with these issues, considering the complex relationships between social research and social policy and the role of research in the policy-making process.

These first three chapters offer an overview of the research process. The next two chapters are concerned with issues that have to be considered before one starts collecting data: how to get access to data sources and how to select whom to interview or observe. Social research is not always welcomed in all quarters and this means that researchers have to make decisions about whether they conceal what they are doing from some or all of their respondents ('covert' research) or whether they will be open about their objectives but risk being repulsed. And some groups are much more capable of resisting enquiries than others. These questions of research **ethics** are addressed in Chapter 4.

Once access has been gained, it is usually neither practicable nor wise to interview everyone and observe everything. Some kind of sampling of data is needed, regardless of whether the research is survey-based or involves observational or documentary methods. Chapter 5 discusses the standard ways of obtaining **representative samples** and considers whether representativeness is always necessary and appropriate.

Once decisions about access and sampling have been made, it is time to go 'into the field'. Chapters 6 to 10 examine various ways of collecting data. During the 1950s and 1960s, there were great advances in the 'technology' of asking standardised questions to representative samples of respondents. This had the result that the interview survey became the data collection technique most closely associated with social research. Chapter 6 discusses the current state of the art, offering advice about how to construct not just **interview schedules**, but also questions for interviewing over the telephone and questionnaires for surveys sent through the mail. Chapter 7 deals in more detail with one of the trickiest aspects of this style of research: how to measure people's **attitudes**.

Although using structured interviews is a common method of data collection, especially in commercial and policy-related research, less formalised and more qualitative methods are also very important. Chapter 8 is about the kind of **focused interview** that is more like a guided conversation and deals with how to construct an interview guide, how to conduct an interview and how to transcribe a recording. Focused interviewing is often combined with observation of people in their 'natural' settings, a style of research called ethnography. **Ethnography**, as a research technique, emerged from anthropology and Chapter 9 traces this history, considering also the practicalities of ethnographic research and, in particular, some methods of analysis of ethnographic data, since it is at the analysis stage that this style of research presents most difficulties.

Focus groups, already frequently used in market research and in politics, are becoming increasingly popular in social research as an additional means of gathering qualitative data. Chapter 10 describes how to organise a focus group, and how the data it generates can be analysed.

Chapter 10 is followed by the first of three 'Exemplar' chapters, each of which shows how the advice presented elsewhere in the book turns out in practice, in actual research projects. The first describes a project that used focus groups to explore the environmental concerns of disadvantaged people. As is so often the case, methodological ideals foundered in the face of practical difficulties, and the researchers had to be flexible and rethink their methods as they went along.

Not all social research involves asking people questions. Many of the classics of sociology were based solely on **documentary evidence**, the topic of Chapter 12. The documents of interest to social researchers include not only public documents such as official reports and newspapers, but also personal records such as diaries and letters, and some objects which, although they document social life, were never intended as records, for example, statutes, novels, photographs and even buildings.

The second Exemplar, Chapter 13, shows how investigating documentary records and evaluating the status of sometimes conflicting evidence is not only the concern of social researchers, but is also fundamental to police work. The chapter describes a project that studied police murder investigations. It shows how the police go about their business of creating evidence for the courts and reflects on the parallels between their methods and the methods that researchers use.

Whether one has chosen a survey, an interview, observation, or documentary sources for one's data, the result is all too often a mass of material, too great in quantity to be analysed unless one is prepared and able to be systematic. The management of quantitative data has been revolutionised by the computer, and computers are now also beginning to be used to assist in handling qualitative data, such as interview transcripts. Chapter 14 discusses the **management and coding** of both types, explaining the technology and the options available. Once you have got quantitative data sets on to a computer, programs can be used to prepare tables and frequency distributions. This is illustrated in Chapter 15, which uses an example to illustrate the steps you need to go through to do simple **analyses of survey data** using the most widely used computer package, SPSS.

You do not necessarily have to collect survey data yourself to do quantitative research. Government departments, research companies and academic social researchers often deposit their data sets as computer files in national archives, from which copies can be obtained for further analysis. This is 'secondary analysis', which is fast becoming one of the most important forms of social research. It opens up quantitative research to those who do not have the considerable resources needed to carry out a large-scale survey. As Chapter 16 notes, **secondary analysis** demands some skills not needed for other forms of social research, including being able to devise ways of testing hypotheses against data originally collected for other purposes. The kinds of difficulty that this raises and the ways that they can be overcome are illustrated in Chapter 17. This Exemplar describes a project based on secondary analysis that examined the effect of the government introducing a wider choice of pension arrangements for women. It traces through the stages of analysis using a dataset derived from a large government survey.

The next three chapters illustrate approaches to analysing qualitative data such as interview transcripts and audio and video recordings. Chapter 18 describes the computer programs that have been developed over the last few years to help with the **analysis of qualitative data**. While it used to be the case that only quantitative data was processed by computer, it is becoming increasingly common to use these programs to assist with analysing interview transcripts and field notes. The chapter examines what these programs have to offer and how they can help.

Chapter 19 suggests one way, based on the framework of **discourse analysis**, to analyse interview data. It uses as an example an extract from a taped interview with a 'punk', in which the punk provides an account of a violent incident. The analysis shows how the account is organised to indicate the innocence of the punks and the provocative nature of police action. Chapter 20 shows how some of the same ideas and methods can also be applied to the **analysis of visual materials**, although analysing the visual also introduces some challenges of its own.

Research only becomes effective when it is written down and published for researchers, policy-makers and others to use and to criticise. The final chapter of the book is about **writing** about one's research. It examines the format of a typical research article and explains some of the historical background to publication conventions in the social sciences.

The coverage and treatment of topics in this book is based on the course taught in the Department of Sociology at the University of Surrey for first- and second-year undergraduates. The contributors are all lecturers and researchers in the Department and not only have had experience in carrying out research in the ways they describe, but also of teaching it, both to undergraduates and to graduate students. The book has been much influenced by feedback from many generations of students, a surprising number of whom have gone on to become social researchers themselves. We hope that you, like our students, will find that the skills of social research can be used both to help in understanding our society better and to support work in many professions and careers.

CONCEPTUALISING SOCIAL LIFE

1

GEOFF COOPER

CONTENTS

Good social research involves more than the identification of a worthwhile topic and the selection and competent use of an appropriate method, vital though these are. This chapter looks at the way in which research is inevitably framed by conceptual and theoretical considerations and shows how such frameworks, properly handled, can enrich and enhance the research.

In one sense, it is not a question of choosing whether to ignore or attend to these issues, since theory *will* be present in the research; but it may be present in the form of unrecognised assumptions that shape what is done in an uncontrolled manner. The explicit use of concepts and theories is therefore part of good research practice, in that the researcher is more in control of the direction, meaning and implications of his or her work.

However, the point on which I place most emphasis in this chapter is slightly different: that theoretical and conceptual frameworks can inspire fresh ways of looking at the social world, and suggest new angles of approach or lines of enquiry. The significance or purpose of particular frameworks may differ. They may, for example, provide a critical view of some feature of society; or they may show us that familiar and apparently unremarkable features of everyday life can in fact be seen as rather strange. What they share is the capacity to re-conceptualise the social world, and thereby to stimulate us to ask new questions of it.

Terminology can be rather slippery in this area. In particular, as the following section indicates, 'theory' can be used in a number of senses. Chapter 2 discusses the use of theory in research, focusing on theory as a specific hypothesis about some phenomenon which can be tested through empirical investigation. This chapter, by contrast, is mainly concerned with theory in the sense of broad frameworks which shape our view of the world.

The chapter is structured as follows. First, the different senses of theory are clarified and we see how different theoretical frameworks, largely derived from the discipline of sociology, can lead us in particular directions and illuminate particular issues. Secondly, we illustrate this with some examples. Thirdly, we consider the relationship between theoretical frameworks, empirical research and society, and indicate that different conceptions of this relationship can have important consequences for our approach. Fourthly, we note two problems that can arise if the relationship between theory and research becomes unbalanced. Finally, it is suggested that attending to the issues discussed in the chapter can provoke us to ask questions not only of the social world, but also of ourselves as researchers, thereby developing a more critical sensitivity.

1.1 THEORIES, CONCEPTS, FRAMEWORKS

'Theory' has become an increasingly difficult term to define with any certainty, since it can refer to quite different things in different contexts. In the natural sciences, it denotes a possible explanation which, crucially, can be tested: thus, in this context and in the most common everyday meaning of the term, a theory is something provisional, tentative and in need of confirmation. In the humanities, literary criticism or history, for example, it can mean something quite different: a style of work which engages with philosophical questions (what is a text? what is history?), sometimes in a formidably abstract manner, often borrowing ideas from other disciplines in order to address them (Culler, 1987).

In sociological work both of these meanings, and others, are found. For example, the term 'social theory' can be used in the latter sense to describe work which engages with philosophical questions, and which is not confined within the boundaries of one discipline (Sica, 1998). 'Sociological theory' –

clearly referring to work within the discipline of sociology, and our main focus here – can be used in the former sense to describe an explanation which takes the form of an assertion that can be tested. However, it can also denote a perspective on the social world that is too general, too broad and too all-encompassing to be confirmed or refuted by empirical research; indeed, the kind of empirical research we choose to do will be profoundly shaped and influenced by the perspective in the first place. Similarly, one cannot compare perspectives by simply checking which one has come up with the right answer about some feature of society, for since each conceptualises society in quite different ways, they are likely to be asking quite different questions. The philosopher Thomas Kuhn (1970) uses the term 'paradigms' to describe these kinds of broad and radically different perspective. They can also be referred to as, for instance, 'theoretical frameworks', 'theoretical perspectives', 'sociological perspectives', or simply 'sociological theories'.

Before we look more closely at these frameworks, it is worth mentioning that there is much more that could be said about the relationship between these very broad conceptions and specific theories that can be tested. For example, some have argued that we should think of the relationship in terms of different levels of theory and, indeed, have suggested that there is at least one more level that comes in between the two (Merton, 1967). We leave this issue to one side in this chapter. One thing we can say is that sociological theories, at whatever level, all share a common general orientation: they focus on the ways in which phenomena (be they institutions, political arrangements, communities, everyday activities, beliefs and attitudes, forms of knowledge, technologies, art, media representations) are socially organised, and they assert that this social organisation has important consequences. However, it is also the case that there are enormous differences between them: for some, 'social organisation' is taken to mean the ways in which people interact, talk and make use of gestures within particular settings; for others, it may mean large-scale structures of domination and subordination which affect the whole society.

There are other kinds of difference. For example, some perspectives are more comprehensive than others in scope, that is in the range of social phenomena they claim to explain, and in the level of detail at which they tend to operate. Confusingly, some even claim that they are not theories at all since they are committed to exploring, without preconceptions, the ways in which people interpret the world (see Rock, 1979, on symbolic interactionism) or the everyday methods by which people routinely achieve social order (see Garfinkel, 1967a, on ethnomethodology), that is, in both cases, to think about the social world on its own terms. These are very important qualifications. Nevertheless, it remains the case that even these approaches have an interest in explaining features of social organisation, and are thus sociological, and have a distinctive orientation, style and conception which can be contrasted with other approaches. The key issue remains the way in which we conceptualise the social world, and it is on the basis of different conceptions or pictures of the world that we can distinguish between different theoretical frameworks.

It should be stressed that these perspectives or paradigms are crucial in shaping the ways in which we *investigate* the world. They highlight particular features of the world as significant, they direct our attention towards certain forms of behaviour and they suggest certain kinds of research question. Some perspectives will have a relatively direct influence on the kinds of research method we use. For example, symbolic interactionism's interest in the ways in which people attribute meaning to the world within particular settings determines that qualitative methods which focus on behaviour in its natural context will be most appropriate (see Chapters 8 and 9). Some perspectives may have a less direct link to method: feminist research, for instance, can equally profitably use statistical methods to examine large-scale structural inequalities, look at the operation of patriarchy in the media via textual analyses of one sort or another, or study social interaction in particular institutional settings by the use of observational methods. The strength of the links between particular perspectives and particular methods, in other words, varies considerably. Nevertheless, each perspective will, at a deeper level, exert a profound influence on the design, orientation and character of the study.

1.2   CONCEPTUALISING SOCIAL LIFE: SOME EXAMPLES

1.2.1 Schools of thought

There are many more perspectives, schools and theoretical approaches than can be listed in the space available, let alone properly explained. (Some observers regard this high level of variation as a problem, others see it as evidence of the discipline's richness. This author tends towards the latter view.) All I want to do here is give a flavour of that variation and illustrate with examples how these different ways of conceptualising the social world bring different facets of social life to our attention and suggest different lines of enquiry.

That said, it is also true that some issues and questions recur throughout more than one perspective, even though they are often envisaged in very different terms. For example, what is the nature of the relationship between the individual and the collective? Is society a structure that limits and constrains the way we act, or rather the sum total of various forms of social interaction in different settings? How do power and inequality operate within society? Is society inherently consensual or riven by conflict? How do the informal rules and norms which seem to govern social life come into being?

On the other hand, we can identify many of the most prominent schools of thought quite easily in terms of the key concepts and issues of concern that set them apart from others. Structural functionalism sees society as a single and unified entity, almost like an organism, and in the main sees its component parts (the family, for example) as being functional for the maintenance of equilibrium. Marxism, by contrast, envisages society as being structured around what it calls a mode of production: it focuses, in particular, on the capitalist mode of production, which is seen as funda-mentally exploitative and unjust. Marxist theory thus places conflict centre stage, and sees its own role as helping to challenge existing arrangements. Likewise feminism sees society as unjust, and seeks to challenge it, but the basis of exploitation here is seen to lie in gender relations, in patriarchy. In both of these cases, theory is closely linked to political movements. Ethnomethodology is interested in how social order is achieved but, unlike structural functionalism, sees this as something which is routinely accom-plished in everyday life by a host of 'methods' – such as knowing when to take a turn in conversation – which are both taken for granted and yet, when properly studied, extraordinarily skilful. By contrast, rational choice theory, to give a final example, seeks to explain social behaviour by positing the individual as a strategic and calculating actor who makes choices according to rational criteria.

It should be noted that the history of the discipline shows that different perspectives come to have a more or less dominant presence at different times. Some may be seen as particularly pertinent to, even influenced by, the prevailing socio-political context. This alerts us to the fact that sociology is very much a part of the society that it sets out to study, as we discuss in section 1.3.

Theoretical perspectives are not always located in schools of thought. Distinctive and sometimes highly influential views of the world may be derived from the work of individual writers, who may be more or less easy to place within a particular school of thought. Let us look at just two examples of such work to illustrate the very different light they cast on the social world.

1.2.2 Erving Goffman

Goffman – sometimes identified as a symbolic interactionist, but thought by many to be too idiosyncratic to be located within any school – studied a wide variety of social phenomena, using a wide variety of approaches. One strand that went through much of his work was an interest in the details of what he called the 'interaction order', that is, the ways we behave in face-to-face interaction with others. Goffman suggests that we continually manage the impression that we make on others, that such things as gesture and gaze are crucially important for monitoring and interpreting the behaviour of others, and that this world of face-to-face interaction is patterned according to subtle but powerful norms and expectations about what is appropriate: a kind of moral order.

In city life, for example, where we are often in close proximity with others (for instance on public transport), we routinely control the direction of our gaze and adopt what Goffman calls 'civil inattention', because direct eye contact may imply certain kinds of direct involvement that are inappropriate. Even the apparently simple business of walking along the street emerges as a delicately structured and complex activity. We continually monitor the gestures and movements of others in order to interpret their behaviour, we recognise certain kinds of behaviour, such as two people in conversation, and take action to avoid walking in between them, and in some cases we have to balance the requirements of communicating with others and making progress. For example, if we see an acquaintance in the distance coming our way, we often feign ignorance until he or she is closer and only then acknowledge his or her presence. This avoids the awkwardness and the physical difficulty of maintaining eye contact and perhaps sustaining a suitable expression on the face, while simultaneously navigating through the pedestrian traffic (Goffman, 1971).

We also have ways of displaying social relationships to others which Goffman calls 'tie-signs'. Holding hands is an obvious one, but in some cases they can become more complicated. Someone on the telephone to a close friend or partner, in the presence of a business colleague, may go to great lengths to keep both parties from feeling left out: talking in a friendly tone into the phone, while simultaneously making gestures of impatience to the other person present is one strategy that is sometimes adopted.

To read Goffman describing how behaviour in public places is patterned can be to recognise features of one's own behaviour but to discover that they are in fact socially organised: they are general properties of social life. We experience a kind of recognition, but the world of everyday social inter-action is transformed and never looks quite the same again. Goffman draws our attention towards the ways in which people are continually controlling and skilfully interpreting the signals they give off to each other, and to the complex tissue of obligations and expectations that we observe, even in our interactions with strangers. He has provided an important resource and source of inspiration for other theoretical and empirical studies, from Heath's work on doctor–patient interaction (Heath, 1986) to Hochschild's (1983) innovative work on the gendered character of 'emotional labour' (work that people are required to do to make their customers feel good).

1.2.3 Michel Foucault

Foucault was not a sociologist, but he has had a good deal of influence within the discipline. (The same could be said of Marx, who is now regarded as one of the key figures in 'classical' sociology.) Often described as a 'post-structuralist', Foucault was interested in explaining how many features of social organisation, which we now take for granted as normal and unremark-able, have come into being. These features include our sense of self, that is, our notions of what is an individual. His work takes the form of historical studies which show that particular, widespread practices can be seen as quite recent inventions. He forces us to ask uncomfortable questions about the way that society operates, the workings of power, and even our own role as social scientists.

One strand that runs throughout many of Foucault's studies is a critical view of the role that certain kinds of knowledge have played in modern western societies. He argues that the 'human sciences', a range of disciplines which turn people into objects of study, have played a key role in the extension of certain kinds of power. Let us look at just one example. In *Discipline and Punish* (1977), Foucault suggests that the widespread assumption that we are now more compassionate and lenient in our treatment and punishment of criminals is misleading. As with much of his work, he attempts to turn such an assumption on its head. We may not be so visibly cruel as before, may no longer have public torture or executions, but we monitor, regulate and control behaviour with a thoroughness that could not have been dreamed of in former times, both within prisons and in the wider population. Foucault suggests that the human sciences have been central to this process. They urge that we have to 'really understand' people, and must therefore study them more closely, and they define what is normal and what is abnormal behaviour, which then provides a basis for judgements of various kinds. Moreover, they have often done so with the very best of intentions, for instance playing a key role in prison reform. However, the effect has been to extend power throughout society to the point where surveillance of many different kinds, by institutions *and* fellow citizens, is a taken-for-granted feature of daily life.

Foucault gives us a very uncomfortable and in many ways gloomy picture of modern western societies. Like any account, it is one which can be questioned, but its value is as a form of criticism. Foucault shows us the extent to which our society is organised and regulated according to ideas about what is normal (whether we are talking of intelligence, physical development, social behaviour or whatever). He fosters a sceptical attitude towards many different forms of expertise and claims to authority, and suggests that we should not assume that the good intentions of particular institutions will guarantee good outcomes. In so doing he opens up new avenues of enquiry.

1.3 CONNECTIONS BETWEEN THEORY, RESEARCH AND SOCIETY

The reader should now have some idea of how sociological theory can be used to construct distinctive views of the social world, views which suggest certain questions, issues and problems that might be explored or pursued through empirical research. The relative usefulness of these views will depend on the general area in which research is to be done, and the kinds of issue that are of interest. Further questions then arise about the nature of the links between theory, research and society.

The following chapter deals with the important issues of how exactly theory should be incorporated into the research process, and at what stage in the research it should be employed. However, there is more to the relationship between theory, research and society than this. Indeed, there is a danger that focusing exclusively on how theory connects to research and research methods can reinforce a particular picture of sociological work which is, in important respects, misleading. This picture is one in which the sociologist occupies a vantage point which is quite separate from the object of study (society or some aspect of it), and from which it can be clearly viewed. To extend the metaphor, he or she merely has to select some interesting theoretical spectacles, and perhaps some appropriate measurement devices from the available tool kit of methods, before proceeding to analyse the phenomena of interest from this position of detachment. The sociologist, according to this view, is quite disengaged from society, and the problems that arise in attempting to study it are simply technical ones (about such matters as choice and correct use of methods). In fact, however, the relationship between sociologist (whether theorist or researcher) and society is more complicated, more contentious and more interesting than this picture suggests. Indeed, some have argued that the existence and prevalence of this picture is itself the product of particular pernicious currents within modern western societies, as we shall see in the next section.

A key issue that needs to be considered in this respect is the obvious fact that sociologists are not the only people to construct theories about society. There are, of course, many different disciplines which can validly claim that this is an important part of their work, but even more importantly, coming up with theories about society is an important part of everyday life and a recurrent feature of everyday talk. These lay theories can take many forms: they may be explicit, as in statements about the relationship between poverty and crime; they may be visible in the form of the assumptions that underlie particular statements, for example about whether one society is more modern than another; or they may be implicit in jokes and clichés such as 'It's a fair cop but society is to blame', which suggests a very specific relation between individual and society. The point here is that people studying society professionally do not have a monopoly on theories about society.

This raises the issue of the relationship between, and the relative importance of everyday theories and 'professional', that is social scientific, theories. There are different approaches to this but I will briefly sketch out two that, though different, take the issue very seriously. Ethnomethodologists take the line that the world is already so full of theories that the last thing that is needed is for social scientists to add more: what is needed is a shift of emphasis and focus (see, for example, Sacks, 1963). Furthermore, they argue that too much sociology has set about constructing its own theory without critically examining the significance of the fact that much of this is derived from common-sense notions (Zimmerman and Pollner, 1973). In so far as ethnomethodologists are interested in theories at all – much of their work being focused on what people do and how they do it, rather than what they believe – it is in everyday theories as *topics* of investigation, as things that can be studied in their own right. They are vehemently opposed to the idea that social science, by virtue of its professional status, can construct allegedly superior theories which can then be the basis for criticism of 'mere' common-sense theory.

Although Pierre Bourdieu shares with ethnomethodology an interest in the understanding of the patterns and forms of everyday activities, his approach to this question is, in one respect at least, quite different. Following, among others, the philosopher of science Bachelard (1984), he argues that a true science is one which makes a radical break with common sense, and that this is the goal to which sociology should aspire (Bourdieu, 1991). Thus, when sociology has reached this level, it is legitimate to take a critical attitude towards everyday beliefs and attitudes, to say that they are mistaken, and to explain which particular social forces are responsible for this state of *illusio*.

To summarise, in the first case the recommendation is that we shift focus and avoid accidentally incorporating everyday beliefs into our work and trying to construct superior theories. In the second, we are urged to improve the quality of our theories (by following a number of principles of good practice) until we can claim that we have managed to break away from the limitations of common sense into true science, from which position we can engage in criticism. In both, there is a recognition of the extent to which sociology is embedded within society, and therefore of the need to think clearly about the consequences of this.

There are other positions that have been taken on this question of course, including ignoring the whole wretched business altogether! However, these two approaches illustrate, albeit in a rather paradoxical way in one case, the value of a distinctive conceptualisation of the world to be studied: for the very closeness of this world, the fact that we cannot assume that we have a clear and detached view of it, alerts us to one important function of a theoretical perspective. It can help us see the social world afresh; it can help us conceptualise it in new ways, even when dealing with things that may be all too familiar to us (as we saw with the example of Goffman). Other things can do this too, notably art. Just as with art's sometimes shocking representations of the world we inhabit, these new views may become commonplace as they are incorporated into mainstream culture over time; and this provides part of the force that helps produce new theoretical work. This can provide a stimulus and framework for the further investigation of the world, and can generate new topics, questions and problems.

1.4 TWO PROBLEMS

It will now be clear that theoretical perspectives are not just important as elements of good research practice, but are also of enormous value in inspiring and stimulating us to ask new kinds of question. That said, the incorporation of theory into research is not always straightforward, and the balance between conceptualisation and empirical investigation can easily be lost. Let us briefly look at two different problems which can arise when theoretical dimensions are either neglected or given undue prominence.

1.4.1 Methodolatry

The first problem was famously noted many years ago by C. Wright Mills (1959), but it is arguably even more relevant today given the extensive development and proliferation of social research in recent times (Williams, 2000). It arises when a concern with the techniques and methods of research overwhelms all other considerations. Rorty (2000), in a different context, has used the term 'methodolatry' to describe this kind of approach, in which too much faith is placed in the power of methods, which then become the obsessive focus of attention. There are a number of reasons why this is problematic, some of which have already been touched on. It omits the conceptual and theoretical work which is an indispensable part of research. Moreover questions of method may start to drive the research and, in effect, take the place of theory. Methods may in themselves imply particular conceptions and assumptions about the topic being studied, and the overall design of a research project will certainly do so. For instance, deciding to base a study on interviews of one kind or another, with a particular sample and using particular methods of analysis, may imply all sorts of things such as the significance of people's views for understanding the topic, the relative importance of different groups in this respect, the assumed correspondence between what they do and what they say, to name but a few. Perhaps more fundamentally, to neglect theory is to miss out on a vital resource for enriching the research.

To approach this in a slightly different way, it can be argued not only that the purely technical approach of 'methodolatry' is mistaken, but that it is itself an expression of social forces. Adorno, for example, argued that obsessive focus on method was 'truly a symptom of the consciousness of our times' and that it was 'closely related to the general tendency to substitute means for ends' (Adorno and Goldmann, 1977: 129). In other words, we become too focused on the most effective and efficient ways of doing things, and lose sight of why we are doing them. Ironically, a purely technical view of research can be seen as a manifestation of the social reality that it sets out to describe. Note that Adorno's comment, whatever we may think of it, shows that theory has another role to play: it can be invaluable in reflecting on the research process itself. We return to this below.

1.4.2 Theoretical arrogance

At the other end of the scale is the problem of theoretical arrogance. By this we do not mean that theorists are arrogant – an empirical question! – but that theory can overwhelm other considerations. There are at least two aspects to this. The first, again noted by Wright Mills, occurs where empirical work is neglected and theory becomes an end in itself. The second is of more significance to the would-be social researcher: here, theory is, in a sense, too powerful, with the result that it prescribes in advance what we are going to find when we start investigating. The criticism has most often been made in relation to the use of large-scale theories which identify structural forces and conflicts that run throughout the whole of society. In the wrong hands, the use of such theories can reduce research to finding, in particular settings, the evidence for the forces that we already know to exist.

This is a difficult issue. A suspicion of 'totalising' theories has recently been expressed under the broad but unsatisfactory heading of 'postmodernism', and the problem of theoretical arrogance is part of the reason for it. But the problem is not new, and it is not always easy to draw a line between appropriate and over-ambitious uses of theory. Nevertheless, the general principle or rule of thumb is relatively easy to state: good research should always allow for the possibility of surprise. Theoretical or conceptual frameworks have a profound influence on what we choose to study, and on the kinds of question around which the research is designed, but they should not determine in advance the answers.

1.5 QUESTIONING OURSELVES

We have seen that theoretical and conceptual frameworks have the capacity to provide new views of the social world, but we have also indicated that the social world includes the activities of sociology and social research. It therefore follows that conceptual frameworks have further value in helping us to reflect upon our position as researchers and develop a more critical sensitivity towards the activity of social research.

We have already touched on some of these issues. What, for example, is the relationship between 'lay' and 'professional' interpretations of the world? Does one have a higher status than the other? These might be crucial issues to consider if we were carrying out an interview-based study. We might also ask questions more specifically of ourselves as researchers since we are, no matter what professional hat we have on, also members of society. Does our personal identity (thinking of such variables as class, race, gender and age) have some significance for the way people respond to us? Or does our membership of a particular professional community predispose us to see the world in a quite different way from that of our respondents, and thus form a kind of barrier to understanding, one that we must take into account (Bourdieu, 1990)? There are many such questions. What they have in common is a recognition that an adequate conceptualisation of the social world has to include the activity of researching it; the researcher is not simply observing from a position of detachment. This inclusive conceptualisation is sometimes called reflexive enquiry and it can be invaluable for improving the quality of our research.

Reflexive enquiry also has ethical importance in that it prompts us to ask questions about what we are doing as researchers, whether we are justified in doing it, and more generally what our responsibilities and obligations are (see Chapter 4). As noted in section 1.2.3, Foucault's work, for example, argues that the human sciences – those forms of knowledge which turn the human into something to be studied – are a relatively recent and rather peculiar invention, and have played a key role in monitoring, examining and judging the populations of modern western societies. Moreover, he suggests that in many cases they have done so with the very best of intentions. This should make us, at the very least, pause for thought before setting out to do more research, particularly in a society in which more and more research is being carried out, to the extent that one might legitimately characterise it as a research society. Reflection upon such issues, and subsequent consideration of the different ways in which our research might be designed, carried out and used, are vital to responsible, sensitive and critical research.

Just as there is no separate vantage point from which to view and describe society, so there is no neutral space from which to describe theoretical and conceptual issues. Any text setting out to describe a range of theories will do so from some position or another, one which sees others from a particular perspective and defines the key issues accordingly. This chapter might be said to have been written from a pragmatist perspective (see Rorty, 2000), since it has stressed the usefulness of frameworks for helping us see the world in new ways and has avoided discussion of, for example, whether some more accurately represent the world than others. Other accounts will have a quite different emphasis.

1.6   SUMMARY

This chapter has argued that theoretical and conceptual issues are indispensable features of social research, and can enrich it in a number of ways. Research is impoverished if these issues are neglected or, conversely, if they are given too much prominence. But more simply, theoretical frameworks are valuable in that they also provide us with new and different conceptualisations of the social world, inspiring us to see it in new ways and ask different questions of it, and of ourselves as social researchers.

1.7   FURTHER READING

For general introductions to sociology, Lemert (1997) and Bauman (1990) are both accessible and critical; Lemert is particularly good on the 'political' dimensions of sociology in terms of who is included and excluded. Wright Mills's classic introduction (1959) is addressed to a different era, but contains much that is still pertinent.

On theoretical perspectives, two excellent starting points are Cuff, Sharrock and Francis (1998) and Stones (1998). In the former in particular, feminist work is under-represented. For a diagnosis of this situation, and an attempt to remedy it, see Abbott and Wallace (1997). Finally, Jenks (1998) is an unusual and very useful collection which provides reliable introductions to many of the key issues and arguments in sociology.

Research, Theory and Method

2

Nigel Gilbert

Contents

In the previous chapter, it was suggested that theory is a vital part of social research, and that good social research depends on sociological understanding and sociological discovery requires good social research. In this chapter, we shall look more closely at the relationship between theory and data and at how the methodological tools that are described in the rest of the book fit into the research process.

2.1 Three ingredients of social research

There are three major ingredients in social research: the construction of theory, the collection of data and, no less important, the design of methods for gathering data. All of them have to be right if the research is to yield interesting results.

We can see these three ingredients in most accounts of good research. Goffman (1959, 1961), for example, spent much of his career exploring the social world of organisations. He writes about hotels, schools, prisons and hospitals. But what is *theoretically* interesting about such places? As a sociologist, his concern is with one of the fundamental problems of sociology, how social relationships are coordinated and regulated. He notes that in many 'establishments', there are common features in the ways employees present themselves to the 'customers' and that this presentation is not just an issue for the individual employee; it is a collective effort. He uses an analogy based on the theatre. In a theatre, a performance is given on stage, but the activity out front is only possible because of the efforts of those who work backstage. In the same way, Goffman argues, the perform- ance of hotel porters, prison officers, mental hospital orderlies and so on relies on the support of other members of the staff.

> For example, in a medical hospital the two staff internists may require the intern, as part of his training, to run through a patient's chart, giving an opinion about each recorded item. He may not appreciate that his show of relative ignorance comes in part from the staff studying up on the chart the night before; he is quite unlikely to appreciate that this impression is doubly ensured by the local team's tacit agreement allotting the work-up of half the chart to one staff person, the other half to the second staff person. (Goffman, 1959: 83)

Goffman's theories about the presentation of self in organisations are intended to be applied across many social settings, indeed, to all 'establish- ments'. That is, his work is not just about the behaviour of people at the Ritz hotel or in Nether Poppleton Mental Hospital, but about these places and all similar ones. Of course, he could be wrong, but, like a good theorist, he sticks his neck out and asserts that he has found something that is to be found in all 'establishments'. There will be more to say about testing such generalisations later, but for the moment it is important to notice that it is a sign of good research that it concerns itself with regularities which transcend the specifics of time or place.

The second ingredient of social research is the collection of data. Theories ought to be firmly based on data if they are to be useful in understanding the social world. What does Goffman do? As the quotation above illustrates, Goffman does provide data to test his theory, much of it splendidly unexpected. He uses data from his own meticulous observations obtained during periods of study of life in institutions, and he uses data from other people's observations, including from novels and even etiquette books.

Which brings us to the third ingredient: the design of methods of data collection which accurately report on the social world. One of the problems with Goffman's work is that, although the data are vividly described, the methods he used to gather his data and to select his examples are not very clearly or explicitly explained. As a consequence, it is hard to be sure that his observations are typical. A second example, concerning crime statistics, will show the importance of understanding what a method of data collection involves.

Crime statistics seem to show that working-class youth commit more crime than middle-class youth (e.g. see the review in Braithwaite, 1981). A generation of sociologists tried to devise and test theories to explain this observation (e.g. Cloward and Ohlin, 1960; Quinney and Wilderman, 1977; Schur, 1971). Some suggested that working-class youth had more opportunity to commit crime and therefore succumbed more often. Others proposed they had fewer opportunities to pursue success and riches through legitimate channels and so were forced to turn to crime. Yet others argued that working-class and middle-class youth were located in different sub-cultures with different norms and that the working-class sub-culture permitted or even encouraged law-breaking.

These different explanations assumed that the official crime statistics were correct. Increasingly, however, criticisms of these statistics accumulated. For example, the basis of the statistics is 'crimes known to the police'. And the police only know about crimes that they themselves have spotted or which are reported to them by the victims. If the police patrol working-class areas more than middle-class areas (a reasonable strategy if the statistics show more crimes among working-class youth), they will tend to notice more crime in working-class areas. They will also find it easier to apprehend working-class youth for criminal acts. It was thought that one way around these biases in criminal statistics is to interview a sample of young people and ask them, in confidence, whether they have themselves been involved in any crimes. Interestingly, the rate of self-reported crime shows little difference between middle-class and working-class young people (e.g. Short and Nye, 1958). Chapter 8 discusses crime statistics and the collection of such self-report data in more detail.

These criticisms of official statistics and the results of self-report surveys presented sociologists with a new set of data and suggested a quite different sociological problem: why working-class youth are *convicted* of crime more often than middle-class youth. Theories began to be proposed which focused not so much on 'criminal' activities, but on the activities of the police and their role in apprehending youth (e.g. Pearson, 1983). Thus new methods of data collection produced new data and new theories.

There are two alternative conclusions that we could draw from this example. One is that there is one right way of looking at the social world and that social research strives to find this way. If we find that crime statistics offer a biased view, other, more valid methods of data collection must be found to get us closer to the truth. Empirical reality is treated as the privileged source of our theoretical understanding of the social world. In its starkest form, this is the position known as **empiricism**. The alternative position denies that one can ever read off theories from observations of the social world. What we as social researchers see as 'empirical reality' is a consequence of the theories which we bring to bear in organising our understanding of it. In short, theories are treated as the privileged source of our understanding of empirical reality. For example, we might conclude that attempts to discover the 'real' or 'true' crime rates among working- and middle-class youth will never be finally successful: different theories suggest different definitions of 'crime rate'.

2.2 CONSTRUCTING THEORIES

But what exactly is a theory?

A theory highlights and explains something that one would otherwise not see, or would find puzzling. Often, it is an answer to a 'Why?' question. For example, why does the sun shine?; why are some people poor and others rich?; why are so many people unemployed in western capitalist societies?; and so on. Thus, one characteristic of a theory is that it can be used as an explanation.

Suppose that someone proposed a theory of unemployment – that the rate of unemployment depends on current interest rates, for example. Then the theory could be offered as a reasonable (if partial) answer to a question about why there are now so many people unemployed: interest rates are high. Of course, we might want to know quite a lot more than this in answer to the 'Why?' question. It would be interesting to know just what the mechanism connecting interest rates and unemployment rates is supposed to be, what counts as a 'high' interest rate, and whether there is anything that could be done to reduce interest rates and thus rates of unemployment. Nevertheless, the theory that interest rates and unemployment are connected does offer a solution to what would otherwise be a puzzle and is not obvious from straightforward common sense, both characteristics of good theory.

As well as providing explanations, theories often provide predictions. For example, if the interest rate was dropping, and the theory is correct, it would be possible to predict that the unemployment rate would also fall.

One of the most famous sociological theories is Durkheim's theory of suicide. Individual acts of suicide are almost always puzzling. Often the first thing families and friends ask after a suicide is, why did he or she do it? But as Durkheim ([1897] 1952) observed, suicide is also puzzling on a wider, societal level. Overall suicide rates in different communities and countries vary widely, yet within any one community they tend to be fairly constant from one year to the next (see Table 2.1). Why is there such variation between the rates in different communities?

Statistics about the suicide rates in particular countries are available from the World Health Organization. There has been a considerable amount of research on how such suicide rate statistics are constructed and what they mean (e.g. Atkinson, 1978). This work indicates that there is no simple relationship between official statistics on suicide and a 'real' rate of suicide;

Table 2.1   *Suicide rates in selected countries*

Country	Male	Female
Bahamas	2.2	0
Greece	5.7	1.2
United Kingdom	11.0	3.2
Spain	12.5	3.7
Italy	12.7	4.0
United States	19.3	4.4
Sweden	20.0	8.5
Denmark	24.3	9.8
Austria	30.0	10.0
France	30.4	10.8
Finland	38.7	10.7
Sri Lanka	44.7	16.6
Hungary	49.2	15.6

Mortality rates per 100,000 population for suicide and self-inflicted injury for 1999 (or the latest year for which statistics are available).
Source: WHO (2000) at http://www.who.int/mental_health/Suicide/suicide_rates.html

indeed, just like crime statistics, the research raises deep questions about the process of labelling certain deaths as 'suicides'. However, again just like crime statistics, the statistics themselves, however they may be constructed, are social facts which warrant sociological investigation. Hungary, for example, has a very high suicide rate compared with other European countries. Hungary has also been experiencing rapid economic growth and a major change in cultural and political values since the break-up of the Communist bloc. We might guess that Hungary's high official suicide rate is caused in some way by these rapid social, cultural and economic changes. This statement certainly answers a 'Why?' question. But as a theory, it is still lacking.

One problem is that, as it stands, it refers only to Hungary. A statement relating to a single case, such as Hungary, would not normally be considered to be a theory. A theory needs to be able to cover a range of settings. But we could look for other countries also experiencing rapid socio-economic changes and see whether they too have high suicide rates. If we found several such countries, we would have a more impressive theory and one that represents a general pattern or 'regularity'.

For example, Sri Lanka has also been subject to major disturbances in the last few years and its suicide rate is also very high (see Table 2.1). Indeed, after some thought and some delving into suicide statistics, one might suppose that 'the rate of suicide increases in times of economic collapse or boom, or generally when there is rapid social and economic change', a conclusion which Durkheim also proposed and which he explained using the concept of anomie. Anomic suicide, according to Durkheim, results when society's regulation of the individual through normative controls breaks down and this is likely to happen where there is social and economic instability.

2.2.1 Induction and deduction

The process that we have just worked through, of finding a single case and observing a relationship, then observing the same relationship in several more cases and finally constructing a general theory to cover all the cases, is known as **induction**. It is the basic technique for moving from a set of observations to a theory and is at the heart of sociological theory construction. This is illustrated in Figure 2.1.

Once a theory has been formulated, it can be used to explain. For example, the theory about suicide rates being high in countries with high rates of social and economic change can be used to explain why the Russian Federation has a high suicide rate (the rates for the Russian Federation are 72.9 for males and 13.7 for females). This process, starting with a theory and using it to explain particular observations, is known as **deduction** (see Figure 2.2). Deduction takes the data about a particular case and applies the general theory in order to deduce an explanation for the data. Thus induction

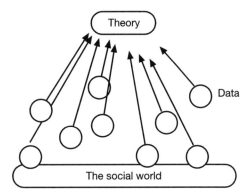

Figure 2.1   *Theory construction by induction*

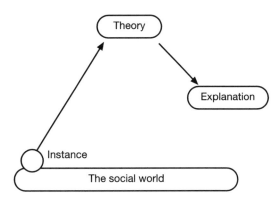

Figure 2.2   *Theory use by deduction*

is the technique for generating theories and deduction is the technique for applying them.

For the sake of defining the terms, we have discussed induction and deduction as though they are quite distinct. Logically, that is true. But in the course of doing research they often get intertwined. First, one has an idea for a theory, perhaps by contemplating the common features of a set of cases and inducing a theory. Then one checks it out against some data, using deduction. If the theory doesn't quite fit the facts, induction is used to construct a slightly more complicated, but better theory. And so on.

It is important to realise that *induction is not foolproof.* It is certainly possible to construct erroneous, misleading or over-simple theories by induction. For example, induction has led us straight to the theory that high suicide rates are the product of economic and social change. Unfortunately, this isn't the whole story. Denmark and Finland both have high rates of suicide compared with other industrialised nations, yet neither has experienced great political or economic changes recently.

These counter instances can be put to good use, however. The theory can be extended in scope and deepened in its explanatory power if we look to see what characteristics Denmark and Finland share which might explain their high rates. The answer, as Durkheim discovered from his data, is that economic and social change is only one influence on suicide rates. The degree of integration of the dominant religion is also important and this is the reason, he argues, that Protestant countries, such as Finland, tend to have much higher suicide rates than otherwise similar countries.

2.2.2 Falsification

This leads to another important aspect of theory construction, the strategy of **falsification**: always look for the awkward cases. If we had stuck with the cases that fitted the original theory about the significance of social and economic change, that is, if we had looked no further than Hungary and Sri Lanka, we would not have formulated the wider theory that brought in the religious dimension.

Falsification as a strategy is important for two reasons. First, by directing attention to 'awkward cases' it helps to improve theories. Secondly, it has been argued that it is a useful criterion for what should count as a theory. The criterion is that it must be possible *in principle* to falsify a theory. That is, it must be possible to imagine some data which if found would demolish the theory.

The preceding theory about suicide rates being linked to economic and political change may not be a good theory, but by the criterion of falsification, it is at least a theory. It is possible to imagine some data that would destroy the theory: a single case of a country experiencing great changes but having a low suicide rate would do. But consider the statement, 'People who kill themselves are suicides.' This is *not* a theory. First, the statement is not an answer to a 'Why?' question. Secondly, it is impossible to think of data which would falsify it. In fact, this statement is a definition of suicide, not a theory.

One of the problems of research is that the search for falsifying observations is, in principle, never ending. No matter how much data one collects that fits the theory, it is always possible that a falsifying instance might turn up next. The consequence is that there is an asymmetry about a researcher's confidence in theory: one can be quite sure that a theory is wrong if there are any data which falsify it, but one cannot be sure that a theory is right, because there may yet be some data which will disconfirm it. Scepticism is therefore the right attitude to assertions that this or that theory is correct.

2.3   CONCEPTS AND RELATIONSHIPS

Durkheim writes, in *Suicide*:

> The fact that economic crises have an aggravating effect on the suicide tendency is well known. ... Even fortunate crises, which have the effect of raising a country's prosperity, have an effect on suicide like economic disasters. ... Every disturbance of equilibrium, even though it may involve greater comfort and a raising of the general pace of life, provides an impulse to voluntary death. (Durkheim, trans. in Thompson, 1985: 108–9)

Durkheim is arguing that there is a causal link between economic crises and suicide rates. Crises cause ('have an effect on') suicide. Such causal statements are often shown graphically, with arrows to mean 'cause'. Figure 2.3 illustrates Durkheim's theory in this way.

The diagram in Figure 2.3 can be read as saying that there is a causal relationship between economic conditions (the occurrence or absence of economic crisis) and high or low suicide rates. We call the things in boxes **concepts** and the lines between the boxes **relationships**. Theories are composed of concepts linked by relationships.

In this example about suicide, there are only two concepts and one relationship. But most theories are a lot more complex. Let us turn from suicide to a rather different example, 'gentrification'. Poor housing areas become 'gentrified' when run-down homes occupied by poor people are taken over by the relatively rich. The process of gentrification has been studied in a number of urban research programmes in the USA and the UK (e.g. Ley, 1996; Smith and Williams, 1986) and is interesting because it is

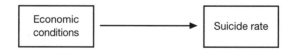

Figure 2.3   *A theory about a cause of high suicide rates*

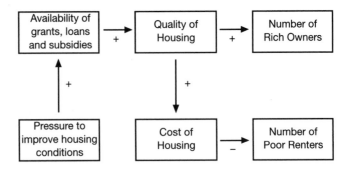

Figure 2.4   *A theory of gentrification*

an example of the unintended consequences of apparently beneficial social policies.

The theory goes like this. Social planners and politicians attempt to improve a poor locality for its residents by providing favourable loans, re-development grants, and so on. The effect is that the overall quality of the area improves. This raises the value of the housing and makes properties not yet improved particularly attractive to developers. The price of housing goes up and with it the rents charged by private landlords. If rents are controlled, landlords take advantage of rising market prices to sell their property. The rise in housing costs pushes the original, poorer residents out and they are replaced by richer owners. The poor neighbourhood has been gentrified, displacing the established residents, often to even poorer housing stock.

Figure 2.4 summarises the theory as a diagram. Each box represents a concept and each line a causal relationship. The causal effect can either be positive or negative. For example, as the quality of the neighbourhood rises, the price of housing also rises – a positive effect. As the price of housing rises, the number of poorer residents falls – a negative effect.

If you wanted to test a theory like this, it would be difficult to do it all at once. It is too complicated; there are too many relationships to consider (although some of the most recent statistical techniques, such as those mentioned at the end of Chapter 15, can help). Instead, it is best to break the theory down into parts, each covering just one relationship. So, one might test the causal relationship between the Quality of Housing and the Cost of Housing and then, separately, the relationship between the Cost of Housing and the Number of Poor Renters. Each such part is known as a **hypothesis** and it is hypotheses that researchers generally test and try to falsify.

2.3.1 Indicators

So far, this chapter has been concentrating almost entirely on theories. It has been argued that theories are things that aim to explain puzzling observa-tions. They are composed of one or more hypotheses, each of which consists of concepts linked by relationships. Theories must be capable of being tested, or falsified. Now we must move on to examine in more detail what is involved in testing a theory.

In order to test a theory, we need to compare the predictions it makes with measurements made of the social world. For example, we need to see whether, as the Quality of Housing increases, so does the Number of Rich Owners, which is what the theory of Figure 2.4 predicts. However, this is more complicated than it seems because concepts cannot be measured directly. Before Quality of Housing can be assessed, one has to have some definition of 'quality' and some means of applying that definition to actual neighbourhoods.

In general, in order to test theories, there must be a way of measuring each concept, that is, for each there must be an **indicator**. An indicator is a method of measurement which aims to measure the concept accurately. If we want to test the hypothesis that the Quality of Housing was related to the value of housing, we would need independent indicators for both these concepts. The value of housing could be measured by averaging the asking price for houses for sale (but there would still be some issues to settle: what is to be counted as a 'house'?; what about a property which has tenants?; what if the price actually paid for property is less than the asking price?; and so on). An indicator for 'Quality of Housing' is more difficult to devise. One indicator that would not be suitable is the value of the housing, for this would then be getting measurement of the two concepts confused. One approach might be to consult a panel of experts, such as estate agents, surveyors or lawyers, and ask them to assess the quality of the housing. Another way would be to conduct an attitude survey of the general public. A third way would be to rely on some more direct measure, such as the average number of months since the exterior woodwork was repainted. Obviously, there is room for debate and for careful thought about the right choice, and factors such as the cost of the research and the speed with which data can be obtained will need to be considered as well.

2.3.2 Validity and reliability

Naturally, researchers want their indicators to be as good as possible. That means that the measurements which they make should be **valid** (accurately measuring the concept) and **reliable** (consistent from one measurement to the next). For instance, suppose that you want to measure people's consumption of alcohol (a concept). You choose to do this using a questionnaire in which you will ask respondents to tell you how much they drank during the last month. In fact, this is not a good indicator of alcohol consumption. People tend to under-report consumption – they say that they drink less than they actually drink – casting doubts on the validity of the indicator. Also, people have difficulty remembering in detail what they were doing as long as a month ago. This means that if you were to ask someone repeatedly over the course of a few days what they had drunk during the previous month, it is quite likely that they would give you different answers, just because they were not remembering consistently. The indicator is not reliable.

In order to know whether an indicator is valid and reliable, we need to understand how it works, that is, the way the indicator measures its concept. Consider a couple of the indicators mentioned in the previous section. Official statistics measure suicide rates in as much as they record the decisions of coroners' courts, bodies which apply procedures laid down in legal statute for assigning causes of death. Coroners, of course, do not have direct access to the cause of death; they themselves use a set of indicators and a body of 'theory' – common sense and legal knowledge – to decide whether a particular death is the result of suicide or some other reason (Atkinson, 1978; Kitsuse and Cicourel, 1963) and this needs to be recognised when we use the indicator. The Quality of Housing in a neighbourhood may be measured by an indicator consisting of the average time since house exteriors were painted because houses in poor condition are rarely repainted, while houses which are in good condition and are being looked after by their owners tend to be repainted regularly, as soon as the paintwork begins to show signs of age.

2.3.3 Measurement theories

As these examples show, the validity and reliability of an indicator will depend on the adequacy of the way in which it measures its concept. One way of thinking about an indicator is that it links a concept (e.g. Quality of Housing) with observable facts (e.g. average time since repainting). The adequacy of this link depends on a theoretical proposition, known as the indicator's **measurement theory**. The measurement theory for the indicator of housing quality is the proposition that 'houses in poor condition are rarely repainted, while houses which are in good condition and are being looked after by their owners tend to be repainted regularly, as soon as the paintwork begins to show signs of age'.

Like any other theory, a measurement theory can, and should, be tested. The more it is tested against data, the more confident one can be in the adequacy of the indicator that relies on that theory. But like all theories, measurement theories can still eventually turn out to be wrong or incomplete. What are the consequences of using an incorrect measurement theory?

One consequence could be that we are led to draw the wrong conclusions when inducing theories from observations. This is what happened in the case mentioned at the beginning of this chapter, that working-class youth seemed to be committing more crime than middle-class youth. The measurement theory implicit in using official crime statistics to measure crime rates (that official statistics validly measure the number of criminal acts committed) turned out to be false. The effect of using the wrong measurement theory was that incorrect theories that attempted to account for a spurious differential crime rate were constructed.

Another consequence of using incorrect measurement theories is that one may falsify correct theories or fail to falsify incorrect theories, because the indicators are not measuring the concepts properly. This has the unfortunate implication that if a theory is apparently not corroborated by the data, we don't know whether this is because the theory is in fact wrong, or whether it is because the measurement theories on which the indicators rely are incorrect. Of course, the solution to this dilemma is to test the measurement theories.

However, this can lead to trouble. As a good researcher, I want to test my hypothesis. I therefore devise some indicators for the concepts in my hypothesis. But before using the indicators, I need to satisfy myself about the adequacy of the indicators. To do this, I need to investigate the measurement theories on which they are based. This will involve devising indicators to test the measurement theories. These indicators will themselves rely on measurement theories. . . . We seem to have embarked on an endless task!

2.4 SOCIAL RESEARCH AS A SOCIAL PROCESS

The answer to this conundrum comes from the fact that research is never conducted without reference to other studies. It can always rely on previous knowledge and previous experience. This means that rather than having to justify every measurement theory, and thus every indicator, researchers can call on other people's work.

Social research, like other scientific work, is situated within a 'paradigm' (Kuhn, 1962), a scientific tradition. The paradigm influences research in several ways. The problems researchers tackle are derived from sociological perspectives which, although in constant flux, have been fashioned through a hundred years of sociological thought. The indicators we use and the measurement theories on which they are based have been honed by many previous researchers through thousands of projects. Instead of having personally to test every measurement theory you use and having to justify every theory you mention, you can rely on standard indicators, standard concepts and standard theories.

Linking new research to the existing paradigm is one of the functions of the 'references' that are sprinkled through journal articles. These references not only acknowledge previous work (saying, in effect, 'the idea I am mentioning is not my own invention, but was previously proposed by someone else'), but also, and more importantly, borrow the authority of earlier research (saying, 'it is not just me who thinks this research method, this hypothesis, etc. is correct, but also the person I am citing'). Chapter 21 discusses the techniques of writing and referencing in more detail.

This is just one example of the way in which we, as sociologists, can examine the social processes that contribute to the construction of socio-logical knowledge. There is no reason to exempt sociology or science in general from investigation by sociologists (Barnes et al., 1996).

Learning about how to do social research is thus not just a matter of becoming proficient at some technical skills, although knowledge of technique is very important. It is also about learning the culture of social science so that you can become a proficient member of the social scientific community.

2.5 CONCLUSION

In this chapter, we have seen that what makes social research different from mere data collection is that it is an activity conducted within a research community. This community provides a body of theory in which the research needs to be located. Sociological theory, like all theory, aims to be explanatory, answering 'Why?' questions. It also aims to be general, offering explanations that transcend the particularities of time, space or personal circumstance.

Theories are generally constructed through induction, extracting the common elements of many specific instances, and are applied to explain other instances by means of the logic of deduction. Theories are made up of hypotheses, individual statements that together relate theoretical concepts.

Theories must be susceptible to falsification, that is, they must be framed in such a way that they can be proved wrong. Testing a theory involves choosing indicators for each of its concepts, using the indicators to collect data, and comparing the data with predictions made from the theory. An indicator should be valid and reliable. This can be determined by examining the measurement theory on which it is based. However, in practice, most researchers most of the time use standard indicators which have been developed and used by other sociologists before them and whose validity is largely unquestioned.

2.6 PROJECT

This chapter has suggested a particular model of social enquiry, one which proposes that social research involves theories, data, indicators and theory testing. In some ways this model can be regarded as itself a theory – a theory about social research. Like any theory, it ought to be capable of being compared with data.

For this project, you should locate in the library a recent issue of one of the major journals in your field. In sociology, this might be one of the *Sociology*, *Sociological Review*, the *British Journal of Sociology*, the *American Sociological Review* or the *American Journal of Sociology*. Find an article in your chosen issue that looks interesting.

Read the article closely to see the way in which the author puts forward his or her argument. Write down, in as few words as you can, the theory being advanced in the article. List the concepts that are used in the theory. For each concept, identify the indicators that the author uses. For each concept and indicator, briefly suggest what the implied measurement theory is.

For some articles, these steps are easy to carry out. In other cases, you may find the theory, the concepts or the indicators hard to pin down. Is this because there is something amiss with the research being reported in the article, or because the model of social enquiry proposed in this chapter does not fit the research in the article you have been examining?

2.7 FURTHER READING

Hughes (1976), Chapters 1 and 2, addresses many of the issues touched on in this chapter in more detail. Stinchcombe (1968) is very good on forms of social theory and how theories are constructed. Blalock (1969) is also good on this, although rather more formal and mathematical.

RESEARCH AND THE POLICY-MAKING PROCESS

3

ALAN CLARKE

Empirical social research, especially when informed by ideas and concepts from sociology, greatly enhances our understanding of the social processes and problems encountered by individuals and groups in society. In this respect social science has an important contribution to make to public debate about contemporary social issues. However, a research study does not have to be deliberately policy-focused for the findings to have relevance for social policy. Indeed, as Finch argues, it is almost impossible for social scientists to engage in research that is not in some way policy-oriented. 'Social scientists are *de facto* part of the social world which we study, and the knowledge which we produce can always potentially be used to some effect; therefore the idea that one can pursue a detached social science which does not engage with public issues is at best naïve' (Finch, 1986: 3).

The social sciences make an important contribution to our understanding of a wide variety of social issues. At a very basic level applied sociology generates 'useful' and 'usable' knowledge on topics that are generally recognised as socially relevant. A great deal of what we know about issues such as the nature and extent of health inequalities, the incidence and causes of family poverty, the impact of racial discrimination and the link between drug misuse and property crimes, comes from the findings of research studies. Given that many of the topics investigated by social researchers are defined by policy-makers as social problems, for which solutions need to be found, it seems reasonable to assume that research evidence will have a positive and direct effect on policy. This would certainly seem to be the case where the very people responsible for developing, formulating and implementing policy solutions are the ones who commissioned the research in the first place. However, just because social research has the potential to produce socially useful knowledge, and applied research is often sponsored by powerful groups who are in a position to shape policy and bring about change, it should not be assumed that the influence of research on policy is necessarily immediate and direct. The relationship between research and policy is much more complex.

As well as developing the practical skills and technical expertise necessary to undertake methodologically sound research, social researchers also need to appreciate the potential their findings and analyses have for influencing social policy debates. In exploring the research–policy relationship, particularly the impact of research on policy, this chapter outlines the characteristic features of applied social research, describes the different models of research utilisation and considers the major models of policy formulation. We begin by distinguishing between basic and applied forms of social research.

3.1   BASIC AND APPLIED RESEARCH

Within the social sciences in general, and sociology in particular, a distinction has always been made between pure or basic research and applied or policy-oriented research. In simple terms, pure research can be described as being discipline-oriented. The aim is to develop a body of general knowledge for the understanding of human social behaviour by means of a combination of empirical enquiry and the application of theory. Constructing, testing and refining theory is what basic or fundamental research is all about. In contrast, applied research is usually defined in practical and instrumental terms. It is not so much concerned with theory-building, as with providing knowledge and information that can be used to illuminate social policy by providing an insight into contemporary social issues.

In sociology, there has always been something of a tension between theoretical work and applied research. Commenting upon the situation in British sociology, Bulmer notes that while the discipline has the potential to make a significant contribution to policy debates, it 'has to an extent held back out of diffidence or fear of being tainted by such contact. A retreat into the comfortable certainties of internal disciplinary debate has often been preferable to engagement with practical policy issues which defy easy solution' (Bulmer, 1993: 26). As Finch (1986) observes, where social scientists have displayed a reluctance to engage in policy-oriented research, it is usually a particular type of policy research they have in mind: namely, research in which the problems and issues to be addressed are not only determined by the policy-makers themselves but reflect the concerns of powerful social groups with vested interests to protect.

Despite the lack of enthusiasm among some sociologists for applied research, there is clear evidence of a growing involvement in policy-oriented work, particularly since the closing decades of the last century. The result is that applied sociology is now an established sub-field of sociology (Smelser, 1994).

The differences between basic and applied research are such that the two types are sometimes viewed as representing two separate social research paradigms. However, as Nas, Prins and Shadid proclaim, despite these differences, basic and applied research can never be totally separated as '(t)here exists much resemblance in research design, theory, methodology and methods and therefore there is much mutual influence' (Nas et al., 1987: 25). This echoes an earlier contribution to the debate by Rossi, Wright and Wright (1978), who acknowledge the fact that both basic and applied social research adhere to the fundamental principles of social scientific investigation, but differ when it comes to what may be termed the 'artful aspects' of their working practices. As they claim, 'the theories, methods and procedures of basic and applied research are quite similar but the *style* of work encountered in each camp is not' (Rossi et al., 1978: 173, emphasis added). Whereas the basic researcher is primarily concerned with developing and testing hypotheses as part of a process of constructing a body of theoretical knowledge, the applied researcher concentrates on the application of theoretical knowledge in conducting empirical research to address specific problems.

In essence then, pure or theoretical work and applied research should not be seen as incompatible: they can be distinguished in terms of purpose. As acknowledged above, basic research is primarily concerned with advancing knowledge through the formulation and testing of theory, whereas applied research is more instrumentally oriented, as displayed by its concern with producing knowledge to inform and direct social change.

3.2 APPLIED SOCIAL RESEARCH

As described in section 3.1 above, there is a difference between basic and applied research. Applied social research is research directed towards practical use. In brief, it 'consists of the application of sociological knowledge and research skills to the acquisition of empirically based knowledge of applied issues' (Rossi and Whyte, 1983: 8). It is also possible to identify different varieties of applied social research.

3.2.1 Types of applied research

While there are many ways of classifying applied social research, Rossi and Whyte (1983) identify three broad types: **descriptive**, **analytical** and **evaluation**.

Descriptive applied social research is the most basic type. This makes extensive use of sample surveys and performs an important 'intelligence and monitoring' function (Bulmer, 1982a: 153). Social surveys provide policy-makers with a wealth of descriptive data covering demographic character-istics, economic factors and social trends. Continuous surveys, such as the General Household Survey (GHS), the Family Expenditure Survey and the British Crime Survey, provide information for those engaged in making policy decisions. For example, data from the GHS can be used to monitor changes in family structure and household composition over time. It is also possible to gain an insight into the changing social and economic circum-stances of specific groups within the population, which may help to identify new areas for policy intervention.

Analytical studies go beyond simple description in their attempt to model empirically the social phenomena under investigation. As Rossi and Whyte (1983) observe, in this respect these studies resemble basic research. However, the difference lies in the kinds of variable on which the analysis focuses. Applied research is defined in terms of intention and not outcome. If the intention is to provide knowledge that policy-makers will find useful, then the variables chosen for analysis will reflect the practical interests of policy-makers and not the theoretical interests of the researcher. Analytical research is problem-oriented and as a form of strategic applied research is 'considerably wider-ranging than intelligence and monitoring. . . . Its pur-pose is to illuminate a problem in such a way as to permit action to be taken to change the situation revealed' (Bulmer, 1982a: 153).

Evaluation research as a type of applied research is characterised by its focus on collecting data to ascertain the effects of some form of planned change. Any policy initiative or social programme is open to evaluation. The primary aim of evaluation research is to determine if a particular policy or intervention is working. The focus of study can be anything from a national policy initiative to a small-scale local programme. For example, social scientists can design studies to assess the impact of government strategies for reducing poverty, or conduct research to evaluate the effectiveness of a crime prevention programme on a local housing estate. Whatever the scale of the research, the idea is that the findings will help policy-makers to decide if a particular policy or programme needs to be extended, modified or replaced.

Thus, evaluation research aims to study the effectiveness with which existing knowledge is used to inform decision-making and guide practical action. This is in contrast to basic research where the emphasis is on discovering new knowledge. Because of its practical orientation, evaluation research can be treated as a specialist area of applied social research. What distinguishes it from other forms of social research is not the methods that are used in the collection and analysis of data, but the purpose to which the methods are put (Babbie, 1995). Those researchers undertaking evaluative studies make full use of the methods, concepts, methodological techniques and theoretical insights provided by the social sciences. They are also committed to the 'rules' of social research (Rossi and Freeman, 1993: 6). However, the primary purpose of evaluation research is to determine the impact or effectiveness of a policy, social programme or other type of planned intervention. According to Bulmer, programme evaluation is 'the most scientistic conception of applied social research, the "hard" end of applied social science' (1982a: 159).

3.2.2 Quantitative and qualitative approaches

A distinction is usually made between two approaches to data collection and analysis: the **quantitative** and the **qualitative**. It is common to find these two approaches presented as representing divergent and opposing research traditions in the social sciences. This situation has been described as positivistic versus interpretative (Giddens, 1976). Emphasis is usually placed on the differences in the philosophical assumptions made about the nature of social reality and the relationship of the researcher to the researched.

According to the positivist tradition, there is an objective, external world that exists independently of human perception, which is amenable to quantitative measurement. The researcher acquires knowledge of this world through following a scientific mode of enquiry similar to that found in the natural sciences. Ultimately the aim is to develop valid and reliable ways of collecting 'facts' about society, which can then be statistically analysed in order to produce explanations about how the social world operates. For example, the social survey provides descriptive documentation of sample populations from which it is possible to make generalisations to the wider population. Furthermore, the social investigator is seen as maintaining an objective stance by using research tools and methodologies, such as questionnaires, experimental research designs and systematic sampling techniques. These serve to safeguard against bias by limiting the amount of personal contact between the researcher and the researched.

It is easy to see why applied social research in the scientific or positivist tradition finds support in policy-making circles. Policy-makers want information to help them to make rational decisions and quantitatively oriented researchers are seen as useful technical experts equipped with the necessary statistical skills to produce precise, objective and scientifically sound analyses of the nature of social problems and the impact and effectiveness of policy solutions.

Qualitative research within the interpretativist tradition is based on a different set of philosophical assumptions concerning the nature of reality and the role of the researcher. First, the positivist notion that there exists a single, objective reality or 'truth', which can be discovered by scientific investigation, is roundly rejected. According to the interpretativist framework, 'truth' is a much more elusive concept. Individuals and groups construct their own version of reality. In short, the social world consists of multiple, subjective realities. Secondly, a central theme in the qualitative perspective is the emphasis placed upon 'naturalism'. In its widest sense naturalism maintains that social phenomena are distinct from physical phenomena in such fundamental ways that they cannot be understood by applying scientific methods and methodologies from the physical sciences. Consequently, the qualitative researcher uses methods such as participant and non-participant observation and non-standardised interviews as a way of getting close to the data and studying social interaction in its natural surroundings. This is in marked contrast to the quantitative approach where the rules of scientific method exhort the researcher to adopt a position of scientific detachment.

When the positivist and interpretativist traditions are described in their pure forms they appear incompatible. The underlying philosophical assumptions are not only different, but they are also mutually exclusive. However, care needs to be taken to separate the debate over two clearly distinct and opposing philosophical stances from the debate about the merits and demerits of quantitative and qualitative research methods and methodologies. As Pawson (1989) notes, contemporary sociological research is essentially pluralistic; researchers often combine quantitative and qualitative research methods within the same study. Mixed-method research strategies are particularly effective in policy-oriented research and the contribution that qualitative research can make to policy evaluation is increasingly being recognised (Doig and Littlewoood, 1992).

Bullock, Little and Millham (1995) identify a number of ways in which quantitative and qualitative approaches can be combined in social policy research. For example, the information provided by qualitative case studies can be used to illustrate, explain and add depth to the findings of quantitative research. Qureshi (1995), in describing a piece of applied social research into the informal care of young adults with learning difficulties and behavioural problems, illustrates how quantitative and qualitative approaches can be linked when it comes to data collection and analysis. Briefly, a large-scale, regional, epidemiological survey was conducted and whenever this identified a young adult with learning difficulties being cared for at home, an interview was sought with the parent responsible for providing the care. The information collected by the survey provided valuable quantitative data on the type and nature of the care received from both statutory and voluntary agencies, and as such was useful to service providers in helping them in the planning and evaluation of future services. Interviews with informal carers were conducted to investigate a number of issues in some detail. Areas that were explored included the problems encountered by parents providing continuing care, parents' reactions to the advice received from the experts, parents' general feelings about the nature and level of support offered by statutory agencies and the type of formal care parents felt would be needed at some future date. Given the sensitive nature of the subject matter, and the need to establish a rapport with interviewees, a qualitative interviewing strategy was employed.

Quantitative and qualitative research procedures are often viewed as providing 'macro' and 'micro' level perspectives on the social world respectively. Quantitative investigation entails adopting a numerical approach to the collection and analysis of data. This usually involves large-scale empirical studies using social survey techniques to collect data from representative samples of the population drawn from a wide geographical area. The aim is to produce useful factual data from which generalisations, often about characteristics of the society as a whole, can be made. In contrast, qualitative research provides a micro-level perspective based on case studies or data collected from individuals and groups. Here the emphasis is on smaller-scale studies exploring the meaning that events and situations have for participants.

Both quantitative and qualitative approaches have an important part to play in policy-relevant research. They can be used to highlight different dimensions of a problem. For example, at the macro-level, a nationwide survey of the victims of crime will provide an estimate of the prevalence and incidence of different types of criminal victimisation and identify those individuals and groups who are most likely to experience victimisation. Quantitative data of this kind can be used to identify those geographical areas and social groups where crime prevention policies need to be targeted. Qualitative case studies of victims of crime can complement the big picture provided by survey data by describing, at the micro-level, the actual impact crime has on the lives of individual victims and their families. This information, along with data on how victims feel about the help and support they receive after the event, is useful to both statutory and voluntary agencies when evaluating current policies and planning future services.

3.3 MODELS OF RESEARCH UTILISATION

Social research has the potential to influence policy decision-making. If social scientists are to improve the contribution that research makes in this respect, then it is essential that they appreciate the different ways in which research findings are utilised. While there are some social scientists who would take exception to the view that they have a direct instrumental role to play in influencing policy by conducting applied research, few would challenge the notion that research findings have the potential to inform policy decision-making. Consequently, social scientists have increasingly turned their attention to the complex phenomenon of research utilisation.

Weiss (1986) argues that before we can comment on the influence that social research has on policy, we need to clarify what we mean by the term 'research utilisation'. A brief survey of the literature reveals that the concept has many meanings (Karapin, 1986). For example, on a general level, a distinction can be made between two broad types of utilisation – 'instrumental' and 'conceptual'. The former applies when there is evidence of policy-makers acting on the findings of specific research studies when amending existing policies and launching new policy initiatives. Conceptual utilisation is said to take place when research influences how policy-makers interpret a social issue or problem. In other words, research can offer an alternative way of viewing a problem and stimulate thinking about possible policy solutions. Thus, it can effectively challenge policy-makers' taken-for-granted assumptions and provide new insights. However, as Weiss notes, 'This kind of conceptual contribution is not easy to see. It is not visible to the naked eye' (1982: 290). Nevertheless, by modifying how policy-makers define and conceptualise a problem, research findings can help shape policy debates, if not directly determine the actual policy choices that are made.

The case of informal carers provides a good example of how research can contribute to policy debates. On a descriptive level, the physical, social, emotional and economic costs of caring for a chronically sick family member have been well documented by numerous studies (Twigg and Atkin, 1994). Thus, policy-makers have a good idea of the kinds of support and assistance carers need. Research from a feminist perspective has done much to highlight the existence of gender inequalities in the provision of informal care and to question the normative assumption, supported by policy-makers, that women are the 'natural' providers of such care. As Finch and Mason (1992) illustrate, the responsibilities and obligations that individual family members feel towards one another are not a fixed and natural property of kinship relations. Furthermore, many people wish to maintain their independence and are therefore reluctant to rely too heavily on their relatives for support. In these circumstances, according to Finch and Mason, 'It makes little sense . . . to build public policies which assume that certain types of assistance will be given more or less automatically' (1992: 179). Thus, feminist researchers have influenced how the debate on informal care has developed by introducing the issue of gender inequality and exploring how kinship obligations operate within families.

A number of different types of model have been advanced to try to explain the utilisation of social research. The four main models to be considered in this section are the knowledge-driven model, the decision-driven or problem-solving model, the political model and the enlightenment model.

The classical **knowledge-driven** model of research use is derived from the natural sciences. It envisages a linear progression from basic research to applied research which, given time, leads to development and, ultimately, application. The underlying assumption is that research produces knowledge that impels action. However, Carol Weiss questions the applicability of this model in the case of social research when she observes that 'Social science knowledge does not readily lend itself to conversion into replicable technologies, either material or social' (Weiss, 1986: 32). Her contention is not that basic research in the social sciences does not have a role to play in policy-making, but that its influence on policy is not in line with the sequence of events described by the knowledge-driven model.

The **decision-driven** or **problem-solving** model can also be described as a linear model. However, in this case it is not the knowledge that is produced by research that promotes practical action, but it is the need to make a policy decision that drives the application of research findings. According to this interpretation of research utilisation, the process begins when policy-makers identify a problem about which they feel something needs to be done. Before they can decide what action to take they need to be fully informed about the nature and extent of the problem. Social research supplies the empirical evidence on which policy-makers can base their decisions.

As Weiss (1986) observes, this model is based on an assumption that policy-makers and social researchers share a common understanding when it comes to defining social problems and recommending appropriate solutions. The relationship between the policy-maker and the researcher is that of customer and contractor. In commissioning a piece of research the policy-maker specifies what the problem is and what information is required. The researcher is then contracted to provide the necessary factual information in order to enable the policy-maker to reach an informed decision. It is deemed essential that the knowledge provided is not only useful for answering policy questions, but is also unbiased. The social scientist is thus cast as 'a supplier of facts – the technician of policy-making' (Finch, 1993: 142). In this problem-solving model 'it is policy rather than theory that disciplines the research' (Booth, 1988: 239). As such, this can be described as a top-down model of policy-making; social scientists trained in the techniques of empirical social enquiry are seen as placing their research skills at the disposal of decision-makers. The stages outlined in this model parallel those found in the 'engineering' model of applied sociology (Bulmer, 1982a; Janowitz, 1970). The researcher is seen as a 'social engineer' or 'socio-technician' (Abrams, 1984: 184), using her or his technical expertise in order to generate conclusive social knowledge that will inform those who are in a position to make policy choices.

The **political** model of research utilisation does not subscribe to the problem-solving view that social research provides policy-makers with objective information that ultimately enables them to make rational decisions on a wide range of policy issues. As Weiss (1986) maintains, some policy-makers may be so committed to a policy strategy for political or ideological reasons that they are unlikely to respond to research findings that challenge their firmly entrenched beliefs. However, as she points out, this does not mean that research is not used, but that it is used in a particular way. Research becomes 'political ammunition' for the side that finds its conclusions support a predetermined policy agenda. In other words, policy-makers may seek out and quote only those research findings that strengthen their position and challenge the counter-arguments put forward by their opponents.

A variant of this model is the 'tactical' model, which according to Weiss describes 'occasions when social science research is used for purposes that have little relation to the substance of the research' (1986: 37). In these circumstances, it is sometimes not the research findings themselves that are used but the fact that research is being undertaken. For example, when policy-makers find themselves under pressure to deal with a problem for which there are no apparent easy solutions, commissioning research can constitute a convenient delaying tactic (Merton, 1973). By funding a research study, policy-makers not only convey the impression that they take the problem seriously, they also buy themselves time before having to make a decision.

The final model of research utilisation to be considered here is the **enlightenment** model. According to this model, the situation is not simply one in which the findings gleaned from either a single research study or collection of related studies have an immediate and direct effect on specific policies. Rather, the research input to policy is best described as indirect and diffuse. Thus while policy-makers' decisions are not determined by specific research conclusions, the conceptualisations and generalisations emanating from the social sciences can influence the way in which policy problems are defined and solutions identified. This process is referred to as one of 'research trickle', whereby new conceptualisations of a problem or issue 'percolate through to both policy-makers and the general public, challenging taken-for-granted assumptions, and creating an "agenda for concern" ' (Tizard, 1990: 437). There are similarities with the 'limestone model', which describes how policy research seeps into the public consciousness (Thomas, 1987: 57).

Following Janowitz's original conception of sociology as enlightenment, a distinction can be made between 'enlightenment-as-clarification' and 'enlightenment-as-advocacy' (Abrams, 1984: 183–5). In the case of the former, the researcher plays a passive role in the policy-making process. Empirical sociological enquiry helps to make sense out of what is a complex social world by questioning preconceived notions and commonplace assumptions about social processes and the nature of social life. The primary task facing the researcher is one of creating a body of valid social knowledge that can be drawn upon by others as they see fit. The sociologist is there to provide clarification and not to promote any particular course of action. In contrast, the enlightenment-as-advocacy model 'impels the sociologist to become a lobbyist for a preferred reading of sociological evidence' (Abrams, 1984: 185).

Whether in the clarification or advocacy mode, the enlightenment model places great emphasis on creating the right conditions for policy decision-making. The knowledge generated by social research is seen as helping to ensure that a biased or distorted view of social reality is not allowed to dominate policy debates. According to this view, the concepts, ideas and empirical generalisations produced by social scientists gradually infiltrate the policy-making process and not only do they give policy-makers a different perspective on enduring social problems but also sensitise them to new issues. Indeed, as Rein (1983) observes, policy-relevant research is not only about helping to find answers to policy problems, but is also concerned with finding the right questions to ask in the first place. In the long run, by introducing policy-makers to alternative possibilities and influencing how they conceptualise policy problems, social research can help to set the agenda in policy debates.

The idea that research provides the intellectual backdrop against which policy choices are made meets with the approval of many social scientists. Although the enlightenment model sees the impact of research upon policy as partial, indirect and diffuse, it nevertheless allows researchers to view themselves as effective participants in the policy-making process. The fact that the knowledge they produce may find its way into policy debates indirectly, such as when the mass media carry reports of research studies, is of little consequence. What is important is that the knowledge actually informs political debate. However, as Weiss observes, there is a downside to the enlightenment process:

> When research diffuses to the policy sphere through indirect and unguided channels, it dispenses invalid as well as valid generalisations. Many of the social science understandings that gain currency are partial, oversimplified, inadequate or wrong. There are no procedures for screening out the shoddy and obsolete. Sometimes unexpected or sensational research results, however incomplete or inadequately supported by data, take the limelight. (Weiss, 1986: 38)

In comparison to the other models of research utilisation, the enlightenment model suggests that the process whereby research influences policy is more open. Consequently, as social researchers have no control over how their findings are reported by others, there is always the possibility that results can be misinterpreted and inferences drawn that cannot be supported by empirical evidence.

Which model best describes how social science research is used by policy-makers? The discussion is usually presented in terms of a comparison between the engineering and enlightenment models. The enlightenment model is attractive to social scientists, partly because of the fact that it does not see the policy agenda as being solely determined by policy-makers. As research is considered to influence policy in an indirect way, social scientists can pursue their scholarly work without necessarily highlighting its policy implications. However, while Finch (1986) is broadly in favour of the enlightenment model, she maintains that it would be wrong to ignore totally the social engineering model. As she claims, 'within an overall framework of the enlightenment model as the realistic goal for most policy-oriented social research, we should nonetheless be hoping to switch to the more direct, engineering mode on appropriate occasions' (Finch, 1986: 156).

It may be the case that no one model of research utilisation is adequate. In examining the usefulness of the different models, consideration needs to be given to the policy-making process itself.

3.4 MODELS OF POLICY-MAKING

The key distinction to be made here is between the **rationalist** and **incrementalist** models of policy-making (Blume, 1979). Bulmer (1986: 5–6) describes five key stages in the rational approach to policy formulation. The sequence begins with the identification of a problem about which it is felt something needs to be done. Those responsible for constructing a policy response outline the goals and objectives that require attention. At the second stage, the different ways of achieving these goals are outlined and the various policy options delineated. The third phase involves estimating the likely outcome of each policy. Following this, the next stage entails comparing the predicted consequences of each strategy to the goals and objectives outlined at stage two. Finally, a decision is made about which is the best policy to solve the problem. According to this rationalist framework, the decision-making process is a linear one and social science knowledge is particularly useful at the second and third stages.

The knowledge-driven and problem-solving models of research utilisation sit fairly easily within the rationalist conception of policy-making. However, the rational model has come in for a great deal of criticism. It is considered to present an unrealistic picture of how policy actually evolves. Many of the key assumptions it makes about the whole process of policy formulation have been drawn into question by the advent of the incrementalist model. For example, the incrementalist explanation of the research input to policy firmly rejects the idea that policy decision-making follows a neat linear progression, starting with the identification of a problem and ending with its ultimate solution. Instead it is argued that policy-making, far from being a rational process, is characterised by a 'disjointed incrementalism' (Lindblom, 1968). In this context, the input of research to policy is best described as diffused, not linear.

As Bulmer (1986) asserts, the contribution that research makes to the development of social policy is not as direct and as systematic as the rational model would have us believe. He maintains that the knowledge and insight provided by the social sciences do have an influence on policy, but in order to gauge the real nature and extent of this impact it is necessary to appreciate the fact that 'policy is a bargained outcome of conflicts between competing groups, proceeding generally in a disjointed incremental manner from one step to another' (Bulmer, 1986: 16). Policy-making does not follow a series of discrete, ordered stages; it is a cumulative, long drawn out process involving interaction between different interest groups each with their own agenda. This image of the policy-making process as diffuse and incrementalist fits with the enlightenment model of research utilisation, which, as described above, emphasises the gradual infiltration of social science concepts and research findings.

Compared to the rationalist model, the incrementalist model, by acknowledging the political nature of the situation, offers a more convincing account of how policy is made. The process is interpreted as 'interactive', in so far as various interest groups exert power in order to influence the decision-making process in their favour. The policy that emerges from this political interaction is arrived at by a process of 'partisan mutual adjustment' (Lindblom, 1979). Individuals and groups use social science knowledge in a partisan fashion, in an effort to promote specific policy options that represent their primary interests. An agreed policy emerges following a process of negotiation and bargaining between the various groups. There is no deep and detailed analysis of all the major policy options, as suggested by the rational approach. The changes that are introduced tend to be relatively small-scale adjustments to previous efforts. All in all, Lindblom's description of partisan mutual adjustment and disjointed incrementalism presents us with an image of policy-making as a process of 'muddling through' (Bulmer, 1986: 11).

Clearly, the relationship between research and policy is a complex one. It should come as no surprise, therefore, that how policy evolves, and how social science research contributes to its evolution, defies easy description. Indeed, as Bartley (1996) observes, research and policy are so entwined that the simple question, does research affect policy?, is not really appropriate. In looking at the debate on the health effects of unemployment, she describes how the various groups involved can be seen as taking part in what may be termed a 'social problem process' (1996: 18). Drawing on the work of Spector and Kitsuse (1977), Bartley maintains that it is important to look at how social issues come to be defined as social problems. A form of entrepreneurialism is involved. Interest groups engage in 'claims-making' activity when they use research findings in order to make 'knowledge-claims' that support their cause. In this way research findings gain the status of facts, or are identified as policy-relevant, as part of the social construction of a social problem. In fact, 'Understanding the relationship between research and policy is the same problem as understanding the construction of knowledge in general' (Bartley, 1996: 18).

Factual or knowledge-claims are made by a group or groups in an effort to get others to recognise the existence of a particular social condition. Once a condition has been identified it needs to be acknowledged as undesirable before any form of policy intervention is seriously considered. This involves individuals and groups making 'value-claims'. Consequently, in the social problem process model, both factual and value-claims feature prominently in policy debates. Unlike the more conventional models of the relationship between research and policy, this approach examines the interplay between facts and values throughout the career of a social problem.

3.5 SUMMARY

Applied social research certainly has an influence on social policy but the nature and extent of this influence is difficult to pin down. The relationship between research and policy is an interactive one and to understand how they influence one another it is necessary to have a view of how the policy-making process operates. Policy-making is less rational and more diffuse than often depicted. Policies evolve over time as part of a long-term process of negotiation, involving a variety of interest groups. Research findings feed into this process in a myriad of indirect ways.

3.6 PROJECT

One of the general conclusions to be drawn from this chapter is that, given the complexity of social life and the intractable nature of the policy-making process, a particular social policy issue cannot be expected to be resolved by the findings of any one piece of sociological research. However, social science research does provide a wealth of knowledge capable of informing policy debates and influencing policy outcomes. One can take an individual piece of research on a contemporary social issue and speculate about how the findings might be used to influence the direction and development of a particular policy.

For this project you should read the article by J. Andersen and J.E. Larsen (1998) 'Gender, poverty and empowerment', *Critical Social Policy*, 18(2): 241–58, and consider the following questions:

1. According to the research findings, how do men and women differ with regard to their general social circumstances, labour market experiences and responses to the lack of material resources?
2. Consider the conceptual distinction that the researchers make between relative poverty/deprivation and social exclusion. What implications does this distinction have when it comes to policy formulation?
3. What general lessons can policy-makers learn from the findings of this study that might help them to devise and implement social reforms and policies to tackle relative poverty and social exclusion?
4. In what sense do you think gender is an issue that needs to be taken into account when devising policies in this area?
5. On the basis of the findings of this study what advice would you give to policy-makers?

3.7   FURTHER READING

A key text providing an overview of the role of social science in the policy-making process is Bulmer (1986). Finch (1986) discusses the relationship between social research and social policy using examples from the field of education, while concentrating on the use of qualitative research techniques and methodologies. For an introduction to the use of social research methods in evaluation research, see Clarke (1999).

PART I

BEGINNINGS

THE ETHICS OF SOCIAL RESEARCH

4

MARTIN BULMER

Ethics is a matter of principled sensitivity to the rights of others. Being ethical limits the choices we can make in the pursuit of truth. Ethics say that while truth is good, respect for human dignity is better, even if, in the extreme case, the respect of human dignity leaves one ignorant of human nature. Such ethical considerations impinge upon all scientific research, but they impinge particularly sharply upon research in the human sciences, where people are studying other people. Sociologists necessarily need to consider ethical issues that arise in the course of their research and this chapter sets out some of the issues.

The sociological research community has responsibilities not only to the ideals of the pursuit of objective truth and the search for knowledge, but also to the subjects of their research. Just as in other sciences, with human subjects in the physiological laboratory, patients in the medical school, or students in the psychological laboratory, so members of the public whom the sociologist encounters while out in the field need to be considered from an ethical standpoint. Researchers have always to take account of the effects of their actions upon those subjects and act in such a way as to preserve their rights and integrity as human beings. Such behaviour is ethical behaviour.

4.1   ETHICS IN SOCIAL RESEARCH

4.1.1 The scope of ethics

Two examples will help to sharpen the point. In 1919, Franz Boas, the dominant figure in American anthropology of the time, wrote to *The Nation* that

> [b]y accident, incontrovertible proof has come to my hands that at least four men who carry on anthropological work, while employed as government agents, introduced themselves to foreign governments as representatives of scientific institutions in the United States, and as sent out for the purposes of carrying out scientific researches. They have not only shaken the belief in the truthfulness of science, but they have also done the greatest possible disservice to scientific inquiry. . . . The very essence of (the scientist's) life is the service of truth. . . . A person who uses science as a cover for political spying, who demands himself to pose before a foreign government as an investigator and asks for assistance in his alleged researches in order to carry on, under this cloak, his political machinations, prostitutes science in an unpardonable way and forfeits the right to be classed as a scientist. (quoted in Weaver 1973: 51–2)

Social science should not be used as a cover for spying. Boas argued that whereas soldiers, diplomats, politicians and businessmen might set patriotic devotion above everyday decency, the scientist's calling, the search for truth, made very special demands. Such behaviour was unethical.

Around 1950, William Caudill, an American anthropologist with interests in psychology, took part in a research project to study some of the social and medical problems of life in a mental hospital as seen from the patient's point of view. Known only to two senior members of staff, he was admitted as a bona fide patient resident in the hospital, and was treated there for two months. He did not reveal to most staff and all other patients that he was a sociological observer. The story that he invented to tell his psychotherapist (who did not know that he was there as a covert observer) was that:

> he had recently been trying to finish the writing of a scholarly book, but felt that he was not getting ahead; worry over his work drove him to alcoholic episodes ending in fights; he was withdrawn and depressed, and had quarrelled with his wife, who had then separated from him. Beyond these fictions, Caudill had given a somewhat distorted picture of his own life, in which he consciously attempted to suppress his own solutions to certain problems and to add a pattern of neurotic defences. (Caudill et al., 1952: 315)

Such duplicity on the part of the sociologist has been attacked by Kai Erikson, who believes that 'the practice of using masks in social research compromises both the people who wear them and the people for whom they are worn, and in doing so violates the terms of a contract which the sociologist should be ready to honour in his dealings with others' (Erikson, 1967: 367–8). Four kinds of wrong are involved. First, the sociologist has responsibilities to the subjects of research. The method has potential to do (unforeseeable) harm. If subjects know they are being studied, at least they have agreed to expose themselves to possible harm. To study them secretly is ethically comparable to a doctor who carries out medical experiments on human subjects without their agreement. Secondly, sociologists have responsibilities to their colleagues. Covert observation is liable to damage the general reputation of sociology and close off further avenues for research. Thirdly, most of those who get involved in covert observation are graduate students. Since covert research poses serious ethical problems and often results in personal stress for the observer, it is unreasonable to use a method, the burden of which will fall upon those still dependent upon their academic elders.

Erikson's final and strongest argument is that covert research is bad science. The complexities of human social interaction are but imperfectly understood. To believe that it is possible to conceal one's identity from others by playing a covert role is highly problematical. It is by no means clear that those who do research in this way really succeed in becoming full participants accepted as such by others. The rationale of the method therefore falls away and the quality of the data collected by its use is liable to bias, distortion and error. We shall return to these general considerations below, but the debate gives a flavour of some of the issues that are involved.

4.1.2 Ethical guidance available to the social researcher

The social researcher faced with potential ethical problems in the conduct of research may have resort to guidance from codes of ethics and ethical guidelines provided by professional associations. Two sets of guidelines are readily available in the UK, from the Social Research Association (SRA) and the British Sociological Association (BSA).

The Social Research Association's *Ethical Guidelines* point the social researcher towards good practice in the conduct of social research. Members of the Association are required to acknowledge them in becoming members, and they appear in the SRA's *Directory of Members*. They may also be consulted on the SRA web site (http://www.the-sra.org.uk) and are reprinted in Bulmer, Sykes and Moorhouse (1999: 53–68).

The British Sociological Association's *Statement of Ethical Practice* appears under the banner 'Professional Standards' on the BSA web site (http://www.britsoc.org.uk/about/ethic.htm). The Association has a set of Rules for the Conduct of Enquiries into Complaints against BSA members under the auspices of the Statement, and its Guidelines on Professional Conduct. The Statement is, however, primarily meant to inform members' ethical judgements rather than impose them as an external set of standards. Sociologists need to be aware of the ethical issues that can arise in their work and use the Statement of Ethical Practice to sensitise themselves to the sorts of ethical issue that can arise.

4.2   ETHICAL BEHAVIOUR IN SCIENCE: THE NORMS

The norms of science advocate the search for truth as the driving force behind the creation of new knowledge (Merton, 1968: 591–603). According to this view, the prime objective of sociology should be the search for the truth. What is the social context in which truth is to be sought? Conventional accounts of social research stress the need to cooperate with informants, establish trust, create empathy between researcher and subject, and be relatively open about what one is doing. Such conventional procedures, it is often suggested, rest upon a consensual view of society in terms of social order. Against this, it is argued that the nature of contemporary society is best described by a conflict model. 'Profound conflicts of interest, values, feeling and action pervade social life. ... Conflict is the reality of life; suspicion is the guiding principle. ... It's a war of all against all and no one gives anyone anything for nothing, especially for the truth' (Douglas, 1976: 55).

The problems faced by sociologists are shared by many other practitioners – for example, doctors and clergymen – some of whom have very well-developed ethical guidelines for decision-making. The ethics of social research are not therefore peculiar, but they do provide an instructive case study of some of the dilemmas that face the social scientist trying to reconcile different objectives. The complexity of ethical decision-making is recognised in this chapter by the variety of views put forward about the principles which are invoked in the identification of ethical issues in social research.

4.3   ETHICAL PRINCIPLES GOVERNING
SOCIAL RESEARCH

Many principles have been adduced to justify taking an ethical view of the activity of social research. One general principle that runs through much of the discussion is the need to strike a balance between society's desire, on the one hand, to expose the hidden processes at work in modern society and, on the other, to protect the privacy of individuals and groups and to recognise that there are private spheres into which the social scientist may not, and perhaps even should not, penetrate (Barnes, 1979: 13–24).

4.3.1 Informed consent

A second very important general principle, which is a linchpin of ethical behaviour in research, is the doctrine of informed consent. This provides that persons who are invited to participate in social research activities should be free to choose to take part or refuse, having been given the fullest information concerning the nature and purpose of the research, including any risks to which they personally would be exposed, the arrangements for maintaining the confidentiality of the data, and so on.

This principle was restated following the end of the Second World War in the Nuremberg trials of Nazi war criminals. The Nazi regime had exposed many subjects, particularly concentration camp inmates, to extreme medical experiments in which subjects sometimes died from the treatment which they received. An example was immersing people for long periods in icy water to test the survival chances of downed air crew in the sea.

The notion of informed consent was embodied in 1946 in the following principle:

> The voluntary consent of the human subject is absolutely essential. This means that the person concerned should have legal capacity to give consent, should be so situated as to exercise free power of choice, without the intervention of any element of force, fraud, deceit, duress, overreaching or any other ulterior form of constraint or conversion; and should have sufficient knowledge and comprehension of the elements of the subject matter involved as to enable him to make an understanding and enlightened decision. (quoted in Homan, 1991: 69; see also Katz, 1972: 292–306)

Informed consent is generally taken to mean that those who are researched should have the right to know that they are being researched, and that in some sense they should have actively given their consent. In medical experiments, a signed consent form is required. This is rarely the case in social research, but the principle does suggest that some attempt should be made to explain to those being studied what the study is for. Thus in a social survey, the respondents will usually be told who is the sponsor of the survey, what in general terms is its subject matter, and what will be expected of them by the interviewer. In ethnographic research, it is usual for ethnographers to be open about their identity as researchers, and to give some general indication of what they are doing, for example that they are writing a book about the group or setting being studied.

In particular, the principle acts as a constraint on those who might be tempted to conduct covert research under the guise of some other role or identity. For example, 'sugging', the practice of pretending to conduct an interview which then turns into a sales pitch, is a practice that many people object to and that the market research industry goes to great lengths to counter. The salesperson is gaining the respondent's cooperation on false pretences and is violating informed consent. Covert participant observation raises similar difficulties, which are discussed further below. A researcher who pretends to be a true participant (for example, a member of a small political party or a religious sect, e.g. Festinger, 1964) is violating the confidence of the people with whom that person is spending his or her time.

4.3.2 Respect for privacy

An ethical dimension to social research that often plays a part in the public perception of social science is the extent to which sociologists are perceived to intrude into areas which are believed to be private. Why such areas are deemed private may vary. Some aspects of behaviour (for example, ownership of wealth or sexual behaviour) are often considered to be the concern of no one other than the person concerned. Sometimes the milieu (for example, the nuclear family) is considered a domain into which the researcher should not enter. Sometimes a public arena (for example, the key political power centres of central government, such as the Cabinet and ministerial offices) are preserves into which the sociologist should not expect access.

Many definitions of privacy emphasise the control by an individual of information about him or herself as a key component. In modern industrial society, information is a commodity, and given the multiple social ties in which people are involved, keeping control of information about oneself and deciding what to release and to whom is often a key means by which one's privacy is protected, and control is maintained over what others can learn about you. But the 'right to privacy' is not a simple matter, since so much information is held about individuals by organisations, and the exchange of information is often necessary for the provision of different kinds of services.

In social research, there are also complications stemming from the institutionalised nature of social life. Entry to research settings may be controlled by gatekeepers who are professionals or administrators in charge (see

Chapter 9). Yet they may grant permission on behalf of clients or customers or patients frequenting the milieu – or may deny entry even if members of those groups are willing to grant it and cooperate in the research. The role of gatekeepers in social research is therefore a critical one, to which separate attention is given in ethical codes and guidelines. In some areas, particularly in socio-medical research, scrutiny of research proposals is institutionalised in ethical review committees where scientists sit in judgement over the research designs and procedures of fellow scientists.

4.3.3 Safeguarding the confidentiality of data

A continuing concern in social research has been not just with the conditions under which data are collected, but with how they are stored and disseminated. Assurances are commonly given to those providing responses to questionnaires or interview questions that these data are needed for purposes of statistical aggregation and the individual will not be identifiable in the resulting analysis.

Increasingly, quantitative data sets are available for secondary analysis via data archives (see Chapter 16) that also control the distribution of data by requiring the registration of users and releasing data only to those who have signed a legal agreement. This provides some safeguard for the uses to which the data are put. Safeguards for quantitative data are further discussed in section 4.4.2.

4.3.4 Harm to subjects and researchers

There has been considerable debate about the ethical implications of harm in social research, involving both harm to those being researched and harm to those who are doing the research (for a review see Warwick, 1982). Although there are no clear conclusions to this debate, there is general awareness that social research may have consequences for those being studied. A graphic example was provided by an ethnographic study in the USA some years ago of impersonal sex among gay men in a public setting. A sociologist, Laud Humphreys (1970), acted as a 'watch queen' in an isolated public toilet located in a park frequented by gay men, in order to carry out an observational study. He also noted down the licence numbers of cars parked near this facility. Later, he obtained the names and addresses of the owners, changed his appearance, and called on these men at home in order to carry out a supposed health survey. In fact, he was seeking information about their social and family backgrounds in order to show how a gay sample of the population compared to a 'straight' sample. When the research became publicly known, a great public furore resulted, since many considered that he had been spying on the men concerned and held information which could be used to their detriment, for blackmail and so on. Humphreys eventually destroyed the data he held identifying the men in the study, deeming the bank vault in another city, where he had stored the data, as not sufficiently safe. The essence of the argument was his potential to cause harm to the men he had studied.

It has also been argued that if sociologists use less than frank methods and pretence to gain access to settings and data, not only do they violate the principle of informed consent (section 4.3.1) but they may also do harm to themselves. The reader may compare the (true) social psychological study *When Prophecy Fails* (Festinger, 1964) with the fictional account of a very similar set of circumstances, *Imaginary Friends* (Lurie, 1967). In both, the sociologist infiltrates a group that believes that the end of the world is about to arrive and attempts to explain how group members adjust their beliefs when the predicted event does not happen. In the fictional account, serious harm results for the sociologist. It has often been argued that the perils of role pretence, dissimulation and deception are harmful for the individual and for sociology as a profession, and this is a dimension of more ingenious research designs in sociology which need to be kept in mind (see Warwick, 1982).

4.3.5 Deceit and lying in the course of research

Argument has waxed fierce at times about the use of deception in research. Lying by sociologists to gain access to data is rare, but misrepresentation has been more common, though still unusual. The extent to which the socio-logical researcher has an obligation to tell the unvarnished truth has been much debated. In principle the issues are not very different from truth-telling in other situations – do we always tell the literal truth to our friends?, do doctors tell the truth to dying patients?, do critics tell the unvarnished truth to artists? – and there is scope for considerable moral argument about the latitude allowed to an individual in such situations (see Bok, 1979). As a general principle, the use of deception in research has been condemned, and concealment of the fact that one is a researcher has attracted criticism. But there are many situations in which it is not possible to be completely open to all participants, and sometimes a full explanation of one's purposes would overwhelm the listener. So it is recognised that there are degrees of openness and concealment possible in social research. Some examples are considered briefly below.

4.3.6 Attending to the consequences of publication

A substantial section of the British Sociological Association's *Statement of Ethical Practice* is concerned with relations with, and responsibilities towards, sponsors and/or funders. There are a number of aspects to this, but one of the most important concerns publication of the results of research. Researchers should try to ensure that they retain the right to publish research results without hindrance, although this is not always possible with certain types of applied research carried out for a client. Maurice Punch, who conducted a study of the independent boarding school Dartington Hall, has written at length about the problems which can arise in this area, and which he himself encountered (Punch, 1986).

There is a more general issue, too, of where the wider social responsibilities of the social scientist reside. Sociologists who have studied particular, disadvantaged social minority groups have often been sensitive to the consequences of publishing studies of them which make previously private information public. Self-censorship is not unknown to protect those who might be harmed by publication. Relations with the mass media also need to be handled carefully, and sociologists who have had dealings at close hand with television, radio or the print media have not always come away from the encounter feeling that their research has been fairly presented (Haslam and Bryman, 1994).

4.4 ETHICS IN QUANTITATIVE RESEARCH

Ethical issues arise in all types of social research, not least in quantitative research. Whatever the type of research, the person designing the study needs to consider the ethical implications and be alert to them. In certain types of research, such as socio-medical research, formal ethical review may be required. But in the vast majority of cases where it is not, the sociologist still needs to be satisfied that the study is ethically sound and that possible ethical issues have been dealt with. In survey research, one important area concerns what the respondent is told about the auspices and purpose of the study, what are the conditions under which the addresses and names of respondents are used, how the data will be published, how anonymity of individual respondents will be preserved, and how the confidentiality of the final dataset will be safeguarded. These are all issues to which thought will need to be given at the design and fieldwork stages of the survey (see Chapter 6).

4.4.1 What it is permissible to ask in surveys: sensitivity

How does the sociological researcher weigh the sensitivity of topics in designing a questionnaire and determine what is permissible? Consider two examples. A policy researcher is investigating the adequacy of social security provision for persons who have recently been bereaved. How does the government grant compare to the actual cost of a simple funeral? The researcher plans to interview the spouses of recently deceased elderly people in order to assess this issue. A second example concerns the study of teenage pregnancy and the availability of contraception. This is also a major current policy concern, which has wider sociological aspects (see Holland et al., 1998; Lees, 1993). Researchers interview adolescents in order to throw light on these issues and test theories. What are the researchers' responsibilities in these cases? The elderly widow or widower may be upset or distressed to be asked questions about the loss of their spouse, and so the issue needs to be handled sensitively. The young person being asked about their sexual knowledge, experience and behaviour needs to be approached with care, possibly with the permission of parents. If the person is under the age of 16, particular problems arise. Lee (1993) has a good discussion of some of the approaches that can be taken to broach sensitive topics in surveys.

4.4.2 Ensuring the confidentiality and anonymity of quantitative data

Social researchers also need to consider their ethical responsibilities in relation to the handling of data resulting from large-scale enquiries, such as the results of a survey. Proper arrangements for the custody of the paper questionnaires or the electronic files resulting from the survey need to be made. The implications of the survey need to be considered. (In the UK, this may involve consultation with the Data Protection Registrar – see the web site: http://www.dataprotection.gov.uk/dprhome.htm).

Various methods have been used to ensure the confidentiality of large datasets. With census data (which cover the entire population), special precautions are taken: the individual data are not released outside the Census office; in small area tabulations random error is injected into the tables; and in the individual and household samples available from the UK 1991 Census (the Sample of Anonymised Records – see Chapter 16), certain mainly geographical variables are suppressed or altered to prevent people deducing facts about individual respondents. With survey data, in addition to omitting respondents' names and addresses, their geographical location is frequently not accurately identified, thus maintaining confidentiality. In longitudinal research, where individuals and households may be followed over a period of time, special precautions need to be taken to keep secret the identities and locations of participants, and these precautions need to be re-doubled if data-matching or linking is involved. A variety of different models are available (see Boruch and Cecil, 1979: 93–126) to ensure insulation of different files from each other, and to keep the identifying links separate from the data to which they relate. Statistical methods, such as random error injection and randomised response (Lee, 1993: 82–6), have often been attempted. The most effective recent innovation seems to be computer-assisted self-interviewing (CASI), in which respondents answer questions themselves on the interviewer's lap-top computer without the interviewer being involved, thus ensuring privacy in the interview and a degree of confidentiality of the resulting data.

4.5   ETHICS IN QUALITATIVE RESEARCH

Many ethical dilemmas also arise in qualitative research and these have been discussed in a number of sources (e.g. Ellen, 1984: 133–54; Filstead, 1970: 235–80; for an example, see Fichter, 1973). In some respects, the ethical dilemmas facing the qualitative researcher are sharper and the freedom of action in research greater, so that the consequent ethical problems that may be encountered are more varied. Self-presentation is at a greater premium in much field research, and this can lead the researcher into problems and dilemmas that frequently have an ethical dimension. The general issues can be demonstrated by means of two specific examples.

4.5.1 Using covert observation: is it ever justified?

Are sociologists ever justified in concealing their identity in order to gain entry to a milieu? In a famous Californian study, Rosenhan (1973) sent eight volunteers to seek admission to different mental hospitals, saying that they 'heard voices' but with instructions to say that the symptoms had disappeared as soon as they were admitted. They were also told not to reveal their identities as researchers. The researchers took between seven and 52 days to be released, with a mean of 19 days, and usually with the diagnosis of schizophrenia 'in remission'. Few of the medical or nursing staff questioned the genuineness of these 'pseudopatients', although a number of the other patients did. One experimenter, who was much exercised about whether to take notes on the ward in case it revealed his purpose, found 'engages in compulsive writing behaviour' written in his notes by one of the nursing staff. Was the director of the research justified in concealing the true identity of members of his research team in order to test the value of labelling theory?

Covert participant observation is clearly a violation of the principle of informed consent. By definition, the subjects of research are kept in ignorance of the true identity of the researcher. They have no opportunity to decide whether or not to participate. Secret participant observation is also frequently an invasion of privacy. To insinuate oneself into a particular setting on false pretences, in order to gather material for research, violates the right of the individual to be let alone and to control her or his personal sphere. On the outside, the individual can hold objects of self-feeling, such as her or his body, actions, thoughts and some of her or his possessions, clear of contact with alien and contaminating things. But in total institutions like hospitals, these territories of the self are violated; the boundary that the individual places between her or his being and the environment is invaded and the embodiment of self profaned. The same is true of staff in such settings, who are not aware that they are dealing with someone who is not as they seem.

A major criticism of covert methods is that they involve out-and-out deception. Researchers are pretending to be people who they are not. This runs counter to the usual norm in empirical research – including observational studies – of building up relations of trust with those whom one is studying. In certain highly exceptional circumstances, deception may be justified by the context in which research is carried out. Bruno Bettelheim's study on the concentration camp (1943) is an example of a covert study that was justified. Bettelheim was imprisoned in the camp. Indeed, he embarked on the study in order to try to survive psychologically in an extreme situation which was not of his own choosing. This research may be justified ethically (if it needs such justification) on the grounds that Bettelheim was held in the camp under duress. But such cases are very rare.

A common defence of the use of covert methods of research is to argue that, although some criticisms of it have force, covert methods do not cause harm to those studied if the identities and location of individuals and places are concealed in published results, the data are held in anonymised form, and all data are kept securely confidential. It is proposed that the benefits from greater social scientific knowledge about society outweigh the risks that are run in collecting data using covert methods. Apart from the problem of being unable to predict the consequences of publishing research, the central issue in any risk/benefit equation such as this is: who is to draw up the balance sheet and determine whether particular methods are justified or not?; whose causes are the right causes in social research?

A further dimension to the problem, less often considered, is what effect covert observation has on the social scientist who is doing the observing. It is noteworthy that several scholars who have used covert methods have subsequently made statements against their use, saying that they would not have used them with benefit of hindsight.

This brief summary (presented in more extended form in Bulmer, 1982b) gives some indication of the dimensions of ethical debate about the use of covert observational methods.

4.6   CONCLUSION: ETHICALLY AWARE
RESEARCH BEHAVIOUR

There are no cut-and-dried answers to many ethical issues which face the social researcher. Very often the issues involved are multifaceted and there are contradictory considerations in play. There is not necessarily one right and one wrong answer, but this indeterminacy does not mean that ethical issues can be ignored. Far from it. The best counsel for the social researcher is to be constantly ethically aware.

4.7 FURTHER READING

Homan (1991) is the best short general introduction to the subject of social research ethics. Although concerned with a slightly different topic, Lee (1993), on researching sensitive issues, is a first-class survey of problems in the practical conduct of social research that has ethical dimensions.

A number of somewhat older works are still relevant to different aspects of the problems of ethics. Barnes (1979) is still the best general discussion of the social responsibilities of the sociologist and how to balance the right to know with the need to respect privacy. In addition to Lee (1993), Boruch and Cecil (1979) discuss the problems of safeguarding the confidentiality of quantitative data. Beauchamp et al. (1982) examine a variety of issues including harm to subject and researcher. Bulmer (1982b) sets out the arguments for and against covert participant observation. A case study of the nature of ethical and legal issues in research in a single area, that of AIDS research, is presented in Gray, Lyons and Melton (1995).

DESIGNING SAMPLES

5

SARA ARBER

CONTENTS

Sampling is fundamental within the social research process and is often one of the first aspects to consider when planning a project. The way in which a sample is designed will depend on the goals of the researcher. Some researchers select samples in order to maximise theoretical understanding, while others are primarily concerned to obtain a representative sample to make inferences about a whole population. In the latter case, a sample is studied to learn something about the larger grouping of which it is a part; this larger grouping is called the **population** or **universe** of enquiry.

If we had sufficient time and resources, we might study the whole population, rather than just a sample taken from that population. Indeed, the population census that is conducted every ten years covers everyone in Britain. However, researching a sample can yield more accurate results than studying the complete population. For instance, in survey research, if fewer people are studied, more resources can be spent on each person, for example, employing more highly trained interviewers, with more supervision and using coders who are more skilled. Decisions about sample designs must always take into consideration the trade off between selecting a larger sample or studying a smaller one more intensively.

Although this chapter emphasises sampling where the 'unit' being studied is the individual, the procedures and theory underlying sampling are equally applicable for other sampling units, such as hospitals, small businesses, towns, households or visits to a museum. The chapter focuses mainly on sampling in relation to surveys, but sampling may also be relevant when undertaking an observational study or a study of newspapers or television programmes. Whatever the method of enquiry, researchers should consider whether they can generalise their findings to a wider group and the degree of confidence with which they can make such generalisations.

5.1 KEY CONCEPTS

Before the range of sampling methods used in social research are outlined, this section will provide a brief introduction to key concepts.

Defining the population

The first step in most research is to define the 'population' to be covered. For example, a study of the sexual behaviour of young people might define the universe of enquiry as people aged between 14 and 19 living in Manchester. It would be necessary to consider whether the population of interest includes young people living away from home as students, or in institutions and the geographical boundaries to be covered (e.g. within the Manchester area). Hence, the **population** is any well-defined set of elements. The researcher then selects a sample from this population.

Sample statistics and population parameters

The term **statistics** is used when referring to a summary about the sample, and **parameters** for a summary about the population. The average (or mean) income of a sample of 300 recent university graduates is a **statistic**. It may be used to estimate the mean income of all recent university graduates, a population **parameter**.

Representativeness

The aim of most researchers is to make the sample representative of the population from which it was selected. For example, there should be the same proportion of men and women in both the sample and the population, and the same percentage distributions on all other variables. If the population characteristics are known, the degree of representativeness of a sample can be checked. For example, one could check the representativeness of a sample of university students against university records to see whether the sample contains the correct proportions of students in each department and in each year.

Sampling error and non-sampling error

When designing samples it is important to be aware of two different sources of potential error. The first is sampling error, consisting of random errors associated with the fact that only one out of many possible samples has been drawn from the population. Sampling error is estimated by the standard error (see section 5.5).

In social research there are always sources of error other than sampling error, and these are liable to bias estimates of population parameters. Some of these non-sampling errors are connected with the sampling process, such as incomplete sampling frames, non-response error and selection error (see sections 5.7 and 5.8). Other sources of non-sampling error are associated with different stages of the research process and include poor questionnaire design, interviewer bias and coding errors. Of course, you should try to minimise all these sources of error (see Chapters 6, 8 and 14).

Sampling frames

A sampling frame is a list of the members of the population under investigation and is used to select the sample. This list should be as complete as possible. The researcher needs to be aware of possible shortcomings, such as omissions and duplications, and should attempt to correct for them. Some sampling frames available for the UK adult population will be discussed in section 5.7.

Non-response

If non-responders differ in significant ways from responders, the researcher has a biased sample (see section 5.8) and inferences to the population will be wrong.

The aim should be to maximise a survey's response rate, since the lower the response rate, the greater the likelihood that the achieved sample will be biased. Interview surveys should aim to achieve about an 80 per cent response rate, although in many cases 70 per cent may be more realistic, and 60 per cent may be acceptable for self-completion questionnaire surveys.

5.2   TYPES OF SAMPLING METHOD

There are two types of sampling method: **probability** sampling and **purposive** (or non-probability) sampling. Probability sampling is where every individual element in a population is chosen at random and has a known, non-zero chance of selection. Therefore the selection process is predetermined and once the units have been selected the goal is to collect data from them all. In purposive sampling, the chance of selection for each element in a population is unknown and for some elements is zero. Probability and purposive sampling are appropriate for different types of research and at different stages of the research process (see Table 5.1).

Probability methods of sample selection are best if the researcher wishes to describe accurately the characteristics of a sample in order to estimate population parameters, for example to establish the needs of older people or the attitudes of residents in an area to a re-development scheme. Probability samples are also most appropriate for analytic studies, which involve testing empirical hypotheses.

Where the researcher's aim is to generate theory and a wider understanding of social processes or social actions, the representativeness of the sample may be of less importance and the best sampling strategy is often focused or judgemental sampling (see section 5.3).

Purposive samples are ideal when developing interview schedules and other research instruments. Developmental and pilot work should be conducted on a wide range of respondents so that the research instruments are adequately tested (see Chapter 6). For example, a survey of attitudes to general practitioners should include pilot work on patients with private

Table 5.1   *Probability and purposive samples*

Probability Samples are best if the purpose is:
  (a)   Description – estimation of population characteristics.
  (b)   Explanation – testing of empirical hypotheses.

Purposive Samples are best if the purpose is:
  (a)   Exploration and theory development.
  (b)   Developing and testing survey research instruments – pilot work.
  (c)   Selection of a small number of first-stage units, e.g. selection of four schools to conduct a survey of pupil's aspirations.

Definitions
Probability sampling is where each element in a population (well-defined universe of elements) has a known and non-zero chance of selection.
Purposive (non-probability) sampling is where the chance of selection for each element in a population is unknown and for some elements is zero.

general practitioners to make sure that the questions in the interview are appropriate for this section of the population. Since few people use private general practitioners, if the interview schedule were to be tested on a random sample, it is quite likely that it would not be tried on anyone with a private general practitioner.

A sample design may involve a mixture of both probability and purposive sampling. For example, in a study of the occupational aspirations of secondary school children, the researcher may only have sufficient resources to study a small number of schools. These should be selected using purposive sampling to represent the range of types of school that are expected to influence their pupils' aspirations. However, within each school, the sample of students to be surveyed should be selected using probability sampling.

5.3   SAMPLING IN SMALL-SCALE AND QUALITATIVE RESEARCH

Although researchers usually seek a representative sample, they often have only sufficient resources to study a small number of people. For example, Oakley's (1974) influential study of housework was based on a sample of 40 married women with at least one child under five. She designed the sample to obtain an equal number of middle-class and working-class women because she hypothesised that class was particularly salient in the lives of these women. The sample was selected from patients registered with two general practitioners in London, one in a predominantly working-class area and the other in a predominantly middle-class area.

Important sociological work is often based on relatively small samples drawn from one local area. Although these samples may attempt to be representative of a specific category of people, they are not probability samples from which precise inferences can be made about the characteristics of the population from which the sample was drawn. Using a probability sample is often unrealistic for small-scale or qualitative research.

Many sociological research studies focus on very specific sub-groups of the population, for whom sampling frames are not readily available. For example, Mansfield and Collard (1988) aimed to understand 'normal' marriages and the processes of adjustment and development within such marriages. It would have been prohibitively expensive to examine a large representative sample of newly married couples. Instead, they studied 65 couples who had married in church, interviewing husbands and wives separately and then together. These couples were re-interviewed five years after their marriage. The researchers' primary goal was an understanding of social processes. This was achieved by interviewing in detail and at length, and conducting interviews on more than one occasion with both partners.

On some occasions researchers redefine their study population to conform to the available lists. For instance, Mansfield and Collard's (1988) research became a study of first marriages solemnised in church because they were unable to obtain a list of civil (Register Office) marriages. It is essential to consider how restricting the sample may influence the conclusions that are drawn. For example, the processes of negotiation between partners in the early months of marriage may differ between couples who had church and civil marriage ceremonies. This difference may arise because couples with civil marriages are more likely to have cohabited before marriage, and they may differ by age and class compared with those who had a church marriage. The researchers should recognise the constraints on interpretation which arise from their method of sampling, and honestly and clearly note them for their readers.

5.3.1 Network or snowball sampling

Network or snowball sampling is sometimes used to obtain a sample when there is no adequate list to use as a sampling frame. It is a method for obtaining samples of numerically small groups, such as members of minority ethnic groups or illegal drug users. It involves contacting a member of the population to be studied and asking him or her whether they know anyone else with the required characteristics (for example, people born in England whose parents came from Poland). The nominated individuals are interviewed in turn and asked to identify further sample members. This continues until no further sample members are obtained. Then another member of the population of interest is identified, preferably from a different area or social class, and the process of asking for contacts with the required characteristics begins again.

Because the snowballing technique involves personal recommendations that vouch for the legitimacy of the researcher, it may be the only feasible method of finding a sample of people engaged in illegal activities, such as drug users (Lee, 1993). It is therefore useful when the potential subjects of the research are likely to be sceptical of the researcher's intentions. Snowball sampling can only be used when the target sample members are involved in some kind of network with others who share the characteristic of interest. This is both a strength and a potential weakness of the method. An advantage of snowball sampling is that it reveals a network of contacts that can itself be studied. A potential problem is that it only includes those within a connected network of individuals. For example, in a study of people with Polish parents, it would fail to find anyone who had no contact with other second-generation Polish people. This would be a serious source of bias if the research topic is the continued maintenance of Polish cultural traditions. In snowball sampling, as in any other method of obtaining a sample, it is essential to assess and report the representativeness of the sample and any likely sources of bias.

5.3.2 Theoretical sampling

Another sampling strategy used in qualitative research is 'theoretical sampling' (Glaser and Strauss, 1967). This approach eschews attempting to obtain a representative sample, arguing that sampling should be entirely governed by the selection of respondents who will maximise theoretical development. The sampling should be designed to locate strategic data which may refute emerging hypotheses. Sampling stops when 'theoretical saturation' is reached, that is, when no new analytical insights are forthcoming from a given setting. Theoretical sampling directs the researcher to collect, code, analyse and test hypotheses during the sampling process. This goal is quite different from that of a researcher seeking a representative sample.

5.4   QUOTA SAMPLING

Quota sampling is a non-probability method which aims to make the sample representative of the population by setting and filling quota controls.

Interviewers have to find sample members to fill pre-specified quotas, which are designed according to the topic being researched. For example, a quota control on employment status would be appropriate in a study of women's purchasing behaviour, since the shopping behaviour of full-time housewives differs from that of women in paid employment. The researcher must know the proportion of people with each characteristic in the population in order to specify the quota controls. These proportions can generally be obtained from the Population Census or from large government surveys, such as the General Household Survey (see Chapter 16). Table 5.2 illustrates the use of three quota controls (age, social class and employment status) for a survey of 100 women aged 21–65. The numbers in the table indicate how many of each type of woman are to be included in the sample.

The independent controls shown in Table 5.2(a) ensure that the sample contains the correct representation on each of the three quota control variables separately. However, the resulting sample may still have an unrepresentative combination of characteristics. For example, all the class IV and V women may be housewives over age 50. To ensure that the sample has the correct combination of characteristics, interrelated (also known as interlocking, interlaced or interdependent) controls can be used (see Table 5.2(b)). However, as quota controls become more complex and the number of variables and categories to be interrelated increases, it becomes more difficult for interviewers to find people to fill each quota cell, and the costs of the research escalate. There is a trade off between the higher costs and the increased representativeness of using more detailed quota controls.

Quota samples are widely used in market research, opinion polling and audience research for three main reasons. First, interviewing costs are much lower than for probability samples because there is no need for call-backs,

Table 5.2 *Example of quota controls for a survey of women aged 21–65*

(a) Independent controls

Age	%	Social Class	%	Work Status	%
21–35	34	Class I & II	30	Not in employment	36
36–50	33	Class III	50	In paid employment	64
51–65	33	Class IV & V	20		
Total	100		100		100

(b) Interrelated controls

Social Class:	I & II		III		IV & V		
Work Status: Age	N	W	N	W	N	W	**Total**
21–35	5	8	6	10	1	4	34
36–50	2	7	2	15	2	5	33
51–65	5	3	10	7	3	5	33
Total	12	18	18	32	6	14	100
	30		50		20		

N = Not in paid employment   W = In paid employment

and travelling distances and times are much reduced. Secondly, administrative costs prior to fieldwork are lower. There are no costs for obtaining a sampling frame and drawing the sample, although there may be costs in setting the quota controls. Thirdly, the period of interviewing can be very short. For some research topics, such as opinion polls about political events and audience views about specific television programmes, it is essential that interviews are completed on the same day and the results published within a few days. A probability sample cannot be used for this kind of research because by the time all sample members had been contacted they would probably have forgotten the event and the results would no longer be newsworthy.

The typical quota sample survey is one where interviewers stand in the High Street to select people to fill their quota cells. However, the sample is likely to be biased for several reasons. First, it may over-represent frequent shoppers and under-represent people who work outside town centres. Secondly, there may be a danger of unconscious bias from interviewers who only stop people whom they think will be friendly and accommodating. Thirdly, interviewers may only stop people whom they think fit into one of their quota cells, with the result that the boundaries of quota categories tend to be under-represented. For example, a quota category of women aged 51–65 may contain few aged 63–65 because interviewers perceive such women as older than they actually are or hesitate to ask their age in case of causing offence.

To overcome some of the biases inherent in High Street quota samples, quotas may be filled by interviewing in specific geographical areas. These can be chosen using probability sampling to provide a set of nationally representative areas. The non-probability element is restricted to the final stage of selecting individuals. Within each sample area, interviewers are instructed to start at a specified house in a certain street, then call at every nth (e.g. third) house, following a specified route, called a 'random route'. When someone answers the door, initial screening questions identify whether anyone present in the household falls into a required quota category, and, if so, they are asked for an interview. Because there are no call-backs, such a 'random route' approach will under-represent those who work long hours or are rarely at home, and over-represent people who spend a lot of time at home. If the person who fits the quota category refuses or says it is not convenient to be interviewed at that time, the interviewer goes on to the next nth house.

A major drawback of quota sampling is that, since it is not a probability sample, it is impossible to estimate the standard error and so the researcher cannot calculate confidence intervals or use any inferential statistics (see section 5.5). In addition, quota samples do not provide refusal or non-response rates, and have been found to under-represent certain groups, particularly people at both extremes of the income distribution (Marsh and Scarborough, 1990). However, as with any sample, it is possible to assess the representativeness of a quota sample by comparing it with known population characteristics.

5.5 PROBABILITY SAMPLING

This section provides an overview of the statistical underpinning of sampling theory. A fuller discussion can be found in most introductory statistics books, and in Moser and Kalton (1971) and Sapsford (1999). If you have previously had little contact with statistics, you may prefer to skim this section and go on to section 5.6.

The aim of probability sampling is to make inferences from the value of a sample statistic to the value of a parameter of a previously defined population with known margins of error. For instance, one might use the mean income of a sample of 300 university graduates ($\bar{x}$) to estimate the mean income of the population of all university graduates (μ).

Any number of samples of 300 university graduates could be drawn from a population of all university graduates, and each sample will have its own mean income ($\bar{x}$). If the means of a very large number of samples are plotted as a graph, the graph is called the sampling distribution of sample means, and will always form a Normal Distribution (a bell-shaped curve). The Normal Distribution has certain fixed properties and is illustrated in Figure 5.1.

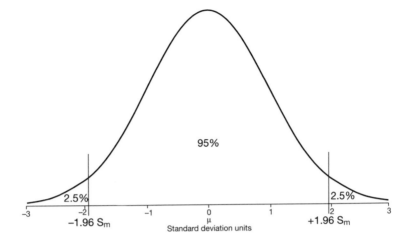

95%

2.5%

2.5%

-3 -2 -1 0 1 2 3
-1.96 S$_m$ μ +1.96 S$_m$
Standard deviation units

Figure 5.1 *Sampling distribution of sample means*

The spread of the curve depends on a quantity called the **standard error** of the mean (S_m). If the standard error is small, the curve is peaked and if it is large, the curve is flatter. The Normal Distribution has the property that 95 per cent of sample means will always fall within the area enclosed by 1.96 standard errors (S_m) on either side of the population mean (μ).

Another way of saying the same thing is that, for any one sample mean ($\bar{x}$), there is a 95 per cent probability that the population mean (μ) lies within the band defined by the sample mean minus 1.96 S_m and the sample mean plus 1.96 S_m. This can be written:

$$\bar{x} - 1.96\ S_m < \mu < \bar{x} + 1.96\ S_m$$

For example, a sample survey of university graduates finds the mean annual income to be £12,500 and the standard error to be £300. Therefore, there is a 95 per cent probability that the population mean (the average income of all university graduates) lies between £12,500 − 1.96 × 300 and £12,500 + 1.96 × 300, that is, between £11,912 and £13,088. If, however, the standard error had been £1,000, there would be a 95 per cent probability that the population mean was between £10,540 and £14,460. The latter would be a much less precise, and therefore less useful, finding.

The standard error indicates the **precision** of estimates of population parameters. One of the aims of sample designers is to achieve a sample with as high a precision as possible, in other words, with a low standard error. Crucial to this is the size of the sample: the larger it is, the smaller the standard error (see section 5.9). The *proportion* of the population sampled has little impact on the standard error, at least for large populations. It is primarily the *size* of the sample that matters.

5.6   SELECTING A SIMPLE RANDOM SAMPLE

The most straightforward way of obtaining a probability sample is to select a Simple Random Sample (SRS) in which each element in the population has an equal (and non-zero) chance of selection. There are three methods of selecting an SRS from a sampling frame: the lottery method, selection with random numbers and, the most widely used method, systematic selection.

Whatever the method of selection, it is first necessary to obtain a sampling frame that identifies uniquely every member of the population (see section 5.7). Suppose a sample of 50 is to be selected from a population of 400 small businesses in a county. The **sampling fraction** (SF) is the chance of selection of each element in the population, and is calculated from the sample size (n) divided by the population size (N), that is $SF = n/N = 50/400 = 1/8$. In the lottery method, names of the 400 small businesses could be put into a hat or drum, thoroughly mixed and a sample of 50 taken out. This is feasible when the population is not very large, but would be unrealistic with a population numbering more than a few thousand.

Random numbers are more frequently used than the lottery method. A unique identification number is assigned to each element in the population. In the case of the small businesses, ID numbers would be assigned from 001 to 400. Random number tables (in the back of some statistics books) or computer-generated random numbers can be used. Using random number tables, the researcher starts at any column in the tables, and examines 3-digit numbers in that column. When the 3-digit number lies between 001 and 400, that small business enters the sample. This continues until a sample of 50 has been obtained. Using this method, the same random number could be selected more than once. There is little to be gained from interviewing the same person twice! So it is usual to sample **without replacement**, that is rejecting any numbers that had previously been selected. Sampling **with replacement** (or unrestricted random sampling) is where each element in the population has the possibility of entering the sample more than once. In the lottery method, this would mean that once a sample member had been drawn its number would be returned to the drum to have the same chance of selection as all the others in the population.

5.6.1 Systematic selection

Both the lottery and the random number methods of selection are cumbersome and time-consuming when a sample is to be selected from a large population. In such cases, systematic selection is more usual. All elements of the population are listed and a fixed **sampling interval** is used to select sample members. The sampling interval is the reciprocal of the sampling fraction. For example, if 50 small businesses are to be selected from a population of 400, the sampling fraction is 1/8 and the sampling interval is

8. Every eighth small business on the list is selected after a random start between 1 and the sampling interval, 8. For instance, if business number 5 is selected first, business number 13 is selected next, then number 21, and so on.

Systematic selection is always without replacement. It is not exactly equivalent to Simple Random Sampling, because once one element has been selected, the selection of all other elements is determined by the order of the list. It is impossible for neighbouring elements on the list to enter the sample. This is generally an advantage, because sample members are likely to be more evenly spread across the population than in a true SRS.

Providing that there is no periodicity that relates to the sampling interval in the list, for example, so long as every eighth business does not share a particular characteristic, systematic selection will result in an unbiased sample. Systematic selection from a list such as the Electoral Register (discussed in section 5.7.1) improves the precision of the sample compared to using an SRS because it spreads the sample more evenly throughout the area. An equivalent SRS could by chance result in a sample in which all members lived in a few streets. In effect, the systematic selection is stratifying the population by street (see section 5.9.1).

Before discussing probability samples more complex than a Simple Random Sample, the next two sections will examine the use of sampling frames and how to minimise survey non-response.

5.7   USING SAMPLING FRAMES

Probability samples require the selection of respondents from some kind of sampling frame. Sampling frames should be evaluated in terms of their completeness of coverage and whether there are any omissions or duplicate entries. Consider, for example, a self-completion questionnaire study of employees in a multinational corporation. It may be possible to obtain names and addresses of employees from the company. However, by the time the questionnaires are sent out, some employees may have left and new employees joined. Those who had left (or died) would be 'out of scope', and their inclusion in the sampling frame would not bias the sample. They would simply be left out of the calculation of the response rate. However, the omission of new employees is more serious because the resulting sample would under-represent recent recruits. To overcome this potential bias, one might seek to update the sampling frame by obtaining lists of new employees and selecting from these as well.

Another potential problem is that employees may have moved between different plants or offices within the same company. If the lists for each plant were updated at different times, the same individual might be on more than one list – a duplicate element – or might be omitted from the sampling frame entirely. Duplicate listings could be checked and one entry deleted, but if the population is large, this might be very time-consuming. The danger of leaving duplicate elements in the sampling frame is that they bias the sample by over-representing occupationally mobile employees.

5.7.1 The Electoral Register

A widely used sampling frame of the adult population in Britain is the Electoral Register, since it covers all people over age 17/18 registered to vote. It is usually used as a sampling frame of the non-institutional population, that is, omitting people in prisons, long-stay hospitals and residential homes. The Electoral Register excludes those ineligible to vote, such as Peers. But much more serious is the exclusion of those who for various reasons have not registered to vote. Because Electoral Registers are compiled annually by each local authority in October and published each February, they are always between five and 17 months out of date.

The Electoral Register is particularly well-suited to systematic selection. Each person on the register has a unique identification number and is listed within their dwelling, dwellings are listed in number order within each street, streets are listed alphabetically within each polling district, and polling districts can be easily amalgamated to form wards and constituencies. The identification number of the last elector in a polling district corresponds to the total number of electors (i.e. the population) in that polling district. It is therefore easy to work out a sampling interval for the systematic selection of a fixed number of individuals from a polling district (or ward).

Electoral Registers are widely available in public libraries and can be purchased from the local authority. They are usually available electronically, but not in a standardised national format, so are easier to use for drawing local rather than national samples. The Electoral Register as a sampling frame has been found to under-represent certain groups, particularly young adults, those in privately rented accommodation, members of minority ethnic groups and unemployed people (Butcher and Dodd, 1983).

It is a more accurate sampling frame for addresses (or dwelling units) than it is for individuals, because individuals within households may be geographically mobile or not registered to vote. Some surveys aim to study households rather than individuals. The Electoral Register can be used to select a sample of households by selecting addresses using a process called **firsting** (Moser and Kalton, 1971). An address is selected into the sample only if the sampling interval falls on the first elector at that address. If this procedure is not used, the probability of selection of an address will vary with the number of electors living at that address.

5.7.2 The Postcode Address File

Since the mid-1980s, the Postcode Address File (PAF) has been used as the sampling frame of choice for the majority of national and large-scale probability samples in the UK. It has advantages over the Electoral Register in being more up-to-date (it is updated quarterly by the Post Office), having a more complete coverage and being available electronically (Foster, 1994; Wilson and Elliot, 1987). It is therefore more easily accessible, more convenient and cheaper to use. A disadvantage is that names are not recorded in the Postcode Address File and it contains no information about the number of adults or households resident at an address. Most addresses contain just one household, but some contain more than one. For these addresses, set procedures need to be laid down in order to give each household one and only one chance of selection.

The sampling frame used by researchers is the 'Small User File' that lists addresses normally receiving under 25 items of mail per day. Thus, those few private households that receive larger quantities of mail are excluded. In addition, about 10 per cent are non-residential addresses, such as shops and small businesses, and therefore need to be excluded from samples of private households.

5.7.3 Multiple list sampling

There is often no ready-made sampling frame available for the population of interest, so the researcher has to piece together a sampling frame from more than one source. Sometimes it is necessary to negotiate access to specialised lists, for example lists of school pupils, patients registered with general practitioners, and members of a society (e.g. the Multiple Sclerosis Society). You may need to be creative in finding lists that cover the population you wish to study, and use skill and diplomacy to obtain access to these lists. It is important to remember that it is necessary to obtain approval from the relevant Health Authority Ethics Committees to use any kind of list of patients within a research study. Ethical approval can take weeks or months and requires the completion of complicated forms.

An example of constructing a sampling frame from several sources is Brannen and Moss's (1988) study of women who returned to full-time work within nine months of childbirth. They defined their population of interest as women born in Britain, living in Greater London, who were having a first birth and who were living with their partner. There were no available sampling frames that covered this population, so the researchers pieced together the sample from three main sources: maternity hospitals, employers and private nurseries. Women were visited on the maternity wards of seven large hospitals and asked if they would mind being contacted again, 47 large employers were asked to pass on the names of women on maternity leave, and the researchers contacted the 33 nurseries in the Greater London area which took children aged nine months or under. From these sources, the names of over 4,000 mothers having first births were obtained, but of these only 295 intended to return to full-time work, and 255 took part in the first interviews.

5.7.4 Screening or two-phase sampling

Two phase or screening samples can be considered when a probability sample is required for a specific sub-group for which an adequate sampling frame is not available. It involves an initial screening phase (or sift) of a larger population in order to identify the required sub-group. The procedure can only be used for sub-groups where the identifying characteristic can be easily ascertained. For example, it would be inappropriate as a method of identifying drug users or groups with a particular sexual orientation, but feasible for identifying a specific minority ethnic group, disabled people or a particular age group (Lee, 1993).

In the first phase, all addresses in a large probability sample are contacted with a short screening questionnaire to establish whether anyone at that address has the required characteristic. This screening phase may be carried out by interviewers if a high proportion of sample addresses contain someone with the relevant characteristic. For example, the Women and Employment Survey used an interview screen to identify a sample of women aged 16–59 (Martin and Roberts, 1984). The Office of Population Censuses and Surveys (OPCS) Survey of Disability (Martin et al., 1988), which aimed to obtain a national probability sample of disabled people in private households, used a postal screen to identify households containing anyone with specific disabilities. A probability sample of eighty thousand addresses drawn from the Postcode Address File were sent a short self-completion questionnaire asking if any household member could not do, or had difficulty doing, various tasks such as climbing stairs or reading. The screening phase should obtain a high response rate and, in the Disability Survey, an 80 per cent response was achieved. Personal interviews may be used to follow up those who did not reply in order to increase the response rate or to estimate if there is a non-response bias.

The second phase selects a sample from the people identified during the first (screening) phase. In the Women and Employment Survey, all women aged 16–59 identified in the screening phase were included in the final sample (Martin and Roberts, 1984). Alternatively, a subset of previously identified cases can be selected using a probability sampling method.

A telephone screen may be appropriate for some topics. An interesting example is a study of the wives of men employed in the off-shore oil industry in Aberdeen (McCann et al., 1984). The researchers were refused access to employee names and addresses by the oil companies in Aberdeen and had to think of an alternative way of obtaining their sample. They assumed a very high level of telephone ownership among oil workers. Random-digit dialling was used to telephone over 10,000 numbers in the Aberdeen area. They asked some simple screening questions: 'Does anyone in the household work in the oil industry?' If Yes, 'Do they work off-shore?' When a potential sample member was identified, the name and address was requested. From over 8,000 households with obtainable telephone numbers, 421 men working in offshore oil were identified. Less than 5 per cent of

numbers were unanswered after three calls, and only 4 per cent of households identified as including offshore oil workers refused to answer further
questions.

5.8 SURVEY NON-RESPONSE

Having selected a probability sample, one needs to maximise the response
rate of those selected, that is, minimise non-response. The researcher should
consider each potential source of non-response and take steps to reduce
each. The two main sources of non-response are refusals and non-contacts.
For example, among selected eligible addresses in the General Household
Survey (GHS) for 1994, 15.4 per cent refused and no contact could be made
with anyone in a further 2.7 per cent of addresses. In addition, in 1.6 per cent
of households there was no contact with one or more household members.
This resulted in an overall response rate of 80.3 per cent (Bennett et al.,
1996). However, the response rate varied substantially between different
areas, varying from 83.5 per cent in Wales to 75.6 per cent in Greater
London. It is usual for surveys to obtain a lower response rate in London and
inner-city areas than in other parts of the country.

Table 5.3 illustrates the survey response rate for the National Survey of
Sexual Attitudes and Lifestyles (Devine and Heath, 1999; Wellings et al.,
1994), which used a nationally representative sample drawn from the Postcode Address File. It shows that 12 per cent of the 50,010 selected addresses
were out-of-scope, in other words they were businesses or institutions that
did not contain a private household. The survey aimed to interview one
person aged 16–59 from each of the sample households, and a further 28 per
cent of addresses did not contain anyone within this age range. Thus, the
sample of eligible addresses was 29,802, only 60 per cent of the original
sample of addresses. Sexual attitudes and behaviour are very sensitive topics
and it was therefore expected that there would be a high refusal rate. In the

Table 5.3 *Sources of non-response in the National Survey of Sexual Attitudes
and Lifestyles*

	N =	%
Total addresses issued:	50,010	100
Out-of-scope addresses (not private households)	5,980	12
No eligible resident (no one aged 16–59)	14,228	28
Potentially eligible addresses	29,802	60
Of which		
Completed interviews (i.e. **response rate**)	18,876	63
Refusals	9,278	31
Non-contacts (i.e. out after at least four calls)	1,027	3
Not-interviewable (e.g. ill, unable to speak English, temporarily away)	621	2
Total eligible sample	29,802	100

Source: Devine and Heath (1999: 113).

event, the refusal rate was 31 per cent (6 per cent of households refused to give any information at all, and in 25 per cent the person selected by random means for interview refused). In addition, there was a non-contact rate of 3 per cent after at least four calls at the address and 2 per cent of selected individuals could not be interviewed because they were too ill, unable to speak English or temporarily away during the period of survey research.

Different sources of non-response will now be considered, together with the strategies that can be used to minimise each.

Refusals

The largest component of non-response is usually made up of people who refuse to be interviewed. The level of refusals is influenced by a number of factors:

1. How interesting respondents find the subject matter. For example, a survey of attitudes to the health service will obtain a higher response rate than one about financial service organisations. If the target population is very specialised and finds the research topic particularly salient, there may be no refusals. In contrast, a very sensitive topic, such as sexual behaviour, may result in a high refusal rate, as in the National Survey of Sexual Attitudes and Lifestyles (Wellings et al., 1994), which obtained a response rate of 63 per cent (Table 5.3).
2. The perceived importance of the study. If the research is thought to be worthwhile or to contribute to improving services or facilities, the response rate will be higher.
3. The perceived 'legitimacy' of the research, in terms of the conduct of the study, the survey organisation and the research sponsor. For this reason, government surveys often achieve higher response rates than those run by commercial organisations.
4. The skill and persistence of the interviewer in providing appropriate and reassuring replies to respondents' queries, and in encouraging hesitant respondents. Interviewer training plays an important role here.
5. There may also be area and cultural differences in willingness to respond.

Information on the first three of these factors should be provided to the respondent through a preliminary letter or a letter left by the interviewer, and in an introduction read out by the interviewer before the interview (see Chapter 6).

Non-contacts

Non-contacts are minimised by increasing the number of call-backs at the selected sample address, calling at different times of day and days of the week. Often the interviewer can arrange an appointment through another household member and make themselves available at a time convenient for the respondent. At least three call-backs are usually recommended. Nevertheless, some people may not be contactable because they are away for long periods of time (e.g. for the summer holidays), temporarily working away from home or in prison.

Not-interviewable

Usually some respondents cannot be interviewed because they are too ill, deaf or unable to speak sufficient English. Whether special measures are taken to reduce this potential source of bias will depend on the aims of the study. Government surveys often use proxy interviews, for example in the GHS, in which a near relative within the same household is asked factual questions on behalf of the respondent, but is not asked opinion, smoking, drinking or income questions. Arranging for proxy interviews is particularly important in surveys of very old people, because the needs of the most frail would otherwise be under-represented.

It may also be important to employ interviewers who speak appropriate languages or interpreters, otherwise the sample would be biased against those with least fluency in speaking English.

Movers

People who have moved will only form a component of non-response when the sample includes specifically named individuals rather than those currently resident at a particular address. An example of the former is Oakley's (1974) research on housework (referred to in section 5.3), which was based on a sample of 65 names of women with young children drawn from two general practitioners' lists. Of these, 16 (25 per cent) had moved or could not be traced, seven were not contactable and two could not be interviewed within the timescale of the research.

5.8.1 Assessing the representativeness of samples

Whatever the magnitude of non-response, survey researchers should always assess the representativeness of the achieved sample and identify the nature and extent of any bias. This can be done by direct or indirect methods (Moser and Kalton, 1971). Direct methods involve further follow-ups and attempts to 'retrieve' non-respondents, for example, by using interviewers who are more experienced to try to 'convert' refusals into respondents. Very brief self-completion questionnaires can be sent to non-respondents to obtain basic socio-demographic information or telephone follow-ups can be attempted. Extrapolations of the characteristics of 'hard core' non-respondents can be made from the characteristics of the retrieved segment, although it is questionable whether these two groups are comparable.

Indirect methods of assessing the representativeness of a sample involve comparing the achieved sample against known population characteristics, such as by age, sex and social class, obtained from the population census or large government surveys. For example, the 1994 GHS results were compared with the age–sex profile for 1994 government population estimates and found to show an under-representation of adults aged 20–29, especially men, and an under-representation of women over age 75 (Bennett et al., 1996).

If significant under-representation is found for a particular sub-group, some researchers may consider replicating the data from those in the sub-group who did respond an appropriate number of times to simulate the results of missing sample members. This procedure is called **weighting**. For example, if there were only half the expected number of men aged 20–24 in the sample that would have been expected from the population distribution, this sub-group could be given a weight of 2.0. However, weighting usually assumes that respondents are in all respects comparable to non-respondents, which may not be the case.

5.9   MORE COMPLEX SAMPLE DESIGNS

Most surveys use a more complex sample design than the Simple Random Samples discussed in section 5.6. When planning large surveys, a compromise usually has to be reached between the desire for high precision (a low standard error) and the constraints of time and money. As we noted in section 5.5, precision is measured by the standard error; the lower the standard error, the more precise the estimates of population parameters from the sample.

Three aspects of sampling that affect precision are illustrated in Table 5.4. The first is associated with the degree of variation in the population under

Table 5.4   *Factors affecting the standard error*

1. *Variation in the population*
   A more varied population will have a larger standard error.
2. *Sample size*
   A larger sample size gives a smaller standard error.
3. *Sample design*
   (a)   More stratification results in a lower standard error.
   (b)   More clustering results in a higher standard error.

The standard error of the mean is estimated using the formula:

$$\text{Standard error } S_m = \frac{\text{standard deviation}}{\text{square root of the sample size}}$$

$$= \frac{s}{\sqrt{n}}$$

study. For example, the variation in income in a sample of the general population is likely to be larger than in a homogeneous sample of comparable size, such as recent university graduates. This variation is usually measured by the **standard deviation** or **variance**.

The second aspect which affects precision is the sample size. The standard error is inversely proportional to the square root of the sample size. For instance, to halve the standard error it is necessary to quadruple the size of the sample.

The third aspect affecting the standard error is the sample design. We will next outline how building stratification into the selection of a sample can produce a substantial gain in precision, while only increasing the cost by a small amount. After this we discuss the use of clustering (or multi-stage sampling) to reduce the costs of fieldwork, especially interviewing. However, clustering has the disadvantage of increasing the standard error of the sample, thereby decreasing the precision of population estimates.

5.9.1 Stratification

Stratification involves dividing the population into separate strata on a characteristic assumed to be closely associated with the variables under study. A separate probability sample is selected from within each stratum. Building stratification into a sample design is recommended because it usually increases precision for very little additional cost. Stratification ensures that the sample is representative on the characteristic(s) used to form the strata.

A Simple Random Sample will *on average* be representative of the population. However, any one sample may be unrepresentative on key characteristics. Suppose we want to study the career aspirations of university students and have sufficient resources to interview a probability sample of 125 students. Using simple random sampling will on average produce a representative sample, but any one sample may under-represent students from particular departments, and over-represent others. Since career aspirations are likely to be closely linked to the subject studied at university, it is desirable that the sample should contain the correct representation according to the students' departments. This can be achieved by stratifying the sample using departments as separate strata.

Prior to sample selection, the sampling frame is divided into departments (strata). This is straightforward because lists of students by department are easily available. Suppose the population consists of 5,000 university students and a sample of 125 is to be drawn. This would represent a sampling fraction of 1/40 and a sampling interval of 40. The 5,000 students would be listed by department and then systematic selection would be used with a sampling interval of 40. A random start between 1 and 40 is selected, say 27. The 27th person in the first listed department is chosen, followed by the 67th, 107th, and so on (see Table 5.5).

Systematic selection from a list ordered by one or more stratification factors automatically forces the sample to be representative on these factors.

Table 5.5   *Selecting a stratified sample of university students with a sampling fraction of 1/40*

Sample size (*n*) = 125	Population size (*N*) = 5,000	Sampling fraction = 140
Sampling interval = 40	Random start for selection = 13	

(a)   *Stratification by department*

	Population Number in department $N =$	Sample Number in department $n =$
Physics	320	8
Chemistry	120	3
Biology	160	4
•	•	•
•	•	•
Sociology	200	5
Total	5,000	125

(b)   *Stratification by department and year*

Physics	Year 1	120	3
	Year 2	100	2
	Year 3	100	3
Chemistry	Year 1	40	1
	Year 2	40	1
•		•	•
•		•	•
Sociology	Year 3	70	2
Total		5,000	125

In this example, the sample will contain exactly the same proportion of students in the Physics department as in the whole university, and similarly for each department.

Another variable that is likely to affect career aspirations is the students' year of study. The researcher could stratify simultaneously by department and by year within department, as illustrated in Table 5.5(b). This would yield a sample which was representative of students by department, by year of study, and by both variables in combination.

Stratification produces a lower standard error because the 'total variation' for any particular variable (e.g. career aspirations) in a population may be regarded as composed of variation 'between strata' and variation 'within strata'. In stratified random sampling, variation 'between strata' does not enter into the standard error because, by definition, this component of the variation in the population will be automatically reflected in the sample. The greater the proportion of a variable's 'total variation' that is accounted for 'between strata', the greater the gain in precision from stratification. For this reason, each stratum should be made as different as possible while maximising the similarity of elements within a stratum.

5.9.2 Clustering and multi-stage samples

A clustered sampling design is one where more than one stage of selection is used. Clustering is used to reduce the time and costs of conducting the survey, but it increases the standard error.

Clusters are often geographical areas (such as political constituencies or postcode sectors) or institutions (such as schools, hospitals or employers). Suppose you want to interview a national sample of 2,000 hospital nurses to obtain their views about current changes in health care. A simple random sample is rarely used for a national interview survey because of the prohibitively high costs of travelling throughout the country to carry out the interviews. Instead, a cluster sample in which the first stage units are hospitals would be preferred. Within such a two-stage design, the key question is the degree of clustering. The range of choices is illustrated in Table 5.6.

At one extreme, it would be possible to take a highly clustered sample of only five hospitals and interview 400 nurses in each. At the other extreme, a very widely dispersed sample could be selected, selecting five nurses from each of 400 hospitals. Because costs arise mainly from paying interviewers for their time, travel and subsistence, the latter design would cost a great deal more than the former.

A clustered sample may also yield substantial savings in administrative and sample selection costs as compared with an equivalent simple random sample. In multi-stage sampling, a complete sampling frame is only required for the primary sampling units, in this case, the hospitals. Negotiating access

Table 5.6 *Variation in degree of clustering in a national sample of hospital nurses*

Aim:	To select a sample of 2,000 hospital nurses.
First stage:	Select hopsitals.
Second stage:	Selection of nurses from within sample hospitals.

Options available:

Number of hospitals selected	Number of nurses selected	
5	400	Lower cost, lower
10	200	precision
20	100	
40	50	
50	40	Optimum
80	25	
100	20	
200	10	Higher cost, higher
400	5	precision

Costs include:
(1) Interviewing costs, subsistence and travel.
(2) Administrative costs of negotiating access to obtain the sampling frame (i.e. lists of hospital nurses from each sample hospital) and drawing the sample.

to obtain lists from a hospital and the time spent in drawing the sample from each list can be costly, and it would be much cheaper to do this only in the selected hospitals.

A clustered sample reduces precision and increases the standard error because elements within a cluster tend to be alike. For example, there is likely to be less variability in nurses' attitudes within hospitals than between hospitals. A highly clustered sample of nurses, selected from only ten hospitals, would have a much higher standard error than a sample of the same size selected from 200 hospitals. The latter would have a standard error which is little different from that of a simple random sample.

To maximise precision in a multi-stage sample, it is advisable to build in as much stratification as possible within each stage of selection. For a national sample of hospital nurses, all the hospitals in the country should be stratified by characteristics such as region and type (teaching, acute general, psychiatric, geriatric, etc.). This would ensure that the sample hospitals are a correct representation according to region and type of hospital. Within each selected hospital, prior to the systematic selection of the sample of nurses, the sampling frame of nurses should be stratified, for example according to grade of nurse. The resulting sample would then have the correct proportions of nurses at each level from senior management through ward sisters to staff nurses.

Samples with two or more stages of selection are called multi-stage samples. A three-stage sample has three separate stages of selection, for example, selection from constituencies, then wards, and finally adults within selected wards. A three-stage sample will generally result in a larger standard error than a two-stage sample. The majority of the large probability samples selected for national surveys are multi-stage samples that include stratification at each stage of selection. For example, in the GHS the first stage of selection is by postcode sectors, which are stratified by region, and within region by three other factors: the proportion of households with no car, in Classes I and II and containing pensioners (Insalaco, 2000). The second stage is to select addresses from within selected postcode sectors. Large national surveys usually use a method of sample selection called 'Probability Proportional to Size' (PPS) sampling. Details of the PPS sampling method can be found in Moser and Kalton (1971: Chapter 8).

5.9.3 Design effects

The estimation of sampling errors for stratified and multi-stage samples is more complex than for simple random samples. A stratified random sample will result in a standard error which is smaller than for a simple random sample of the same size, while the standard error for a clustered sample will be greater than for a comparable size simple random sample. The relationship between the standard error of a complex sample design and that of a simple random sample of the same size is called the Design Effect or Deff (see Moser and Kalton, 1971: Chapter 5). The design effect therefore measures the effect of the sample design on the precision of population estimates (Insalaco, 2000). The magnitudes of design effects vary between different variables within a survey; but a discussion of design effects is beyond the scope of this book.

5.10 PROJECT

1. A Catholic magazine included a self-completion questionnaire on the attitudes of Catholics to recent changes in the Catholic church and received over 10,000 replies from its readers. What could these data tell you about the attitudes of Catholics?
2. The government wishes to understand more about the reasons why juveniles commit offences. They decide to select a probability sample of 300 offenders from boys attending ten Youth Detention Centres. What could you learn about juvenile delinquency from this sample?
3. How would you obtain a sample of the following groups?
   (a) Illegal drug users in order to study the process of becoming a drug user.
   (b) Adults who are diabetic in order to study the effect of diabetes on family and social relationships.
   (c) Second generation Italians, i.e. people who were born in Britain and whose parents were born in Italy, for a study of the maintenance of Italian cultural practices.
   In each case, first define more precisely the population to be studied, then suggest alternative sampling strategies. How well would your proposed sample represent the population you initially defined?
4. Outline how you would select a probability sample of:
   (a) 5,000 women aged 16–59 which is nationally representative. (This is the sample selected in Martin and Roberts, 1984.)
   (b) 400 older people from a medium-sized town for a survey of unmet health needs.

5.11 FURTHER READING

De Vaus (1996, Chapter 5) is a survey methods text that provides a good but brief introduction to sampling. Kalton (1983) is a statistically sophisticated discussion of survey sampling concepts and sample designs. It requires a reasonable grasp of elementary statistics. Kish (1965) is a more advanced text, but very comprehensive on the technical aspects of sampling.

Lee (1993, Chapter 4) provides an excellent discussion and evaluation of the range of techniques that can be used to obtain samples of numerically rare or deviant populations. Lohr (1999) is comprehensive, but concentrates on the statistical aspects of taking and analysing different types of sample design. It includes useful exercises. Lynn and Lievesley (1991) provides a practical guide to drawing national samples.

Despite being 30 years old, Moser and Kalton (1971, Chapters 3–7) still provides a comprehensive discussion of survey sampling. Parts are quite advanced in the treatment of the statistical underpinnings of sampling theory. Sapsford (1999, Chapters 3 and 4) has a clear discussion of sampling theory and useful examples of some practical aspects of sampling.

PART II

INTO THE FIELD

QUESTIONNAIRES

6

ROSEMARIE SIMMONS

CONTENTS

Most people have encountered survey research, in one form or another, as either participants in surveys or recipients of information from surveys. Often surveys are used to predict outcomes, for example, the MORI polls conducted prior to elections, which attempt to gauge the voting behaviour of the adult population. Commercial organisations use the results of surveys to make decisions about the development of products, their pricing, their market penetration and the profiles of their customers.

Sociologists also regard surveys as an invaluable source of data about attitudes, values, personal experiences and behaviour. Surveys allow researchers to gather information from a specified target population by means of face-to-face or telephone interviews, or postal questionnaires. One of the most important parts of any research survey is the development of the questions. The success of a survey will depend on the questions that are asked, the ways in which they are phrased and the order in which they are placed.

The challenge for the researcher is how to select questions that will obtain the most valuable and relevant information. This is a skill to be learnt like any other in social research, and this chapter provides guidelines to help you devise such questions. The chapter will also make the distinction between questionnaires and interview schedules; discuss the use of open-ended and closed questions; show how to avoid ambiguous, leading, double-barrelled and hypothetical questions; describe the types of question that can be asked and the order in which they should be placed; and finally, discuss the varieties of format for questionnaires and interview schedules.

6.1   CHOOSING A METHOD OF QUESTIONING

Social research involves detective work. You begin with a problem and then ask a number of questions about it, such as, 'what?', 'who?', 'where?', 'when?', 'how?' and 'why?'. In some research, the most important question may be 'What are the consequences?' Consider the subject of discrimination:

- *What* constitutes discrimination? It is necessary to begin by identifying what is meant by discrimination. A starting point would be to look at existing literature on the subject and to work out ways in which the concept can be measured.
- *Who* experiences discrimination? You will need to focus on the particular groups that may be discriminated against, for example, people with disabilities, minority ethnic groups, or gays and lesbians. You may be interested in a certain age group, or those in a particular socio-economic group, or those living in an urban or rural environment.
- *Where* does the discrimination take place? Is it specific or general, for example, in the workplace, in schools, or simply on the streets?
- *When* does the discrimination occur? How regularly? For what length of time? Is it a large part of the subjects' everyday lives?
- *How* does it occur? This question may cover several aspects of behaviour, from investigating formal discriminatory practices to the measurement of levels of abuse. You may decide to explore ways in which institutions deal with discrimination, or concentrate on how prejudice affects the lives of those who experience related acts.
- *Why*? The main purpose of the study may be to seek an *explanation* for discrimination and why it occurs in certain areas and not others.

Most research studies will include questions within these categories.

At the outset of any research project, it is essential to identify the most appropriate method of carrying out your study. The method you choose is likely to be determined by the time and budget available, as well as the subject matter of your research.

If you want to find out what it feels like to experience homelessness, it would be more appropriate to use qualitative methods, such as conducting in-depth interviews to explore in detail the ways in which individuals cope with living on the streets. However, if you want to assess people's attitudes towards the government's expenditure on the Millennium Dome, it would be more effective to carry out a quantitative study, using self-completion questionnaires. This method would allow you to obtain a large-scale representative sample that would produce data which can be analysed statistically.

In practice, most studies combine both qualitative and quantitative methods, for example, beginning with focus group discussions to identify categories and relevant areas of study, followed by in-depth interviews with key informants and, finally, a survey targeting a much larger population. At the outset of any study, you will need to decide on the most appropriate and workable solution to the research problem.

6.1.1 Postal surveys

Postal surveys are a popular way of conducting research studies where the views of large populations are needed. These surveys use self-completion questionnaires.

The questionnaires follow a standardised format in which most questions are pre-coded to provide a list of responses for selection by the respondent (coding is discussed in Chapter 14). The questions must be phrased in a way that respondents find easy to understand, and so that it is easy for them to see how they can record their responses.

The main advantage of self-completion questionnaires is that a large population can be surveyed relatively cheaply. Costs are lower because interviewers are not used, and pre-coding and computerisation speeds up analysis. It is also possible for respondents to complete questionnaires at a time convenient to them.

The main arguments against using postal questionnaires have generally been that the response rate is low. For example, some postal surveys do not achieve more than a 20 per cent rate of return. The response rate will depend on a number of factors, including the subject matter of the survey, the target population under survey, the recipients' perception of its value, and the ease of completion of the questionnaire. In addition, even when respondents do complete questionnaires, their answers may be incomplete, illegible or incomprehensible. This poses a problem for those who have to transfer the data to a computer.

A further important consideration is that the researcher generally needs information about the target population in advance of the study in order to develop survey questions that are appropriate for the recipients. As many of the questions will list pre-coded answers, exploratory research to obtain these categories will have to be done before developing the self-completion questionnaire.

6.1.2 Face-to-face interviews

Some projects benefit by employing a face-to-face interview survey method. For example, a study that is concerned with a detailed study of household waste management might benefit from an interviewer being present in a home to guide the respondent through a large range of disposal options.

Interviewers will need to be provided with some form of document to guide questioning; this may consist of both pre-coded and open-ended questions (see section 6.4). It is important here to note the distinction between an **interview schedule** and an **interview guide**. A schedule contains set questions in a pre-determined order that is adhered to in each interview. This type of instrument is generally used in a large-scale survey.

An interview guide, on the other hand, is used for a *focused* interview and will list areas to be covered while leaving the exact wording and order of the questions to the interviewer. In some cases, the interview guide will be quite sketchy to allow for the possibility of non-directive interviewing in which the interviewee's replies determine the course of the interview.

Interviewers may record responses directly on to an interview schedule by pen or use a tape-recorder to record the interview for later transcription. Portable computers, programmed with interview schedules, are becoming increasingly popular.

Interviewing can have both advantages and disadvantages. Interviews can be more flexible and, in the hands of a skilled interviewer, extract more information from the individual than a postal survey. The disadvantage is that it is expensive to carry out interviews because of the cost of paying interviewers and travel expenses.

Often, interviews are used in preliminary research before a postal survey is carried out in order to develop ideas for questions and to determine what pre-coded answers should be offered in the postal questionnaire.

6.1.3 Telephone surveys

Interview schedules are also used for interviews conducted via the telephone. Telephone surveys have similar merits to those involving face-to-face interviews, but have the added benefit that it is possible to reach a wider population at less cost.

Although telephone surveys are less popular with social scientists than they are with market research companies, they can be an effective way of conducting social research. Developments in computer technology have now made telephone interviewing easier. A computer-assisted telephone interviewing (CATI) system is able to sample the specified population, provide guidance for the interviewer's introduction, display the interview schedule item by item with appropriate filter questions (see section 6.5), and record the interviewees' responses.

Telephone surveys do have disadvantages. The main problem is that certain groups such as the poor, the young, the sick and disabled, and those who are frequently away from a telephone (perhaps in the course of their work) may be under-represented. Sensitive questions are difficult to ask at a distance, and it is less easy to supply stimulus material such as prompt cards (see sections 6.4.1 and 6.7) to the interviewee.

Furthermore, telephone interviewing is very different from face-to-face interviewing and the training of interviewers in telephone technique must be thorough. Interviewers cannot interpret the reactions of the interviewee by observation so they must learn to present questions clearly and listen carefully for any signals that might indicate lack of understanding. A further problem concerns concentration; if the interview is not prearranged, the interviewer may not get the full attention of the interviewee.

It might well be assumed that since all three of these methods, postal, face-to-face and telephone surveys, have significant deficiencies, the chances of obtaining valid and reliable data are very small. This is not so, argues Dillman (1978), who claims that many difficulties can be overcome by using a 'total design method'. By giving minute attention to every aspect of the survey process, from the training of interviewers to the devising of questions, from the letters asking for participation to the paper on which questionnaires are printed, the quality of response for all types of survey can be improved. This approach is to be thoroughly recommended: giving careful attention to the planning and execution of the research project will enhance the likelihood of producing useful results.

6.2 HOW TO BEGIN

Before embarking upon any research exercise, it is important to explore any previous studies that have been carried out on the subject. This will not only provide a framework for developing questions for the new research, but will also ensure that the project builds upon previous work. Start, therefore, by obtaining academic papers, books and reports based on related research. The use of the Internet is invaluable for exploratory work. Questionnaires and interview schedules that have been used in a study are sometimes included in published work and can prove a useful foundation for one's own research.

A first draft of a questionnaire will be based largely on questions derived from previous studies and on 'brain-storming', that is, writing down all questions that could be useful. It is not enough that questions should reveal interesting information; the data obtained *must* relate directly to the study. Often, it is quite difficult to decide which are the important issues, but preliminary background reading will usually help to elaborate a set of hypotheses that will help to sort the relevant from the irrelevant (see Chapter 2).

If you were to investigate whether e-mailing to friends was the most popular means of written communication, you would need to begin by defining 'popular'. Does this mean 'most liked' or 'most often carried out', or both? You would probably want to know whether different sections of the population had different patterns of communication. A number of variables would therefore have to be considered: age, sex, marital status, employment status, educational level, social class, and so on. You may be able to think of several areas that have a bearing on the research topic, but each question must have a direct relevance to one of the variables of the hypothesis – be ruthless in weeding out questions that do not. It is advisable to keep the hypothesis and the objectives of the research very firmly in mind when developing questions.

When drafting questions, you also need to consider **reliability** and **validity** (see Chapter 2 and section 7.4). A study can be said to be reliable if similar results would be obtained by others using the same questions and the same sampling criteria. In order to make it possible for repeat studies to be carried out, first, questions should be worded clearly and unambiguously so that they can be asked in the same way in follow-up studies. Secondly, instructions for both administration and completion should be the same for all questionnaires or interview schedules. Thirdly, the sample of the population under study should be well defined and the details provided in the research report.

A study can be said to have validity if it actually measures what it sets out to measure. This is more difficult than it sounds. For example, what set of criteria can be used to measure what contributes to 'good health'? Some researchers may use variables such as physiological factors, relationships or employment status, while others may choose spiritual or psychological criteria (see the discussion of measurement theories in Chapter 2).

6.3   TYPES OF INFORMATION

Four main categories of information can be obtained from a survey. They are listed below with examples of how questions might be phrased.

Attributes

Attributes include personal or socio-economic characteristics, such as sex, age, marital status, religion and occupation.

Obtaining valid and reliable information about occupation is more difficult than it might seem at first. You could ask some simple questions, as in Example 1. However, what constitutes paid employment? Would, for example, two hours work per week in a bar put the respondent into the 'employed' or 'unemployed' category? A good example of the kind of careful and thorough questioning needed to get over these kinds of difficulties can be found in the interview schedule used in the General Household Survey (Bridgwood et al., 2000: 216).

Example 1

Are you in paid employment?	Yes No
If <u>yes</u>: What is your occupation?	....

Example 2

Have you ever belonged to a political organisation?	Yes No
Are you a member of a political organisation at the moment?	Yes No
Do you intend joining a political organisation in the future?	Most likely Likely Unlikely Most unlikely Don't know

Behaviour

Behaviour constitutes what the individual has done, is doing, and may possibly do in the future (see Example 2). There may, of course, be difficulties in defining what is meant by a political organisation and it may be necessary for the researcher to make it clear to the respondent what is meant by the term. For example, should Greenpeace, the ecological pressure group, and the Institute for Economic Affairs, a politically committed research institute, be counted as political organisations?

Attitudes

Attitudes imply evaluation and are concerned with how people feel about an issue (see Chapter 7). Questions about attitudes usually employ scales: a statement is made and individuals are asked to indicate their level of agreement in a positive or negative direction (see Example 3).

Example 3

I think anyone with a conviction for drinking and driving should be banned indefinitely	Strongly in favour In favour Neither in favour nor against Against Strongly against

Example 4

The number of people living on the streets in London has increased in the past five years.	True False

Beliefs

Beliefs can usually be assessed by asking whether something is seen as true or false (see Example 4).

6.4 FORMS OF QUESTION

In both interview schedules and questionnaires, there are two forms of questions that can be asked: **closed questions** and **open questions**.

6.4.1 Closed questions

Closed questions are developed in advance, complete with a number of possible answers that can be given. Each respondent is asked to choose from one of the listed options. For example, a closed question asking about the highest level of educational attainment would ask respondents to choose from a list of categories such as basic education, a degree and professional qualifications. Other questions, such as 'Are you married?' have the appearance of open questions, but are only answerable by 'yes' or 'no'.

Closed questions have advantages because they can be pre-coded and the responses can easily be put on a computer, saving time and money (see Chapter 14). They also have particular advantages in studies using self-completion questionnaires because they are less time-consuming for the respondent to complete.

However, such structured questions also have the disadvantage that they force the respondent to choose between the answers provided. When faced with a question such as: 'Do you enjoy your work?' the respondent may wish to say 'yes and no', 'it all depends', or 'I like the social contact'. This difficulty can be overcome to a certain extent by asking for more information. When the respondent is asked to indicate either 'yes' or 'no', this can be followed by a 'why?' or 'please provide further details', allowing for more elaboration. Where lists are given, a category of 'other' should always be provided for those who cannot find an appropriate pre-coded response.

Ranges can be given which make completion and coding easier. For example, when asking about income, the options in Example 5 can be offered. In face-to-face interviewing, such ranges of answers can be printed onto a prompt card and given to the respondent.

Example 5

> Under £5,000 per annum
> £5,000–£9,999 per annum
> £10,000–£14,999 per annum
> £15,000–£19,999 per annum
> £20,000–£24,999 per annum
> £25,000–£29,999 per annum
> £30,000–£34,999 per annum
> Over £35,000

Example 6

> Which do you feel are the most important factors in staying healthy?
>
> *Please rank the following in order of importance to you. Number them from 1 = most important, to 7 = least important.*
>
> Taking regular exercise
> Having a good diet
> Being in a stable relationship
> Having regular health checks
> Living a low stress lifestyle
> Being engaged in productive activity
> Knowing about what contributes to good health

6.4.2 Ranking scales

A ranking scale is a form of closed question that can be valuable when trying to ascertain the level of importance of a number of items. A list of choices is provided and the respondent or interviewee is asked to rank them (see Example 6). It is advisable to limit the range of alternatives because it may be difficult for the individual to rank a large number. This is particularly important when carrying out face-to-face and telephone interviews, where more than four or five items can be unmanageable. It is helpful in face-to-face interviews to allow the respondent to look at a prompt card showing the choices.

6.4.3 Open questions

Open questions are those that allow individuals to respond in any way they wish. For example, asking an open question 'What do you think can be done to improve your local environment?' will allow the respondent or interviewee to state any measure from reducing noise pollution to instituting steep penalties for dropping litter.

Open-ended questions can be most usefully employed by skilled inter-viewers who can allow interviewees to develop answers much more fully than they would if they were completing questionnaires.

It is also very useful to use open questions when beginning a new research project. If investigating the ways in which students cope financially while at university, the researcher would do well to begin by asking open-ended questions of a small sample of students. From such a small-scale study, it would be likely that a list of possible answers would emerge, for example, working in a bar, borrowing from the bank, living with relatives, and so on. If a larger study were to be carried out, answers to these open questions could then be used to devise pre-coded categories for closed questions.

Open questions do have their drawbacks. In questionnaires, it is relatively simple for respondents to tick pre-coded categories, whereas unrestricted answers require more thought. A further disadvantage of using open questions is that they produce responses that may be ambiguous, wide-ranging and difficult to categorise. Answers can be time-consuming to code, interpret and analyse, and therefore expensive to deal with when conducting large-scale studies.

The type of study will determine whether open or closed questions are best, but it is worth bearing in mind that:

> closed questions should be used where alternative replies are known, are limited in number, and are clear cut. Open-ended questions are used where the issue is complex, where relevant dimensions are not known, and where a process is being explored. (Stacey, 1982: 80)

> Their advantage is that they allow a respondent to answer on their own terms, enabling the researcher to discover unexpected things about the way people see a topic. (Seale and Filmer, 1998: 130)

In most questionnaires and interview schedules, both open and closed questions will be included. However, when large numbers of individuals are to be studied by self-completion questionnaires, it is best to use a majority of closed questions.

6.5 DEVELOPING QUESTIONS

Your choice of questions will obviously depend on the subject matter of your study. However, a number of important guidelines need to be considered.

Relevance to participants

It is essential to assess whether respondents will have the knowledge to answer the questions, whether the questions are relevant to them and whether they wish to reveal the information.

Clarity

A fundamental point is to ensure that questions can be clearly understood and are not subject to any ambiguity. Although this applies both to interview schedules and questionnaires, it is particularly important when producing a document for self-completion. If someone is interviewed and does not understand a question, he or she can at least ask for some elaboration, but when the questionnaire is the only means of communication, confusion will discourage the respondent. Furthermore, any misunderstanding will mean that any response given is invalid.

Getting the wording right may present a problem, particularly if a wide-ranging population is under study. The wording should not appear too simplistic for some, seeming to insult their intelligence; on the other hand, it must not be too sophisticated for others. If words or phrases are complicated, then misunderstanding may result. It is preferable to avoid jargon: words like 'social interaction', 'alienation' or 'socialisation' may be everyday terminology to sociologists, but their meanings may not be fully understood by others. It is worth remembering that significant numbers of the population may be functionally illiterate and that for many, English will not be their first language. Of course, if the sample comes from a particular group, for example, engineers, medical practitioners, or lawyers, it would be appropriate to use the vocabulary common to these groups.

It is important to have the same frame of reference as those under study and this is one of the most difficult aspects of producing questions. Certain words may be interpreted in differing ways, depending on individual perspectives. For example, common words like 'equality' or 'independence' may mean different things to different people. Other more technical words such as 'fault' or 'fracture' will be understood differently by tennis players, horse riders and geologists. Therefore, questions need to be developed carefully to match the sample to be used.

The important principle is to use simple words and uncomplicated sentences.

Leading questions

Television or radio interviewers' questions are sometimes preceded by 'Wouldn't you agree that . . .?', or 'Isn't it the case that . . .?'. The object is to *lead* an individual into agreeing with a particular statement. Researchers, however, need to take a more objective stance and avoid leading questions. For example, if you are carrying out a study of attitudes towards government policy, you should not ask: 'Don't you agree that the present government's policy on crime is an excellent one?' or 'Isn't it the case that, since the present government came into office, the life of pensioners has improved?' Rather, an open-ended question such as 'What do you think of the government's policies on crime?', or a closed question listing various elements of the policies and asking the respondent to rate which they regard as most valuable, would yield more objective and helpful results. It is important to establish what the respondent thinks is important, without being directed by the researcher.

Double-barrelled questions

Double-barrelled questions are those which ask two questions in one. For example, if the question 'Are you employed, and do you enjoy your work?' is asked, it may be that the answer to the first part is yes, while the answer to the second part is no, so that the respondent is not sure how to answer. The questions should be separated: 'Are you employed?'; if *yes*, 'Do you enjoy your work?' Two questions in one will lead to confusion.

Another example is a question in which a person is asked, in one sentence, whether he or she knows about something and what he or she thinks of it: 'Do you know anything about the work of Greenpeace, and what is your opinion of it?'

It is also advisable to avoid double negatives. If you were to ask someone whether he or she agrees that 'Those not over 18 should not be allowed to drink alcohol in pubs, restaurants or at home', it is not clear what an answer 'no' is intended to mean.

Hypothetical questions

For most studies, hypothetical questions are best avoided. These questions usually begin with 'What would you do if . . .?' or 'Would you like to . . .?' What the respondent or interviewee says he or she might do when faced with a given situation may not be a good guide to his or her actual future behaviour. There are some questions that inevitably produce favourable replies: 'Would you like to have a higher income?' is unlikely to be met with a negative response.

There are, of course, instances where it may be useful to ask people to imagine what they would do in a certain situation: 'If you witnessed someone stealing a wallet, would you intercept?' Whether such hypothetical questioning is useful will be dictated by the subject matter of the study. Hypothetical questions are sometimes used at the outset of a study, as part of a focus group discussion, where such questions stimulate ideas and debate between participants.

Secondary information

In most instances, it is inadvisable to ask respondents or interviewees about someone else's views, that is, request secondary information. An individual may not be able to state the opinions or perceptions of another person with accuracy. Neither will respondents necessarily be able to describe the experiences of someone they know. However, if the other person is not easily available for interview, it is common practice to ask a member of his or her household for *factual* information about that person (for example, his or her age, sex, occupation, and so on). This is called using a 'proxy' for the intended interviewee.

Periodicity

When investigating behaviour which requires the individual to specify a time or a number, supply specific categories. Thus, when asking how often the respondent attends the theatre or reads a newspaper, offer the alternatives: daily, 2–3 times a week, once a week, twice a month, and so on. Terms such as 'often', 'frequently', or 'regularly' are too vague and should be avoided.

Sensitivity

Attention must be given to ensuring that the way in which questions are phrased is handled sensitively so that respondents are not offended or alienated. For example, your study may be interested in the sexual behaviour of young adults and questions will, of necessity, be personal in nature. Piloting to test responses will help guide the development of acceptable questions.

However, a key problem with researching sensitive issues is to know whether respondents are being truthful – they may over- or under-report some activities. Sudman and Bradburn (1983) suggest that there are three main areas where over-reporting may occur:

1. 'Being a good citizen', that is, voting behaviour, relationships with government officials and community activities.
2. 'Being a well-informed and cultured person', for example, newspaper and book readership, and attendance at concerts and plays, involvement in educational activities.
3. 'Fulfilling moral and social responsibilities', that is, contributions to charity, helping family and friends, and being in employment.

Conversely, there may be under-reporting of certain aspects of individuals' lives, such as illness and disability, criminal behaviour, sexual activities, smoking, illegal drug-taking, drinking alcohol, and financial status.

Because of the dangers of either over-reporting or under-reporting, questions need to be phrased so that they do not intimidate those taking part in the study. Careful preparation of questions, using foresight and experience to predict those which may prove to be sensitive, will ensure that you get the best response from participants.

6.6 THE FORMAT OF A QUESTIONNAIRE

A questionnaire should be designed with the respondent in mind. It is also important to include information to explain the purpose of the study.

In a postal survey, it is essential that a covering letter is included as part of the questionnaire so that it does not go adrift. For a postal questionnaire, the date by which the questionnaire needs to be returned should also be given (generally, two weeks from the distribution date). Either a stamped addressed envelope or a 'Freepost' envelope must be included.

The questionnaire should explain at the beginning what is needed, give clear instructions throughout and, if necessary, provide illustrations. It is particularly important to ensure that participants understand whether a single response to a question is wanted, or whether several responses to one question would be appropriate.

Here is a checklist of key points to remember:

1. All closed questions must be pre-coded, allowing space for as many alternatives as possible. Always include an 'other' category.
2. For some open-ended questions, prompts may be needed.
3. Ensure that you have appropriate column numbers to help with transferring the data to a computer file (see Chapter 14).
4. Remember to include filter questions and provide clear directions so that the respondent needs only to read the questions that are appropriate to his or her circumstances.
5. Each question must be numbered. If appropriate, section headings and sub-sections are useful as guidance for both respondent and researcher. When the topic changes, an introductory sentence should be provided.
6. Neither split questions between pages, nor ask a question on one page and ask for a response on the other.
7. An identification number must be put on every questionnaire to enable checking and reminders to be sent if questionnaires are not returned.

The questionnaire should be no longer than necessary. For most studies, it should take less than half-an-hour to complete. So, list the questions you require, edit as much as possible, and try to limit the layout to no more than six sides of paper. It is more likely that there will be a good response rate if a concise questionnaire is provided.

The order in which questions are asked is important; the questions should not jump from subject to subject. A question about marital relationships, followed by one about work experience, then one on home ownership before a return to the subject of marital relationships, would be an example of poor ordering. When positioning the questions, try to follow the same sequence one would in normal conversation, with each question arising logically from the one before.

Questions should not only fit together but also be grouped together according to subject. If the ordering of questions is unpredictable, it will frustrate respondents and make the study appear ill-considered and amateurish.

It is also essential to provide clear linking sentences, particularly when moving on to a different topic. Phrases such as: 'Moving on to . . .', 'Thinking about your experience of . . .', 'The next set of questions concerns . . .', or 'I'd now like to ask you about . . .' can be used.

The interest of the respondent needs to be engaged and maintained. It is best to begin with simple and easy questions that are non-threatening. Once the individual begins to complete the questionnaire, or take part in the interview, the chances of successfully obtaining the more sensitive items of information improve. Even if the later questions are left unanswered, it may still be the case that earlier responses will be valuable for the study.

Questions concerning background and socio-economic data are normally best asked at the end of questioning. However, there are exceptions. For example, if you are examining experiences of hospital care, you would need to ask early on whether the respondent had children, so that those who were childless could be re-directed or excluded.

Postal questionnaires should begin with closed questions, where responses can simply be ticked, rather than open questions which may require the respondent to give considerable thought to an answer. It is preferable to ask open questions at a point when the respondent has become committed to the questionnaire.

Both questionnaires and interview schedules usually need to include filter (or skip) questions to guide respondent and interviewer through the questions, avoiding those which are irrelevant to the respondent. Interviewees who have not had a child should not be asked questions about children. This is the purpose of the instructions to the interviewer on the right hand side of the page in Example 7.

Producing the questionnaire in a booklet form looks professional and makes the document easier to handle. Generally an A4 paper size allows questions to be well-spaced and clearly printed.

Choose a font for the document that is attractive and easy to read, such as Arial, and use a range of sizes to make instructions and questions clear to the respondent. If the budget allows, use good quality paper, preferably coloured so that it stands out from the mass of other paper which might be received. Remember that the questionnaire's appearance will have a significant influence on whether respondents feel like completing the form.

A note of thanks expressing appreciation for the assistance given should be placed at the end of the questionnaire.

When each questionnaire is returned, it needs to be checked for missing information and to ensure that it is legible prior to data capture.

Example 7

Q.1 Do you have any children?	Yes No	*if yes, go to question 2* *if no, go to question 4*
Q.2 What ages are your children?		
Q.3 Do they still live with you?		

It will be necessary to send reminders to those who have not returned questionnaires. Plot the rate of return on graph paper and send reminders when the response rate begins to fall. The questionnaire forms will need to be coded to enable you to check which ones have been returned. If you think coding may put people off responding, and yet you wish to send reminders, send them to everyone, saying that if they have not already done so, they should return the forms. Usually, reminders include another copy of the questionnaire and are sent two weeks after the date given for the return of the questionnaire.

6.7   THE FORMAT OF AN INTERVIEW SCHEDULE

The interview schedule, or interview guide, will be handled by a trained interviewer. It is important that the same guidelines are followed by every interviewer and, therefore, the instructions must be explicit.

All interviewers must carry some means of identification (with a photograph) and, if required, a letter of authority from the funding body (see Example 8).

Even if the interviewee has received prior notification of the interview by letter or telephone, the interview schedule must begin with a brief introduction, stating who the interviewer is, which organisation he or she represents and the purpose of the interview. Confidentiality and anonymity should be stressed.

Interview schedules, like questionnaires, must provide filter questions to ensure that the interviewer can move smoothly from section to section. This

Example 8

Good morning/afternoon/evening. I am .... from the University of Poppleton.

We are conducting a survey on behalf your local Council, to find out what people think about their services. A representative sample of people in the Borough has been selected for interview in this survey. This will give you the opportunity to 'have a say' and your taking part will make a great contribution to the study.

Everything you say will be treated confidentially. No names will be attached to any information you provide.

The interview will take about 30 minutes.

If the potential agreement is shown:

Would it be convenient to carry out the interview now, or if preferred, I could come back (or telephone) at another time? When would be most convenient?

is particularly important in telephone interviewing when silences over the telephone while the interviewer sifts through the questions may confuse or annoy interviewees. Several filter questions and examples of other features of interview schedules are shown in Figure 6.1, an extract from a housing survey.

For some closed questions, it can be more convenient to offer grouped answers on a prompt card. For example, in most instances the exact dates of birth of respondents is not of interest, but simply their age group. Participants

---

IF HOUSEHOLD TOOK UP TENANCY IN 1996 OR LATER (IN LAST 5 YEARS)

ASK SECTION 1, if not, GO TO SECTION 2.

SECTION 1. INITIAL TAKE UP OF TENANCY

1. When you moved into your present house/flat did you move?:   (1)
    From Council Waiting List _____   1
    From temporary Hostel (Homeless) accommodation   2
    Moved because of modernisation programme ____   3
    Transfer or exchange of Council property _____   4
    Other (Specify) _____   7
    NA/NR _____   9

    (a) Is your present house/flat temporary (short-term)   (2)
         accomodation?
         Yes – temporary accommodation _____   1
         No – permanent home _____   2
         Don't know _____   8
         NA/NR _____   9

2. When you first took up the tenancy what was the internal   (3)
    decoration like?
    Very good _____   1
    Good _____   2
    Acceptable _____   3
    Poor _____   4
    Very poor _____   5
    Don't know _____   8
    NA/NR _____   9

    If 'Poor' or 'Very Poor'
    (a) How did you feel about this?   (4)
         Extremely upset/very disturbed/desperate _____   1
         Very unhappy _____   2
         Unhappy _____   3
         Did not mind/not concerned _____   4
         Quite happy _____   5
         NA/NR _____   9

    (b) Did you receive a decoration allowance (because of the   (5)
         poor decorative order of the property)?
         Yes _____   1
         No _____   2
         Don't know _____   8
         NA/NR _____   9

Figure 6.1 *An extract from the Public Housing Survey*

Example 9a   Example 9b   Example 9c

Your Age
18–25
26–35
36–45
46–55
56 and over

Financial reward
Social contact
Self-esteem
Benefits
Something to do
Other

Strongly agree
Agree
Neither agree nor disagree
Disagree
Strongly disagree

also find it more convenient (and, in terms of age, sometimes less embarrassing) to indicate a range (see Example 9a).

Cards can also be used to list various alternatives from which the interviewee can choose. For example, when asking the question 'What are the most important aspects of being employed?', the card can list the responses shown in Example 9b. Cards can be used for attitude questions. For example, the responses offered for the proposition, 'The Government should reduce the tax on fuel' might be shown in Example 9c. Supplying prompts will also help respondents remember events which they might otherwise have forgotten.

If there is a long list of statements to be read or shown to interviewees, it is possible that items at the top of the list are attended to more closely than those in the middle or at the bottom. To reduce this potential bias, the items in the lists can be rearranged with some interviewers using one order and others using an alternative order.

An interviewee cannot look at a card when being interviewed by telephone so an alternative technique is to read all the items and obtain a yes/no answer to each one separately. The number of items will need to be limited to three or four for this to work.

6.8 PREPARING FOR FIELDWORK

When developing a questionnaire or interview schedule there are two preliminary steps you should take. First, try your draft out on people you know. Secondly, 'pilot' the questionnaire or schedule on a small sample drawn from the same population as the main study.

It can be very useful to try a questionnaire or schedule on friends and colleagues who will cast a critical eye over the questions and the order in which they are placed. This will also help to ensure that instructions and guidelines are clear. It is surprising how often a question that seems perfectly satisfactory to the author proves to be ambiguous to others. It is better to discover this before it is too late. The questions can then be revised and a working document produced.

The next stage is to conduct a pilot study. As a guide, in a proposed survey of 2,000 respondents, the pilot sample should include between 10 and 20 respondents. This initial group must have similar characteristics to those of the population to be studied. From the pilot, the researcher will be able to assess whether the line of questioning is appropriate and whether the document is understandable and simple to use.

Remember that people are under no obligation to take part and will need to be encouraged and feel valued in order to comply with your request. The theory of social exchange propounded by Blau (1964), among others, argues that individuals' actions are motivated by the 'rewards' they are likely to receive from others. Although there may be certain 'costs' in performing any particular action, most individuals try to ensure that these are outweighed by the benefits they receive. In general, the material rewards offered by researchers to participants taking part in a study are likely to be low. However, if individuals feel that they have been specially selected and that their participation is highly valued, this may be sufficient reward. The costs are the time taken to provide answers and the mental effort required. If the questions make the individual feel anxious or embarrassed, these costs may in the end outweigh any rewards.

An effective introductory letter is especially important when carrying out postal studies because it helps secure the cooperation of potential partici-pants. When an individual receives an unsolicited questionnaire through the post, his or her immediate reaction may be to ask any or all of the following questions: 'What is the study about?'; 'Who is carrying it out?'; 'How long will it take to complete?'; 'What are they trying to sell to me?' An introductory letter may allay some of these doubts and anxieties.

Begin by introducing yourself and your organisation, and briefly state the aims and objectives of the research. In most instances, the individual has nothing to gain by taking part and it is therefore necessary to emphasise why the study is important and make the individual feel that he or she will be making a valuable contribution to research by participation. You will also need to state why the individual was chosen for the study so a brief outline of the sample is useful.

It is also vital to stress that confidentiality will be maintained and that information provided will only be used by those involved in the research. State that the report derived from the study will only include statistical information and unattributable quotations.

Letters should be personalised by a signature. Attention can be drawn to a telephone or e-mail number so that individuals approached can seek more information.

6.9 CONCLUSION

This chapter has provided some guidelines and offered some practical assistance so that most of the difficulties of preparing questions can be foreseen and avoided. The fundamental idea underpinning the approach outlined here is that attention must be given to all aspects of the questioning process if a satisfactory response rate and valuable data are to be obtained.

The researcher must give thought to what is to be investigated, what form and types of question are relevant and whether the questions ask for information that is available to the participants. Questions should be clear, composed of everyday words and simple sentences, and the order in which they are presented should be logical. Questionnaires and interview schedules should be drafted, tested, edited and tested again, before being used for the survey.

6.10 PROJECT

Now you have been given some guidelines, try to put these into practice by developing a self-completion questionnaire. Imagine that you have been asked by a local authority to carry out an investigation into attitudes towards the recycling of waste. You have been asked to select a representative sample of the population (see Chapter 5) and ask questions about whether respondents recycle their waste, if so to what degree, if not, why not, etc. For example, what have respondents recycled during the past month? You will need to devise a working definition of what is meant by recycling activity to guide the design of the questions. The Council are particularly interested in how people might be encouraged to recycle more, so questioning along these lines will be necessary.

As this will be a self-completion questionnaire, try to include as many closed questions as possible, with pre-coded categories. So that correlations can be made when you analyse the data, choose a number of variables that may be relevant, for example: age, sex, employment status, income, marital status, housing status, and so on.

Prepare a draft, test it with a friend, and then try the final questionnaire out on a small sample (e.g. five people).

6.11 FURTHER READING

A very useful book which comprehensively covers all aspects of questioning is Sudman and Bradburn (1983). It is particularly helpful on the subject of designing questions on 'sensitive' issues and also addresses the problem of ensuring that the answers gained accurately represent the views of the respondent. Questionnaire development is also fully explored in De Vaus (1996). Oppenheim (1992) provides useful tips on producing questionnaires. Seale (1999) includes essays on the philosophy, methodology and history relating to social science investigation, as well as guidance on conducting research. For the analysis of data gained from in-depth interviews, Silverman (1993) provides helpful guidance.

Measuring Attitudes

7

Mike Procter

The content of many surveys can conveniently be divided into two components: 'objective' and 'subjective'. The first of these certainly needs to be printed in quotation marks, since there is a point of view according to which all social facts are social constructs.

Nevertheless, it often makes sense to distinguish between, on the one hand, the approximately objective, factual variables, such as age, gender, and even social class, since this is typically classified on the basis of ostensibly factual information about the respondent's occupation, and, on the other hand, the variables that result from asking the respondent for a subjective reaction: an opinion on a social issue or something of the sort.

This latter component is often referred to as attitudinal. ('Opinion' and 'value' are near synonyms to attitude.)

7.1   WHAT IS AN ATTITUDE?

An attitude is a hypothetical construct: no one has ever seen or touched one, and its existence and properties must be inferred indirectly. This is, in itself, not an embarrassment: there are plenty of other perfectly respectable examples of unobserved constructs, including not only most of social science but also large chunks of physics. What is important is that the particular concept should be linked in well-understood theoretical terms to other concepts, and that it should be possible, at least in principle, to make empirical observations that can produce evidence either consistent or inconsistent with those theoretical links (see Chapter 2). It has to be admitted that in practice there is not as much theory or evidence as one would like. However, the idea of an attitude is so natural that despite these failings it remains central to much research in sociology and social psychology.

What seems to be common to most definitions is that an attitude is a predisposition to behave in a particular way. If a friend eats no meat, her vegetarianism could be based on health concerns; if she attends hunt saboteur meetings, the anti-hunt stance could be due to class identification; and if she demonstrates outside the pharmacology department's animal laboratories it might be part of a general mistrust of globalisation and transnational corporations. Alternatively, you might explain all three of these behaviours in terms of a particular attitude to animal welfare. There is a tension here: Occam's razor goes in favour of simplification, but this may be an *over*-simplification. Later in the chapter, I shall show how we may be able to decide between these two hypotheses.

To avoid over-simplifying, I should mention the long-standing debate sometimes referred to as the 'attitude–behaviour problem'. This refers to the common (indeed, almost universal) finding that there is no simple relationship between verbal and non-verbal indicators of an attitude.

This finding was dramatically illustrated by a landmark study published before the Second World War. LaPiere (1934) described how, for two years starting in 1930, he travelled extensively throughout the USA with a Chinese couple. He reported that they were received at 66 overnight lodgings and served in 184 eating establishments during their travels, and only once were denied service – by a proprietor who said he did not provide accommodation for Orientals. However, when LaPiere sent out questionnaires six months later, asking each of the 250 establishments that served them whether they would accept Chinese guests, only one of the 128 respondents replied that they would. The general point to be made is that if there is an underlying attitude it will not be the sole determinant of either the verbal or the non-verbal behaviour, and strong relationships can be expected only if the entire situation is very carefully analysed. In particular, it seems likely that

LaPiere's restaurateurs, motivated chiefly by commercial considerations, believed that they would be less likely to lose custom by discreetly admitting a Chinese customer who was actually in the foyer than by risking a scene. The latter problem did not exist for the postal questionnaire.

In short, a verbal statement is only a **behavioural indicator** of an attitude and the attitude–behaviour problem is really just one aspect of the more general one of imperfect relationships between different behaviours.

7.2 A PRELIMINARY EXAMPLE

Before getting more deeply into the theoretical and methodological problems of attitude measurement, let us consider the problem of measuring political radicalism through a questionnaire, either self-completed or administered in the course of a survey interview. A number of points will emerge to be dealt with in more detail in later sections.

You might begin by thinking of a simple question to ask: for instance, 'Do you consider yourself to be politically radical?' Respondents could be invited simply to answer 'yes' or 'no', or to choose one of, say, five answers from 'yes, very' to 'no, on the contrary'. (In principle, they could be allowed to make an open response, but in practice this would be too complicated to analyse in a typical survey sample of 1,000 or more.)

There are several objections to such an approach. The one I will emphasise here is that the researcher is asking the lay respondent to make a social-scientific judgement: the question assumes that the respondent uses the term 'politically radical' in essentially the same way as the researcher, even when applying it to him or herself. Even if there were agreement on the beliefs that tended to be part of radicalism, a person's judgement is likely to be situation-dependent: when I am with some of my colleagues (ageing 1960s' revolutionaries) I might think myself a conservative; in the company of some students I might think myself a dangerous radical. Only an 'objective' observer, such as a researcher aspires to be, may be expected to apply the same criteria in a roughly consistent way across a range of individuals and settings.

It would perhaps be more reasonable to ask the respondent to answer a question that does not demand as much prior analysis on his or her part. For instance, we could ask which political party he or she belongs to or identifies most closely with, and then use our knowledge of the parties to classify people into radicals and non-radicals, or to locate them on a radical–conservative scale. A different problem here is that people sometimes identify with parties for non-ideological reasons – because of class identification, or family tradition, perhaps, so that you measure the wrong concept.

Alternatively, we could try to formulate a question that would encapsulate our concept of radicalism more directly. Suppose we saw it in terms of the Labour Party's celebrated Clause Four, which called for the common ownership of the means of production, distribution and exchange. Then we would ask our respondent to indicate an opinion of that view, either by a simple agreement or disagreement, or on a scale from complete endorsement to complete rejection.

What are the problems now? The first is that a single item is a very unsatisfactory way of measuring an underlying attitude.

An analogy may help. Suppose that you want to get a brief message from one mountain top to another by using teams of shouters, who are recruited in pairs. The big difficulty is that (for religious reasons about which there is no room to go into in detail here) every 'signal shouter', who will obediently shout the same message in unison with the other signal shouters (the words 'Party tonight!', say) is accompanied by a 'noise shouter'. All the noise shouters will shout different words. If you have just one pair of shouters, the noise is just as audible as the signal, which may well not be received. But if you use ten pairs, the message will be shouted ten times as loud, whereas the different noises will tend to cancel each other out, so that the signal has a much greater chance of being correctly received. Something rather like this can be observed at the last night of the Proms, London's summer classical music festival, where, during an interval in the music, a small, carefully rehearsed section of the Promenaders shouts a humorous message in unison, which is quite audible over the random chatter of thousands.

The same analysis can be applied to measurement problems.

It is convenient to see any behaviour as being determined by an equation of the following form:

$$B = A + R$$

Here B means an item of Behaviour (in the case of attitude measurement it will be verbal behaviour), A means Attitude, and R means Randomness. In words, a particular item of verbal Behaviour (a statement of opinion, say) is determined partly by a relevant Attitude and partly by a large number of other influences, which can be regarded as essentially Random.

If we consider two related statements (related in the sense that they may be regarded as manifestations of the same underlying attitude), called B_1 and B_2, then their two equations will be identical in form, though slightly different in detail:

$$B_1 = A_1 + R_1$$
$$B_2 = A_2 + R_2$$

It is often reasonable to assume that A_1 and A_2 are essentially the same thing (because both statements are, as already specified, to do with the same attitude), but that R_1 and R_2 are different random influences.

Suppose, now, that we consider both B_1 and B_2 (for the same individual). This **compound behaviour** now contains a double dose of both the attitudinal determinant and the random influences. The difference between these is that the attitude is duplicated (like the shouted signal), and therefore reinforced, whereas the random influences (like the shouted noise) are not duplicated, and thus become dilute. So the share of the compound behaviour that is due to the attitude is greater than is the case for either of the individual statements.

To put this in more concrete terms, any single statement, intended as an indicator of an underlying attitude, will always be heavily contaminated with other influences, and thus measure the attitude rather poorly; several statements, all chosen so as to reflect the same underlying attitude, will do so collectively far more effectively.

Some technical details will be added to this observation below, under the heading of reliability and validity (section 7.4).

The second problem is that it is certainly unrealistic to see political radicalism solely in terms of an attitude to Clause Four. To put it in more technical terms, most attitudes are multidimensional. In the present context this means that we would almost certainly want to include in our conception of radicalism other issues that are logically unconnected with the question of common ownership. Examples that occur to me (though one would usually use less subjective sources, as will be outlined later) include nuclear disarmament and pacifism, redistribution of resources within a nation and between nations, racial and gender divisions, sexuality, freedom of information, trial by jury and other civil liberties, and so on. Each of these is a very broad heading, and might be represented by a range of specific statements. For instance, the redistribution area might include statements about levels of income tax and inheritance tax, and about direct confiscation of wealth; and about terms of trade and financial relations between developed and 'third world' countries.

Appropriate analysis would probably show that, rather than a single dimension of radicalism, there are several, and that, although there may be some tendency for a respondent who is in favour of reducing expenditure on armaments also to be in favour of increasing overseas aid, there will be many individual exceptions, so that, in brief, the two views may be seen as belonging to two distinct dimensions of radicalism.

All of this implies that it is always desirable, and often essential, to adopt a multiple-indicator approach. This means putting together a collection of statements thought to be relevant to the concept to be measured. First, of course, the concept itself must be defined as closely as possible, with what help one can get from a search of the literature. The statements are then assembled from a variety of sources, including written materials of various kinds (the press, pamphlets, polemical books) and oral statements taken from group discussions and unstructured interviews. They are edited to try to avoid the pitfalls discussed in Chapter 6. The final versions of the items are then put to a sample from the appropriate population and the responses analysed so as to determine how best to use them to represent the attitude. In practice one usually starts with too many statements, so as to be able to select a subset of the best.

A number of approaches have been proposed within this general framework and these are described in section 7.3. However, in order to understand them, it is necessary to know about a key statistical concept: correlation.

7.2.1 Correlation

The correlation coefficient is a number between 0 and 1 (calculated from a rather complicated formula – or by clicking the appropriate button in a computer program) that indexes the strength of the relationship between two variables. If the correlation is zero, then the two variables are completely unrelated: for instance, if there is no tendency whatsoever for agreement with one of two statements of opinion to imply agreement with the other. On the other hand, a correlation of 1 means perfect association: here it would mean that agreement with one statement would unerringly imply agreement with the other. Correlations can also be negative: a value of -1 would mean that everyone who agreed with one statement disagreed with the other. (One might get something approaching this situation because the wordings of the two statements were in some sense 'opposite ways around': one that favoured first-strike use of nuclear weapons and another that favoured immediate unilateral disarmament, perhaps.)

Of course, in practice we always find correlations of intermediate value. You can either interpret these essentially qualitatively – 'a higher correlation means a closer relationship' – or you can try something slightly more technical. To be precise, if you square a correlation coefficient, the resulting value (which must necessarily be positive, of course) can be interpreted as the proportion of the variance in one variable that is shared with the other.

7.3 TECHNIQUES OF ATTITUDE SCALE CONSTRUCTION

There are a large number of methods of constructing attitude scales, which will be described rather briefly in this section. Many of them are of importance more because of their frequent mention, especially in the older literature, than because they are still recommended.

7.3.1 Thurstone scaling

Leo Thurstone (1928) was the first important pioneer in this field. He suggested a method that involved the following steps:

1. Collect statements of relevant opinion, chosen in such a way as to range along the presumed scale of attitude, from most favourable to most unfavourable. Edit them for clarity, etc. End with about 100 statements.
2. Recruit a panel of about 300 judges, and ask them to sort the statements into 11 numbered piles, from most to least favourable, with a middle, neutral category. Each statement thus receives 300 scores. The average of these is that statement's scale value.

3. Twenty statements or so are selected for further use, in such a way that they cover the range of the scale and avoid statements on which the judges disagree too widely.
4. In use with a study sample (as opposed to the panel of judges), the final set of statements is offered to the respondents, who are asked to indicate the ones with which they agree. Their scale scores are then the averages of the endorsed items' scale values.

However, this method is extremely expensive in time and other resources and is rarely used today.

7.3.2 Likert scaling

Rensis Likert (1932) developed a method that, as well as making different statistical assumptions, had the great advantage over Thurstone scaling of dispensing with the initial large panel of judges.

1. The initial collecting of opinion statements proceeds as before.
2. The statements are administered to the study sample (without a preliminary panel of judges).
3. Respondents are asked to respond to each item by placing their response on (typically) a five-point scale, most often

    strongly agree ... agree ... can't decide ... disagree ... strongly disagree

    These are usually coded 5 ... 1.
4. For each item the 'item-whole' correlation is calculated between that item and the sum of the remaining items. Items with excessively low correlations are eliminated from further analysis, on the grounds that they must be failing to tap the attitude that is measured by the other items. The computer program SPSS (see Chapter 15) includes a procedure called RELIABILITY which carries out all of these calculations.
5. Scale scores for individuals are determined by summing the retained item scores.

An important difference between Thurstone and Likert scale items should be explained. A typical Thurstone item is worded in such a way that some respondents will agree with it, some will disagree because it is too favourable to the issue in question, and some will disagree because it is too unfavourable. For instance, a statement designed to measure attitudes to the present government might say 'about half their policies have been successful'. Strong supporters and opponents would both reject this statement (and would be catered for by parallel statements attributing higher and lower success rates). On the other hand, a Likert item would say 'the policies of present government have been successful'. This would be rejected by all opponents of the government, but could be accepted by all their supporters, however enthusiastic.

Likert items are called 'monotonic' and Thurstone items 'non-monotonic'. To understand these terms, think of each person as occupying a position on a vertical line extending from most 'con' (at the bottom) to most 'pro' (at the top) with respect to the government (or other social object). Statements of opinion are arranged on the same line, in increasing favourableness from bottom to top. A moderate Likert item will be rejected (for simplicity, suppose we only permit two responses, agree or disagree) by all respondents positioned well below it and accepted by all those well above it. There will be individuals in the immediate vicinity of the item who hesitate: the more favourable they are, the greater the probability that they will accept. On the other hand, a Thurstone item will be rejected by respondents too far above it or below it. As we consider individuals who are close to the item, going from bottom to top, the probability of acceptance will first rise and then fall again.

In essence, monotonic means 'order-maintaining': as we go up the attitude continuum, the probability of accepting a Likert item at first remains steady at 0, then rises over its immediate vicinity, then remains steady at 1; having risen it never falls again. A non-monotonic Thurstone item, on the other hand, first rises in probability and then falls again.

Nowadays most attitude items are constructed so as to be monotonic (and are often referred to as 'Likert items', especially if the responses form a five-point scale), although the analysis usually follows the factor model described below in section 7.5.

7.3.3 Guttman scaling

Louis Guttman (1944) was one of a team of eminent social scientists recruited to the US Army during the Second World War. The method that bears his name has been extremely influential (even though it is not often used in its original form) because Guttman continued for many years to develop his methods into more general forms.

The essential idea behind his original formulation is that of a cumulative scale. One problem with, say, a Likert scale is that though a particular set of responses will always add up to the same total score, the same total score may arise from many combinations of responses. For instance, a score of 10 on a five-item scale could come from 'disagree' (scored 2) on each item, or from one 'strongly agree', one 'disagree' and three 'strongly disagrees'. In practice, one would seldom get quite such different combinations, but clearly it would be preferable if the same score always meant the same thing.

It is easiest to give an example of such a desirable property from achievement testing. Suppose your class is given a maths test consisting of three questions which require respectively addition, multiplication and differentiation. Each answer is scored 'pass' or 'fail'. In principle there could be eight different patterns of pass/fail ($2 \times 2 \times 2$), but in practice there would only be four: some would pass all three items, some would pass the first two but fail the third, some would pass only the first, and some would fail all three. To put it slightly differently, a score of 2, for instance, would in practice identify someone who can add and multiply but not differentiate: we would not expect to find someone who can differentiate but not multiply.

One attitude item can also be regarded as more difficult than another, in the sense that it will be endorsed only by a respondent with a stronger positive attitude. For instance, a respondent with a moderately negative attitude to smoking might agree that television advertising of cigarettes should be banned. Someone with a stronger negative attitude, who agreed with a ban on smoking in all public places, would almost certainly also agree with the first item. There would probably be few individuals who would reverse this: who agreed with the public smoking ban but thought television advertising should continue. Of course, since there is no logical connection between the two items, whether this neat relationship actually holds is an empirical question, and the development of a multi-item cumulative scale of this kind (often simply called a Guttman scale) involves a complicated statistical analysis.

In more recent years, Guttman, Lingoes and others have developed multidimensional extensions to this method, called generically Smallest Space Analysis. In parallel with this, other groups of researchers have developed very similar analyses called multidimensional scaling. At one level these may be regarded as alternatives to factor analysis (see section 7.5) which make more realistic assumptions about the measurement properties of the data. Specifically, many of these methods assume only ordinal measure (see section 14.1.2), whereas factor analysis is usually regarded as requiring interval measure, for which the difference between 'agree' and 'strongly agree' should be quantitatively the same as that between 'strongly disagree' and 'disagree'.

7.3.4 Magnitude estimation

Magnitude estimation has its origins in the attempts of psychologists to measure the relationship between the strength of a physical stimulus (the intensity of a light, the pressure level of a sound, a weight resting on the hand, an electric current) on the one hand, and the strength of the corresponding experience on the other. The same stimulus is offered at a range of different objective intensities, and the subject is asked to give a subjective numerical rating to each one. The results, averaged over a dozen subjects, are plotted. It turns out that people can handle this task in a quite consistent way, although the details differ between sense modalities.

Sellin and Wolfgang (1964) found that their respondents could give similarly consistent ratings on a social perception task. They constructed brief narratives focusing on the theft of goods worth a varying amount, other details of the offence being held constant. Ratings of the perceived seriousness of each offence were plotted on the vertical axis, with the actual amount on the horizontal axis. As with physical stimuli, respondents (judges, police officers and students) spontaneously gave ratings that followed a consistent curve. Emboldened by this success, Sellin and Wolfgang asked for seriousness ratings on other offences not involving a quantifiable loss, such as smoking marijuana, assault and sex abuse. It seemed reasonable to assume that seriousness was being rated in the same way as when a money amount was mentioned; if this is so, one can assign a seriousness score to any offence and estimate the aggregate seriousness of a year's offences in a way that makes far more sense than merely counting 'crimes known to the police'. For instance, there is the basis for assessing the effect of a decrease in crimes against the person and an increase in property offences.

Since Sellin and Wolfgang, magnitude estimation has been used much more widely, to obtain, for instance, quantitative measures of a candidate's political popularity. Respondents have been asked, instead of giving an oral numerical response, to draw a line, the length of which reflects their strength of feeling. Originally this was done on paper, with obvious inconvenience from the researcher's point of view, but respondents can now use a joy-stick (meant originally for playing computer games) to draw the line on a computer screen, which automatically measures the length and 'acquires' the data for instant statistical analysis.

7.3.5 Expectancy-value scaling

Fishbein and Ajzen (1975) propose a method of not just measuring but also analysing attitudes, the expectancy-value (E-V) approach. This is based on the assumption that we consider a number of dimensions in evaluating any social object, and refers back to early theoretical formulations that refer to affective and cognitive components in attitudes. Respondents are asked to what extent they approve of each of a set of dimensions (the affective, or 'value' component), and then to what extent they believe each dimension applies to the issue being considered (cognitive, or 'expectancy'). Each expectancy is combined with its value to get an overall E-V score. For instance, overall preferences between energy technologies (nuclear, fossil fuel, tidal power, etc.) were evaluated by asking to what extent (in probability terms) each was characterised by low cost, risk of catastrophe, long- and short-term pollution and favourable technological spin-offs. Before this, the liking or disliking for each dimension was elicited. The contribution of each dimension to the overall evaluation was estimated by multiplying the probability score by the liking score. A technology would tend to be favoured overall if liked dimensions were seen as having high probability, and disliked dimensions had low probability. For instance, catastrophe was highly disliked, but seen as very unlikely for tidal power.

The advantages of the E-V approach are, first, a convenient format and, secondly, the possibility of analysing the reasons for an overall score. In the example just given, it was found that overall attitudes measured separately seemed to be far more highly correlated with negative than with positive dimensions: respondents tended to approve of a technology because of the absence of bad points rather than because of the presence of good ones. This in turn would tell policy-makers that if they wanted to gain public acceptance for nuclear power, say, it would do little good to emphasise low costs

and favourable spin-offs; what was needed instead was to change perceptions of the dangers of catastrophe and long term pollution.

7.4 Reliability and validity

A pair of key methodological concepts that have been touched on in section
2.3.2 are reliability and validity. The distinction between them may be seen
in these terms: reliability is about whether a measure works in a consistent
way; validity is about whether the right concept is measured.

Reliability and validity are most often described in terms of correlation
or some closely related concept. Validity is conceptualised as correlation
between the measure (any measure, not only attitudinal) and a relevant
independent criterion. The crudest version of this is called face validity, and
here no formal correlational analysis is attempted, though the underlying
ideas remain. For instance, an end-of-term test may consist of multiple-
choice items based on statements taken from the course lecture notes or
textbook. Usually no evidence for the validity of these items is offered other
than that they 'obviously' measure knowledge of what the course is about.
When we are trying to measure something as slippery as an attitude, this
should never be regarded as sufficient justification: it is not difficult to find
examples of obvious errors based on such a glib approach to the problem.

The simplest case of a proper correlational analysis is called predictive
validity. For instance, the validity of an aptitude test, to be used for selecting
candidates for a course of training, may be defined as the correlation
between the test score and some subsequent measure of success, such as a
passing-out exam or an on-the-job performance measure. The criterion
measure must be assumed to be a perfect indicator of success, obviously
questionable in itself.

Clearly the problem is far more severe when there is no objective external
criterion – as when, for instance, we try to devise a measure of an attitude.
A conceptually convincing solution (that is, however, difficult to apply) is
offered by the idea of construct validity (Cronbach and Meehl, 1955). This
requires that the measure being evaluated should represent a hypothetical
concept that is well embedded in theory, so that the nature of the relationships between it and other concepts is well understood. Then, by analysis of
the statistical relationships between the various measures, and comparison
of these relationships with the corresponding theoretical relationships, the
appropriateness of the measures can be assessed. To give a more concrete
example, if theory requires that the correlation is 1, but the correlation
between measures is 0.5, then the validity of each measure (assuming them
to be equally good) is 0.71. The details of the mathematical reasoning will
be skipped, but notice that $0.5 = 0.71 \times 0.71$. Having established the validity
of a measure in this way, it can be used to help in calculating true
correlations with other variables, and so on. The difficulty, of course, is in
getting a sufficiently precise theoretical baseline from which to begin. In

reality, a lengthy process ensues, in which an initially insecure baseline is gradually reinforced by adding more and more similarly wobbly buttresses. It is a perfectly sound engineering principle that the same strength can be achieved by a single strong component or several weaker ones, and this seems a plausible analogy to follow.

Reliability is measured without reference to external criteria. It includes two slightly different concepts: **stability** and **consistency**. Stability is usually measured by administering the same instrument twice to the same respondents, the time interval being chosen so as to minimise the effects of memory while avoiding the likelihood that 'real' change may have taken place. A stable measure will be indicated by a high test–retest correlation. A low correlation may mean an unstable measure, prone to be affected by short-term irrelevancies such as mood, distraction, or differences in the circumstances of completing the instrument; or it may mean an attribute that is genuinely very changeable, such as, apparently, voting intentions. Because of this ambiguity, the concept is seldom accorded much importance nowadays. Consistency is generally considered to be more significant. An early form of assessment entailed splitting the constituent scale items into two sub-scales, computing total scores separately for the two halves, and finding the correlation between the two sub-scales. A high correlation would mean consistency between the halves. Of course, the exact value of the correlation would depend on just how the split was made: first half versus second half, odd versus even, etc. Almost universally used instead is **Cronbach's alpha** coefficient (Cronbach, 1951), which is approximately the average of all the possible split-half correlations, and thus measures the consistency of all items, globally and individually.

A conceptually very powerful approach to the problem of establishing validity is offered by Campbell and Fiske (1955). They point out that reliable variance in an item will come partly from a consistent dependence on the concept it is designed to measure, and partly from irrelevant characteristics of the method. For instance, some respondents show a consistent (hence, reliable) preference for one end of a Likert-type scale – usually the 'strongly agree' end, the so-called 'acquiescent response set'. Or the very fact that we are relying on a verbal response may mean that a respondent with literacy problems will lack confidence and thus consistently avoid the extreme categories. To avoid such problems we should use several different methods. For example, we can include essentially the same item twice, but with reversed meaning, and compare people's responses. Then the pattern of correlations between items, using the same and different methods and tapping the same and different attitudes, can yield important insights into the true validity of our measures.

In conclusion, it may be noted that it is very simple to calculate a quantitative measure of the reliability of an instrument, because it is based entirely on internal criteria, but almost impossible to do the same for validity. Perhaps the best advice is to bear the problem in mind, and find ways of improving validity, even if it cannot be definitively measured.

7.5   FACTOR ANALYSIS

If a set of attitudes is indeed multidimensional (as argued in section 7.2), how is it to be analysed? There are several ways to approach this problem, but probably the most commonly used is a statistical method called **factor analysis**. This is generally regarded as an advanced method, but the results are not too difficult to understand, and what follows is an example of such an analysis. (You could duplicate these results using the computer program SPSS, which is described in a little more detail in Chapter 15.) My example is rather simpler than the problem of political radicalism discussed earlier. Respondents to a general purpose survey in the USA (the General Social Survey carried out every year by the National Opinion Research Center) were asked the question shown in Table 7.1.

Respondents were invited to answer 'yes' or 'no' to each reason; 'don't know' was also permitted, but excluded from analysis. These items are monotonic, so, although they have only two possible values rather than the traditional five-point scale, they could in principle be analysed according to the Likert model.

The 'words' in parentheses after each reason for abortion are the names by which the corresponding variables will be referred to in the computer analysis that follows.

You may not like the wording of some of the reasons. For instance, some may find the patriarchal implications of reason F irritating or even offensive. Others might say that, realistically, even today many women (and even more women's parents) would find the idea of having a child without being married pretty horrifying, and therefore it is an important hypothetical situation to ask respondents to consider. The choice of wording, like most research decisions, is not value-free. On the other hand, these questions came out of the standard process of examining spontaneous statements of opinion in open-ended discussions. In short, this example is an instance of secondary analysis where we are dependent on someone else's decisions, with all the potential difficulties (and advantages) discussed in Chapter 16.

The items were selected so as to cover the main range of grounds that might be used to justify abortion. By using several statements rather than just one (such as 'Do you think abortions should be legal always, most of the

Table 7.1   *Attitudes to abortion*

Please tell me whether or not you think it should be possible for a pregnant woman to obtain a legal abortion . . .

A. If there is a strong chance of serious defect in the baby (ABDEFECT)
B. If she is married and does not want any more children? (ABNOMORE)
C. If the woman's own health is seriously endangered by the pregnancy? (ABHLTH)
D. If the family has a very low income and cannot afford any more children? (ABPOOR)
E. If she became pregnant as a result of rape? (ABRAPE)
F. If she is not married and does not want to marry the man? (ABSINGLE)

Source: General Social Survey, 1996, National Opinion Research Center.

Table 7.2 *Correlation matrix*

	ABDEFECT	ABNOMORE	ABHLTH	ABPOOR	ABRAPE	ABSINGLE
ABDEFECT	1.00					
ABNOMORE	.41	1.00				
ABHLTH	.57	.27	1.00			
ABPOOR	.40	.79	.27	1.00		
ABRAPE	.61	.39	.58	.38	1.00	
ABSINGLE	.41	.79	.26	.83	.39	1.00

time, sometimes, seldom or never?') the overall reliability of a derived score will be much improved. In addition, the researchers leave open the possibility that people's attitudes in this area may be multidimensional. Of course, in a sense, a person's responses to these items will be six-dimensional, since they are making six responses, but the use of factor analysis entails the assumption that the six items are not entirely independent, but can be understood in terms of a smaller number of underlying attitudes. The question is, how many?

The first thing that the factor analysis program does is to calculate the correlation between each pair of variables (see Table 7.2). You will notice first that every single correlation is positive: a respondent who approves of abortion on any ground tends also to approve on any other ground. However, the coefficients vary quite a lot, from 0.26 up to 0.83: ABPOOR, ABSINGLE and ABNOMORE are closely related, as are ABHLTH, ABRAPE and ABDEFECT, but the correlations *between* the two subsets are smaller. From this, one might suspect that people's views tend to fall into two categories, and indeed factor analysis can be seen as a more systematic way of investigating patterns of correlation.

The factor extraction takes place in a 'black box' that it would be inappropriate to delve into in an introductory discussion. A summary of the results is presented in Table 7.3.

An **eigenvalue** is a concept in matrix theory, the area of maths that underlies all multivariate statistics. For present purposes, it can be regarded as the variance of each factor – a measure of its importance in explaining the measured items. Because there are six items, the total variance is 6.0 and the percentage of variance explained in each case is the eigenvalue divided by 6. In Table 7.3 $51.71 + 18.24 = 69.95$, the second figure in the cumulative percentage column, so altogether these two factors successively summarise almost seven-tenths of the original variation.

Table 7.3 *Factors and the variance they explain*

Factor	Eigenvalue	Percentage of variance	Cumulative percentage
1	3.10	51.71	51.71
2	1.09	18.24	69.95

Table 7.4   *The relationship between the factors and the attitude items*

	Factor 1	Factor 2
ABDEFECT	0.09	0.73
ABNOMORE	0.86	0.03
ABHLTH	−0.09	0.79
ABPOOR	0.91	−0.01
ABRAPE	0.05	0.76
ABSINGLE	0.91	0.00

But what are these factors? They are inferred from the correlations among the items, but they are understood as underlying the items. Each entry in Table 7.4 indicates the extent to which the row item is determined by the column factor. ABDEFECT, for instance, is determined largely by factor 2, whereas ABNOMORE belongs almost entirely to factor 1. As you look down the columns you can arrive at an interpretation of each factor: factor 1 is to do with attitudes to abortion on social grounds, or with 'elective' termination, whereas factor 2 is to do with medical grounds, or matters outside the woman's control. (Yet again, it is impossible to express this in a value-free way: coping with this is part of the researcher's responsibility.)

Although there are two distinct factors, they are not independent: the factor analysis reports that there is a moderate correlation, 0.49, between the two factors. Approval on one set of grounds tends to go with approval on the other set. Common sense (which can be confirmed by further analysis) suggests that the correlation is less than perfect mainly because many people approve on medical but not on social grounds.

Of course, discovering the structure of people's attitudes is only the beginning. Having identified the two factors, a program like SPSS can assign to each respondent a score on each factor, based on his or her individual item scores. Then the real analysis begins. Instead of having to tabulate each of the six items by various explanatory variables, we need only tabulate the two factors, thus simplifying both the computer analysis and the subsequent interpretation. As an illustration, Tables 7.5 and 7.6 show the result from examining the relationship between factor 1 and sex, and between the same factor and level of education. (This is a simple two-category classification, divided into those who had some higher education and those who did not.)

All the variables in these tables are dichotomous: sex is naturally a two-state variable, and the others have been recast into similar classifications for simplicity of analysis. (In professional research this might be regarded as a

Table 7.5   *Attitude to abortion on 'social' grounds: percentage approving by sex*

	Male (%)	Female (%)	
Tend to approve	51.0	49.8	50.5
Tend to disapprove	49.0	50.2	49.5
	(728)	(922)	(1650)

Table 7.6 *Attitude to abortion on 'medical' grounds: percentage approving by educational level*

	Less educated (%)	More educated (%)	
Tend to approve	46.5	58.6	48.9
Tend to disapprove	53.5	41.4	51.1
	(1134)	(512)	(1646)

rather wasteful way to treat data.) As far as the two factor scores are concerned, there is no natural dividing line, so for reasons of statistical efficiency they have been split into roughly equal-sized categories. As explained earlier, it is impossible to say exactly where the neutral point lies.

The creation and interpretation of tables of this kind is outlined in Chapter 15. For now, I shall focus on just a couple of figures in each table. In both tables, each cell contains the number of individuals in that combination of row and column categories, expressed as a percentage of the column total (shown in parentheses). Notice that 51 per cent of men tend to approve of abortion on social grounds, compared with 49.8 per cent of women. This is really no difference at all. First, such a difference is almost certainly not statistically reliable – simply because of random sampling variability we could easily get precisely the opposite result in another sample – and in any case, 1.2 per cent difference is not enough to get excited about. So the conclusion must be that there is no real difference in men's and women's attitudes in this respect.

But there is a substantial difference in attitudes to abortion on medical grounds between less and more educated respondents: a tendency to approval is expressed by 46.5 per cent and 58.6 per cent of the respective groups. To put it slightly differently, a more educated person is 12.1 per cent more likely to be in the more approving group.

To summarise, then, a set of six attitude items can be successfully condensed into two factors, which can then be used as variables in their own right. The advantages are not only in simplification: it will generally be found that, because of the reduced 'noise' in the derived variables, the relationships with explanatory variables are more distinct than is the case for the raw variables. That is, of course, the essence of construct validity.

7.6 SUMMARY

The measurement of attitudes deserves great care and close attention to detail. The general point to recognise is the necessity to improve reliability and validity. At a minimum that means adopting a multiple indicator approach wherever practicable. If you are seriously interested in this area of research design, you should look through some of the suggestions for further reading and build up a repertoire of methods, so as to avoid always forcing your respondents into the same mould.

7.7 PROJECT

To do something worthwhile with your own data probably means a class project. Decide on a researchable area, probably one that other students will be interested in, since you will need willing research subjects. You could, for instance, examine attitudes to participating in higher education. This may well be multidimensional: for instance, some people are more concerned with the 'pure' benefits of education – general intellectual development, self-actualisation, and so forth – whereas others will emphasise the practical advantages to the individual and to the nation. Do a bit of reading around, to get an idea of the necessary breadth of coverage. Start collecting items. Keep a note of statements made in the press, especially student journals; record group discussions and extract coherent opinions. Edit your collection, bearing in mind the rules discussed in Chapter 6. Assemble between 10 and 20 items into a questionnaire, adding a few factual questions – gender, age, course of study, parents' occupations, etc. Ideally, design and attempt to achieve a proper sample (though that is a project in itself). Set everyone in the class a quota: you will need at least 200 completed questionnaires. Put the data on to a computer and (if you know enough about factor analysis, or can get more detailed advice) use my example as a model. For a relatively small dataset you may be able to manage without a specialised package like SPSS if you can get advice on a good spreadsheet program like Excel or Lotus 1-2-3: you won't be able to do factor analysis, but you can weed out items that don't seem to correlate with anything else, and then add together the remaining scores. Finally, look at the relationship between your scales and students' background characteristics. Which disciplines seem to be related to which justifications for education? Are there class background differences?

If you cannot collect your own data, you will find that many datasets are available for secondary analysis (see Chapter 16) and these are particularly suitable for attitude research: as well as the NORC GSS from which my illustration was taken (see Davis and Smith, 1992), there are the annual British Social Attitudes Survey and the Euro Barometer series sponsored by the European Commission. If you have access to suitable computing facilities you can learn a lot by obtaining one of these datasets from your national Data Archive and hunting through it for groups of connected attitude items. The British Social Attitudes Survey, in particular, is the subject of an annual report (e.g. Jowell et al. (1999)) that might give you some ideas on where to start.

Recently some datasets have become available for public analysis and downloading via the Internet. To get your own copy of the NORC General Social Survey used in the factor analysis example, point your browser at http://csa.berkeley.edu:7502/archive.htm, and follow the instructions on screen. The subset I used took only a few seconds to download from the archive in California.

7.8 FURTHER READING

Many of the classic papers are brought together in Summers (1970). Oppenheim (1992) gives a useful guide to many of the practical details of scaling. A more technical overview is presented in Spector (1992). Jacoby's (1991) survey provides a general conceptual framework for social science measurement. The expectancy-value approach is best described in Fishbein and Ajzen (1975). Lodge (1981) has written an excellent practical guide to magnitude scaling. To learn about factor analysis you should start from a foundation in basic statistics, including correlation and regression; then Norusis (1993) gives a very clear account directly related to SPSS output.

QUALITATIVE INTERVIEWING

8

NIGEL FIELDING AND HILARY THOMAS

CONTENTS

Sociologists have always been interested in the attitudes and beliefs of social groups, and much methodological refinement has come about by engaging with the problems posed by trying to get at other people's feelings. A key method of attitude research is the interview, and, as we will see, it has a central role in a diversity of research designs.

8.1 VARIETIES OF RESEARCH INTERVIEW

Interviewing has a strong claim to being the most widely used research method. Whenever we are getting our bearings, whether as a researcher or a new arrival in a foreign land, the quickest, most instinctive method is to ask a question. It is therefore no surprise that interviewing takes many forms. The normal way of differentiating types of interview is by the degree of structure imposed on their format.

In the **standardised** or **structured** interview the wording of questions and the order in which they are asked is the same from one interview to another (see Macfarlane Smith, 1972; and Chapter 6). The piece of paper the interviewer holds is called the interview schedule, and that word 'schedule' seems to convey the formality of this type of interview. It is most familiar from market research; most of us have been stopped in the street or visited at home by an interviewer bearing a schedule to be completed by ticks in the boxes corresponding to our answers.

The next type of interview is **semi-standardised**. Here the interviewer asks major questions the same way each time, but is free to alter their sequence and to probe for more information. The interviewer can thus adapt the research instrument to the level of comprehension and articulacy of the respondent, and handle the fact that in responding to a question, people often also provide answers to questions we were going to ask later.

The endpoint of this typology is the **non-standardised** interview, also called **unstructured** or **focused** interviews. Here interviewers simply have a list of topics which they want the respondent to talk about, but are free to phrase the questions as they wish, ask them in any order that seems sensible at the time, and even join in the conversation by discussing what they think of the topic themselves. The bit of paper the interviewer holds is called an interview guide, and once again the second word, 'guide', conveys the style of this approach, where interviewers take their own path within certain guidelines.

This chapter is mainly about non-standardised interviews, because the standardised types are discussed in Chapters 6, 7 and 14, and because the non-standardised interview best fulfils Lofland and Lofland's (1994) case that the essence of the research interview is the 'guided conversation'. Also, because of its simplicity of design and correspondence to conversational procedures that are routine in social life, it is often the type of interview that students conduct in their own research projects. Where necessary, comparisons are made with the more standardised types.

After examining the uses of interview data, the chapter considers the conduct of interviews, the design of an interview guide and the practicalities of transcription, coding and analysis. The second part covers problems of interview methods and the ways these can be overcome, with an emphasis on promoting and assessing validity and on the different perspectives on validity found in different theoretical traditions.

8.1.1 Characteristic uses of interview data

Like other qualitative methods, non-standardised interviews are valuable as strategies for discovery. Standardised interviews are suitable when you already have some idea of what is happening with your sample in relation to the research topic, and where there is no danger of loss of meaning as a result of imposing a standard way of asking questions. However, if you are on new ground – for social research or yourself – a more flexible approach is best. Lofland summarised the objective of the non-standardised format as being 'to elicit rich, detailed materials that can be used in qualitative analysis. Its object is to find out what kinds of things are happening rather than to determine the frequency of predetermined kinds of things that the researcher already believes can happen' (Lofland, 1971: 76).

As well as the typology based on degrees of standardisation there is another preliminary distinction to make. Interviews can be administered either one-to-one or to a group. In the former, respondents are seen individually, while in the latter the interviewer, or a group leader, guides the discussion among a small group of respondents. Recently, market research has embraced what Merton and Kendall (1946) called 'focus groups' as a way of studying consumer preference, and the method has spread to the study of political and policy preferences (see Chapter 10). To social scientists, the strength of group discussions is the insight they offer into the dynamic effects of interaction on expressed opinion, which is discussed further below.

Many studies begin with 'pilot interviews', to gather basic information about the field before imposing more precise and inflexible methods; this is why interviews are the most often used research method. Such interviews use a broad topic guide with as few direct questions as possible. The flexibility of non-standardised methods is a major attraction and many influential and sophisticated analyses have been based entirely on interview data.

This versatility is apparent in the list of uses to which interview data can be put. Interviews can be used to identify the main behavioural groups to be sampled, and to provide insight into how they should be defined. Interviews can be used to get acquainted with the phrasing and concepts used by a population of respondents. Interviews are often used to establish the variety of opinions concerning a topic or to establish relevant dimensions of attitudes. Interviews are also used to form hypotheses about the motivation underlying behaviour and attitudes, although this use is much debated (see section 8.8).

These are the major applications, but non-standardised interviews have important subsidiary uses. For those who accept that motivations can be studied this way, interviews can also be used to examine non-motivations, why people do not do certain things. For instance, in London, postal surveys were conducted on why people failed to apply for welfare benefits for which they were eligible. The surveys had poor response rates, perhaps for reasons similar to the low take-up of benefits themselves. A research organisation commissioned to pursue the matter discovered that individual interviews were the best way to guarantee a response from the semi-literate, the frail, the elderly and the plain suspicious – the main target groups for the campaign to maximise take-up of benefit. Another subsidiary application is when we need detailed and extensive data, such as case histories of patients, or detailed records of behaviour, such as criminal careers. In recent years the 'life history' interview has come into vogue, particularly in feminist research (Devault, 1990).

The non-standardised approach is also valuable where the subject matter is sensitive or complicated. For instance, a research agency had to establish attitudes to nuclear waste as part of a social impact study. The problem was that reaching an informed view required technical information of considerable complexity. No survey questionnaire or standardised interview could provide the information in sufficient depth or attune it to the varying levels of comprehension likely to be present in the population. Non-standardised interviews allowed the researchers to fine tune the explanation and satisfy themselves that the respondent had sufficient grasp to reach a considered view. Of course, care must be taken that the technical explanations are not biased.

In a similar vein, the flexibility of this approach is a boon where topics have varying salience to the sample population but where it is difficult to anticipate which will register with particular respondents using knowledge only of broad indicators such as age. When the applicability of research instruments cannot be predetermined by sampling assumptions, non-standardised interviews can help. This is how Robb (1954) compiled his sample of East Enders who were anti-Semitic; aware that East Enders were reputed to be anti-Semitic, he used interviews to identify such views and select his sample.

8.2 COMMUNICATION IN INTERVIEWS

Two principles inform research interviews. First, the questioning should be as open-ended as possible, in order to gain spontaneous information rather than a rehearsed position. Secondly, the questioning techniques should encourage respondents to communicate their underlying attitudes, beliefs and values, rather than a glib or easy answer. The objective is that the discussion should be as frank as possible.

Frank discussion can be impeded in several ways. There may be attempts at *rationalisation*. Respondents may offer only logical reasons for their actions, withholding evaluative or emotional reasons that may give a truer insight. We have already noticed the problem of a *lack of awareness*; as well as a lack of information, many people are not used to putting their feelings into words. Respondents may fear *being shown up*. People often avoid describing aspects of behaviour or attitudes that are inconsistent with their preferred self-image; questions about such things as personal hygiene or involvement in deviant behaviour are examples. Respondents may tend to *over-politeness* to the interviewer. Being shy or over-anxious to impress can distort response. A common problem here is where respondents give those answers which they anticipate the interviewer wants to hear. This is a good reason to be careful about your initial explanation of the focus of the interview.

There are several solutions to these obstacles to frank communication. The manner of the interviewer is important. A relaxed and unself-conscious interviewer puts respondents at ease. Research on interviewer effects suggests that interviewers should not be drawn from either extreme of the social scale, that their demeanour should be neither condescending nor deferential, that they should display interest without appearing intrusive (Singer et al., 1983). There is more on interviewer effects below. Another broad tactic is to personalise the discussion to get at underlying attitudes. For example, do not simply talk about 'police policy' in the abstract, ask respondents to tell you about their experiences with the police.

However, this advice is rather broad. There are special questioning techniques to deal with particular communication problems.

When attitudes to a number of items need to be investigated, the **repertory grid** is useful, particularly in measuring attitude change over time, such as during a period of socialisation into, say, a new job. Initially, dimensions of attitude – **constructs** – are identified. The researcher presents three stimuli to the respondents (a **triad**), and asks them to say which two are most alike and how they differ from the third. The procedure is repeated with a number of triads. Let's say we are studying attitudes to noise. Presented with traffic noise, aircraft noise and noisy children, the respondent may say noise from aircraft and children is intermittent, whereas traffic noise is continuous where they live. Thus, 'continuity of noise' emerges as a salient dimension of opinion. The virtue of this is that one elicits constructs (like 'continuity of noise') directly from the respondent rather than supplying a construct which may be meaningful to the researcher but less so to respondents. Respondents then relate the set of constructs to each other to form a grid, and, if the procedure is repeated over time, changes can be identified (Norris, 1983). For example, a constable's degree of identification with the triad of detective, patrol officer and police sergeant can be measured at different stages of training.

Several projective questioning techniques are designed to encourage respondents to give views indirectly. There is **sentence completion**, for example, 'The noise from the motorway _____'. Another is **indirect questioning**, which works on the basis that people are more prepared to reveal negative feelings if they can attribute them to other people. You might ask 'How do you think other young people feel about noise?' Not knowing others' views, respondents will offer their own. Another technique is **personalisation of objects**, in which emotion or other affective qualities are attributed to inanimate objects. For example, 'If your house were a person, how would it feel about re-development?' The technique is thought most appropriate for child respondents, but it is surprisingly effective with adults.

8.2.1 Probing and prompting

Prompting involves encouraging the respondent to produce an answer. In standardised interviews care is taken to get a response without putting words in the respondent's mouth. The mildest technique is merely to repeat the question. If this fails, the interviewer may be permitted to re-phrase the question slightly; if so, the interview schedule will often list acceptable re-phrases. It is thought more important that the stimulus (question) be delivered in precisely the same way to each respondent than to allow the interviewer to improvise to get an answer (Foddy, 1992). In standardised interviews failure to elicit a response after such attempts will result in missing data. In non-standardised interviewing, the interviewer has more latitude.

Probing involves follow-up questioning to get a fuller response; it may be non-verbal or verbal. An expectant glance can function as a probe as much as a direct request like 'please tell me about that'. Probes are acceptable in standardised interviews, but are likely to be pre-specified. Their use is entirely acceptable in non-standardised interviews, because we probe frequently in normal conversation and our objective is to have a 'guided conversation'. However, the probe should be as neutral as possible. It should not incline the respondent towards a particular response.

The less standardised the format the more flexible these injunctions. Indeed, life history and other discursive interview formats may contain prompting of a kind which is heresy in standardised interviews (Atkinson, 1998). It may take the form of the interviewer's comment that he or she has heard others express some view or other, and what does the respondent think of that. Sometimes the interviewer will even say what he or she thinks or has experienced. The fact that non-standardised interviewers, especially in feminist methods, talk about 'sharing' their view with the respondent gives an idea of the opposition between those who prefer stimulus–response conventions and those who believe interviewing should be an 'open' method involving a genuine interplay between researcher and respondent. As in all research methods, what is permissible ultimately depends on the analytic task to which the data will be applied.

Probing is a key interviewing skill. It is all about encouraging the respondent to give an answer and as full a response as the format allows. Frequently it involves getting respondents to choose from alternatives. For example, if, in a standardised format, a respondent answers the question 'Are you very satisfied, not very satisfied or not at all satisfied with your present home?' with the statement 'I couldn't really say', this implies hesitation rather than an absence of opinion. Here the interviewer can say 'Which comes closest to your views?' and repeat the question. If the answer still does not fit, the interviewer is usually instructed to repeat the pre-codes.

Probing is especially important in open-ended questions, and even highly standardised formats will usually include a few of these. To get respondents to expand their answers the following probes may be used, in increasing order of imperativeness:

- an expectant glance
- um hm, mm, or yes, followed by an expectant silence
- what else?
- what other reasons?
- please tell me more about that
- I'm interested in *all* your reasons.

That last one would probably make most respondents uncomfortable and is best kept for the truly evasive! Following Dohrenwend and Richardson (1956), Burgess offers a scale which enables one to evaluate the interviewer's degree of directiveness, allowing interviewing styles to be calibrated to the interview situation (Burgess, 1982: 111–12). The rule of thumb is to probe whenever you judge that the respondent's statement is ambiguous. Generally, anything that would make you wonder what the respondent meant in a normal conversation would be worth probing (in normal conversation we tend to be more tolerant of the unexplained or unclear, perhaps because we know we can check later with people we will see again). So responses like 'This is important' should always be probed, perhaps by asking 'What do you mean by "important"?' The interviewer's task is to draw out all relevant responses, to encourage the inarticulate or shy, to be neutral towards the topic while displaying interest. Probing needs skill because it can easily lead to bias. That is why effort is put into measuring directiveness. The best way to acquire this skill is to practise interviewing, initially with someone prepared to help you review your performance and later in pilot interviews with people like those who form your sample. A video camera can be helpful in reviewing and honing your interviewing skills.

8.2.2 The value of group discussions

Earlier it was mentioned that group discussions are especially valuable for those who want to assess how several people work out a common view, or to elicit the range of views. The majority of research interviews are one-to-one, but researchers interested in consensus formation, interactional processes and group dynamics find the group discussion useful. They allow you to see how people interact in considering a topic, and how they react to disagreement. They also help identify attitudes and behaviours that are considered socially unacceptable.

Apart from this use, which is tailored to particular analytic interests, group discussions are quicker and cheaper to conduct than individual interviews with the same number of respondents. However, they have their own disadvantages, too. Not everyone who has been invited will attend, but if some of them have shown up, you will have to run the session regardless. The elderly, disabled and members of elites are particularly unlikely to attend group discussions. If these are important in your sample you may need to target them individually.

Group discussions are also rather unwieldy; it helps to share the running of the session, or split the roles so that one person maintains the discussion while the other looks ahead to new topics and introduces them, or so that you take the lead for one topic and a colleague takes it for another. Finally, it is hard to get a clear recording in a group discussion; you will need more than one microphone, and should check that your equipment can handle people speaking at different volumes and distances from the microphones before conducting the actual session.

This may make it sound like discussions are too difficult to bother with. However, their value was demonstrated convincingly several years ago when one author (Fielding) was helping some students convene a group discussion on domestic violence. Women from a local refuge were invited and eight came. Several students – males and females – shared the running of the session, and one concentrated on the equipment. We found that the women were prepared to share information of remarkable emotional intensity about harrowing experiences we regarded as deeply private and which we had not thought we would be able to address in the interviews. It seemed that, because they all shared the experience of having been abused, once one respondent launched a line of discussion the others were more than willing to join in. We were certain that we would not have got the amount and depth of data using one-to-one interviews, particularly as we could not have matched genders without denying some students the experience of inter-viewing. It was difficult to end the session. The women wanted to continue, and were generating their own topics, which led us on to new and relevant ground. The session finally ended when the building was locked up for the night.

Latterly the 'focus group' variant has come into prominence in a variety of research applications, so much so that Chapter 10 is devoted to them.

8.2.3 Telephone and online interviewing

Recently, two technological developments have added to the techniques available to the interviewer. The first is the heavy market penetration of telephone ownership in western societies, accelerated by the popularity of mobile phones. The second is the emergence into the consumer domain of computer-mediated communication. As the proportion of the population accessible by telephone has risen, telephone interviewing has become a more important tool of social research (and market research). Telephone inter-views have the advantage of generally being cheaper than interviewing face-to-face, and some testify that useable data is more forthcoming because people tend to stay focused on the topic. Except for the grossest character-istic, gender, interviewer matching will not usually be an issue. Where there is time pressure, telephone interviews may be an efficient alternative to field interviews.

But telephone interviews have their drawbacks. Special recording equip-ment is needed (a 'bug' attached to the interviewer's handset) if the inter-view is to be in semi-standardised or non-standardised format (respondents are particularly unlikely to tolerate note-taking during a phone call). The interviewer needs very effective communication skills to keep the interaction 'natural' while keeping an eye on the interview guide and helping the respondent stay on topic. Potentially important nuances may be lost because we communicate by body language as well as speech. To secure participation we may have to make preliminary calls to arrange convenient times for the interview. It will not be possible to show the respondents materials which might inform their response. Because of the ubiquity of market research interviews – and their misuse as a disguised sales pitch – potential respondents may be suspicious and refuse to participate. Despite all this, the technique is regularly used in social research. It can be particularly useful where the interviewer already has an 'in' with respondents, such as when conducting research on employees of the organisation sponsoring or endorsing the research (for example, carrying out phone interviews with police in Home Office research). The technique seems to be particularly successful when collecting factual information as compared to matters of attitude and affect (feeling). In a national survey of social work and police practice in child sex abuse investigations we pre-circulated the interview schedule so respondents could gather necessary information from files before the interview (Moran-Ellis and Fielding, 1996).

There is less experience with online 'interviewing' and some may dispute whether it is interviewing at all. Nevertheless this emergent method already has its advocates. The most common form, interviews administered via e-mail, enjoys the advantage that respondents can respond when convenient and the interviewer can likewise provide any necessary probes when they like. Online interviewing is not limited by distance and so the method lends itself well to cross-national research. Another advantage is that data collected this way are 'self-transcribing': one simply prints the responses or imports them into word processor files. Online interviewing can also be done in 'real time', using 'chat room' technology. This allows a greater degree of spontaneity, although some find this medium strangely disembodied and, where there are several participants, the discussion can be chaotic, requiring skill to keep everyone focused. If the method is used to access an international sample, it will also have to negotiate differences of time zone. In both asynchronous and real-time approaches, participants' stakes in the proceedings are low. Also, it is not usually possible to verify the declared characteristics of respondents; you may think you are 'talking' to a young man but it could be a middle-aged woman and you will have no way of knowing. There are, then, real concerns about validity, but the method shows intriguing promise, particularly as technology advances (Mann and Stewart, 2000).

8.3 HOW TO DESIGN AN INTERVIEW GUIDE

The best way to learn the ins and outs of a research procedure is to try it out for yourself, provided you recognise that your first efforts must be taken as practice rather than the finished product. To get you started on refining your interview technique we will borrow from the Loflands' discussion of the basics of designing a guide with which to conduct a non-standardised interview (Lofland and Lofland, 1994). Having identified a topic which is appropriate to study by interviewing, the first step is thinking over what you find problematic or interesting about it; the Loflands call these things 'puzzlements'. Jot down questions that express each puzzlement. Try to spread the range of the enquiry by asking friends what they find puzzling about the topic, too. What you are doing is teasing out what is puzzling about the phenomenon in the context of your particular 'cultural endowment'. We are located in a particular social context, with particular biographical backgrounds, and our point of departure is always what is puzzling relative to our own cultural perspective.

The next step is to write each puzzlement, or research question, on a separate sheet of paper. Now sort the sheets into separate piles that seem to be topically related. These clusters of topics may have to be arranged several times to obtain an order that seems to express the social phenomenon. In the process, some puzzlements will be discarded; growing knowledge means you can see they are irrelevant to the phenomenon in which you are interested. Others will emerge as being related, so you can amalgamate them. The puzzlements, expressed as questions, can then be decanted from the sheets of paper onto one list. It should display a logical, orderly sequence, taking the form of an outline.

The last step before piloting your interview guide is to design probes. Remember, this is a non-standardised interview, so probes may be couched in informal terms or written flexibly so that the exact words you use to the respondent can be fine-tuned to your estimation of their comprehension and ease of response. Devising the probes is as important as generating the main questions on the guide.

Let's take the example of a study by Lyn Lofland of urban careers, how people get on when they move to a new city. The outline of the interview guide looked like this:

I.   Pre-residence images
II.   Initial contact
III. Subsequent career
IV.   Experience of the city

As you can see, the guide is fairly minimal. Nearly all the work goes on in the detailed probes. We can see this when we look at the main question featuring in II, 'initial contact'. The question, whose informal wording you should note as it is typical of the non-standardised style, was:

> Can you tell me exactly how you went about finding a place to live, how you got your first place, and so forth?

Such a question would fail to measure up to standardised requirements. It asks more than one question at once, and ends with a non-specific clause.

But if the interviewer has gained rapport, that kind of question is fine in a non-standardised format. So here are the probes:

> Probe for: Conception of city areas; Areas would not consider; Contacts with landlords, real estate people (estate agents); Financial constraints; Any need to find place quickly; Internal or external conflicts and compromises; Network involvement (e.g. friend found place, relatives, etc.).

Clearly the probes are in 'sociologese' and would confuse the respondent if spoken in the words on the guide. They are instructions to look at particular sub-topics, reminders to the interviewer to be sure to check on each. They don't have to be put into the exact words which you will ask because the non-standardised format is discursive, letting respondents develop their answers in their own terms and at their own length and depth. So the interviewer has to keep all the probe sub-topics in mind as the respondent talks, mentally ticking off the ones the respondent mentions and remembering to ask about the ones the respondent does not mention. The idea is to have a list of things to be sure to ask about. One may know so little about the phenomenon that probes cannot be devised in advance. Often the probes will emerge spontaneously, as in any conversation. Remember, the non-standardised interview tries to be a guided conversation, and the bit of paper you hold is only a guide.

8.4 INTERVIEWER EFFECTS

As we have already noticed, the standardised and non-standardised approaches vary greatly in the role they permit the interviewer to play in the interaction with the respondent. A long tradition of methodological research warns of the many effects the interviewer has on the respondent's statements. While advocates of non-standardised interviewing value and analyse the part played in the discussion by the interviewer, proponents of standardised approaches regard these effects as undesirable and seek to maintain forms of quality control which reduce the impact of the interviewer on what the respondent feels able to say. Whichever approach is preferred, it is sensible to take note of some key findings of this tradition of research on interviewer effects.

The classic study dates from 1954 (Hyman), but in 1974 Sudman and Bradburn published a definitive review of what had already become a considerable body of literature. There was an early concern with whether the demographic characteristics of the interviewer and respondent should be matched; this literature, being largely American, displayed an early preoccupation with race. Hyman found that white interviewers received more socially acceptable responses from black respondents than from white respondents. Similarly, black and Oriental interviewers obtained more socially acceptable answers than did white interviewers, with the differences predictably being greatest on questions of race. Such findings were borne out by many subsequent researches. In fact, as well as race, characteristics such as age, sex, social class, and religion have proven to have an impact for which an allowance has to be made. Socially acceptable responses are particularly likely to represent convenient ways of dealing with interviewers rather than expressing the respondent's actual view. For these reasons, standardised interviews try to match interviewers to the characteristics of the research population wherever possible.

Another body of findings concerns the effects of the interviewer's behaviour and conduct of the interview on the responses. One study showed that variations in respondent 'verbosity' resulted from the willingness of the interviewer to probe (Shapiro and Eberhart, 1947). Aggressive interviewers elicited more information. It has also been shown that response rates and the extensiveness of response are different between experienced and inexperienced interviewers, which suggests that, as well as matching, it is important to practise your techniques and include a full programme of pilot interviews in your research design. These are vital in helping you to get acquainted both with your interview schedule or guide and with respondents of the sort you will encounter in your main data-gathering.

While interviewer effects must be acknowledged and controlled if they endanger the validity or reliability of response, there are limits to the extent of matching that can be achieved. There are also limits to the efforts that can be made to conduct the interview the same way every time, and differences in respondents and the context of interviews may make it less meaningful to think in terms of similarity. It could be argued that it may be easier to confide in a stranger, that female interviewers may be less threatening to both female and male respondents and that deference may encourage rather than inhibit response. Such doubts about matching suggest why it is crucial to have as full and accurate a record of the interview as possible, for scrutiny during analysis. The record is not only the foundation of our analysis but the best index of the effects we may have had on the things the respondent says. This brings us to the business of transcription.

8.5   TRANSCRIPTION

There are now some sophisticated technologies for the transcription of interviews. In recent years, computer software for transcription has improved considerably. Such software converts speech or audio files into text. Software like 'Dragon Dictate' and 'IBM ViaVoice' is now able to achieve rates of accuracy as high as 90 per cent. However, note that to achieve this level the software must be 'trained' to a particular voice. This is acceptable for its primary application – replacing secretaries who take dictation – but means that when used for transcription, users have first to train the software to their voice, and then read back the interview tapes to the software, because training the software to all the respondents' voices is impractical. Also, though it sounds good, 90 per cent accuracy still leaves you correcting one word in ten.

A more appealing approach may be that of qualitative data analysis software (see Chapter 18) with direct coding capability. Software like Code-A-Text and C-I-SAID enables the user to apply codes representing the themes of the analysis to audio or video files. This cuts out transcription altogether; when you want to hear respondent 8's comment on social class you use the feature and it plays the relevant part of the interview. This does entail a significant shift from working with text on paper, though, and may have implications for analytic work. With both direct coding and transcription software there is a further point: as discussed below, when you transcribe you get analytic ideas. Cutting out or cutting down transcription may save on tedium but could be at analytic cost. Hereafter we will focus on straightforward transcription of one-to-one, non-standardised interviews.

The first choice is whether to write down everything the respondent says. This is the choice between verbatim and selective transcription. Verbatim transcription offers the advantage that all possible analytic uses are allowed for. You may not know what will be the most significant points of analysis when you are doing the transcription; doing it verbatim means you have not lost any data that may later become significant. But the disadvantage of verbatim transcription is that it is laborious and time-consuming. The advice is that even if you plan to be selective with most of the interviews, you should still transcribe the first few verbatim. These will help guide your analysis and probably reveal lines of analysis you had not thought of. You may even be able to adjust your guide for subsequent interviews to pick up on things your transcription reveals as unexpectedly important. Whether to transcribe all your interviews verbatim may also depend on how many you are doing. If your sample is small, say 20 or less, you should probably transcribe the lot verbatim.

Another choice you need to make is whether to tape record the interview or write notes. If you are doing a standardised interview using a highly pre-specified schedule, you will probably not need to tape record but develop the skill of completing what is in effect a questionnaire as the respondent talks. But if you are conducting non-standardised interviews, you will be joining in the conversation too, and without recording you will inevitably lose data as well as have to engage in a very stilted and peculiar interaction as you pause every few utterances to write down what the person says. The advice is to tape record whenever possible.

Most people worry about the prospect of negotiating with respondents to tape record the interview. But recording does convey that their responses are being taken seriously. In most cases it is worth pushing hard to tape. Notes are not only very slow but open to doubts about validity. When police interviews in Britain went from contemporaneous note-taking to tape-recording, detectives found that average interview times fell dramatically. An interview that took four hours with note-taking now took half an hour. Responses also became more factual, and accusations of 'verballing', putting words in the respondent's mouth, fell to virtually nil (Irving and McKenzie,

1988). Nevertheless, the researcher should ensure that the request to tape is explicit, that confidentiality is offered, and that the respondent knows he or she can ask for the machine to be switched off while giving a particular answer. Care should be taken over the decision to tape record when interviewing members of vulnerable groups. The researcher needs to weigh up any possible harm to respondents should they be identifiable as a result of being interviewed on tape and in some cases whether they may become distressed or otherwise feel threatened by being interviewed 'on the record'. If in any doubt, make time to discuss the matter fully and ensure that the final decision is one with which both parties are genuinely satisfied.

It is also worth remembering that many people now use tape-recordings in their work. Businesspeople record notes to themselves and memos for audio-typing, social workers and probation officers tape discussions with their clients or notes to themselves after client interviews. You can make taping more palatable by offering to supply the respondent with a transcript so its accuracy can be checked (of course, this commits you to full transcription). This is a useful 'foot-in-the-door' device too, because you will then have a further contact with the respondent to discuss the transcript, which often yields more data, including comments by the respondent on what he or she thought of the interview. This can be useful both analytically and in gauging the validity and reliability of responses. If the respondent is worried about the uses to be made of the interview data, you can also offer to anonymise the quotes you use in the final write-up and to destroy the recording once it is transcribed.

If the respondent is really reluctant, you may be able to get recording accepted by starting to write notes. This will be unbelievably slow. After a few minutes you can ask whether they still object to the tape recorder! Also, because so many people now use tapes in their work, and because many occupational groups are now more accountable, it may be that your respondent not only assents to recording, but pulls out their own recorder to make an independent record of the session. Don't be shy.

Transcribing is a slow process, a typical ratio being one hour of interview to four to six hours of transcription, but if undertaken by the researcher, it has the advantage of familiarising you with the data. Type your questions in a different font or in upper case to help distinguish between the two contributions to the exchange. Set generous margins to allow space for coding and analytical notes. Number lines or sections for referencing purposes. Do not be tempted to 'tidy' the language or grammar of the respondent; where some clarification is required, identify your additions, for example by reserving square brackets for this purpose. Jotting down thoughts about the data during transcription contributes to the subsequent analysis and may relieve the tedium of transcription. Check each transcript by listening to the tape and reading the written version, a process particularly important if transcription is undertaken by someone other than the researcher doing the analysis.

A final point concerns audio-typing transcription services. These are available in many towns, and some people have secretaries who can transcribe for them. Even so, it is worth transcribing at least some, and preferably all, of the interviews yourself. This is because you have ideas as you transcribe, and transcribing makes you very familiar with the data. It helps you to start making connections and identifying themes for analysis. In fact, you should keep a pad handy when you transcribe to write down these thoughts as they occur to you.

8.6 PRACTICALITIES OF ANALYSING
INTERVIEW DATA

Key to successful qualitative analysis is the need for the researcher to become thoroughly familiar with the data and to devise a practical system that enables rigorous comparison to be made between interviews while retaining the context of data within each interview.

It is useful to listen to each tape-recording as soon as possible after the interview. This provides an opportunity to make some brief notes about content, especially to note information such as age, marital status, occupation, etc., which was collected systematically and which will form the sample characteristics. These notes might be held in the form of a card index. It is easier to calculate, for example, the mean age of a sample from a card index than from the eventual transcripts. Note also the length of the interview, if this was not done at the time. Listening to the entire tape at this stage will bring to light any technical difficulties with the quality of the recording when unclear or unrecorded material can be replaced by notes from memory. Adding fieldnotes about the setting, the conduct of the interview, the interviewee, and so on, will help to bring back the context of the interview later in analysis.

8.6.1 Coding and analysis

Qualitative analysis involves systematic, rigorous consideration of the data in order to identify themes and concepts that will contribute to our understanding of social life. Themes and concepts that are identified and coded in one interview are then compared and contrasted with (any) similar material in the other interviews. New themes that emerge in subsequent interviews necessitate further consideration and analysis of previously coded interviews. The analytical and practical issues of this process stem from a need to both compare and contrast segments, or pieces, of data from different interviews and to maintain the chronological integrity of each interview. The analytical challenge is the identification of thematically similar segments of text, both within and between interviews. The practical counterparts are the labelling and subsequent retrieval of similarly coded segments together with a reference to their original location (interview/line number).

Codes may have a number of origins. Themes, topics and subject areas may be generated *a priori* from the interview research questions or the interview checklist. These will be supplemented from fieldnotes, jottings during transcription and transcription checking, and of course from the transcripts themselves. Where coding is done on paper some means of identifying codes, for example with different coloured pens, highlighters, etc., should be established. It may be most practical to develop the set of codes in the margins and later, when the coding frame is established, to outline the exact text area pertinent to each code. Codes may well overlap in the text so keep the eventual coding frame as simple as the analysis allows. Note where potentially useful material for quotation overlaps the boundaries of a particular coded segment, for example by starring the relevant section.

Having identified and noted the codes, a system of retrieval that enables the researcher to retrieve all instances of each individual code must be devised. This may involve listing the instances on separate sheets, perhaps with the addition of a grid or matrix. If the transcript is to be cut up, ensure that a whole version of each transcript is retained. Ensure that each cut segment is referenced to the particular location (interview/line number). Note that overlapping codes may require additional printing/photocopying. Cuttings can then be reassembled into thematic sections by code or group of codes. Merging of codes may happen at this stage.

As systematic comparison and contrast of material within themes proceeds, a useful way to capture these thoughts is to begin writing up a particular theme to develop a feel for how to present the analysis. This will incorporate descriptive findings but should also show insight into the emerging analysis. Relationships between themes and linkages between types of respondent may begin to emerge. Note similarities and dissimilarities. Keep asking *why* differences are emerging. Incorporate examples from the text to illustrate and help unpack your emerging analysis but be wary of depending on 'favourite' quotations and evidence from particular respondents.

8.7 SOME PROBLEMS OF INTERVIEW ANALYSIS

As we have already seen, researchers worry about the effects interviewers may have on the validity and reliability of the data. The charge of interviewer bias has been levelled particularly at non-standardised interviews. Active commitment to a particular perspective during the interview certainly affects the results. On the other hand, it is easy to overstate the problem of interviewer bias. Selltiz and Jahoda suggest that 'much of what we call interviewer bias can more correctly be described as interviewer differences, which are inherent in the fact that interviewers are human beings and not machines' (1962: 41). They point out that social scientists are universally dependent on data collected by oral or written reports and these are 'invariably subject to the same sources of error and bias as those collected by interviewers' (1962: 41). In dealing with bias, the advice of eminent sociologist Robert Merton still holds true (Merton and Kendall, 1946: 555). He maintains that:

1. Guidance and direction from the interviewer should be at a minimum.
2. The subject's definition of the situation should find full and specific expression.
3. The interview should bring out the value-laden implications of the response.

As Merton's carefully-balanced advice suggests, we cannot simply ignore the matter of interviewer bias. So far we have identified several sources of error or bias arising from carrying out the method badly: misdirected probing and prompting, ignoring the effects of interviewer characteristics and behaviour, neglecting the cultural context in which the researcher is located, and problems with question wording. These are mostly susceptible to quality control measures. But, more profoundly, the logic in analysing interviews is based on several assumptions that can be challenged, and we need to be conscious of these possible criticisms.

The first problem is the assumption that language is a good indicator of thought and action. Attitudes and thoughts are assumed to be a direct influence on behaviour and, in turn, language is presumed to be an accurate reflection of both. Nowadays such assumptions would make a social psychologist cringe (Potter and Wetherell, 1987; see also Chapter 19). A legion of studies show that expressed attitude is a problematic indicator of what people have done, or will do. The relationship between attitude and action has to be empirically tested in all cases, so that collecting information about people's attitudes is only one part of any study concerned with explaining or predicting behaviour. Of course, there is some value in documenting people's attitudes, provided we do not claim that by doing so we have proven what they do, nor offer predictions about what they will do. These problems are one of the reasons that multiple method studies are desirable – you can combine attitude measures with, say, direct observation, to confirm whether people actually do what they have told you they do. A classic reference for those interested in social scientists' efforts to tighten the fit between expressed attitude and actual behaviour is Deutscher (1973), and there is a discussion of ways of measuring attitudes in Chapter 7.

It certainly is not hard to compile reasons to doubt what people say to us in interviews. It is hardly a revelation to note that people sometimes lie or elaborate on the 'true' situation to enhance their esteem, cover up discreditable actions or for any of a whole gamut of motives.

A good case is that of 'self-report studies' in the sociology of deviance, as we noted in Chapter 2. Social scientists have long been aware of the many deficiencies of crime statistics. Ambiguities abound. For example, would you consider the theft of a chequebook with 30 cheques left in it to be one theft or 30? If all 30 cheques are fraudulently 'passed' it counts as 31: the theft of the chequebook plus each fraudulent encashment. The government has to issue 'counting rules' to help the police decide how to report for the statistics. As to crimes cleared up, for many years it was standard practice to count a crime as cleared even if the defendants were found innocent in court, and to clear a crime known to have been committed by several people if only one of them was caught. For such reasons criminologists have long worried about the so-called dark figure of crime.

In the 1960s American social scientists thought they had solved the problem with a technique called self-report. It was based on interviews, usually with young people, who were shown lists of offences and asked if they had committed any in the last year. The results were staggering, typically showing that up to 99 per cent of crime was going unreported. The difference between known and admitted crime was especially acute in the case of middle-class youths (Empey and Erickson, 1966). Because crime theories are largely based on official statistics, which suggest crime is largely a lower-class phenomenon, the results were important. But then doubt set in. Most studies were of juveniles, for reasons of easier access (often through schools). Could one generalise to adults? Most of the studies were in the mid-western USA, because this is where most of those using the technique worked. Were the results valid for city kids? But, most importantly, there were no checks on the validity of the responses. It is possible that respondents might have exaggerated their offending to impress the interviewer, but it is equally likely that they would minimise their involvement, fearing the interviewer would give the information to the police. There was a flurry of further tests, with some using polygraphs to try to see if the respondents were lying, others checking what they said with school records and parents to see if what the children reported was plausible, and others offering the respondent the chance to change their answers prior to such validity checks to see if they retracted their admitted involvement. The best conclusion of all this work is that self-report is not an adequate substitute for official statistics. And in the 1970s another technique largely supplanted it, victim surveys. This is not to say that self-reporting is straightforwardly wrong, and in conjunction with other methods it is still used. What it does say is that anyone using the technique must be aware of the methodological problems arising from the question of the fit between accounts and action, and devise means to allow for it in the analysis.

We have already encountered some of the problems with 'social desirability' as an influence on the validity of responses. Admitting to involvement in some socially disapproved behaviour can be subject to cultural factors and therefore provide false data. A good case is rates of mental illness in different cultural groups. In New York it was found that, holding class constant, Puerto Ricans had a higher apparent rate of mental illness than did Jews, Irish-Americans or blacks. However, on subjecting the mental health inventory to a social desirability rating, it was found that Puerto Ricans regarded the items as less undesirable than did the other ethnic groups and were probably more willing to admit to them (Dohrenwend, 1964).

Cross-cultural research is especially susceptible to problems in interpreting interview responses. It is often difficult to establish equivalence of meaning in work involving translation, especially if the material is attitudinal (e.g. Is a British publican's repudiation of public drunkenness as fervent as a teetotal Muslim's?) Faced with the Marathi language group in India, which has no concept corresponding to the generalised other (e.g. 'people', 'they'), most researchers would despair. Of course, there are different cultures in every society. The classic culture-based term is 'democracy', which varies tremendously in meaning according to cultural nuances.

There are some even more straightforward problems with which to wrestle. It has been found that some people have a consistent tendency to answer 'yes' or 'no' independently of the content of the question. Also, people are woefully inaccurate. One study found 30 per cent inaccuracy in whether the respondent had voted in an election held a few weeks previously, and similar problems have been found in studies of birth control, social welfare and health information (Gorden, 1975).

It seems, then, that the least tractable problem is the assumption of correspondence between verbal response and behaviour. We can overcome most technical problems, by interviewer training, careful question design and probing, and comparison with results using other methods. But it seems that we need a better theory of why people do and do not act as they say they do. This brings us to our final topic.

8.8 ANALYTIC STANCES TOWARDS
INTERVIEW DATA

Sociologists differ greatly in their assessment of the status of interview data. This section reviews three of the principal perspectives, but this is not exhaustive. The discussion draws heavily on Silverman (1985).

The first approach is that of positivism, the longest-established, and still dominant, perspective on social science methods. This school of thought is geared to a statistical logic mainly based on survey research. Interview data are regarded as giving access to 'facts' of the social world and treated as accounts whose sense derives from their correspondence to a factual reality. Where the account imperfectly represents that reality, checks and remedies must be applied.

For positivists, the idea that responses might be an artefact of the interview setting or its conduct would challenge their validity. Positivists aim to generate data that hold independently of the setting and interviewer. They are keen on standardised interviews and suspicious of non-standardised approaches. Each interview must follow a standard protocol, asking each question precisely the same way each time and in the same order. Interviewers should not show surprise or disapproval, offer impromptu explanations of questions, suggest possible replies or skip questions. If care is taken, the 'facts' will be established, affording a reliable and valid basis for inference.

The second approach is that of symbolic interactionism. For interactionists, interviews are social events based on mutual participant observation. The context of the production of interview data is intrinsic in understanding the data. No clear-cut distinction between research interviews and other forms of social interaction is recognised. For interactionists, the data are valid when a deep mutual understanding has been achieved between interviewer and respondent. The practical consequence is that most interactionists reject prescheduled standardised interviews in favour of open-ended interviews. The latter allow respondents to use their own way of defining the world, assume that no fixed sequence of questions is suitable for all respondents, and allow respondents to raise considerations that the interviewer has not thought of.

While interactionism has a strong relativist tinge (believing that the meaning of social action is relative to the researcher's perspective) it retains an orientation to those threats to validity which worry positivists. For example, Denzin (1981) lists the following problems to which non-standardised interviews are a solution: the problem of 'self-presentation', especially early in interviews; the problem of fleeting encounters to which respondents are uncommitted, leading to possibilities of fabrication; the relative status of interviewer and respondent; the context of the interview. These can only be seen as problems if it is assumed there is a truth or fact which lies behind them. It is a kind of positivism-plus, where the plus is a full attention to the context of the interview as a form of interaction.

But there are some who are so doubtful about the status of interview data that they abandon a concern with the content of responses in favour of examining its form. For ethnomethodologists, interview data do not report on an external reality displayed in respondents' utterances but on the internal reality constructed as both parties contrive to produce the appearance of a recognisable interview. They treat interview data as a topic and not a resource. For them, when standardised, multi-interviewer studies produce invariant data this does not establish the credibility of the data but the practical accomplishment by which intrinsically variable stimuli were made to produce the same results. As Cicourel put it:

> In spite of the problem of interviewer error, somehow different inter-viewers with different approaches produced similar responses from different subjects. The question then becomes one of determining what was invariant or, more precisely, how were invariant meanings com-municated despite such variations. (Cicourel, 1964: 75)

This approach derives from a perspective on social order which is preoccupied with the everyday production of orderly interaction. Some argue that it is indifferent to disparities of power between interviewers and respondents, preferring to see them as cooperatively engaged in producing the interview. However, the problem of 'facts' is solved, since the issue of truth does not arise, except in so far as a community version of reality is assumed. Everyday knowledge is not identified with truth. Indeed, questions of truth are marginalised, since they relate to content, not form.

While these three are important positions on the analysis of interview data they are not the only ones. Nor can it be said that they do not overlap; it is possible to find research which is informed by more than one perspective. We cannot authoritatively conclude that one is 'better' than the other, but what we must acknowledge is that, in pure form, they are tied to very different theories of the social world (see Chapter 1). Your choice of which approach to take will reflect not only your theoretical orientation but, hopefully, your thoughts on which provides the fairest reflection of your data.

8.9 PROJECT

All of us have been to school. In this exercise you will pair with a partner and conduct a brief interview. Each will act as interviewer and respondent in turn. The exercise takes about an hour. Begin by thinking over your school experiences and choose some aspect of school about which to ask questions.

Choose an aspect about which you are curious. It could be relations with teachers, or how people prepare for exams, or the value of religious education, or many other things. Since you will only be interviewing for about ten minutes, you only need to prepare for the beginning stage of the interview. You should write down several questions addressing the research issue, and also write a standard 'project explanation', a general statement of the research issue which you can say to your respondent to get the interview going.

Take ten minutes to design your questions.

Now choose which of you wants to act as interviewer first. Carry out your interview. The time allowed is ten minutes. There is no need to take notes on the respondent's replies.

The next stage is debriefing. The interviewer should identify in writing the skills they managed well and those that need improvement. To do this you should discuss it with your respondent. This should take five minutes.

Now swap roles with your partner, carry out another ten-minute interview and another five-minute debriefing.

When you have finished both rounds, discuss with your partner your experience of interviewing and the accuracy of your debriefing notes about what was good and what needed more work. This should take 15 minutes.

8.10 FURTHER READING

Arksey and Knight (1999) is a comprehensive, up-to-date source with a wealth of useful tips, examples, project ideas and other resources. Gorden

(1975) is a comprehensive book with good attention to problems of communication. Mishler (1986), a social psychologist, emphasises the need to take account of reflexivity and the interaction between interviewer and respondent in analysing interview data. Norris (1983) offers a beginner's guide to repertory grid. Rubin and Rubin (1995) provides a good overview of non-standardised interviewing incorporating recent perspectives. Chapter 8 of Silverman (1985) is devoted to interviewing and is particularly good on theoretical approaches to interview analysis.

ETHNOGRAPHY

9

NIGEL FIELDING

CONTENTS

This chapter concerns ethnography, a form of qualitative research combining several methods, including interviewing and observation. I examine the emergence of ethnography before discussing the practicalities of conducting ethnographic research, including the maintenance of relations in the field, fieldwork roles, and methods for recording field data. Considerable attention is paid to matters of analysis, since the eclecticism of ethnographic methods means that ethnographers often confront problems in converting reams of data into a coherent analysis. The intimacy of field relations prompts a discussion of fieldwork ethics.

The origin of ethnography lies in the classical tradition of anthropology which evolved during the colonial period of the British Empire, although elements of the method date back to antiquity. The ruling principle of *Thucydides' History of the Peloponnesian War* (Grene, 1959) was strict adherence to carefully verified facts, so that the work would be 'a possession for ever, not the rhetorical triumph of an hour'. But it was not only a matter of chronicle, for the speeches which constitute a quarter of the *History* shed a vivid light on the workings of the Greek political mind, the motives of contemporaries and the arguments which they used. The concern to balance detailed documentation of events with insights into their meaning to those involved is the enduring hallmark of ethnography. We can already discern ethnography's customary mix of observation, documentation and speech (interviews, nowadays). But for these concerns to be separated from the discipline of history and become a distinctive method for the study of unfamiliar cultures we must wait for the time of the British Empire.

While early anthropologists sometimes accompanied scientific expeditions, the armchair approach was more common. British colonial administration relied on district commissioners, local representatives of the colonial power who dealt with all matters affecting the British interest. Such men were ideally located to document the way of life of the indigenous peoples. Yet, however thoughtful, they were men of action and hardly 'intellectuals' by training or inclination. A system grew up whereby scholars in Britain effectively used district commissioners as fieldworkers, collecting data to be sent for analysis at home. The material was produced to a standard format which enabled similar questions to be explored in any colonial society. It was called the 'notes and queries' approach after a guidebook first published in 1874, which provided the so-called 'man on the spot' with a set of questions to ask native informants (Van Maanen, 1988: 15); it is worth noting the important role that informants were already playing in ethnography.

There is great continuity in the practice of ethnography, despite the dwindling number of cultures which can truly claim isolation from the outside world (a fact which has seen the emergence of 'the new urban anthropology', which seeks to adapt anthropology to the study of the anthropologist's own society). Bearing in mind the historical examples, consider this summary of Caroline Humphrey's study *Karl Marx Collective: Economy, Society and Religion in a Siberian Collective Farm* (1983):

> This book, the first ethnography based on fieldwork in a Soviet community by a Western anthropologist, describes the contemporary life of the Buryats, a Mongolian-speaking people in Siberia, through a detailed analysis of two collective farms. After describing Buryat historical traditions and ethnic relations, Dr Humphrey sets out the official theoretical model of the Soviet collective farm, its statutes and forms of social control. She then analyses how far the reality conforms to the model; in what respects it does not; and how the Buryats respond to the inconsistencies between theory and reality. (Humphrey, 1983: Publisher's catalogue, Cambridge University Press, 1983: 60)

The first thing to notice is that this study is pathbreaking, as ethnography often is. It explores some hitherto obscure niche of social life. It is not a rule that ethnography must study the unknown, but, as we shall see, some of the constraints on it as a method can be excused by its value as a 'method of discovery'. As a means of gaining a first insight into a culture or social process, as a source of hypotheses for detailed investigation using other methods, it is unparalleled.

The second thing to notice about Humphrey's study is that it involves a small sample, just two collective farms. Ethnography does not have to be limited in sample size, but because of the emphasis put on 'depth', 'intensity', 'richness' and so on, it usually is. Gathering detailed material is demanding, and few ethnographers are able to devote such effort to more than one or two settings. But notice also that, by focusing on two farms, Humphrey is able to employ a key element of social scientific analysis: the ability to compare and contrast between settings in which similar activities occur.

The third characteristic emphasis in Humphrey comes in the mention of 'the official theoretical model'. That word 'official' is very revealing. We cannot utter it without acknowledging that things could well be otherwise than they appear on paper: there must be an 'unofficial' reality, too. Social scientists make an important distinction between 'formal' and 'informal' organisation – for instance, the law in the books and the law as practised on the streets. Thus, Humphrey explores the fit between the official model and the reality of the collective farm. Finding the fit less than perfect, she shows how the Buryats handle the breakdown between theory and reality. Ethnography is often a debunking exercise, especially when it is used to shed new light on the darker corners of our own society.

9.1 THE MEANING OF ETHNOGRAPHIC RESEARCH

Contemporary ethnography has another important progenitor, the social reformers of the early twentieth-century US cities. The sociologists associated with the 'Chicago School' came from backgrounds in journalism and social work, and were keenly aware of the failings of their own society. They brought to ethnography a campaigning, critical edge and a sympathy for the underclass who were the principal subject of their studies. The idea of 'appreciation' became a key part of their 'naturalistic' stance (studying people in their 'natural settings') towards ethnography, a stance which emphasised seeing things from the perspective of those being studied before stepping back to make a more detached assessment. These early sociologists were mindful of the American Indian adage that one should 'never criticise a man until you have walked a mile in his moccasins'.

Another way of rendering the spirit of the adage is to argue that the researcher must be involved in the ongoing, daily world of the people being studied. As Goffman put it:

> any group of persons – prisoners, primitives, pilots or patients – develop a life of their own that becomes meaningful, reasonable and normal once you get close to it, and . . . a good way to learn about any of these worlds is to submit oneself in the company of the members to the daily round of petty contingencies to which they are subject. (Goffman, 1961: ix–x)

Goffman thought that every social group had something distinctive about it and the best way to understand it, to see how it was 'normal' no matter how zany it may seem to outsiders, was to get close. He was just following Hughes and the other Chicagoan mentors who taught generations of students to 'get the seats of their pants dirty' in 'real' research which, naturally, had to take place in the 'real' world, not the library.

The principles we can derive from this include the idea that ethnography always involves the study of behaviour in 'natural settings', as opposed to the experimental settings of clinical psychology. Further, it is committed to the idea that an adequate knowledge of social behaviour cannot be fully grasped until the researcher has understood the 'symbolic world' in which people live. By 'symbolic world' we simply refer to the meanings people apply to their own experiences, meanings developed through patterns of behaviour that are in some way distinctive. To get a full and adequate knowledge of these special meanings the researcher must adopt the perspective of the members, in an effort to see things as they do.

Ethnography has been referred to as 'a curious blending of methodological techniques' (Denzin, 1981). According to McCall and Simmons, it includes

> some amount of genuinely social interaction in the field with the subjects of the study, some direct observation of relevant events, some formal and a great deal of informal interviewing, some systematic counting, some collection of documents and artefacts; and open-endedness in the direction the study takes. (McCall and Simmons, 1969: 1)

That last point is important because it takes us away from techniques and towards analysis, suggesting a preference for adapting the research focus to what proves available and interesting rather than imposing an outsider's sense of what is going on. But whether the ethnographer is a Brit in Borneo or a professor on an assembly line, the techniques to record and make sense of the experience are likely to include interviews (usually more like a conversation than a standardised interview, and often involving key informants), the analysis of documents, direct observation of events, and some effort to 'think' oneself into the perspective of the members, the introspective, empathetic process Weber called 'verstehen'.

Thus, my ethnographic study of the National Front, an extreme Right racist organisation, combined participant observation at marches, demonstrations and meetings, where I passed as a member, plus interviews with party officials and opponents of the party, plus content analysis of party documents, and a good deal of reflection on the differences between my beliefs and those espoused by members (Fielding, 1981).

The ethnographer's encounter therefore involves becoming a part of the 'natural setting'. To do this he or she has first to learn the language in use; this not only means jargon and dialect, but special meanings and unfamiliar uses of familiar words. This modicum of understanding gives sufficient purchase on action in the setting to allow the compilation of fieldnotes. From inspection of these, and reflection in the field, the researcher can begin to identify the rules that govern relationships in the setting and discern patterns in members' behaviour.

9.2 FRONT MANAGEMENT AND FINDING A ROLE

The process of participation involves the researcher engaging in impression (or 'front') management. It involves a vital decision, because the role always has an element of deception and this can present ethical dilemmas. Like many others, Lofland and Lofland argue that, before choosing ethnographic methods, we should ask ourselves 'am I reasonably able to get along with these people? Do I truly like a reasonable number of them, even though I disagree with their view of the world?' (1994: 94). If we cannot answer 'yes', field observation becomes too much a matter of masking one's feelings. In special circumstances detailed below, covert observation may be acceptable; this will entail considerable front management, particularly where covert work is chosen because the group is hostile to research. It is best left to those who are comfortable with deception; several ethnographers who have used this technique have an acting background. A useful observational tactic is the cultivation of an impression of naiveté and humility, so that members feel obliged to explain things that seem obvious to them; the literature even speaks of taking on the role of the 'acceptable incompetent' (Daniels, 1975). Would-be ethnographers could well consider adopting a role which would allow them to ask naive questions, such as the apprentice or new convert.

An important problem ethnographers face in the field is that of 'going native', a term with an obvious origin in anthropology. It has to be remembered that adopting the perspective of members is a methodological tactic. One is participating in order to get detailed data, not to provide the group with a new member. One must maintain a certain detachment in order to take that data and interpret it. But it is also important to note another problem less remarked in the literature, though it may be more common. This is the problem of 'not getting close enough', of adopting an approach which is superficial and which merely provides a veneer of plausibility for an analysis to which the researcher is already committed.

In deciding how close to get, ethnographers must choose a role somewhere between the 'Martian' and the 'convert' (Lofland and Lofland, 1994). The most basic choice is whether to tell members of the setting what you are up to. Those who accept the need for covert observation usually justify it on the basis that some groups, especially powerful elites, would otherwise be closed to research (Fielding, 1982). I justified my use of covert observation in the National Front research (Fielding, 1981) on the basis that this racist group was particularly hostile to research. However, a covert approach is almost always inappropriate in anthropology, where the deceptive role is frowned upon and may represent a breach of professional ethical codes. Whatever their discipline, researchers should remember that deception is not required in most circumstances.

There are many problems in covert ethnography. The first is that you must play the role which warrants your presence in the setting; if you are masquerading as an industrial worker, you will have to spend most of your time actually working on the assembly line. Your freedom to wander and observe is limited to what is appropriate for the role which has gained you entry. You may be fascinated by the management canteen, but as a shopfloor worker that is not open to you. Your range of enquiry is also limited to what is appropriate for that role. Also, unless your role includes writing, it will be difficult to take notes in the setting.

Why, then, choose covert observation? Apart from the justifications mentioned above, actually occupying the role you are studying offers an intimate acquaintance with it. There is probably no better way to understand the experiences of members, and the meaning they derive from their experiences. Further, provided you are proficient in the role, you are much less likely to disturb the setting, avoiding the risk of studying an artefact of your presence rather than normal behaviour. But it must be emphasised that covert observation is an intensely demanding method and that you must be able to satisfy yourself that breaking the ethical objections to it is warranted by your research problem.

Choosing an overt approach does not solve all the problems. It is increasingly accepted that the most faithfully negotiated overt approach inescapably contains some covertness, in that, short of wearing a sign, ethnographers cannot signal when they are or are not collecting data. Nor is even the most scrupulous researcher entirely able to anticipate the purposes to which the data will be put. In reality, overt and covert approaches shade into each other, so that most observational research involves a 'delicate combination of overt and covert roles' (Adler, 1985: 27).

In overt observation, access is accomplished through an explicit nego-tiation with a 'gatekeeper'. The gatekeeper will be interested in what your research can do to help – or harm – the organisation. Be prepared to have to sketch in some likely findings, and to offer feedback. If access is promised, remember that the organisation may have an interest in letting you in. This needs to be taken into account in deciding what information to provide. You should avoid promising too much through gratitude. In particular, if you are preparing a dissertation or report, think carefully before committing yourself to providing a separate report for the organisation. You should also allow for the possibility that the gatekeeper's permission may be given without the knowledge or consent of the others being studied.

It is normal to accomplish access through some established contact; my study of police training (Fielding, 1988) came about because the training establishment director had been a student of my former thesis supervisor. In gaining access this way one also gains a 'sponsor' in the organisation, to whom one is accountable. After all, if things go badly you can leave, but the 'sponsor' will remain. Access-givers often serve as key informants about the organisation. Informants are the unsung heroes of ethnography: it is usual to develop several key informants with whom you discuss your research. While they can help you avoid analytic errors, you should remember that they may have ulterior motives in cooperating, such as influencing your account. It should also be remembered that their cooperation may endanger their own position in the organisation (Fielding, 1982, 1990).

All this may make access sound a fearsome business. But we should not be too demure. Many settings are public despite the observer's trepidation; for instance, even the most bizarre political and interest groups hold public meetings, because they wish to gain converts.

Overt observers are able to move about the setting more freely, to ask questions which are clearly research-related and to withdraw to write notes whenever they like. The role still presents problems. Most organisations contain factions and when people know research is taking place they will be keen to discover whether the researcher is affiliated to one or other faction. It is recommended to maintain neutrality relative to internal divisions.

The researcher may become the scapegoat for things that go wrong; in evaluation research, where budgets stand or fall on the findings, this may be a realistic perception! Where a stance of neutrality proves impossible to sustain, it is typical for the observer to align with the single largest grouping in the setting while trying to remain aloof from internal disputes. In evaluation research this often involves a separation of roles, with the observer compiling material which is then analysed by a colleague not bound by relations developed in the field.

Another problem is that of personal involvement. Observers often feel bound to help members in exchange for their tolerating the research; services range from giving lifts and stuffing envelopes to illegal activities. The problem is acute in studies of crime and deviance: in one case, the observer agreed to hide a gun in his house for a criminal expecting a visit from the police (Polsky, 1971).

These problems all relate to the issue of marginality, the idea that the ethnographer is in this social world, but not of it. It leads to fears about whether one has been accepted, and to feelings of loneliness. In covert research there are also worries about whether the deception has been discovered. It is possible to deal with these by observing on a team, so there are others to share the experience. If this cannot be done, there should at least be regular meetings with other researchers who know what it is like. But it can be argued that this sense of marginality is actually crucial for the success of the work. This is because it is out of this experience of being simultaneously an insider and an outsider that creative insight is generated. When we construct our analysis we reflect on the self that we had to become in order to pass in the setting, and how that temporary, setting-specific self differs from the person that we are normally. We can begin to identify the things that are distinctive about the people who inhabit the setting, and these are an important basis for our analytic categories. Mention of analysis brings us to fieldnotes.

9.3   RECORDING THE ACTION: FIELDNOTES

The production of fieldnotes is the observer's *raison d'être*: if you do not record what happens you might as well not be in the setting. In order to take full fieldnotes it is sensible to gradually develop your powers of observation (Emerson et al., 1995). I will discuss mental notes, jotted notes and full fieldnotes. Before doing so it is worth making an observation on the functioning of human memory. Erosion of memory is not related to time so strongly as it is to new input; that is, the more stimuli to which you are subjected during a day the more detail is forced out. It is a good idea, then, to write up fieldnotes after a round of observation before engaging in further interaction. It may be possible to sleep before writing fieldnotes but it would not be sensible to end the day by going to a party!

The 'taking' of mental notes is a skill journalists develop; they do so by practice, sometimes quizzing each other about what they can recall. Good reportage and observation is marked by accurate description of how many people were present, who in particular was present, the physical character of the setting, who said what to whom, who moved in what way, and a general characterisation of the order of events (Lofland and Lofland, 1994).

Reporters have one obvious aid, the notepad. In sensitive settings it may not be feasible to scribble notes, which partly accounts for journalists developing the capacity to take mental notes. But as soon as possible these will be transferred to writing. In taking jotted notes you do not record everything that took place, as in full fieldnotes. Rather, you note key words, phrases or quotations which represent more extensive chunks of verbal and non-verbal behaviour, and which will stimulate the memory when you are at leisure to reconstruct the events as comprehensively as such notes and your memory permit.

The jotted note may be most useful when covert observation is taking place, but even when subjects are well aware they are being observed it can be disruptive for one member of the setting to be busily note-taking. It is sensible to jot notes at inconspicuous moments. A stock ploy is to develop the reputation of having a weak bladder, enabling frequent retirements to scribble notes. The object of jotted notes is to jog the memory when writing full fieldnotes. It is worth including items from observation on previous occasions which one forgot to record at the time. Often the process of observation stimulates one's mind in such a way that events thought significant but forgotten are returned to conscious awareness.

In taking full fieldnotes it is possible to move beyond the homilies above and to be quite systematic in suggesting a standard procedure. First, it is essential to write up observations promptly. It should be delayed no later than the morning after observation. Most people lose good recall of even quite simple chains of events after 24 hours; detailed recall of conversation sufficient to enable quotation is lost within a couple of hours. Secondly, writing fieldnotes requires discipline; you should expect to spend as much time writing fieldnotes as in the observation.

A third matter is the question of tape-recording versus writing. While recording speeds things up, it has the disadvantage of leading to a less reflective approach. Being slower, writing often leads to a better yield of analytic themes. Most researchers find the process of writing fieldnotes productive, not just of description but of first reflections on connections between processes, sequences and elements of interaction. It is commonly the case that innovation occurs when the mind is not directly exploring the problem at hand.

A fourth routine matter is that it is essential to produce several copies of the full fieldnotes or to hold them on secure computer files. One set forms a complete running commentary. The others will be cut up (sometimes literally, when employing the 'cut and paste' approach to analysis) or marked by outline codes during analysis.

The contents of fieldnotes are the subject of considerable consensus among methodologists. Since different analytic uses may be made of them, it makes sense to maximise the elements of description and to gather such data systematically. The several rules applying to content are based on the idea that fieldnotes need to provide a running description of events, people and conversation. Consequently, each new setting observed and each new member of the setting merits description. Similarly, changes in the human or other constituents of a setting should be recorded. Fieldnotes should stay at the lowest level of inference: they should be 'behaviouristic' rather than seeking to summarise (see Figure 9.1). Fieldnotes should be directed to the concrete, and resist the urge to use abstractions. Such abstractions and analytic ideas that occur – and it frequently happens in the field – should be recorded separately or in a distinct column in the margin of the page.

Any verbal behaviour that is included should be identified as verbatim or otherwise. A system of notation should be adopted; one convention is that full quote marks (") denote verbatim quotation, while single quote marks (') indicate a précis of what was said.

Finally, it is essential to record your personal impressions and feelings. Doing fieldwork has emotional costs, and one needs data on one's own attitude to document one's evolving relationship to others in the setting.

Summarised or over-generalised note
The new client was uneasy waiting for her intake interview.

Behaviouristic or detailed note
At first the client sat very stiffly on the chair next to the receptionist's desk. She picked up a magazine and let the pages flutter through her fingers very quickly without really looking at any of the pages. She set the magazine down, looked at her watch, pulled her skirt down, and picked up the magazine again. This time she didn't look at the magazine. She set it down, took out a cigarette and began smoking. She would watch the receptionist out of the corner of her eye, and then look down at the magazine, and back up at the two or three other people waiting in the room. Her eyes moved from the people to the magazine to the cigarette to the people to the magazine in rapid succession. She avoided eye contact. When her name was finally called she jumped like she was startled.

Figure 9.1   *Fieldnotes (*based on Patton, 1987: 93*)*

Among other things, such information helps compensate for shifts in perspective due, for example, to 'going native'. Covert observation poses special problems in recording, leading to various ploys – the use of hidden tape recorders, note-taking in toilets, or hasty exits when something important has to be written up precisely. These problems may lead to the researcher having an effect on the setting. Note should therefore be taken of memory distortion, confusion of issues and speakers, and general field fatigue (Bruyn, 1966: 106).

9.4 COMES THE CRUNCH: ANALYSIS

While there are several approaches to the analysis of ethnographic data, the mechanical procedures researchers use are straightforward and readily summarised, as in Figure 9.2.

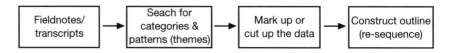

Figure 9.2 *Analysis procedure*

Appreciation of the meaning of action and events to members is not gained by simply 'telling it like it is' for them. Mere mirroring is insufficient. One gains insight from comparing the participant observer's normal and setting-specific self, appreciating the difference in such a way as to understand on what separate assumptions about reality both are founded. Meaning emerges, then, from experience of the tension between distinct selves. As Spiegelberg puts it, the investigator must not attempt to 'go native' but to move back and forth between his or her own place and understanding and that of the other (1980: 42). To appreciate the procedure of analysing ethnographic data it can be useful to compare different analyses made of the same data; Coffey and Atkinson (1996) and Cresswell (1998) both offer such accounts.

Leaving the setting begins when one is confident that one has identified the chief assumptions on which this particular worldview is based. This enables an increasingly selective focus in observations, with description of matters now seen as peripheral being skipped. The themes which best represent the setting have been identified.

9.5 VALIDATION

Making critical assessments of the reality of some unknown area of social life places a heavy responsibility on ethnographers. They must make sense of something which will remain unknown to most of their readers; precisely because the method is one of discovery, it is unlikely that the audience will have any direct way of validating what the ethnographer claims. But the concept of relativism tells us that the ethnographer is never a detached observer: our view is inescapably relative to our own perspective. 'Objective' observation is hopeless to achieve.

Given that 'objective' observation is impossible, what grounds might there be for the credibility of the ethnographer's account? The participating observer is involved, not detached. Understanding is derived from experience. Beginning to share in the member's world enables one to gain access to one's own personal experience. Clearly, such knowledge is introspective. While one's description and conclusions may be public, the introspective knowledge is not. Followers of the method have therefore pursued a test of **congruence** or principle of verifiability. The idea is that in any natural setting there are norms or rules of action in which members are competent. Understanding on the part of the observer is achieved when the observer learns the rules. The adept observer is able to provide others with instructions on how to pass in the same setting. Following such a recipe, one should ideally be able to have similar experiences and hence personally appreciate the truth of the description. In Hughes's description of the principle of verifiability, 'understanding' is achieved when the researcher knows the rules and can communicate them to both members and colleagues in such a way that if a colleague were to follow them, she or he could also become a member of the actor's group (Hughes, 1976: 134).

A more sophisticated approach is that of the 'grounded theory' of Glaser and Strauss (1967). It requires

> the development of a systematic understanding which is clearly recognizable and understandable to the members of the setting and which is done as much as possible in their own terms; yet it is more systematic, and necessarily more verbal, than they would generally be capable of expressing. It uses their words, ideas and methods of expression wherever possible, but cautiously goes beyond these. (Douglas, 1976: 124–5)

This is necessary because members are immersed in a setting natural to them, and are seldom concerned to express its essence in a symbolic fashion for outsiders. Yet without such symbolic interpretation one's ethnographic description is hollow, a mere catalogue of events and constituents.

Douglas (1976) takes the matter of verification to what some regard as its illogical conclusion. Ethnography's general orientation to 'naturalism' means that most observation is informed by a stance of 'appreciation', of trying to see things from the member's perspective. This approach tends to celebrate the knowledge of members on the basis that they, not outsiders, are the experts about their natural setting. But this is not enough for Douglas, who is preoccupied with the ways members can deceive outsiders. He suggests procedures such as 'testing out' and 'checking out' as antidote. The former involves comparing members' accounts with 'the most reliable ideas and generally patterned facts the researcher has from his prior experience' (1976: 146), while the latter involves 'comparing what one is told by others against what can be experienced or observed more directly'. Among his many examples is the case of massage parlour proprietors. Ethnographic interviews with them suggested that their popularly-supposed sideline offering illicit sex (often called 'relief massage') was false. Douglas just could not believe this; their expensive cars and houses did not seem consistent with the volume of legitimate trade. Among Douglas's checks was to send graduate students in search of a massage, a device that soon undermined what the proprietors had been telling him. For Douglas, the proper 'investigative' research attitude is 'tough-minded suspicion', a position that contrasts utterly with that of naturalism.

The problem is that Douglas's hard-bitten scepticism obstructs the attempt to construe the world as members do, with a view to gaining an understanding of its distinctive characteristics (Fielding, 1982). Yet Douglas's concentration on the delicate balance between appreciation and being conned, between the participant persona and the observer role, does alert us to the fact that the effects of the researcher's presence on the setting is as inevitable as it is hard to gauge.

A case in point is Van Maanen's study of urban policing (1982). Van Maanen had trained as a police officer as part of his observational research but his esteem among his police colleagues was dramatically improved when, after witnessing the beating of a black man in the back of a police van, he refused to comply with a subpoena of his fieldnotes on the incident. Luckily for him, the case brought by the victim was settled out of court, because there are no legal grounds for refusing to surrender fieldnotes. Two years later he returned for more observations. He initially did not realise that some of what the police did on his return was for his benefit; they were, if you will, 'playing to camera'. He suddenly saw this when they did something that broke with his previous knowledge of their demeanour:

> I . . . witnessed a bizarre encounter in which a young boy, perhaps 10 or 11 years old, was verbally assaulted and thrown to the pavement because he had aimed a ceremonial upright third finger in the direction of a passing patrol car – a gesture from a child that would have been routinely ignored or returned in my previous experience. (Van Maanen, 1982: 137)

When he had been with them every day, he felt he could maintain a role that did not disturb their routines. But when he came back the action did not flow from the logic of the situation at hand, but from what the police thought he might appreciate, as a published 'expert' who was apparently sympathetic to street justice. As he put it:

> in the abstract, relations in the field are such that the researcher is provided with trusted information of the sort necessary to both understand and empathize with the observed, but the researcher's presence

itself creates little change or disturbance . . . concretely, however, such relations wax and wane over the course of a study, approach or exceed the upper and lower limits with different individuals on the scene, and vary according to the practical situation. . . . (Van Maanen, 1982: 138)

Such considerations weigh heavily with feminist and postmodernist ethnographers. Rather than seeking to satisfy what they see as the outmoded criterion of objectivity that they associate with positivism, they seek validation in criteria of 'empowerment'. Feminist ethnographers value the way ethnography involves researchers working closely alongside the group being studied, and seek to produce analyses which can improve the lot of the women they research. An emphasis is put on the ethnographer's 'standpoint'. Many postmodernist ethnographers are also preoccupied with the issues of relativism and subjectivity, the idea that what we see and report depends on our own perspective and social location (Brettell, 1993). Rather than seeking to control for this, they make themselves advocates of the disprivileged groups they study. For them, a successful analysis may not be one that meets challenges to validity but one which impacts positively on the situation of the researched group (Denzin and Lincoln, 2000). This approach is sometimes tagged 'critical social research'. There are dangers in ideologically-based criteria, though. If the aim is to 'empower', this begs real questions about affecting the social world we study. It also means that groups with whom researchers do not sympathise may be under-researched; this could, for instance, end research on powerful elites.

All this challenges our established canons of verification. The test of congruence may comprise the ideal check on the validity of observations, but it has to be recognised that many consumers of research do not have time to perform it. In fairness to them, and to satisfy ourselves, observers still need to be self-critical. Lofland and Lofland (1994) identify seven ways of evaluating the quality of observation in terms of possible error and bias. First is the directness of the report; direct observation is more reliable than second-hand observation. Second is the spatial location of the observer. Proximity may be social as well as spatial. Third, problems arise from skewing of reported views by the informants' social location. Informants may not have said the same to other members of the setting. Fourth, one needs to guard against self-serving error in describing events by asking whether the observations fit rather too neatly into one's analytic schema. Fifth are plain errors in description of events; one may not be an accurate observer. Sixth and seventh are problems of internal and external consistency. One's analysis needs to cohere around the themes identified, while external consistency is evaluated by checking agreement of key aspects against independent studies.

The Loflands' concerns are ably dealt with in the criteria of subjective adequacy suggested by Bruyn (1966). It is worth keeping a notebook evaluating one's observations, using Bruyn's six criteria after writing each set of fieldnotes. Bruyn's first index of subjective adequacy is time: the more time the ethnographer spends with the group, the greater the likelihood of adequacy. Second is place: the closer the observer works to the group, the greater is the likelihood of adequacy. Third, Bruyn takes account of social circumstances, on the grounds that the more varied the status opportunities within which the observer can relate to the members and the more varied the activities witnessed, the more likely the interpretations will be true. Fourth is a sensitivity to language, on the argument that the more familiar the observer is with it, the greater is the accuracy of observation. The observer notes, but also becomes adept in, the argot, slang or jargon in use, and is alert to ordinary phrases which bear a setting-specific meaning.

The fifth index is intimacy. Here Bruyn suggests the observer record how she or he experienced and encountered social openings and barriers in seeking accurate interpretation of setting-specific meanings. Intimacy, or how close one is allowed to get, can be constrained by one's own reserve as well as by members. In the sixth index, 'social consensus', the criterion of adequacy is fulfilled by maximising confirmation of the group's expressive meanings, either directly – by checking interpretations with members – or indirectly – by observing what members say about an interpretation.

9.6 Sequential analysis

It is commonly recognised that the analysis of ethnographic data is demanding, not least because ethnography produces a mass of data. One of Miles and Huberman's studies of a school system produced over 3,000 pages of fieldnotes (1984). You must remember that not all the detail you have arduously gathered can be regarded as equally precious. If your procedure fulfils the various criteria of adequacy, you should have faith in your ability to select the most significant data. These items of description must then be compressed so they adhere around several manageable themes or, formally, analytic schema (Agar, 1986). The essence of the procedure is that one works up from the data, rather than selecting some theory by convenience, whim or prejudice and then dipping into the data for fragments that support it.

Howard Becker has suggested a procedure termed 'sequential analysis' (1971), similar to Simmel's (1950) *zirkel im verstehen*, in which one continually checks data against interpretation until satisfied one has grasped meaning. In Becker's approach the analysis of ethnographic data is carried out sequentially in the sense that analysis begins while one is still gathering data. In the periods between observation one may 'step back' from the data, so as to reflect on their possible meaning. Further data gathering is then directed to particular matters to which the observer has become sensitive by provisional analysis. Subsequent observation may oblige the researcher to abandon the original hypothesis about that part of the process and pursue one more consistent with the setting. Thus, hypotheses, or, if you prefer, hunches, about the functioning of natural settings are gradually refined. This is a distinct advantage over methods like surveys, where, once the instrument is designed, analytic interests cannot affect the data collected.

The evaluation of hypotheses hinges, then, on indices of the adequacy of data such as those suggested by Bruyn, plus consideration of the fit of one's observations to theory. Regarding the latter, the point is that such theory must be grounded rather than be 'grand' theory. Ethnography generates hypotheses for further testing through the researcher's ability to apply a theoretical perspective to observations and pick up uniformities and irregularities in the data. As McCall and Simmons note:

> These uniformities and departures, which provide theoretical richness, are seldom manifest in the data themselves but are obtained only through carefully designed theoretical sampling and analysis based upon the researcher's frame of reference . . . data are not rich in and of themselves but may be *enriched* by proper use of discovery techniques. (1969: 142, emphasis in the original)

Three kinds of conclusions emerge from ethnographic studies. First, and most demanding, the observer may be able to produce complex statements of necessary and sufficient conditions for a particular pattern of action or setting. Secondly, the observer may be able to typify some of the observed phenomena as 'basic' to the studied activity, on the grounds that they exercise a persistent influence on diverse events. Thirdly, the observer may be able to identify a situation as an example of an event or phenomenon described in abstract terms in a theory. This latter is the least demanding application.

Turning to the mechanics of analysis, towards the end of fieldwork the observer draws up an outline comprising his or her current idea of the principal themes to emerge from the data, along with any analytic ideas which have accumulated during fieldwork (this is where keeping an analytic theme notebook is useful). The data, such as fieldnotes or transcriptions of interviews or documents collected in the setting, are then indexed to the points on the outline. Though time-consuming, all the data should be indexed in this way. When the time comes to compile a first draft of the report one may then discard the weaker or simply repetitive data relating to particular points on the outline.

A somewhat more rigorous procedure is to compile the outline itself from ideas emerging only from the data. The data are read for analytic themes, which are listed. This list is then ordered by placing related items together in compounded items and, when condensed as much as possible, put in order according to an overall theme which seems to relate all the individual items. Because the selection of data pertinent to one of several analytic themes requires its separation from the rest of the field data, so that it may be collated with the other data on the theme, this procedure is sometimes called 'cut and paste'. Nowadays this operation can be performed using qualitative data analysis software (see Chapter 18 for a detailed explanation). Conventional word-processors allow you to retrieve selected segments to facilitate sorting into themes, but dedicated software provides many other extremely useful features.

Good qualitative analysis is able to document its claim to reflect some of the truth of a phenomenon by reference to systematically gathered data. Poor qualitative analysis is anecdotal, unreflective, descriptive without being focused on a coherent line of enquiry. It is important not to misrepresent the generalisability of findings from one setting. Ethnography's demanding nature means you are seldom in a position to claim that findings generalise to all such settings. The compensation for this is the depth of understanding gained of that one setting, which can be a rich source of ideas for work using methods such as surveys which can claim generalisability.

But the decision to use ethnographic methods must be ethical as well as practical. Some consider it unethical to conduct any research that does not give the subjects the right to refuse to be studied, while at the other extreme are those who maintain that 'any investigation that does not deliberately damage the reputation of those studied is ethically justified' (Denzin, 1981: 33). Many professional bodies use the criterion of informed consent; in agreeing to research, subjects must be told its likely consequences, among other things. Yet it may not be feasible to predict the use to which research can be put. For example, a detailed ethnography of a group of mountain villagers may seem innocuous until, years later, the region is engaged in revolt and the agents of a foreign power develop a keen interest in the group's beliefs so they can be won to its side. Are we to desist from our study when harm *might* result at some unknown future time?

What goes in the balance against potential harms is the value to social scientific knowledge of the study. This value may be obvious, as when a group is powerful and little is known about it. But it can be hard to guess. It is doubtful that Rosenhan (Bulmer, 1982b) could have predicted the enormous impact of his team's research on mental hospital diagnoses, for the simple reason that no one would have guessed they were so abjectly unreliable. The study involved placing 'pseudo-patients' in mental hospitals. On arrival they feigned hearing voices, but once admitted and diagnosed they ceased simulating any symptoms. All but one was admitted with a diagnosis of schizophrenia. Not one was caught out, providing crucial evidence about the reliability of psychiatric diagnosis and the labelling of patients. Nor were their diagnoses changed when they switched to normal behaviour, despite many of their fellow patients guessing that, as one of them put it, 'you're a journalist or a professor, you're checking up on the hospital'. One case file contained perhaps the ultimate description of compiling fieldnotes – 'patient engages in writing behaviour'! But he was never questioned about what he was doing. The staff of a hospital Rosenhan was in touch with were so appalled at the results that they agreed to the same being done at their hospital. Staff were told to expect impostors and to rate all admissions with this in mind; 23 out of 193 were suspected by at least one psychiatrist. In fact, Rosenhan had not sent in a single pseudo-patient.

Tough cases like this give some idea of what is at stake. No one could seriously doubt the value of this work, but neither could they deny its dangers. For instance, it is not hard to imagine that the psychiatrists' professional competence would be severely undermined, and their effectiveness with real patients affected negatively. The reaction of some mental health systems to such studies has been to ban social research of any kind from their institutions (Bulmer, 1982b). What these ethical complications do is to support the case for 'situation ethics' attuned to the specifics of the case, in preference to broad, general principles which collapse when confronted with dilemmas.

While dramatic, such problems only hint at the host of fieldwork issues which provoke ethical complications. There are cases where it has emerged after the study has been published that relationships between researcher and researched go beyond the published account. In one prominent, recent case it turned out that a research participant who had taken destructive action against 'his' ethnographer had been motivated by a sexual relationship with the ethnographer, a relationship which was not acknowledged in the original published account. In another recent case, ethnographers who studied high-level drug dealers failed to acknowledge until some years later that they had themselves been participants in the drug-dealing operations. Neither revelation necessarily undermines the insights of the original work, but would certainly lead us to weigh the evidence differently. Perhaps the most glaring example, though, is that of Margaret Mead's famous studies of sexuality among Pacific islanders. This research was of fundamental importance in the development of American policy on sex education and other aspects of sexual behaviour, it being used as a key comparison case to establish the nature of sexual mores in 'simple' societies. Decades later it emerged that Mead's island informants had deceived her, partly to maintain the flow of rewards she used to encourage their participation. Sensing her own prejudices and inclinations, they fed her accounts consistent with those (Freeman, 1998).

These difficult cases do not mean we are left without rules of thumb. Here are some guidelines. First, all researchers should be honest enough to report their mistakes and failures, and to do so as part of their overall analysis. Secondly, researchers should not spoil the field for those who may follow. Thirdly, researchers must acknowledge that some groups have virtually no power and are especially vulnerable. They have a right to not be researched, an example being the decision by one ethnographer not to publish a study of American draft resisters during the Vietnam War (contextual details could have revealed their location). Fourthly, unless there is a danger of reprisals affecting the physical security of the ethnographer, subjects should be given the right to comment on findings, by being provided with transcripts of interviews and draft publications. This is not just good practice but can yield more data. It should be clear to subjects what comments are legitimate; it is normal to allow points of accuracy and information to be added, while reserving the analysis to yourself.

9.7 PROJECT

This project is an exercise in collecting observational data. The emphasis is on developing your skills of observation and gaining experience of the techniques of recording social events. First, think about a research design before your fieldwork. Decide what research topic is appropriate to study through observation. For instance, you might be interested in the unstated rules that govern queuing behaviour, and so watch people lining up for buses. Or you might be interested in how people interact when they are engrossed in video games, and find your way to the Student Union to watch them. Another idea is to watch how people order drinks in the pub, noting gender differences. Several students might work on the same topic so that they can (literally) compare notes.

Secondly, carry out field observation. Record your observations by writing fieldnotes. Now write a description of the research procedure and the sort of data you gathered. Mention any problems in using the method and evaluate how it went.

The exercise works best if there is someone with whom you can discuss it and who has also tried it out. When you are thinking over the experience, or discussing it, here are the sorts of question you need to ask to assess the adequacy of your observations:

1. How accurate an observer am I of sequences of action? of dialogue?
2. Have I the ability to write 'concretely' or do my notes contain generalisations and summaries?
3. Was my research aim realistic? Was it adequately specified at the outset? Was it interesting? Was it 'sociological'?
4. Was I comfortable doing the observation? Did I tell anyone I was researching? If I did not tell anyone I was researching, do I think anyone guessed?
5. What other methods could I have used to get this data? Now that I have tried observation, was it the best available method to get this data?

9.8 FURTHER READING

Burgess (1982) is a comprehensive, edited collection that serves well as a sourcebook and field manual. It is particularly good on naturalistic and American sources. Denzin and Lincoln (2000) is an eclectic and comprehensive resource with particularly good attention to postmodern approaches. Emerson et al. (1995) offers much advice on the vital activity of preparing fieldnotes.

Fetterman (1989) offers guidance about every step in the process of conducting an ethnography. Goodale (1996) profiles a number of fieldwork issues and ways to negotiate them. Hammersley and Atkinson (1994) is a thorough treatment of ethnography with particularly good attention to issues of analysis and writing up.

Patton (1990) is good on sampling in ethnography and on the practical application of observational methods. Seale (1999) gives a stimulating, pragmatic account of epistemological foundations of ethnography and ways of handling challenges to its validity, and Yin (1984) provides an excellent introduction to the case study approach.

Focus Groups

10

Ann Cronin

Contents

Over the last 50 years, the focus group has become synonymous with market research. The ability of commercial enterprises to succeed in an ever-expanding consumer-oriented global economy depends on accurate up-to-date information about consumer behaviour. While a range of methods are used, for example surveys or questionnaires, the focus group has become the key method for the collection of qualitative data (Krueger, 1994; Morgan, 1993). In addition to their commercial use, focus groups have more recently become associated with the world of politics. Here the focus group provides an insight into the views of the electorate about existing and future policy. Initially used in political campaigns in the USA in the 1980s, they achieved a somewhat notorious reputation under the Labour government in this country (Barbour and Kitzinger, 1999).

While the commercial and political use of focus groups is sociologically interesting in itself, this chapter is concerned with them as a research tool in social research. Although the high profile accorded to the focus group in both market research and political canvassing is not matched within social research, it has a valuable role to play in the generation of qualitative data. Recognition of that value has led in recent years to renewed interest in the use of focus groups in social research. Indeed, its origins lie within sociology (Morgan, 1988). In the 1950s the American sociologist Robert Merton and his colleagues used focus groups, in combination with other research methods, to examine the impact of wartime propaganda (Merton and Kendall, 1946; Merton et al., 1956).

This chapter provides an introduction to the methods involved in organising and conducting focus groups and in managing and interpreting the data they generate. It is divided into five sections. The first defines the term 'focus group' and provides a brief overview of its use in social research. The second examines the processes involved in preparing for a focus group. The third section provides a step-by-step guide to running a focus group. It also considers some of the problems that may arise during the course of focus group discussion and offers possible solutions. The fourth section considers the analysis of focus group data.

10.1   WHAT IS A FOCUS GROUP?

This section begins with a brief definition of a focus group before moving to examine the type of data generated through focus group discussion and the role of the moderator. An extract from a focus group transcript illustrates the points made in this section.

A focus group is quite simply a **group interview** or a **group discussion** (Barbour and Kitzinger, 1999; Hawe et al., 1990; Krueger 1994; Morgan 1993). Elaborating on this, we can say that a focus group consists of a small group of individuals, usually numbering between six and ten people, who meet together to express their views about a particular topic defined by the researcher. A **facilitator**, or **moderator**, leads the group and guides the discussion between the participants. In general focus groups last one and half to two hours and are tape recorded. Sometimes a video is made as well. The tape-recording can be transcribed for analysis.

Akin to the individual interview discussed in Chapter 8, the focus group enables the researcher to explore participants' views and experiences on a specific subject in depth, for example the use of the Internet or the experience of growing old in our society. So, as with the individual interview, the focus group discussion involves the **exploration of ideas** and **interpretation** of what people say. However, it differs from the individual interview in that the focus group is dependent upon **interaction** between participants. As Morgan notes, 'The hallmark of focus groups is the explicit use of the group interaction to produce data and insights that would be less accessible without the interaction found in a group' (Morgan, 1988: 12). Thus a focus group is not a replacement for the individual interview; the type of data generated through focus groups is very different from that generated through individual interviews.

10.1.1 The role of the facilitator

The level of interaction between participants, which ultimately has a bearing on the type of data produced, is largely dependent on the role taken by the group facilitator. Morgan (1988) talks of low and high levels of moderation, although his own preference is for 'self-managed' groups. Those wishing to know more about 'self-managed' groups should read Morgan, because in this section I concentrate on low- and high-level moderation and offer a third position – of medium-level moderation. However, as Morgan points out, it is best to view moderation of focus groups on a continuum and adopt the position best suited to your research needs.

Low-level moderation means that the facilitator's role in the discussion is kept to a minimum. In this scenario it is usual for the facilitator to introduce the broad topic, for example 'crime and young people', and then withdraw from the discussion. This non-involvement with the group can be demonstrated by physically withdrawing, thus preventing the group turning to the facilitator for guidance or direction. The data produced are therefore entirely dependent upon the interaction of the group members.

Faced with the daunting prospect of running a focus group with eight to ten people for the first time, this might seem an attractive option! Furthermore, data produced in this way can be said to be free of researcher influence and, certainly, this is a valid reason for choosing to adopt this level of moderation. It is clearly useful when the aim of the research is to gain an insight into the perspective of the participants without the researcher imposing any limits on their understanding of the subject. However, be prepared for the discussion to wander away from the set topic or for the development of group dynamics not conducive for a full exploration of the subject. For example, some individuals may dominate the proceedings. This may make analysis of the data difficult. Of course, if your interest lies in the study of group dynamics, this level of moderation is ideal. However, if you are more concerned with gathering specific information, this may not be the most appropriate method.

In contrast, high-level moderation means that the facilitator assumes a high degree of control over the direction and nature of the discussion. Questions are asked in a specific order and there is little opportunity for participants to deviate from the topic or to raise issues of concern to them. This approach may be appropriate if you require information of a very precise nature, for example, feedback on the phrasing of a questionnaire. However, this level of moderation is not appropriate for gaining in-depth qualitative material about attitudes, behaviour and experience. It is also likely to impede rather than facilitate group discussion and interaction.

In practice the majority of focus group facilitators opt for a level of moderation somewhere in between these two extremes. The moderator performs a guiding role in the discussion, ready to interject, ask questions and probe for further information when necessary. In an individual interview, the dialogue is largely dependent upon the interviewee responding to the questions and prompts of the interviewer. However, a focus group facilitator will not ask or expect that all participants will answer every question in turn, or ensure that everyone answers each question (Krueger, 1994; Morgan, 1993). Furthermore, even with medium-level moderation, the facilitator will often 'step back' and let the discussion develop between the participants.

In contrast to low-level moderation, this approach has the advantage that, as a facilitator, you can maintain a greater degree of control over the direction of the discussion, hence ensuring that the data are relevant to your research question. It is this middle level of moderation that I will consider. However, you should be able to see how it could be adapted for either high- or low-level moderation.

10.1.2 Understanding focus group data

The unique way in which focus groups are conducted means that the type of data produced is also unique. This can best be illustrated with a short extract from a transcript of a focus group discussion. The focus group consisted of eight students, four men and four women, all members of a college's Student Union lesbian and gay society. The group had been convened to discuss views about levels of crime in the area and its effects on personal behaviour. The facilitator's words (myself as it happens!) appear in bold.

Do you personally feel scared to go out at night?
– I do, I do. I always get a taxi home from work if I'm working.
– Yeah, we always walk the main roadway. If we have to go to a shop at night we walk down the High Street rather than walking down the . . .
– You always get shouted at.
– It's always full of squaddies and that sort of, you know, homophobic and they don't like students . . .
– . . . Got a taxi at the station and there's this bloke saying well surely you should feel like you're in one of the safest towns like in the country because there's the Army everywhere and I was like, "No".
– But the locals are like this as well aren't they?
– Yes.
– The locals are more of a problem.
– I get that impression as well that the actual problems are caused by locals from _____ rather than the squaddies themselves . . .
Right.
– And I think the locals think that as well actually don't they?

– Yes.

– All the trouble we get is from locals, it's definitely the locals that are a problem.

– They seem not to like students as well.

In this extract, my initial question, 'Do you personally feel scared to go out at night?', directed the participants to focus on a particular topic yet remained sufficiently open for the ensuing discussion to consider wider issues, namely the identification of key groups perceived to be responsible for causing trouble in the area. As a researcher who does not live in the area, this type of information gave me an insight into different groups in the community, thus enabling me to ask questions I had not previously considered. Furthermore, these data were not the result of one person talking, or from me as the facilitator asking each person in turn the same question, but arose through the interaction of the participants. This type of exchange is very typical of focus group discussion. That is, in the normal course of a focus group participants will raise issues relating to the subject that you have not previously considered and comment on each other's experiences and attitudes (Barbour and Kitzinger, 1999).

To summarise, this section has so far considered what a focus group is, the role of the moderator and the type of data generated from focus group discussions. The discussion will already have given you some idea about the sorts of thing focus groups can be used for in social research, and it is this issue that is explored in the next section.

10.1.3 When to use focus groups

Focus groups produce qualitative data, and so we can apply many of the reasons for conducting in-depth interviews to focus groups. Focus groups can be used either as a 'self-contained' method or in conjunction with other research methods. Their use at the preliminary stage of a project can provide insight on a topic and inform the development of an interview schedule or questionnaire. Alternatively, in the final stage of a research project, they can be useful for gaining feedback on research findings obtained through other methods. Because focus groups are useful for examining people's knowledge about a subject, they have a broad application in social research. For example, we might want to explore similarities and differences between participants on a subject such as capital punishment. The interactive nature of the focus group is ideal for this sort of research. Finally, focus groups can be used to test topics and the phrasing of questionnaires. However, it is important to remember that the data from a focus group consisting of eight people will lack the depth of information that could be obtained from eight individual interviews, although may be broader in content. This needs to be taken into account when selecting the appropriate research method for your research project.

10.1.4 Topic and membership of focus groups

In my own experience, borne out by the literature (e.g. Barbour And Kitzinger, 1999; Morgan, 1988), there are few topics unsuitable or too sensitive for discussion in a focus group, so long as attention is given to the composition of the group. For example, when examining domestic violence it would be inappropriate to have a focus group consisting of both victims and perpetrators. However, convening two groups (one for the victims and one for the perpetrators) would be feasible. The key factor is that groups containing people who have shared experiences or the same social identity will be more successful than those with disparate views and backgrounds. Additionally, people often benefit from being a member of a group and having the opportunity to share experiences with people who understand them.

This raises a related issue, should focus groups always consist of strangers or is it acceptable to have people who know each other? There are no hard-and-fast rules and the answer to this question will often depend on the nature of the research and availability of participants. For example, if you obtain your sample from a student population, it is highly likely that people will know each other. However, you need to bear in mind that the group dynamics between groups of friends will differ from those between strangers and this may affect the quality of the data.

10.2 SAMPLING STRATEGY

Students considering using focus groups for the first time often ask: How many focus groups should I run?; How big should they be? These questions are about sampling size and strategy. This section discusses some of the issues you will need to consider when deciding on the number and size of focus groups.

10.2.1 How many focus groups?

Barbour and Kitzinger (1999) identify three factors to consider when looking at sampling size and strategy: the nature of the research question, the range of people who need to be included and the limitations imposed by time and cost. Bearing in mind the discussion in the previous section, you also need to consider whether the focus groups will be self-contained or form part of a process of 'triangulation' with other research methods, for example, individual interviews or surveys.

Consideration of these issues leads to what Barbour and Kitzinger term 'structured rather than random sampling' (1999: 7). In the planning stage of your research you will need to decide how to find samples from your target population. Focus groups depend on purposive sampling, that is a sampling strategy that selects participants according to the project's goals. For example, if you wish to consult older people on local government policy you will need to draw up a list of organisations run by and for older people.

Purposive sampling is different from the sampling used in quantitative surveys. The goal of surveys is to generalise the findings to larger populations by collecting numerical data, and this requires a random sample. The main goal of a focus group is to gain insight and understanding by hearing from representatives from the target population. As with any research methodology the recruitment of participants is one of the most important elements of the research study. In some instances, the participants need to be drawn from a cross-section of a population, and care will need to be taken to choose people from, for example, different age ranges, housing and/or employment status, or ethnicity (see also Chapter 11).

Having determined the number and composition of your focus groups you need to gain your sample. Below are a few suggestions for how you might do this:

- Ask someone to nominate participants.
- Use a sampling framework such as populations lists.
- Send out questionnaires to a population asking for participants.
- Advertise for participants.
- Snowball sampling.

When planning your research do not underestimate the time and effort it takes to recruit a sufficient number of participants for just one focus group, let alone four or five or more.

10.2.2 Size of groups

Ideally, focus groups should consist of between six and ten people. However, this is a matter of debate. It has been suggested that four or five allows for more in-depth discussion of participants' stories. Others suggest that if the subject is particularly sensitive, then three may be a suitable number. While this debate indicates that there are no hard-and-fast rules, in my experience the conversation in groups smaller than six is very limited. Nevertheless, while the minimum number might be a matter of debate, often depending on the nature of the research, it is unwise to go above ten. There is a tendency among those new to focus groups to assume that the greater the number of participants, the greater the return in terms of data. However, running groups that consist of more than ten people poses a number of problems, which result in the ensuing data lacking both depth and substance. As a facilitator you will find it difficult to maintain control over a group with more than ten people. Furthermore, participants do not feel the need to contribute, relying on the group to carry the discussion (Morgan, 1988). Latané, Williams and Harkins (1979) nicely refer to this phenomenon as 'social floating'. The important point to remember is that focus groups provide an understanding of the range and depth of opinions, attitudes and beliefs, rather than a measure of the number of people who hold a particular view or opinion. Therefore, be prepared to substitute quantity for quality.

10.2.3 Research examples

Two examples from my own research will help to clarify these points. In the first example, the research question was the effect discrimination has on physical and mental health. The research design consisted of five focus groups followed by 20 in-depth interviews. The number of focus groups was determined by the limited funding available for the project and the identification of five groups considered to be the recipients of both institutional and personal discrimination. The five focus groups were chosen from lesbian women, gay men, users of mental health services, members of ethnic minorities and unemployed people. Four in-depth interviews from each group supplemented the findings, adding depth and substance to the issues raised in the discussions. The focus groups were conducted first and the findings informed the development of an interview schedule.

In the second example, the aim of the research was to assess the extent and nature of community involvement in a large urban area with an ethnically and culturally diverse population. In order to take this diversity into account it was necessary to run 25 groups with people from different ethnic minorities, older people, young people and single parents. So in this case the need to include the voices of as many different sections of the community determined the number of focus groups. In this case the focus groups were self-contained. Both these examples demonstrate that the number of focus groups and the composition of those groups will be specific to your research needs and based on your research question.

10.3   ARRANGING A FOCUS GROUP

This section examines issues related to organising a focus group. It begins with practical considerations regarding venue and equipment before moving on to discuss developing a focus group schedule and running a focus group discussion.

10.3.1 Venue and location

Your choice of venue should suit both the research project and the types of participant you wish to recruit. Suitable venues may be community halls, school buildings, council offices, a room in the Student Union, or an individual's home. The venue should be one where people feel comfortable enough to sit and talk for a couple of hours. If possible choose a venue which is familiar to the members of the focus group, thus aiding attendance and participation.

Green and Hart (1999) provide an interesting account of the way in which different locations can affect levels of participation. To this I would add my own experience of running a number of focus groups in a very run-down community centre. My first reaction on entering the room set aside for the focus groups was horror combined with anger at the lack of respect for the participants. It was dirty, poorly furnished and the lighting was bad. However, during the course of running the focus groups, a number of the participants commented on the appropriateness of the venue, adding that if the groups had been held at the rather grand town hall they would not have attended. Not only was this a good indication that the venue was an appropriate one, but it also gave me an interesting insight into the relationship between the local population and local government, an issue that had a bearing on the research question.

It is a good policy to check the chosen venue prior to the meeting to ensure that:

- All participants will be able to see and hear each other.
- There will be a minimum of distractions and interruptions.
- Observing or recording can easily be carried out.
- It is not too warm or too cold.
- The venue is accessible to all members of the group.

Refreshments such as tea, coffee, soft drinks and biscuits should be provided. The key point to remember when choosing a location is that the venue should provide an appropriate and 'sympathetic' social setting for the group discussion. Finally, the list below provides a checklist of equipment necessary for running a focus group:

- Cassette recorder(s) with cord/leads.
- Remote microphone.
- Extra batteries.
- Blank cassette tapes.
- Flipchart and pens.
- Pads/pens for the moderator.
- Copies of the focus group schedule.
- A list of participants.
- Pens/paper for participants (if necessary).
- Handouts (if appropriate).
- Masking tape to hang things on walls (if appropriate).

10.3.2 Running a focus group

Merton et al. (1956, cited in Morgan, 1988) cite four criteria necessary for a successful focus group discussion: **range**, **specificity**, **depth** and **personal context**. This section uses these criteria to highlight some issues to consider when constructing a focus group schedule and running a focus group.

Range refers to ensuring that your focus group schedule enables the maximum number of relevant topics to be covered. Although you will have a good idea of the issues you want to discuss, the questions should not inhibit the participants from raising topics of interest to them. **Specificity** means ensuring that the facilitator encourages participants to move beyond the abstract to situate their talk in actual lived experience. This will help to shed light on the sources of attitudes and beliefs and add clarity and **depth** (Merton's third criterion) to the points being made. Finally, there is a need to take account of the **personal context** of participants' lives, that is, the social role they perform or the social category to which they belong. Attention to such issues enables us to gain a better insight into the social construction of people's attitudes and beliefs.

The issues raised by Merton's four-part criteria relate particularly to the phrasing of questions. Much of the advice given about the construction of interview schedules in Chapter 6 is applicable here, for example the use of open-ended questions, so I will confine myself to just a few key points. 'Think back' questions are useful for encouraging participants to provide a social context for their responses. For example, 'Can you tell me about the last time you visited the doctors?' It is best to avoid using 'why?' questions. Such questions assume that people always behave in a rational manner and can account for their behaviour in this manner. They can also make people feel that they are being interrogated and judged. Similarly, while occasionally it is helpful to give an example to illustrate a point, it is best to avoid using this strategy too often. Examples can constrain answers to the topic of the example and prevent participants from talking about their own experiences. Likewise, if a participant provides a long or very complicated example to answer a question, do repeat the original question. Finally, while a focus group schedule usually consists of questions to stimulate discussion, it is possible to use other means to generate talk. For example, visual, written or audio material, a list of attitude statements or a short questionnaire can all be effective. Such stimulus materials can be used on their own or in combination with questions.

Having outlined some of the issues that need to be taken into account when designing a focus group schedule, we will now consider how to run a focus group. You need to start by giving the group members an **introduction** to the research topic. Too much information is counter-productive as it may confuse the participants and leave them unsure about their role. Make a brief statement about what you intend to do with the data collected in the focus group, for example, the basis of a dissertation. Do assure confidentiality on your part and remind participants to respect the confidentiality of all members of the group. The aim is to provide a friendly and welcoming atmosphere in which participants will feel sufficiently comfortable and relaxed to talk. I always let people know that I am not seeking right or wrong answers and am interested in hearing what they have to say. I tell them that I may ask what might appear to be obvious questions, but this is because I want their understanding of the subject and not simply my interpretation of it. Bellenger, Bernhardt and Goldstucker (1976) quite aptly refer to this as 'incomplete understanding'. You might like to consider introducing 'ground rules' at this point, although they can inhibit discussion. However, I do ask participants not to hold private conversations with the person next to them but to direct all comments to the group. I do not ask people not to interrupt each other as this makes for very stilted conversation and inhibits discussion. Do make use of those occasions when all the participants start talking at once: this is generally a very good indication of the salience of the topic under discussion.

After introducing yourself it is useful to begin with an **opening circle** in which participants say their name and other relevant personal information. Make a note of participants' names and where they are sitting. This will enable you to direct questions at particular participants and to draw in the quieter members of the group. It is helpful to use the opening circle to elicit participants' views on the subject under discussion. This is useful for debunking 'group-think' (Janis, 1982; Morgan, 1988) and enables you to make an initial judgement on areas of agreement and disagreement. Do make a note of anything of interest and refer back to such items in the discussion.

Following the open circle, use one or two **introductory questions** to introduce the topic under discussion and to encourage participants to think about the **range** of topics involved in the subject. One way of doing this is to ask participants about their understanding and definition of the subject, which may differ from your own. So, for example, in a study of health beliefs, the question 'what does health mean to you?', enables participants to discuss their own understanding of health as it relates to the social context of their lives (physical, mental, social, and so on).

These questions will be followed by the **key questions** driving the study. Ideally there should be between two and five of these. Any more and you will not allow sufficient time for in-depth discussion. Remember that you can use probes to follow up responses, which will allow you to explore the issues in depth. Finally, there are **ending questions** that, as the name suggests, are designed to draw the discussion to a close, but can take a variety of different forms. You might like to throw out a general 'all things considered' type of question. For example, you might end a discussion on the causes of crime by saying, 'Bearing in mind the issues raised in the discussion, what do you consider to be the main causes of crime?' Altern- atively, you could have a closing circle. The advantage of a closing circle is that it will allow all participants to say something that is particularly useful if the group contains quiet members who have not contributed to the main discussion. Alternatively, you might like to summarise the key points of the discussion and ask participants if they agree with this summary. Regardless of the method you use in this closing period, the main purpose is to provide people with a final opportunity to raise issues of concern that have not yet been explored and/or to make a closing statement. Do not be surprised if this closing phase goes on for some time as some people use this opportunity to say what they really think.

10.3.3 Dealing with focus group problems

This section outlines some of the problems you may encounter when running a focus group and offers solutions for dealing with them. It is quite likely that in a group of eight people you will have one or two people who are shy or reluctant to join in the discussion. These people need to be gently drawn into the discussion, for example by directing a question at them. However, if you do this, do be prepared to give them plenty of time to answer.

In addition to the shy person, it is very common to have at least one person who will try to dominate the conversation. While such contributions might be interesting, it is important that they do not prevent other people from speaking. While there is no simple solution to dealing with such people, the following are suggestions you might like to consider:

- Acknowledge his or her contribution and then ask other people what they think.
- Avoid eye contact with the dominant person.
- Directly ask him or her to be quiet and let the others speak.
- Take a break and ask him or her to leave.

Other common problems include people who have private conversations with their neighbours, people who wander off the subject, or inattentive participants. Very often a gentle reminder of the purpose of the group is sufficient to correct the problem, but at other times more drastic action is required. For example, in the case of a private conversation between two individuals, you might decide to call a five-minute break and ask people to sit in a different order when reconvening the group. Finally, do not be afraid to take control of the group when appropriate. Participants will expect you to and will feel reassured by it. The golden rule here is to be firm and direct, while remaining friendly and open.

10.4 ANALYSIS OF FOCUS GROUP DATA

In this section I provide a brief outline of the analysis of focus group data, merely highlighting some issues you will need to consider. I strongly recommend that you read widely on this subject, beginning with the suggested books at the end of this chapter.

A focus group generally lasts about 90 minutes and will yield a transcript of 20–30 pages. Multiply this figure by the number of groups you are conducting and you will begin to understand the enormous amount of data generated by focus group discussions. This can seem daunting when it comes to analysis. However the data produced by a focus group is directed by the focus group schedule that you developed. The data will therefore include at least your initial conceptualisation of the problem you are investigating.

Morgan offers two approaches to the analysis of focus group data: 'a strictly qualitative or ethnographic summary and a systematic coding via content analysis' (Morgan, 1988: 64). To these can be added discourse analysis, conversation analysis and an approach that focuses on group dynamics, although the latter is more closely associated with social psychology than sociology. Similarly, while qualitative methods of analysis differ considerably from the more quantitative approach adopted by content analysis, it would be feasible to combine the two (see Chapters 12, 18 and 19). My own preference is for a qualitative approach and it is this method of analysis that I will concentrate on here, although those who wish to know more about content analysis can consult Bertrand, Brown and Ward (1992), Knoedel (1993) or Frankland and Bloor (1999).

Nevertheless, regardless of the approach you take, the main point to remember is that the group is the unit of analysis, not the individual participants. This means that, first, your analysis needs to take into account the group context and, secondly, you are looking for themes, issues, areas of agreement and disagreement that arose at a group level and not simply from individuals within the group. Therefore, you need to be able to distinguish between the opinions of individuals and group opinions (Barbour and Kitzenger, 1999).

As a starting point, begin with the systematic coding of the data from each focus group, generating hypotheses as you proceed. In the early stages you will not be able to make comparisons between the focus groups, but this is something you will be able to do as your analysis proceeds. Differences between the groups should be related to the social composition of each group. For example, in a study of adult education it is very likely that you would have taken socio-economic status into account when deciding on your sample and the composition of the groups. This would need to be addressed in an analysis of, for example, the effect income has on the participation and completion rates of adult education courses. The edited collection by Barbour and Kitzenger (1999) provides numerous illustrations of the analysis and writing-up of focus group data. As a starting point, see the chapter by Myers and Macnaghten on the application of conversation analysis to focus group data.

10.5 PROJECT

The government wishes to establish the views of people regarding the possible legalisation of drugs. You have been commissioned to study this issue by means of focus group discussions. The budget for the research would pay for up to 15 groups, but expenditure of that order would need to be justified. Briefly consider the following:

- How many groups should be convened?
- What should their composition be?

- How should they be organised?
- Where should they be held?

Develop a short topic guide. To get started you might like to consider the following issues:

- Attitudes towards drugs and drug taking.
- Experience of using drugs.
- Attitudes towards the legalisation of drugs.
- Consequences of legalisation.

10.6 FURTHER READING

Morgan (1988) offers excellent guidance on every aspect of organising focus groups and analysis of focus group data. It is particularly good for its discussion on using focus groups with other research methods. Barbour and Kitzinger (1999) is an edited collection which draws on a range of different disciplines to examine both the advantages and disadvantages of using focus groups in social research. Krueger (1994) provides a practical step-by-step guide to running focus groups.

EXEMPLAR: THE ENVIRONMENTAL CONCERNS OF DISADVANTAGED GROUPS

11

KATE BURNINGHAM AND DIANA THRUSH

CONTENTS

This chapter provides an example of a research project in action. In 1999, we were commissioned by the Joseph Rowntree Foundation (JRF) to undertake a year-long study exploring the environmental concerns of disadvantaged groups within the UK. At the time of writing, we are right in the middle of this research. This chapter provides an insight into the often somewhat messy reality of research in practice in contrast to those neatly structured versions of methodology which appear in proposals before research commences and, after it has finished, in papers discussing the results.

The chapter begins by providing some background to the research and outlines the methodology as it was stated at the outset of the project. We move on to discuss our experience of carrying out the study, considering in detail the interviewing of key informants and recruiting for focus groups. Through examples of issues encountered during the project, we emphasise the need for flexibility and reflection during the process of research.

11.1   BACKGROUND

During the 1980s within western societies there was a dramatic upsurge in environmental concern and in membership of environmental groups. While concern about environmental quality is widespread, research indicates that levels of concern, individual domestic action (e.g. recycling, green consuming) and membership of groups are highest among young people, those with higher levels of education, members of the middle class, the politically liberal and urban residents (see Greenbaum, 1995; Witherspoon and Martin, 1992). Moreover, the environmental movement in the UK is noticeably white, with few members or employees drawn from minority ethnic groups (Taylor, 1993; Wright, 1998). This profile suggests that groups within the UK population who might be described as 'disadvantaged', for example, members of minority ethnic groups, poor people (unemployed, on low incomes, older people, etc.), are often effectively excluded from the environmental movement which, as a consequence, is unlikely to reflect their agendas, concerns and interests.

Given that they are often those worst affected, disadvantaged groups might be expected to have particular perspectives on environmental problems. Research in both the USA and the UK has demonstrated the extent to which poor communities are often subject to environmentally polluted or hazardous environments. This is true for inner-city residents subject to the pollution associated with traffic (McNally and Mabey, 1999), communities close to polluting or hazardous industries (McLaren et al., 1999; Phillimore and Moffatt, 2000) and rural communities subject to the polluting effects of chemicals used in agribusiness. Economically depressed areas are also more likely than richer areas to accept further environmentally damaging facilities or industries. Not only do such areas often lack the necessary levels of community organisation to resist siting proposals, they may positively welcome the investment (whether in jobs or compensation) associated with the development (Blowers and Leroy, 1994; Bullard, 1993).

Just as environmental 'bads', such as pollution, have a disproportionate effect on certain sections of society, access to environmental 'goods' is also unequally distributed. Sufficient energy, clean water and healthy food are often out of reach of the poorest members of society (see Boardman (1991) on fuel poverty; Donkin et al. (1999) on access to healthy food; Herbert and Kempson (1995) on water debt).

The fact that members of 'disadvantaged' groups are seldom represented within environmental groups does not necessarily mean that the environment is of no interest to them, but it is likely that the focus of their concerns, what the environment means to them, and the environmental measures they are concerned to see implemented will differ from the agendas of the mainstream environmental movement. The environmental movement within the UK has historically focused largely on issues of countryside and habitat conservation and more recently on campaigns associated with global environmental change (McCormick, 1995). In contrast, the concerns of disadvantaged communities are likely to focus on more immediate issues of local amenity, health and safety (Burrows and Rhodes, 1998; Macnaghten et al., 1995).

There is now increasing recognition among environmental groups and policy-makers of the need to address social and environmental issues together in the pursuit of environmental sustainability. In tandem with this is a realisation of the need to include the diversity of lay perspectives into environmental decision-making (Bloomfield et al., 1998; Royal Commission on Environmental Pollution, 1998). Such participation is advocated for a range of reasons: to reduce conflict within the planning process and enable people to have a sense of ownership of outcomes; on the grounds that lay people have important knowledge which should be included if the best environmental decision is to be reached (Brown, 1991, 1993; Irwin, 1995); and as part of a commitment to improve democracy and enable people to contribute to decisions which will affect their lives. Nonetheless, to date the perspectives of disadvantaged groups on environmental issues have seldom been incorporated into environmental planing, policy- and decision-making.

It is within this context that we are carrying out our research. The aim of this study is to develop a detailed understanding of the environmental concerns and interests of disadvantaged groups and of their perspectives and understandings of the environmental movement. The study addresses the following issues:

- What do 'the environment' and 'environmental problems' mean to members of disadvantaged groups?
- What concerns do they have for the immediate environment of their own homes, their localities and for the wider national and global environment?

- What kinds of environmental improvements (at all levels) would they like to see?
- Whom do they identify as responsible for environmental 'bads' and who is responsible for implementing improvements?
- To what extent are they involved in environmental action (individual and collective) and what barriers exist to their environmental action?
- Do disadvantaged groups think that environmental policies and the green movement are worthwhile and to what extent do they address the issues that concern them?

11.2 DEFINING 'DISADVANTAGED GROUPS' AND 'ENVIRONMENTAL CONCERNS'

One of the first tasks in many research projects is to develop working definitions of the key concepts to be explored. For us this involved outlining what we meant by 'disadvantaged groups' and 'environmental concerns'.

11.2.1 Disadvantaged groups

Contemporary discussions of disadvantaged groups draw heavily on debates about social exclusion, which has a strong spatial dimension. The Social Exclusion Unit defines social exclusion as 'individuals or areas suffering from a combination of linked problems such as unemployment, poor skills, low incomes, poor housing, high crime environments, bad health and family breakdown' (Social Exclusion Unit, 1998). The government's approach to tackling social exclusion focuses on areas with a high proportion of individuals or households who are experiencing a range of deprivations, either singularly or in combination. An area-based approach, however, may gloss over the fact that not all individuals and households in a deprived area will experience deprivation and, conversely, not all disadvantaged people live in deprived areas. The area-based approach has been particularly criticised by those concerned with rural poverty. Many households experience extreme poverty in rural areas that are viewed as desirable and picturesque residential environments (Cloke et al., 1995). It also fails to acknowledge that people may be part of a disadvantaged 'community of identity', for instance by virtue of their ethnic minority status.

For the purposes of our research we defined disadvantaged groups as people living on low incomes within both urban deprived environments and in rural environments. Within this broad definition we sought to include within our research individuals experiencing different aspects of deprivation: for example, those with a long-term illness or disability, unemployed people and those on low incomes, lone parents, members of ethnic minorities and older people.

11.2.2 Environmental concerns

Surveys of environmental concerns within the population tend to be based on a limited definition of environmental concern. Questions asked in surveys (particularly British Social Attitudes Surveys) have followed the general focus of the UK environmental movement, being primarily concerned either with attitudes towards the countryside or about adherence to green values.

By defining environmental concern in this way, surveys fail to address attitudes towards the local environment, whether in terms of individuals' homes or the area in which they live (which may be phrased in terms of concern about amenity, health or safety rather than environment *per se*). They also adopt a narrower conception of environmental concern than the one embodied in discussions of sustainable development, which argues for the need to consider environmental issues alongside economic and social issues rather than in isolation from them. In order to access this broader definition of environmental concern (encompassing a local dimension and taking a sustainable development rather than a 'green' perspective), recent qualitative studies of people's perspectives on the environment have framed their initial questions in terms of participants' perception of quality of life (Macnaghten et al., 1995) or 'the most important problems in our society today' (Kasemir et al., 1999).

In common with these recent projects, our research uses a broad definition of environmental concern. We are interested primarily in identifying what disadvantaged groups view as the key problems of their environments (whether or not these are framed as 'environmental'), and in understanding their perspectives on environmental problems and environmentalism more broadly. Rather than devising indicators of environmental concern (as in attitude surveys), we adopt a qualitative approach that allows respondents to talk about issues in their own terms.

11.3 METHODOLOGY

The research was planned in three distinct stages:

1. Literature review.
2. In-depth interviews with key informants and site selection.
3. Focus groups and in-depth interviews with members of disadvantaged groups.

The aim of the literature review was to provide the intellectual background for the research and to inform the methodology. This aspect of the research will not be discussed here.

The purpose of the key informant interviews was to give insights that might be missed in a review of published material, to help us select suitable sites for our case studies and to suggest topics for inclusion in our focus groups. These interviews were planned in two phases. First, we interviewed individuals connected with environmental groups and organisations representing the concerns of disadvantaged groups. Having identified suitable sites for our case studies, we then planned further key informant interviews with individuals working within those areas in order to learn about specific local concerns, to discuss appropriate recruitment strategies and to find venues for the focus groups.

The third phase of the research involved conducting focus groups within specific localities. We were committed to a qualitative approach as we wanted to allow respondents to discuss issues in their own terms and to explore some of the complexities of environmental concern which are not illuminated by survey research. We opted for focus groups as the primary investigative tool because they would enable us to listen to the views of a greater number of people in a shorter time than would be the case with one-to-one interviews. While focus groups provide less detail about individuals' views than one-to-one interviews, they do have the advantage of providing a window on to areas of agreement and dispute between local people. This was something that particularly interested us.

We envisaged that we would conduct approximately 20 focus groups and follow these with some 30 in-depth interviews with sectors of the population whose views had not been represented within the groups. We did not specify actual sites or the composition of groups in our research proposal but suggested that the following types of location might be selected:

- Inner-city location (4 groups at one site).
- Suburban location (4 groups at one site).
- Rural location (4 groups at one site).
- Locations close to hazardous and polluting industries or facilities (e.g. the nuclear industry, the chemical industry, incinerators, amenity tips, high-density traffic areas) (8 groups overall – 4 at two sites).

11.4 THE RESEARCH IN PRACTICE: SITE SELECTION AND KEY INFORMANT INTERVIEWS

11.4.1 Site selection

Site selection proceeded in tandem with the key informant interviews. As the research progressed, we refined our site categories to the following:

1. A rural area in which some people are socially disadvantaged.
2. A socially disadvantaged urban locality.
3. An area where socially disadvantaged people are living close to a potentially polluting installation (e.g. incinerator, industry, etc.).
4. An area where socially disadvantaged people are living close to a busy road.

We used the interviews to help us identify possible sites and choose between alternatives.

Our final selection of sites was as follows: the Peak District; Possilpark in North Glasgow; Cefn Mawr in North Wales, where people live very close to a chemical factory; and Bromley-by-Bow in East London, where people live very close to the A102 Blackwall Tunnel Northern Approach. The decision to select four sites instead of the five originally planned is explained in section 11.5.1.

11.4.2 The key informant interview guide

We wanted to use these interviews to gather a range of information. We used a semi-structured interview guide (see Chapter 8) which simply introduced a number of topics for discussion. These were:

- Agenda of the group/organisation concerning disadvantage and environmental concern/action.
- Their experience of talking to/working with disadvantaged groups.
- How our research relates to their work/who they deal with.
- Areas of interest to them in our project (i.e. increasing the relevance of our research).
- Their knowledge of other relevant research.
- Further contacts for key informant interviews.
- Ideas on site selection and methodology.

11.4.3 Identifying key informant interviewees

We used an informal snowball approach to identify potential interviewees. Initially, names were suggested by members of our project advisory board. While many research projects will not have an advisory board it is always a good idea to ask those who know something about your research area if they can suggest individuals who might be useful key informants. In the course of our interviews, we asked each interviewee for the names of other people who they thought it would be relevant for us to consult and so our list of potential contacts expanded. As the list grew, we selected interviewees in line with particular areas of interest within the research.

The earliest interviews we conducted tended to be wide-ranging discussions around the issue of social disadvantage and the environment. Later, we began to select interviewees with particular areas of knowledge and experience and thus the interviews became more focused. As the process of site selection developed, we also chose to interview people who could help us to choose appropriate areas and identify key informants within potential sites.

For example, one of the first individuals suggested to us worked for the Public Health Association (PHA) for the UK, an organisation that engages in political lobbying on the links between poverty and health and provides information to communities on inequalities in health. He gave us a list of

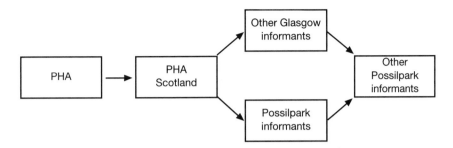

Figure 11.1   *The process of identifying key informants in Possilpark*

further contacts, one of whom worked for the PHA in Scotland. As the project developed we decided to select our urban deprived site in Glasgow. We then interviewed our contact at PHA Scotland about potential sites and relevant key informants. After discussions with a number of key informants, we decided upon Possilpark, a deprived area in the north of the city. We were able to go back to our informant in the PHA Scotland and obtain from her a list of people working on projects with local people in the Possilpark area. These individuals in turn provided names of others working with disadvantaged groups within that community and so we were able to build up a detailed picture of the particular issues of concern for people in that area (see Figure 11.1).

11.4.4 The key informant interview process

When we wrote the proposal we envisaged that we would tape record all key informant interviews and transcribe them in full. Once we began to do these interviews, however, we began to question whether this was in fact necessary or useful. We did not intend to analyse our key informants' accounts as data, rather we were using them to inform and guide other parts of the project.

Full transcription of interviews provides the best record of an interview and enables other researchers to scrutinise or re-use your data (see section 8.5). Transcribing is, however, extremely time-consuming. Given that we were not planning to analyse our key informants' accounts in depth, and our very tight timetable, we decided to save time by simply taking notes during interviews and using audio recordings to fill in gaps in the notes later. In addition, as the tenor of the interview was one of informal information exchange, it often seemed inappropriate to ask our informants if we could record them. As we were not committed to producing transcripts of every interview, we were then able to be flexible about using the tape recorder when it seemed appropriate and useful.

After each interview, we typed up our notes immediately. This is essential as the longer you leave it the harder it becomes to decipher your notes and to remember any comments that you did not get down on paper during the interview. It also enabled us to share the content of the interviews with each other and to move ahead with contacting others suggested by the interviewee and to order any references that had been recommended.

11.4.5 The role of key informants

At the outset of the research, we saw the role of key informants as helping us to understand the particular environmental concerns of disadvantaged communities, informing our site selection and methodology and, within our selected sites, introducing us to local context and concerns. The interviews proved invaluable in all of these respects; however, they also proved useful in ways that we had not anticipated, notably in enabling us to conduct research 'for' not just 'on' our subjects.

Research 'for', not just research 'on'

At the end of our study we want to disseminate our findings as widely as possible. As with most academic research, we will use the traditional avenues of presenting our work at conferences and submitting papers to journals. These methods are ideal for conveying your findings to others within academic circles but research disseminated in this way rarely reaches those outside academe. Our key informants provide us with an excellent channel for disseminating our research to an audience more interested in the practical relevance of our work. We plan to send a summary of findings to all our key informant interviewees and also to summarise findings from each particular case study to those who served as informants for that site. For many of our local informants, the data we collect on local concerns will be of direct interest and use. Some of those we have talked to have an element of public consultation as part of their brief and many of the questions we ask are exactly those for which they need answers. By feeding our results through in this way, we will be able to give something back to those who have helped us in our research.

Through contact with key informants, we hope that we will also be able to donate something to members of the disadvantaged groups that form the focus of our study. Disadvantaged people may benefit indirectly if insights from our study prove useful for improving local projects and initiatives. In addition, key informants have also suggested other ways in which we can give something back to local people, as part of the process of our research. One of our sites, Bromley-by-Bow, is located in Tower Hamlets, one of England's poorest boroughs. As a consequence, the area has been heavily researched by those interested in issues surrounding urban deprivation and regeneration. In response to this spotlight on the area, local people have been trained by a research unit at London University to enable them to carry out research themselves so that they are no longer simply the researched but also researchers. One of our local informants introduced us to one of the organisers of this local research team and we were then able to use local people to recruit and organise our focus groups. As well as having important benefits for our research (see section 11.5.2), this also meant that our project contributed to the experience and income of some local people and was thus another way in which we could give something back to those living in the area.

Practical help

Our key informants have been far more useful in practical terms than we ever envisaged. We have mentioned above how they helped us by identifying local recruiters in Bromley-by-Bow. In this area and in all the others they also identified suitable venues for the focus groups. Some informants also offered to recruit and organise groups for us. For example, in Possilpark one of the key informants ran a disability forum. We were keen to interview long-term sick and disabled people and she was willing to recruit individuals who used the centre, to organise the group in the centre and to arrange transport for people to attend the group and refreshments once they were there. In the Peak District our key informants helped us to refine our recruitment categories (see discussion in section 11.5.3), identified individuals for the focus groups and set up focus group meetings for us. This kind of practical help was especially useful given that our research involved researching difficult-to-access groups (for instance those experiencing rural poverty) in a number of geographically dispersed locations.

11.5   THE RESEARCH IN PRACTICE:
PLANNING AND RECRUITING FOR
FOCUS GROUPS

11.5.1 The number of groups and sites

As outlined above, our original plan was to hold 20 focus groups spread over five locations. As the project progressed and we gained a deeper understanding of the concepts of social disadvantage and environmental concern, it became clear that our focus group topics were very wide ranging, from discussions of local quality of life to perceptions of what is meant by 'environmental problems'. Comparable research exploring local understandings of sustainability (Macnaghten et al., 1995) and perceptions of environmental risk (Walker et al., 1998) has employed a research design where each focus group meets on two occasions to enable such diverse issues to be discussed in depth. We decided that this sort of design would be more appropriate for our study than having groups which only met once.

Changing our research design in this way, however, meant that we had to reduce the total number of groups recruited in order to keep within our project budget and time frame. We had to think carefully about the relative advantages and disadvantages of recruiting 20 groups that would meet only once compared to recruiting around half that number to meet twice. One of our key concerns was that by recruiting fewer groups we would access a less representative cross-section of the population of interest within each locality. After discussion with other researchers, we decided that the advantages of meeting each group twice outweighed the disadvantages but that extra care needed to be taken to identify and recruit appropriately within each site.

Our research budget included funds for paying professional recruiters to assemble focus groups. These costs can be quite considerable. By changing our research design so that each group would meet on two occasions, we were able to cut the cost of recruitment as fewer individuals overall needed to be recruited. Thus we did not have to restrict the total number of groups to ten but were able to afford twelve. We decided to arrange these twelve groups over four sites (instead of our original proposal of five), with three groups to be recruited at each site and each meeting on two occasions.

11.5.2 The importance of local knowledge

Recruitment for focus groups is greatly improved and made much easier if recruiters have local knowledge. This is important both in terms of understanding the local population profile (e.g. if the area has a predominately elderly population it may be very difficult to recruit a group of lone parents) and in selecting appropriate places in which to recruit (i.e. having knowledge of where specific groups of individuals meet, knowing what local organisations and clubs etc. exist and knowing in which areas of the locality the target population are likely to be found). Recruiters with local knowledge are also likely to be sensitive to local issues and concerns in a way that an outsider might not and are thus able to recruit more effectively.

In addition, we needed to use recruiters who spoke the same language as those we wished to include in our study. For instance, in Bromley-by-Bow we wanted to recruit a group of Bangladeshi women for whom English was unlikely to be the first language. For this group we also used a local bilingual researcher to facilitate the focus group discussion and to translate it for us. Recruiters' accent and dialect may also determine whether or not they are able to communicate easily with potential participants. In Possilpark, we decided to use Glaswegians both to recruit participants for the research and to transcribe the focus group discussion in recognition of the fact that someone from outside the area might have difficulty understanding the local dialect.

In proposals for research funding, it is therefore worthwhile to include the cost of employing local recruiters. In fact, it may not be any more expensive than trying to do all the research yourself if research sites are geographically dispersed since the costs of travel and subsistence can be considerable. With small research projects, however, it is often the case that one researcher has to undertake all the recruitment and interviewing alone. In this case it is important to build up as much knowledge as possible about the geography, demography, politics and social issues within the locality before recruitment commences. This can take various forms such as consulting documents (e.g. Local Authority Plans, census data, local histories), walking the area and conducting interviews with key informants. Although we were able to use local recruiters, we also familiarised ourselves with each locality in these ways. This enabled us to discuss local issues with recruiters with some confidence as well as ensuring that our focus group topic guides were sensitive to local issues.

11.5.3 Recruitment categories and criteria

Our project required us to recruit members of disadvantaged groups. This is a very vague term, however, and we had to specify carefully the types of people we wanted to include in the study. We decided that we should have some groups of the following:

- Older people.
- Lone parents with a low income.
- Single unemployed people.
- Parents of young children with a low household income.
- Long-term sick/disabled people.
- Members of minority ethnic groups.

These will be referred to as 'recruitment categories'.

The exact composition of groups within each locality was based on information about the local area gleaned from our key informant interviews and from recruiters. This turned out to be another area in which some flexibility was necessary and in which local knowledge proved important. For instance, we initially decided that we would like to recruit a group of unemployed men in the Peak District. As we spoke to key informants and learnt more about the area, we realised that recruiting such a group would be difficult. In a rural area, there is rarely the concentration of unemployment found in many urban areas and so finding an appropriate place in which to approach individuals for recruitment might have proved very hard. In addition, poverty tends to be more hidden in rural places as there may be stigma attached to admitting it. We also learnt that men were likely to have a number of casual or part-time jobs rather than to be simply 'unemployed'.

While it might not have been impossible to recruit people to fill our original category, it was likely to have been a very difficult, lengthy and thus costly process. It was suggested to us that it might be more appropriate to recruit a group of farmers living on low incomes. Such a group was easier to identify and would provide us with particular insights into rural poverty and environmental concerns that would be valuable for our research. Rather than seeing changes to our recruitment categories as a problem, they can be viewed as an opportunity to improve the research. By remaining flexible we ended up including individuals who experienced aspects of social dis-advantage that we had not considered at the outset.

Our key informants proved invaluable not only in helping us to identify appropriate recruitment categories, but also in recruiting individuals for the focus groups. Several of those we spoke to were involved in organisations which provided a service for disadvantaged sectors of the population (e.g. disability forums, age concern, community centres) and were able to help us to assemble groups based on their contacts.

One of the effects of recruiting groups through key informants who already have access to groups of individuals is that participants in the focus group are likely to know each other. In addition, individuals known to key informants are likely to be those who are involved in local groups or activities and thus not the most excluded or isolated within a locality. The views of such individuals about the quality of the local environment may well differ from the perspectives of those who do not participate in community activities. Methodologies for focus group research caution against recruiting groups where individuals know each other and recruiting 'unrepresentative' participants by focusing on a few sources of recruitment (see Chapter 10). These are important considerations; however, the reality of recruiting (especially recruiting difficult-to-reach groups in far-flung locations) sometimes means that groups do involve people who know each other and are mainly made up of people who are involved in some community activity. The important thing is to be aware of these issues, to acknowledge them where they do occur, and to interpret the data in the light of this information.

Once we had decided upon broad categories of participants (i.e. older people, lone mothers, farmers, etc.) in each locality, we then prepared detailed recruitment questionnaires outlining the criteria that individuals had to fulfil before being accepted as a participant within a specific group. This involved a process of operationalising some of the vague concepts we were using such as 'low income'. We decided to define low income on the basis of the current minimum wage and accepted participants whose income was at this level or lower. This is a crude measure of income but it is difficult, when recruiting for focus groups, to elicit precise information about individuals' income. Income is often considered to be a sensitive issue and questions about it may make potential participants hostile to the research. Asking people about their income within broad bands is the most common approach and was the only practicable one for our project. Even asking people to identify the band into which their income fell proved difficult in some instances for our recruiters. Some of those approached were suspicious about what the research was for, believing that it may be undercover work for the Benefits Agency trying to find out if they were claiming benefits fraudulently or doing cash-in-hand work while registering as unemployed.

We also found that some of the criteria we had assumed were straightforward turned out not to be so. For example, in Possilpark we decided to recruit one group of lone mothers and another of parents on low income. Our recruiter found that a number of the women they approached to participate in a focus group had partners who were currently in prison and she was unsure whether to categorise such individuals as lone mothers or as those living in a family situation with a partner and children. We had not originally considered the possibility of including individuals in this situation within our research. This was clearly, however, a relevant group to consider within this specific locality. We decided that such individuals could be recruited as participants in the low-income family group.

11.5.4 Timing

It is important to organise groups at a time when the participants you want are able to attend. This means that you need to think carefully about their probable daily routines. For example, organising a focus group of lone mothers early in the evening is unlikely to be successful as most will be occupied with feeding their children and putting them to bed. Lone mothers who are not working are more likely to be able to find childcare during the day than early in the evening.

It is also important to be aware of other events that are happening in the same period as your focus groups, which might make it hard to recruit people at specific times. For instance, Euro 2000 (football tournament) was taking place during the period in which our focus groups were scheduled. As far as possible we were careful not to schedule groups, particularly those involving young men, at times that clashed with matches. Scheduling groups in the Peak District also required sensitivity to the farming calendar as there are certain periods (e.g. harvest, lambing) when the intensity of work leaves little time for any other activities.

The other important consideration in timetabling focus groups relates to the facilitator rather than the participants. If meetings are scheduled too closely together, the facilitator is likely to become tired and will not be able to listen to participants or probe for details effectively. Enough time should be left after each group to allow the facilitator to sort out participants' expenses. This time may also be used to chat informally with participants; such post-group talk often provides insights or explanations that were not voiced during the taped session and are thus very valuable in interpreting the data. It is also important to schedule time between groups to allow the facilitator to reflect on the issues that have been raised by participants and to note down any ideas or impressions that have formed during the session. These are often very useful for the eventual analysis of the data and are quickly forgotten if not written down immediately.

11.6   SOME TENTATIVE FINDINGS

As our research is as yet incomplete we are not ready to present any detailed conclusions but we can indicate some of our findings.

Participants in our focus groups talked confidently and passionately about the day-to-day problems of the particular places in which they lived. Issues such as dirty streets, damp houses and dangerous traffic were topics that troubled many of those we spoke to. Concerns often focused on the relationship between these issues and health and quality of life, especially for children. These were not generally seen as 'environmental' issues, however. Participants were largely unfamiliar with the language of environmentalism and tended to regard 'the environment' as something they knew little about.

Environmental problems that seem 'obvious' from the outside were often viewed differently by those who lived with them day to day. For instance, the busy roads in Bromley-by-Bow were seldom mentioned spontaneously as a key problem, and the factory in Cefn Mawr was regarded with ambivalence – it was seen as a putative risk to health but also as an important part of the local community. This highlights the need to view local environmental problems in context; a busy road or polluting factory is only one facet of life in a particular place and may not be the most significant.

For many people in our focus groups their overarching concerns were with the poor quality of their housing, the lack of facilities for young people, crime and poor local amenities. Despite their frankness about such problems, a constant refrain was that 'it's the same anywhere though'; participants were at pains to emphasise that their locality was no worse than anywhere else. Alongside this, we witnessed real loyalty to, and pride in, their localities and each of our case study areas was described as 'friendly'. This insight suggests that we should be careful about how we present the idea that poor people tend to live in poor environments. Local people rarely characterise their environments in this way and express concern and anger that outsiders might label the place they regard as 'home' as 'a dump'.

11.7 CONCLUSIONS

The Oxford English Dictionary defines an exemplar as 'a typical example or appropriate model'. What we have tried to show is that a 'typical example' of social research is rather different from the closely defined stages often presented in writing about methodology. In our project the 'stages' of social research have overlapped, decisions about method have been made throughout, not decided once and for all at the start, and pragmatic considerations about how much time and money are available have often guided the research as much as any theoretical or methodological considerations.

Qualitative researchers are exhorted to keep an open mind as far as possible about what they will discover through their research, to let the findings 'emerge' from the data rather than deciding a priori what will be important and setting out to find that (see Chapter 9). This recommendation is usually made with reference to the analysis of data, and consequently it might be assumed that this is the appropriate mind-set for the researcher to adopt once the data have all been collected and it is time to develop an analysis. In practice, however, the analysis of data is not a discrete stage that occurs at the end of data collection but a process that is ongoing throughout the research. As soon as data collection begins, researchers start to develop hunches, make connections and think of new questions to ask. This ongoing process of analysis must be able to shape the methodology of a project as it progresses. At the start of a project you often don't know what will prove to be relevant, interesting or important. If you stick too rigidly to the questions, concepts and methods that you envisaged that you would use, the research will be the poorer for it. Flexibility and a willingness to change or discard original decisions about methodology should be seen as the hallmark of a good piece of qualitative research rather than as indicating problems with the project.

It is important to remember that every research project is different. Ours is a complex project both in terms of the broad scope of our topic and the fact that we have a large team of recruiters and interviewers in four very different areas of the UK. Although the examples we have presented are specific to our research, there are some general recommendations that are widely applicable. Running through all of these is the emphasis on flexibility and the need continually to rethink aspects of methodology in line with things you learn as you go along:

- Talk to other people. Don't think you know it all. Be prepared to learn from other researchers and people with experience of the issues you're researching.
- Be clear about the purpose of each stage of your research.
- Value local knowledge. Get to know as much as you can about the issues/area you're researching before you begin interviewing.
- Be prepared to change your recruitment categories and criteria – sticking rigidly to your original ideas may mean that you will miss sectors of the population relevant to your research.
- Be aware of the effects on your sample of how (i.e. where, through what organisations, etc.) you recruit participants and of the effects of operationalising recruitment criteria in certain ways.
- Be pragmatic. Keep in mind how much money and time you have available.
- Be flexible throughout and be prepared for surprises.

Using Documents   12

Keith Macdonald

Contents

The two main methods in social research are usually thought to be either the survey, using questionnaires, or qualitative research in one form or another. But there is a third method, with a longer history and of no less importance, documentary research. Many early sociologists – Marx, Durkheim and Weber for example – used documentary research and, although advances in technology have enabled researchers to handle large sets of survey material, and to record speech and interaction on audio and video tape, documentary research remains an important research tool in its own right, as well as being an invaluable part of most schemes of triangulation (Denzin, 1970).

Survey and questionnaire research is fundamentally different from ethnography and fieldwork research. The former collects information from a predefined situation and population, to answer fairly specific questions or to test hypotheses; the latter tends to be a much more general enquiry, guided by the overall question, favoured by symbolic interactionists, 'What is going on here?' (Glaser and Strauss, 1965). The former is analogous to the work of natural scientists, with a concern for controlling for variables, with known parameters, while the latter is much more like detective work. You may not know what you are looking for, or what you are looking at, until the investigation starts.

Documentary research may at first sight seem to have an affinity with the survey model, but in fact documentary research is much closer to the detective work of field research, with all the excitement of the detective story and all the hard graft of checking reams of evidence.

This kind of undertaking should be seen as an application of the deductive method, espoused by Gellner (1988) and Gumilev ([1970] 1987: xvi, 10, 43) (see also Chapter 2). Gellner says of his approach, 'Basically it is deductive. Conclusions are extracted from clearly stated assumptions; various possible conclusions are then checked against the available facts. Assumptions are revised if the implications fail to tally with available facts' (1988: 13). Gellner does not go into much more detail, but Gumilev gives a fuller account of his approach, and his 'trade secret'.

In *Searches for an Imaginary Kingdom* Gumilev is concerned with the history and society of the people of the Asian steppe in the early Middle Ages, and his aim is similar to Gellner's when he writes of producing 'an organic conception'. His starting point is the inconsistencies, inaccuracies and even downright lies to be found in the documentary sources that have survived from that period. From this follows the need to adopt the tactics of a (fictional) detective. These untrustworthy witnesses have to be cross-questioned and their motives assessed (Gumilev, 1987: 10, 362). How was it written? What was it really? Why did it take place in that way? What was the point? Who had a motive? Who benefited? In Gumilev's example of the twelfth-century report, circulating in Europe, of a powerful Christian state in Central Asia called the Kingdom of Prester John, one must ask to whose advantage was this rumour? Who was in a position to start and disseminate it? Whom did they wish to deceive and why?

He concludes by spelling out the practicalities and the advantages of the deductive method, and in so doing makes explicit what I and, I suspect, most historical sociologists and documentary researchers generally do in practice.

The author has striven to show that understanding events and accumulating accounts of them are different things. The moment of enlightenment does not precede studying the problem and does not crown it, but lies somewhere in the middle, a bit nearer the beginning. If no sparks have been struck between the scholar and his material, there can be no synthesis. Searches in the proper sense of the word start later, for it is only worthwhile searching when you know what you are looking for.

> Usually the creative factor is concealed – it is so much quieter so, and
> the author leads the reader from the known to the unknown new matter
> by a selection of quotations from ancient sources and a strictly logical
> argument. This is the way I have proceeded till now: but this time . . . I
> wanted to disclose the 'trade secret'. (Gumilev, 1987: 378)

I believe that the same may be said of documentary research in sociology.

12.1   WHAT IS A DOCUMENT?

Documents are things that we can read and which relate to some aspect of
the social world. Some documents are intended to record the social world –
official reports, for example – but there are also private and personal records
such as letters, diaries and photographs, which may not have been meant
for the public gaze at all. But in addition to the purposeful record, there
are those things that may be overtly intended to provoke amusement or
admiration or pride or aesthetic enjoyment – songs, buildings, statues,
novels – but which nonetheless tell us something about the values, interests
and purposes of those who commissioned or produced them. Such creations
may be regarded as 'documents' of a society or group which may be 'read',
albeit in a metaphorical sense.

The sociologist's emphasis on this point is that while public monuments
and 'official' art can readily be seen as social products, documents which are
intended to be read as objective statements of fact are also **socially
produced**. This is not to imply that all official documents are like the
statistics that were published in Stalin's Russia, or the war reports issued in
Nazi Germany; they are not propaganda. But they are produced on the basis
of certain ideas, theories or commonly accepted, taken-for-granted principles, which means that while they are perfectly correct – given certain
socially accepted norms – they do not have the objectivity of, say, a measure
of atmospheric pressure recorded on a barometer. This view of official
records has been shown clearly in the case of suicide verdicts (Atkinson,
1978), which cannot tell us exactly how many people killed themselves, but
only how many were socially defined as having done so in accordance with
the array of social rules and practices used by coroners and police to arrive
at a socially acceptable judgement.

In a very different context, Hindess (1973) has shown how official census
statistics may be compiled on the basis of categories that are derived from a
particular theoretical viewpoint. Attempts to reanalyse the data along other
theoretical lines are quite misguided. So, a set of minutes, the accounts of a
public company, or official statistics are produced in a socially acceptable
form that seems to those involved to give a 'reasonable' account of their
actions. When one reads that between 1979 and 1991 the basis for collecting
British unemployment statistics was changed 30 times (*Independent on*

Sunday, 11 August 1991), it becomes clear just how unstable this 'reason-ableness' can be. Furthermore, the archive in which documents are stored is also socially produced: What is to be kept? How, where and how long they are to be kept? And what is to be thrown away?

12.2 TYPES OF DOCUMENT

The term 'documents' includes a vast range of materials to be found in all sorts of places and all that can be done here is to give a review of five broad categories, which, though necessarily brief, will exemplify the nature of the materials and the problems encountered by the documentary researcher.

12.2.1 Public records

The oldest writings in existence are public records. Writing was devised by officials in the ancient civilisations to record the taxation and tribute that the state received and the rations it issued to its servants. It is ironic that these early bureaucratic records have only survived by accident, for they were intended as temporary records and were made on soft clay tablets. They exist today because the buildings in which they were stored were burnt down. The tablets were baked in the process, buried under rubble and then built over, thus preserving them for posterity.

The modern state has an enormous apparatus for generating fiscal and economic records. Because these records deal with quantifiable matters it tends to be assumed that they have an objectivity that other kinds of documents may lack, whereas in fact a financial or statistical record is a social product just as much as any other. Those who produce these statistics may make every effort to follow the scientific canons to ensure the reliability and validity of their work, but that does not alter the underlying fact that any indicator of economic performance or incidence of crime, or anything else that the state sees fit to measure and publish, is based on working assumptions, some of which, at least, could have been decided otherwise.

In addition to the need to understand the conventions which surround the compilation of official reports and statistics, one must be aware of the dis-tortions that can arise as a result of the actions of the people to whom the statistics refer. A notable example of this is the under-recording of certain groups in the Census. Recent immigrants, for instance, may not understand the purpose of the Census and evade being recorded because they assume it is connected with taxation or with legislation regarding overcrowding or some other reason. Similarly, the introduction of the Community Charge in Britain in 1989 and 1990, whereby a 'poll tax' was levied on every individual, led to a significant reduction in the number of registered voters because omission from the Electoral Roll meant that a person would not be taxed (*The Guardian*, 19 June 1991).

Public documents available to the social researcher include the Census and the UK Electoral Register, and the Registrar General's annual reports on the vital statistics of the nation. Government departments produce their own national statistics – industry, education, crime, housing and so on, summaries of which are published for the United Kingdom in the *Annual Abstract of Statistics* or the *Monthly Digest of Statistics*. There is also a steady flow of reports from individual departments, from government enquiries and so on. Local authorities publish similar material, as do health authorities, nationalised industries and many other public sector bodies. There are also collections of statistics published by international organisations such as the United Nations, the International Labour Organisation, the European Commission and numerous others.

Another important kind of official record is the verbatim account of British Parliamentary debates to be found in *Hansard*, together with the reports of Parliamentary Committees. Verbatim reports of judicial proceeding are also kept, but these are not so readily available to the public, except that important cases from the point of view of case law are published in the *All England Law Reports* and the *Times Law Reports*.

In addition to these, there are the unpublished papers of government departments, which are deposited in the London Public Record Office and only become available after a period of 30 years. At this point the question of the construction of the archive becomes very significant for the researcher. Even if there is no attempt to hide things from public gaze, the idiosyncrasies of departmental officials can prove extremely frustrating. Some records are subject to the Official Secrets Act, and these may be kept secret for longer than 30 years.

12.2.2 The media

The *Times Law Reports* are, of course, published by the newspaper of that name, and the selectivity that they display follows well-understood principles. The selectivity displayed by the paper itself is a matter of editorial policy and may be much less readily comprehended. Nevertheless, editorial policy is usually fairly clear to a regular reader of *The Times* or of any other paper, at least in regard to what they print. What they leave out is another matter altogether and requires much closer study of the media and current events generally. It is fairly easy to discern that the more serious papers print more foreign news than the popular tabloids, but unless one consults newspapers published in other countries, one can have little idea of the selectivity imposed by a particular editor. The bias and selectivity imposed by editorial policy is only one of a number of areas in which the researcher *must* be on guard. Newspapers are subject to:

● Errors, which may be technical (such as spelling, typing, or printing), when lines or longer sections of print get transposed, or in matters of fact (such as people's ages, which newspapers are very fond of including in their reports but about the accuracy of which they are often careless).

- Distortion, which may stem from the preferences of the proprietor or editor, or from the journalist producing the copy. On the other hand, it may arise at source, as when an account of events is given by a politician who was a participant in them, or when a journalist relies on an organisation's press release. Yet again it may arise inadvertently from the actions of a sub-editor who changes the meaning of an item in the process of compressing it into the space available, or who conveys an erroneous impression in the search for a punchy headline. The most fundamental form of distortion is, of course, that of propaganda, where the source of the news is engaged in wholesale creation of a particular view of events. In wartime, for example, it is undertaken in what is perceived to be the national interest or with the object of systematically deceiving an enemy. A more subtle form is the use of 'spin' by the press officers of many organisations, especially political parties. This does not go as far as the downright lies of wartime propaganda, but with the use of emphasis, omission, timing and so on, aims to create a particular response to the matter being reported.
- Audience context, which is an aspect that may be easily overlooked. It refers to the fact that the production of any medium of communication is undertaken with an audience in mind, and unless one knows how that audience 'reads' the content, it may be possible that the researcher will fail to grasp the message. Not only cultural norms, but jokes, deliberate mistakes, irony and so on depend on the existence of a common frame of reference between writer and reader. Unless the researcher is privy to their common understandings, serious misapprehension may result. The claim by a German newspaper to have established that the bagpipes were a German invention aroused fury in Scotland, but merely raised a smile in Germany, where it was regarded as either untrue or unimportant.

Finally, the researcher must remember that in many cases it is not the original document that is under scrutiny, but some form of copy, such as a microfilm or microfiche and that its reliability depends on the work of a copyist. Omissions and transpositions are not unknown.

12.2.3 Private papers

The researcher must also be cautious about the documents of a private individual, for these are also open to distortion and manipulation, especially if the person concerned is a public figure or an author whose work is so widely read and discussed as to put him or her in the public sphere.

For example, Seymour-Smith (1990), in his biography of the writer Rudyard Kipling, examines several earlier biographies and shows that they contain serious distortions and omissions that resulted from the pressures and deceptions of Kipling's widow and family. Their desire to control the account of his life that reached the public was such that they eventually destroyed a sizeable part of the archive of material on which a biographer might wish to work.

Such attitudes are even more likely to be present in the case of a politician, whose private papers refer not only to matters of interest to critics and academics, but to events that were of consequence to the nation or even to the world. So, some private papers deal with public matters.

There are also, of course, large numbers of private papers that refer to private lives and personal careers. A single individual or family can sometimes throw considerable light on the times in which they live, as in the case of the Paston Letters (Bennett, 1922), which come from a fairly well-off family in the fifteenth century but are sufficiently voluminous to provide social historians with one of the best sources of material on the late Middle Ages. In a case like this, the researcher is the beneficiary of a careful family who treasured their papers, but is essentially at the mercy of those by whom the archive is created and to whom it is entrusted; it is entirely at their whim what is collected and preserved. It is possible to improve on this state of affairs if one is dealing with the recent past, because then one can purposefully collect the diaries and letters of people in a certain category, as in the case of *The Polish Peasant in Europe and America* (Thomas and Znaniecki, [1918–20] 1958). It is possible to take this a step further by soliciting the material from informants and asking them to search their memories and give accounts of past events. An outstanding example of this method is the work of Middlebrook (1978, 1983), who selects one day, like the first day of the German Spring Offensive in 1918, or the day of the US Air Force bombing mission to Schweinfurt and Regensberg in 1943. Starting from the official records and histories, he then seeks out the actual participants still surviving by, for example, advertising in the local papers of the regions from which the regiments involved were drawn, and obtains first-hand accounts. So *The Kaiser's Battle* (Middlebrook, 1978) draws *inter alia* on the testimony of over a hundred German participants and several hundred British.

12.2.4 Biography

The accounts that Middlebrook (1978, 1983) obtained from the participants in particular events are examples in miniature of another kind of document, namely biography and autobiography. The term 'biography' is employed in two differing senses by sociologists. The first refers to an account obtained by a particular style of interviewing. Rather than providing a factual snapshot of how things are at the present time, the informant is encouraged to describe how his or her life, or some aspect of it, has changed and developed over time and to do so in a way that reflects his or her own conception of self, identity and personal history (Chamberlayne et al., 2000). The object of this kind of biographical sociology is to demonstrate that original knowledge can be derived from the study of individual life stories while keeping hold of an essentially sociological frame of reference. Such investigations begin with the identification in individuals of distinctive life strategies, trajectories, or kinds of self-recognition, which become the building blocks from which a larger understanding of society can be imagined.

> Socio-biographical accounts usually seek to identify in individual
> utterances, elements that are socially recognisable, which are typical of
> some social form or other. . . . The individual case becomes the point
> of discovery and starting point for inferences about social structure.
> (Rustin, 2000: 45–8)

Most of the contributions to Chamberlayne, Bornat and Wengraf (2000)
are concerned with the biographical interview, and Rustin's contribution is
the only one which ranges wider. Curiously, however, the examples he
quotes are all from poets, novelists and playwrights. There is some justification for this, for, as he says,

> Works of 'fiction' have paradoxically come closer to the truths of
> subjective experience than either generalising works of science, which
> fail to capture the particularity and immediacy of lived lives, or factual
> descriptions of individuals, whose common defect is a lack of coherence
> or connectedness, a sufficient sense of 'the essential'. (Rustin, 2000: 39)

This may be too harsh a judgement on auto/biography, but there is no
doubt that fiction and biography can overlap. More than one critic has
commented that Siegfried Sassoon's (1937) 'fictional' trilogy of novels
about the First World War is closer to the truth of his times and his
experiences than his friend Robert Graves's 'biographical' *Goodbye To All
That* (1927 [1954]). Some novelists, particularly historical novelists, base
their work on detailed research. An example is the work of Patrick O'Brian,
whose sequence of 18 books on the Royal Navy at the time of the
Napoleonic Wars (e.g. O'Brian, 1970, 1997) illuminates many aspects of life
and society, and even the use of language, of that period. Some novelists
have almost made historical circumstances actors in their stories. Examples
may be found in J.G. Farrell's *The Siege of Krishnapur* (1973) set in the
Indian Mutiny, and *The Singapore Grip* (1978) which portrays the social and
economic life and the military defeat of British colonial society. Paul Scott's
Raj Quartet novels (1966–75) about India include extracts from newspapers
and other contemporary documents.

Nonetheless, some sociologists argue that works of fiction are produced
for and by an educated social elite and therefore

> to some extent reflect the values and interests of those groups. . . . They
> are therefore an unreliable guide to the realities of the social life they
> write about. . . . Relations between literature and society are both more
> complex and subtle than can be conveyed by the idea of a straight-
> forward, mirror-like reflection. (Filmer, 1998: 278)

But Filmer does not regard this problem as insurmountable and goes on to
explain what he terms the *intrinsic* approach to the sociological study of
literature. This operates on the premise that literature 'is a *reflexive* feature of
the society in which it is produced, engaging with it through critical

reflection on social practices' (Filmer, 1998: 279). He then provides an illuminating illustration of these techniques in an analysis of Charles Dickens's *The Pickwick Papers*.

The other use of the term biography is the everyday meaning that refers to a work that draws on whatever materials are available to an author to present an account of a person's life and achievements. Ready access to this mode of documentary research may be found in *Sociology* (1993, 27(1)), a special issue on 'Biography and autobiography in sociology'. This volume does contain some reference to the biographical interview, but places more emphasis on auto/biography in the conventional sense, and on accounts that may have been invited by an investigator but which are written by the informant unaided and unprompted. The contributors put a high value on this souce of data, for example:

> In looking, therefore, at biographies, social scientists might find rich material for the way in which the formal categories of social life are given human meaning. The use of biography is not just to illustrate a social theory but to explain its meaning. (Evans, 1993: 12)

> C. Wright Mills sees the interaction between life-experience and history as the definition of sociology. From such a viewpoint accounts of lives are more or less interesting, depending on how effectively they are able to distil both social structure and a story of an individual life without, in the process, either swamping the personal or subjectivising the social. (Erben, 1993: 15)

Later in this chapter we consider the problems of reliability in documentary research, but it is worth mentioning at this point that auto/biography is all too likely to have aims other than the presentation of objective truth. Nowhere is this more graphically illustrated than in the case of the English king, Alfred the Great. Historians, seeing him as a political figure, have for centuries regarded the *Life of King Alfred* as basically factual. Only in recent years has painstaking research (Smythe, 1995) shown that this account was seen by its author, a monk, as being in the tradition of 'Lives of the Saints'. As hagiography, its aim was to convey moral and religious lessons, not to recount the political and military realities of Alfred's era accurately. In pursuit of this aim, the author, who in fact lived two generations or so after Alfred's death, claimed to be Bishop Asser, who was Alfred's contemporary.

12.2.5 Visual documents

Seymour-Smith's (1990) study of Kipling (see above) is an example of how literary analysis can take on a sociological role. Other examples can be found in the writings of Quigly (1984) and Fussell (1975, 1989). In these cases literary work is being treated as a 'document' and its analysis needs skills that are more often found in a sociologically minded critic than in a sociologist. But in *Wartime: Understanding and Behavior in the Second World War,* Fussell (1989) quotes from a comparative analysis of posters in the two world wars, and thus moves into a field in which some sociologists do feel able to contribute, that is in the study of visual 'documents'.

It was noted at the beginning of this chapter that interpretation seems to be a more obvious requirement when dealing with visual materials, such as photographs, advertisements, record sleeves, paintings, posters, statues, buildings, films and so on. Photographs present a particular problem, because although they make a claim to authenticity ('the camera cannot lie'), the photographer can leave things out of shot, and negatives and prints can be doctored in various ways (Becker, 1979). There is a celebrated example of a photograph of Lenin addressing a crowd from a platform, at the foot of which can be seen, in the original version, the unmistakable figure of Trotsky. In later versions, when Trotsky had fallen out with Lenin's successor, Stalin, and fled to Mexico, he has been blotted out.

With paintings, sculpture and architecture, however, it is unlikely that the artist is trying to deceive the beholder, but it is often necessary to have some knowledge of the circumstances in which an object was produced before it can be interpreted as a social 'document'. This need is nicely exemplified by Berger (1972: 82–112), who examines a number of seventeenth- and eighteenth-century paintings to show the way in which patrons of painting of that period were concerned with their possessions, and how this trend can be associated with the emerging power of capital (1972: 86). He even reports a dispute between himself and an art critic about this interpretation. But the point is that Berger and the other authorities that he quotes rely for their analysis on a wide range of social historical data, and indeed on the comments of the painters themselves. So Berger has successfully made his point, but he has not done it on the basis of the paintings alone. This raises the problem of what tests of reliability and authenticity must be applied to the supporting data, a matter that will be considered below. Other outstanding examples of the bringing together of artistic and sociological analysis may be found in Fredrick Antal's studies of Hogarth (1962) and more especially his *Florentine Painting and its Social Background* (Antal, 1987).

Cohen's (1989) study of the political implications of public statues erected in provincial France during the nineteenth century provides another example. Again it is apparent that any 'reading' of the objects themselves would be a risky undertaking because of the difficulty of being sure of the motives lying behind their erection. However, when combined with analysis of local government records and newspaper reports, the part that statues played in the political conflicts of the period becomes clear and their subject matter, their timing and their location intelligible.

12.3   EVALUATION AND INTERPRETATION

Many of the problems that the documentary researcher may encounter are about how to evaluate material and these can be grouped under four headings: authenticity, credibility, representativeness and meaning. Scott (1990) gives a valuable treatment of these issues and what follows draws on his ideas.

12.3.1 Authenticity

'A CHECK MAY BE WRITTEN ON A COW' ran a headline in the *Memphis Press-Scimitar* in 1967. It is well known that you cannot believe everything that you read in the newspapers, but this particular article referred to a nineteenth-century case in England which allowed this practice and quoted as authority the Chase Manhattan Bank. One cannot tell by what route this supposed legal principle reached the *Memphis Press-Scimitar*, but the original source was the dramatisation on BBC Television of one of A.P. Herbert's (fictional) *Misleading Cases in the Common Law*, originally published in the 1930s (and set in that period, not in the nineteenth century). Herbert (1977) recounts a number of other occasions in which his litigious character, Mr Haddock, has escaped into real life, thus illustrating one of the problems of authenticity in documentary research, namely that writers (or copyists) may quite innocently, or perhaps carelessly, convert fiction into fact or perpetuate the errors or deceptions of others.

But deliberate falsehoods are rare: cases like the Zinoviev Letter or the Hitler diaries do not come our way very often (Scott, 1990: 43, 175). But it is always possible that records or factual accounts may have been falsified for the author's own purposes at the time, and the researcher must always be suspicious of unexpected changes of paper, ink, typeface, handwriting, and so on, and must check consistency and plausibility, internally and externally.

In order to test whether a document is genuine, complete, reliable and of unquestioned authorship, Platt (1981), who has encountered the problem of deliberate deception in documentary research, proposes a set of questions.

- Does the document make sense or does it contain glaring errors?
- Are there different versions of the original document available?
- Is there consistency of literary style, handwriting or typeface?
- Has the document been transcribed by many copyists?
- Has the document been circulated via someone with a material or intellectual interest in passing off the version given as the correct one?
- Does the version available derive from a reliable source?

12.3.2 Credibility

Credibility refers to the question of whether the document is free from error or distortion. The latter may occur when there is a long time between the event and the account of it being written down, or when the account has been through several hands and the author of the document was not present at the event. Credibility can be affected by the interest of the author, which might, for example, be financial, to enhance a reputation or to please the readers. Such possibilities should always lead the social researcher to ask who produced the document, why, when, for whom and in what context, so as to be assured of its quality.

12.3.3 Representativeness

Can the documents available be said to constitute a representative sample of the universe of documents as they originally existed? If the archive appears to contain all the material produced in that category then the problem does not exist. But once it is established that there is something missing, the questions of what is missing, how much and why it is missing become important. When the survival of documents is quite haphazard, as it is with the material from ancient civilisations, conclusions must always be tentative or at least historians must be prepared to revise their accounts if fresh evidence is unearthed. With more recent archives it must always be a matter of judgement, based on the amount of missing material, whether the blanks have any pattern to them and whether anyone could have had an interest in destroying certain documents. In this, as with the questions of authenticity and credibility, the researcher's approach must be essentially that of the detective, in the sense that everything is potentially suspect and anything may turn out to be the key piece of data, including things which ought to be there but are missing, like Sherlock Holmes's 'the dog that did not bark'.

12.3.4 Meaning

Establishing the meaning of a document usually involves working at two levels: the surface or literal meaning, and the deeper meaning arrived at by some form of interpretative understanding or structural analysis. Although there is a clear difference between the extreme forms of these two modes, it is possible to see the two as merging in some instances since form is only conceptually distinct from content, or the message from grammar, and human beings habitually handle both without any trouble.

Understanding the surface message may be troublesome, although this is more often a problem for historians than for sociologists, who do not in the ordinary way have to decipher hieroglyphics or cuneiform writing. But the social researcher will find that language use varies between different groups, cultures and periods.

The deeper meaning of a document or a text may well prove more difficult. The simpler kind of question about meaning is exemplified by the problem of how important particular themes are to the author (or the newspaper, or whatever is the unit of investigation) and the answer to this question is usually sought through quantification, by means of content analysis (Weber, 1990). The importance of a topic is measured by the number of times it is mentioned, the number of column inches devoted to it, the square inches of the photographs displayed, the number of times it appears in the index, the number of readers' letters that the editor decides to publish, and so on. This method, being a quantitative one, carries with it a number of technical issues to do with sampling, representativeness, coding and statistical reliability which, for reasons of space, we must leave to one side (but see Chapters 5 and 14).

Practitioners of literary and other criticism would undoubtedly argue that the measurement of the relative salience of a theme by the frequency of its occurrence is simplistic and does no kind of justice to an author's intentions. It is, of course, the case that most of what social researchers study is not produced by artists, so this criticism of quantitative method loses some of its point. Nonetheless, in dealing with anything more complex than newspapers, content analysis on its own does appear rather unsubtle, and so sociologists for many years have searched for something more sophisticated that would do justice to the more complex kind of document. In the earlier part of the century, the notion of 'interpretative understanding', following the ideas of Dilthey (see Rickman, 1961), achieved some importance, especially among German historians. This emphasised the need to understand the particular techniques and definitions that lay behind the production of the text in order to grasp the author's meaning and intentions. The researcher picks out what is relevant for analysis and pieces it together to create tendencies, sequences, patterns and orders (Ericson et al., 1991: 55).

More recently the task of textual analysis has drawn much more on the semiotic approach to be found in the structural linguistics of Saussure ([1915], 1959), especially as developed by Barthes (1967). The former defined **semiotics** as 'a science that studies the life of signs within society', the object of which is to get to the underlying message of the text. This is to be found, not only in the words and phrases, but in the system of rules that structures the text as a whole. It is therefore this underlying structure and the rules it embodies that can tell the researcher what its cultural and social message is. The analyst seeks to connect a *signifier* (an expression which may be words, a sound or a picture) with what is *signified* (another word, description or image). The distinction between content analysis and semiotics is concisely set out by Slater (1998).

An example of a piece of research which explicitly rejects content analysis in favour of semiotics is to be found in McRobbie (1978, 1991), a study of *Jackie*, a weekly magazine aimed at teenage girls. The author describes magazines as 'specific signifying systems where particular messages are produced and articulated' (1991: 3). Quantification is rejected in favour of the understanding of media messages as structured wholes.

> Sociological analysis proceeds by isolating sets of codes around which the message is constructed. These conventions operate at several levels, visual and narrative, and also include sets of subcodes [in *Jackie*] such

as those of fashion, beauty, romance, personal/domestic life and pop music. These codes constitute the 'rules' by which different meanings are produced and it is the identification and consideration of these in detail that provides the basis to the analysis. In short, semiology is concerned with the internal structuring of a text or signifying system, with what Barthes calls 'immanent analysis'.

From the large range of codes operating in *Jackie*, McRobbie identifies four around which to organise her study, and from this analysis delineates 'the central feature of *Jackie* insofar as it presents its readers with an ideology of adolescent femininity' (McRobbie, 1991: 92).

While this method undoubtedly provides a more coherent set of guidelines for the analysis of text than its predecessors, Scott (1990) argues cogently that semiotics still does not give us a means of judging between rival interpretations of a text. He draws on the work of Giddens (1976) and his view that a text, taken in isolation from its social context, is deprived of its real meaning. This is provided by a socially-situated author and audience who are necessary for the text to have any meaning at all. 'Texts must be studied as socially situated products' (Scott, 1990: 34). A graphic, though fictional, illustration of this point can be found in the novel *Foucault's Pendulum* (Eco, 1988: 134, 534) where a document is found in circumstances that suggest that it could be a plan, devised in the fourteenth century, to perpetuate a secret society for the next 600 years. To achieve this interpretation a system of rules is worked out to explain the text, just as semiotics proposes. The characters in the book proceed to work on this reading of the text for a sizeable part of the novel, until someone proposes a different and rather more plausible context for the document, and suggests a new system of rules whereby the text is read as a laundry list! A real-life example is provided by Garfinkel's (1967b) paper, ' "Good" organizational reasons for "bad" clinical records' (reprinted in Turner, 1974). This research started out as a study of a population of patients attending a psychiatric clinic, but Garfinkel found that the data in the clinician's files were sadly deficient as a means of showing the characteristics of the patient population and how patients had been selected for treatment. Garfinkel concludes that the clinic's records are kept so as to serve the interests of medical and psychiatric services rather than to serve the interest of research. Therefore the 'expressions that the documents contain will have to be decoded to discover their real meaning in the light of the interest and interpretation that prevails at the time' (Garfinkel, 1967b: 126). This kind of work may be regarded as closer to discourse analysis. Although discourse analysis sounds as though it concentrates on language and possibly even speech, it may be applied to 'official documents, legal statutes, political debates and speeches, media reports, policy papers, maps, pictorial and exhibition materials, expert analyses, publicity literature and press statements, historical documents, tourist guides, interviews, diaries and oral histories' (Tonkiss, 1998). Tonkiss gives a useful outline of this method, which is also covered in Chapter 18 (below). Another good example may be found in Gilbert and Mulkay (1984).

12.4 THE NEED FOR TRIANGULATION

In documentary research everything must be checked from more than one angle. Nothing can be taken for granted. A document may not be what it appears to be, the archive may have been collected for motives we do not understand, and the context may be crucial in determining the nature of the object before us. This makes documentary work very different from, say, survey research, where validity and reliability are secured within the method itself. The layout of the questionnaire, the meaning of the items, the reproducibility of scales and the representativeness of the sample are all concerned with a particular pre-defined topic, method and data source. But in other modes of research, the notion of **triangulation** has become a salient feature of research methodology (Denzin, 1970, 1978). In this framework, validity is seen as having both external and internal aspects and the achievement of validity, and indeed of the research task as a whole, requires a triangulation of research strategies.

Denzin (1970) proposes four kinds of triangulation. The first is **data triangulation**, which has three sub-types: time, space and person; that is, data should be collected at a variety of times, in different locations and from a range of persons and collectivities. The second is **investigator triangulation**, that is, using multiple rather than single observers of the same object. The third, **theory triangulation**, consists of using more than one kind of approach to generate the categories of analysis. This is the most difficult kind of triangulation to achieve and it is noteworthy that Denzin (1970: 297–301) can only adduce a hypothetical example, and the three theoretical approaches he draws on are in fact quite closely allied. Finally, the fourth, **methodological triangulation**, has two sub-types: within-method triangulation, for example using, in a questionnaire, a combination of attitude scales, forced choice items and open-ended questions; and between-method triangulation, which is self-explanatory and which is probably the more important.

The general approach that he advocates, and to some extent the actual methods he suggests, provide sound guidance for the documentary researcher. It is, however, rather more difficult to give a toolkit for this kind of work because the data materials are so various. But hopefully the principle is clear and its practice can be appreciated from the following quotation from *Belfast in the '30s: an Oral History*:

> In the first place we carried out . . . 'investigator triangulation'. That is, each transcript was checked by two or three researchers to ensure that it said what people had meant to say. In the second place, we systematically did a cross-method triangulation, in that every piece of oral evidence that could be was checked against a range of written sources:

newspapers, parliamentary reports, documents, etc. Finally, there was a considerable amount of data triangulation possible within the oral sources themselves. (Munck and Rolston, 1987: 12)

12.5 PRACTICAL GUIDELINES

Documentary work normally involves reading through large quantities of written material. Great savings of time and effort can be achieved if it is possible to scan the material into a computer. The way is then open for the use of the software described in Chapter 8 of this volume, for the analysis of qualitative data. However, the researcher has to devote some time to acquiring the necessary skills to use these programs.

If that time is not available, an alternative is to make use of a conventional word-processing package. For example, the 'Find' facility enables one to locate particular words or phrases in a document, or it may be possible to use 'Index' in a similar fashion.

It is also possible to analyse lists according to a number of criteria, by using the 'Table' facility. For example, a list of students, showing their college and their degree class, can be converted into a table showing, say, college size by degree class. First code the entries by, say, three sizes of college, by putting 1, 2, or 3 at the beginning of the entry. Next use 'numerical sort' to group them, and then move all the 1s into the top left-hand cell, the 2s into the second cell in the first column, and so on. The entries can then be moved individually into the appropriate degree class column and a count made of the number in each cell.

12.6 PROJECT

Imagine that you have been recruited as a Research Officer on a project set up to study financial scandals in the twentieth century. Outline some ways of tackling this, using documentary sources. Indicate how you would achieve triangulation. What sorts of document do you think could be used in this project? What sorts of problem would you expect to encounter in getting access to and working with these documents?

12.7 FURTHER READING

Scott (1990) is an essential book for anyone interested in doing documentary research. It provides a particularly valuable introduction to the problems of evaluating and interpreting documentary materials.

Platt (1981) is a pioneering article that highlights the problems of handling documentary evidence. Plummer (1983) is a readable introduction to the importance of personal documents such as letters, diaries and life histories in social research. Weber (1990) is a short but clear introduction to the technique of content analysis, with an appendix that deals with the use of computers in text analysis.

Becker (1974) is a very stimulating article which examines the relationship between sociology and social documentary photography.

Sociology (1993) 'Biography and autobiography in sociology', Special Issue, 27(1): 1–178.

Exemplar: Investigating the Investigators – Studying Detective Work

13

Martin Innes

Contents

[The suspect][1] beat the head of the victim with a number of objects including an electric fire, frying pan and saucepans causing severe head wounds. The offender then appears to have taken a shower in the victim's premises and then returned to the bedroom where the attack took place and started a fire at the foot of the victim's bed and left the premises. At some stage the offender hand-washed the clothing that he is believed to have been wearing at the time of the offence.

---

[1] The brackets indicate that identifying details have been removed. Ensuring the anonymity of those involved in the incidents was a condition of access to the data.

This is an extract from a police case file on a domestic homicide investigation, where a man had returned home from an evening drinking at the pub and killed his common-law wife. The extract was prepared for the pre-trial hearing and the document from which it is taken is intended to detail the 'outline' facts of the police case against the suspect.

Stories about murder and murder investigations, similar to that above, are regular features in both factual and fictional media representations. Despite this, or perhaps in part because of it, police murder investigation has not been the subject of much academic research. While there has been considerable growth in the literature on policing over the past three decades, which has done much to improve the state of our knowledge about many of the social and technical aspects of policing, there has been only sporadic interest in the procedures that the police employ to investigate and solve crime. In this chapter I provide an overview of a three-year qualitative research project conducted on murder investigations. I review a number of issues relevant to the craft of qualitative research and map out some intriguing parallels between the tasks performed by police detectives when investigating a crime and those performed by social researchers. The chapter starts with a short description of the project and the sorts of issue I encountered in the research. It then moves on to discuss how detectives approach their work, and concludes by drawing out some of the affinities between the methods of crime investigation and social research.

13.1 AN OVERVIEW

In selecting the topic of police murder investigations for research, I was influenced by a number of factors. First, it seemed an interesting area in which to conduct research because it raised a number of sociological questions, such as what is the relationship between investigative actions performed by individual detectives and the process of enquiry as a whole. Secondly, it appeared to be an area about which little had been written. Thirdly, a personal family connection meant that I was fairly confident I would be able to obtain access to sufficient data to study this aspect of police work.

The study was based with one police force in the south of England, and as such it was effectively a case study; it examined the investigative practices and strategies employed by a particular police force in responding to criminal homicides. The advantages of a case study approach are that it allows for an 'in-depth' treatment of the subject, where a large amount of detail about the practices and processes being studied can be understood in relation to a particular social context. The main limitation of a case study approach is that there is always a concern about the representativeness of the particular case being studied and thus whether the findings can be generalised to other similar cases. In respect of murder investigations, the presence of national police guidelines meant that it seemed reasonable to assume that the investigative systems that I observed were sufficiently representative of those used by the other 42 police forces in England and Wales.

I decided that qualitative techniques were likely to be the most appropriate methods for getting at the sorts of issue in which I had an interest. Furthermore, from my own point of view, I felt more comfortable with the epistemological bases and assumptions of qualitative research (see Silverman, 1993). As I will describe presently, the methodological focus shifted as the study progressed, but in total, I observed five enquiries in progress, conducted a range of semi-structured interviews with officers of all ranks, performed qualitative content analysis of 20 police case files and briefly reviewed a further 50 case summaries.

13.2   The process of research

With the benefit of hindsight, I can now see that the research that I conducted on police homicide investigations was a process that developed and emerged over a period of time. Over the course of the project, the focus of my research activities shifted and altered in response to a range of influences. These included developments in my understanding of the subject I was studying, the need to perform different tasks, such as formulating a research question, collecting and analysing data, and writing up the results, and changes in my relationship with the organisation I was studying. Some of these developments were deliberate and part of the natural 'career' of an empirical research project, resulting from the need to collect and analyse the data before writing an account of the results. However, some of the developments that were to prove of vital significance to the eventual findings of the research were not anticipated when I began the project. Indeed, it is this requirement to be able to adapt to the situational requirements of the research setting and the research subjects that is one of the key skills of the good qualitative researcher (see also Burgess, 1984).

One of the most important shifts in the focus of the study occurred while I was immersed in the field. In designing the project, I had concluded that due to the exploratory nature of the research, ethnographic techniques would be the most appropriate method of data collection. Observation is the preeminent method for gathering data about social processes in 'naturally occurring contexts', examining how people act in particular situations (Silverman, 1993). However, once I commenced the non-participant observation it soon became apparent that I needed to adapt the methodology, because in designing the research, I had overlooked a number of qualities related to the nature of police homicide investigations. The first was that murder investigations regularly involve anything up to 30 police officers working on separate tasks, which collaboratively contribute to the overall trajectory and dynamics of the investigative process. Consequently, there was an issue as to how a single researcher could adequately observe and document the array of simultaneous activities that were constitutive of the police investigation. The second quality that I had overlooked was to prove to be an opportunity to resolve the previous oversight. I had failed to anticipate the large amounts of information that were typically produced by police investigations. Typically, a murder investigation would generate hundreds, if not thousands of documents from which the case for the prosecution would be constructed. These could be interpreted sociologically to reveal a lot of detail about the process of investigation. As a result, in the final analysis, I made far greater use of the police case files and qualitative content analysis techniques (Altheide, 1996) than I had originally envisaged.

Reflecting these problems, the methodology shifted from its original reliance upon ethnographic observation, to making more use of the principles associated with 'between' and 'within' methodological triangulation (Denzin, 1970). Data were collected via a combination of observation, semi-structured interviews and qualitative content analysis of police case files. This latter aspect was particularly important, as it provided an opportunity to understand how the investigative process as a whole worked and how the actions performed by individual detectives, observed through ethnographic observation, were both framed by and helped to constitute the process as a whole.

13.3   THE BIG QUESTION!

A clearly formulated research question is an extremely useful tool to guide the research process. A clearly stated question provides an explicit focus for the study. Without such a question, there is a constant danger of drifting away from the central issues that should be addressed by the researcher. But it is important to acknowledge that 'the big question' which constitutes the central focus for a qualitative social research project may not be evident in the initial stages of a project. Rather, it is likely that new research questions will emerge as one becomes familiar with the subject area, and these may serve to supplement or replace the original questions. As Hammersley and Atkinson (1994) have suggested, coming to realise what the research is 'really about' is a common development in qualitative research. This reflects Blumer's position in relation to studying an obdurate social reality where the 'determination of problems, concepts, research techniques, and theoretical schemes should be done by the direct examination of the actual empirical social world . . . the nature of the empirical social world is to be discovered, to be dug out by a direct, careful, and probing examination of that world' (Blumer, 1969: 48).

When I began my project I knew that I was interested in the role of the police in responding to criminal homicides, but for a long time I could not understand what I was *really* trying to achieve through my research. I was doing fieldwork and collecting lots of interesting data, but could not see any direction to it. Gradually though, I came to realise that what I was looking at, and what I was really interested in, was the question of 'How do the police investigate murders and why do they do it like this?' The data I was collecting focused upon the investigative methods police use in their enquiries – and the combination of factors that impact upon this aspect of their work. This was my 'big question' and once I had identified it, it provided a focus for the subsequent data collection and analysis.

The alert reader will have noticed that my 'big question' was actually composed of two parts, which encapsulate two different analytic foci within the research. The notion of 'how' something is done suggests a focus upon the practices, procedures and activities by which a task is accomplished. This is different from asking 'why' a particular task is accomplished in this way. A 'why?' question, when used conjointly with a 'how?' question, directs attention to the role of context, experience and interpretation in shaping a situated social actor's practices.

An example drawn from my research illustrates the ways in which how and why questions can be used. From my reading of the academic literature, I had established that an important issue was how, in the initial stages of an investigation, detectives define whether an incident should be treated as a crime (see, for example, Ericson, 1993; Hobbs, 1988). In responding to a suspicious death, police officers have to distinguish whether the deceased was killed by another person (criminal homicide), whether he or she committed suicide, or whether he or she died of natural causes. My observations of this aspect of their work quickly established that due to the often 'messy' and confused nature of suspicious deaths, establishing whether a crime had occurred was not always easy for detectives. I therefore decided that one of the questions that I would address was 'How do detectives establish that a crime may have occurred?'

In an interview with an experienced detective, the basic rationale underpinning the police's investigative response was explained to me.

> You have to think that each case is a murder, until proven otherwise you have to treat each case as a 'worst case scenario', because if you don't and later on something comes up which suggests that your interpretation was wrong and this person was probably murdered, you're gonna have a real problem because the evidence is likely to have gone and you're left holding 'a crock of shit'. On the other hand, if you start off collecting all the evidence on the basis that it could be a murder, you may waste a couple of days finding out you were wrong, but at least you are sure.

If we turn to consider why the police adopt this approach in response to suspicious deaths, we can see that they draw upon past experiences of dealing with these sorts of situation. Experience has demonstrated that it is better to start an investigation as a homicide enquiry, when the maximum amount of evidence is likely to be available, than to have to start the investigation some time after the body is first discovered, when it is likely that important evidence will have deteriorated in quality or have been destroyed altogether.

Similar issues were illustrated in another case that I observed, where the body of a middle-aged woman was found in her flat. She had died as a result of multiple stab wounds and the knife used to inflict these injuries was found beside the corpse. Through interpreting the scene, the detectives were quickly able to establish that the victim had been killed by an intruder and that the injuries were not self-inflicted. How did they do this? First, they identified that although the wounds could have feasibly been self-inflicted, the pattern of injuries was not consistent with how people commit suicide. Secondly, the flat was in a state of disarray, with drawers and cupboards left open and it appeared that someone had been searching for something. They used this to infer that the killing occurred as part of a burglary that had 'gone wrong'. Thirdly, forensic searches of the flat revealed traces of the victim's blood on the taps in the bathroom, which suggested that the attacker had tried to clean him or herself after killing the victim. The allied question of how they defined the incident as a homicide is why did they use these methods? Interpretations of the state of the scene and forensic analyses of it have in the past proven to be effective ways of identifying whether a crime has been committed. This further illustrates how and why detectives draw upon past experiences to inform the ways in which they approach particular situations. In summary, both of these examples show that the heuristic separation of the questions 'How is something done?' from 'Why is it done like that?', is a useful way of directing the collection and analysis of empirical data.

13.4   GAINING INSIGHT, GAINING PERSPECTIVE

An increased familiarity with the subject was vital in allowing me to clarify the aims and objectives of the project. The processual quality of research is even more evident in what I term the activity of 'gaining insight' and the subsequent shift to 'gaining perspective'.

Qualitative research, and in particular observational methods, are selected by researchers because they facilitate a close-up view of the actions of particular groups and allow for a degree of empathetic understanding to be built up about their subject's situated perspective. It is this 'naturalistic' familiarity that is central for understanding how and why people do what they do. The researcher is seeking a degree of insight about what it is like to inhabit the social world of another. Certainly this was the case for me when I was researching the police. I wanted to know what the police did and the influences that conditioned the formulation of their social actions.

However, while seeking a 'depth' of understanding is the principal aim when collecting qualitative data, in order to establish a 'thick', detailed and nuanced description of what has been studied (Geertz, 1973), once you shift to analysing data, this insight must be augmented through 'gaining perspective'. Gaining perspective means being able to appreciate how the object, people or phenomena studied are located within a particular social context and how they link with issues of wider sociological import. This enables a move from providing purely descriptive interpretations of the data to providing explanations. In my case, the study of detectives allowed for an array of issues relating to organisational processes and systems, information management and communication, and the construction of symbolic meanings, among others, to be addressed. It is in the shift from gaining insight to gaining perspective that sociological concepts and theories come into play.

13.5 THEORY: PROCESS AND PRODUCT

In thinking about social research as a process, an important question that should be addressed is the role of concepts and theories. Broadly speaking, theoretical concerns can be integrated within the research process as a resource to guide the collection and analysis of data, or alternatively, the generation of concepts and theories can be treated as an objective of the research. In terms of understanding the nature of theory as a product of research, Glaser and Strauss's (1967) distinction between 'substantive theory', relating to the specific area of social life being studied, and 'formal theory', which is more a general, rule-like proposition relevant to the study of social life, is useful. In the case of my research, theory was used to inform the research process and in addition some 'substantive' and 'formal' conceptual development was one of the products that resulted from the study.

An example of the development of substantive theory from my work is provided by the concept of 'signifiers of intent'. I developed this concept to capture a particular aspect of the interpretative work that detectives routinely engaged in as part of the investigative process. In order to prosecute a suspect for the crime of murder, police must demonstrate that the individual caused the victim to die through his or her actions and that this was his or her deliberate intention. However, as both Douglas (1971) and Strauss (1993) have discussed, intentions and motives are 'subjective', internal states that are difficult to prove objectively. In murder investigations, the police cope with such problems by examining the behaviour of a suspect prior to the crime, in an effort to see if he or she did anything which can be used to infer that he or she intended to kill the victim. For example, on one of the cases that I observed, involving the killing of two young men in a public house, the investigation team spent a lot of time trying to establish if one of the suspects had brought a knife used in the attack with him to the pub, or whether he had picked it up from the bar during the assault. The detectives were of the opinion that if it could be shown that the suspect had brought the knife with him, this could be used to suggest that he had acted in a premeditated fashion. Similar processes were observed on a number of cases where actions performed by the suspect in advance of the killing were interpreted by police as signifiers of intent.

In terms of how theory was integrated into my study, the symbolic interactionist perspective was central to my conceptual concerns. I had always found symbolic interactionism and allied sociological perspectives quite engaging, offering a persuasive account of how individuals, as members of social groups, act, negotiate and render understandable their social worlds.[2] As I began to collect data about murder investigations, I was looking for ways of interpreting and making sense of the material that I had available. In the literature on symbolic interactionism, I discovered a range of concepts and a general emphasis that made sense of my data. In particular, the stress that interactionists place upon the importance of social action, and the dialectic that exists between action and context,[3] provided a useful approach to understanding how police officers made decisions and the various influences that affected what they did. Similarly, the strong identification made with 'process' as a key concept seemed to fit much of what I was seeing in the field. At a more epistemological level, the claim made by symbolic interactionist sociology that what are accepted as meanings and 'truths' are collectively produced as a result of human interaction, was directly relevant to explaining the detective work I was observing.

The essence of the detectives' role as homicide investigators was that they would be confronted with the body of a victim and have to interpret and define this situation to produce an account that explained how and why the victim died. In performing this task, detectives routinely encountered a range of difficulties. In particular, the victim could not provide them with an account of what happened, the suspect was strongly motivated to provide an account that restricted his or her apparent legal culpability, and any witnesses often provided the police with conflicting versions of events. In order to establish who did what to whom in the fatal interaction, the police use information collated from a range of sources to assemble a detailed account of events. Essentially, their role is concerned with 'constructing the case for the prosecution' from the available information (McConville et al., 1991). The police do not know the absolute 'truth' of what happened, nor do they have to. As a set of institutions and practices the law identifies for police 'what are to be counted as the facts' (Tamanaha, 1997). Thus detectives do not have to be able to state 'the truth' in order to gain the conviction of a suspect in a court of law. They operate to a legal standard of 'beyond reasonable doubt', which is achieved by producing sufficient evidence to support their claims as to what they believe took place. Symbolic interactionist theory provided a resource that could be used to explore these issues.

---

[2] For various examples of the symbolic interactionist perspective, see Blumer, 1969; Rock, 1979; Strauss, 1993.

[3] Erving Goffman's (1959, 1961) studies are particularly good examples of this aspect of the interactionist approach.

It is not necessary to treat existing theories and perspectives in a reified or sacrosanct way. An important aspect of empirical research is the opportunity to refine and develop existing concepts through critical treatment. This was certainly one aspect of the research that I conducted. A criticism that is often levelled at research inspired by symbolic interactionism is that it lacks sufficient emphasis upon the role of social structures in directing and shaping the behaviours of individuals. Such criticisms are in fact only partially true and not necessarily borne out by a careful reading of a number of key works in the interactionist tradition. Nevertheless, an awareness of such issues prompted me to develop a more explicit account of the influence that 'structural' factors have upon how detectives performed their work.

My analysis suggested that there were three key influences that had a direct impact upon the response offered by the police to criminal homicides. These influences were: the qualities and circumstances of the incident itself; the administrative and bureaucratic properties of the police organisation; and the law and the legal process. These factors served to structure the process of investigation and thus the actions performed by individual officers. In an effort to deal with these issues I developed the concept of 'process structure'.

The concept of process structure is more akin to the development of 'formal' theory and aimed to capture the fact that as a result of the 'structural influences' identified above, the actions performed by investigators tended to follow a discernible sequence, which could be divided up into a series of stages. Thus the process of investigation could be seen to have a specific structure or framework that served to order the actions of individual officers. This idea of a structured process should not be altogether surprising, as one of the key functions of an organisation is the regularisation of social action. Weick (1995) suggests that organisations are mechanisms intended to sort forms of ongoing interdependent actions into 'sensible' types, in an effort to achieve 'sensible' outcomes. The police organisation shares these basic properties. The concept of process structure aims to account for how, through a combination of procedures, policies and routines, the police response to homicide is ordered and patterned. This concept, which I have developed through an empirical study of a particular aspect of policing, is relevant to studies of organisations more generally and other aspects of social life.

13.6 PARALLELS BETWEEN SOCIAL
RESEARCH AND CRIME INVESTIGATION

In studying the work of police detectives, it became apparent to me that there were a number of intriguing parallels that could be identified between how detectives accomplish their tasks and how I, as a social researcher, was going about mine. The most important and fundamental similarity is that both research and crime investigation are forms of 'information work'. I used the term information work in my study of detectives to capture how the principal focus of their activities is the identification, interpretation and construction of information. As discussed earlier, the facts of a case are not inherent to the incident, but rather are produced as a result of the actions taken by police officers and other actors in the legal process. The facts of a case are selectively emphasised elements of the accounts and interpretations to which the police have access. This notion of information work applies equally well to conducting research. The researcher is engaged in trying to identify relevant information and make use of it in a particular way. For both detectives and researchers, explaining the information work that is conducted is focused around three key issues: methodology, evidence and case construction.

13.6.1 Methodology

Methodology in social research refers to the techniques and epistemological pre-suppositions, which contribute to how information is identified and analysed in relation to a research problem. It considers the ways in which the data, on which the researcher will base his or her findings, are produced. Methodological concerns are informed by a particular worldview, an assessment of the nature of the subject to be researched and the sorts of material that are available to research the problem. The selection of a methodology is crucial for the project, as it will, to a certain extent, determine the nature of the findings.

The concept of methodology is equally applicable to the practices of crime investigation. Indeed, I used the concept of the 'investigative methodology' within my study to document the ways in which police officers employed information-gathering strategies and techniques in order to collect data and thereby build an understanding of who did what to whom, when, where, how and why. The methodology that the police used was designed to generate sufficient information to provide an authoritative answer to these questions, and thereby state how the crime happened and who was responsible.

An example of an investigative methodology in practice and the ways police seek to collect information from a range of potential sources is provided in an instruction issued by a senior detective to his team:

1. Formal interview with [suspect's name].
2. Trace and interview customers of [pub name – where victim and suspect were last seen by a witness together].
3. Enquiries with neighbours along the canal bank.
4. Family background enquiries.
5. Examination of scene.

In this case, the suspect had been identified and arrested by police at the scene of the crime. In a different investigation, this time where the suspect had not been identified, we can observe similar information-collection strategies being employed.

> At this stage because there is no obvious motive for this crime, the lines of enquiry will be as follows:
>
> 1. Enquiries with close family of the deceased, including ex-wives for background information.
> 2. Enquiries with business associates, again for background information.
> 3. House-to-house enquiries in the High Street.
> 4. Criminal intelligence enquiries, to include [neighbouring police force] due to deceased's known criminal connections.
> 5. Research NCIS [National Criminal Intelligence Service] records in light of the information provided in 4 above.

Comparing these extracts demonstrates the extent to which police use established procedures to direct their lines of enquiry in an effort to generate relevant information from potential sources. It is this sense of organisation that the concept of investigative methodology aims to capture.

These extracts also indicate how police seek to identify and combine different types of information derived from separate sources in constructing their account. The investigative methodology can be seen to share a number of principles with a social science methodology informed by a strategy of 'data triangulation' (see Chapter 12). For both police and social researchers, triangulation allows for a comprehensive account to be assembled that overcomes the limitations associated with any single source of data.

One of the key heuristic devices that police use to organise and coordinate the investigation is what I have termed the 'Cluedo questions'. Police can use these questions in a reflexive fashion, to evaluate their work in an effort to ensure that they have covered the fundamental aspects of a particular incident. If they cannot provide conclusive answers to the following list, then they know that their account may be unsuccessful in proving the involvement of the suspect when it is presented and scrutinised in court.

- Who killed the victim?
- What killed the victim?
- Where was the victim killed?
- When was the victim killed?
- Why was the victim killed?
- How was the victim killed?

Similar questions can be asked by sociologists of their work and used to structure the methods they are employing. They serve as a useful tool to ensure that the findings are thoroughly grounded in the evidence and not based upon speculation or weak inference. This brings us to a consideration of the role of evidence in crime investigation and research.

13.6.2 Evidence

Both detectives and social researchers are required to use evidence in order to warrant or substantiate their claims. In legal discourse, evidence is a fact or thing on the basis of which a second fact can be inferred. If one accepts this definition, there is a temptation to view evidence unproblematically, and ignore the extent to which its probative value rests on the way it is defined and interpreted. If one observes barristers in a courtroom setting, it is apparent that they do not simply present evidence 'neutrally'. They make suggestions about how the item should be interpreted and understood in the context of the case, and thus the meaning it should be ascribed. Evidence does not 'speak for itself'. It acquires its meaningful qualities as a result of being interpreted and defined by police officers in the context of a structured process of enquiry. The defence and prosecution will often contest how the other side has interpreted a piece of evidence and the conclusions that each side has drawn from it. The police are aware of these matters and as part of their investigative work seek to demonstrate that all possible alternative interpretations of the evidence are ill-founded.

This is an aspect of evidence of which social researchers should be mindful. The evidential qualities of an object or account are not inherent; rather they become evidence as a result of the way they are interpreted and used. The findings of research should be supported by the careful selection of evidence. And just as detectives do, it is often useful to check what alternative claims the evidence could support. Detective work takes place in an adversarial environment where the police are aware that their opponents will try to discredit the evidence they present and the conclusions which they base upon it. As a result, they try to use several pieces of evidence to warrant a claim in constructing their case and they routinely consider the alternative interpretations available. This is a pragmatically applied version of Popper's advocacy of falsification (see Chapter 2). If a researcher tries to disprove a conclusion, but finds that he or she cannot, confidence in the plausibility and credibility of the conclusion will grow.

13.6.3 Case construction

In discussing the role and uses of evidence, I made it clear that evidence was to be treated as a social product, that is, as an artefact of the investigative process. With respect to policing, evidence is rendered meaningful as part of the processes of case construction. The case against a suspect, setting out and documenting his or her alleged involvement in a crime, is not simply discovered by police, but is socially constructed. The investigative actions of police uncover a large amount of information, some of which is relevant to their understanding of the incident and some of which is not. In constructing their case, they select the information that they feel contributes to an understanding of the crime and place it in an order so as to provide a comprehensive and coherent account that details how the crime took place and who was involved. This assembling and ordering of information is a key aspect of investigative activity, enabling the police to ensure that their account tells 'the right kind of story'.

A similar notion of case construction is relevant to the role of the researcher in preparing the products of a research study. Making a case from the collected materials and presenting it so 'that a skeptical outsider can see how a pattern is grown to enable comprehension of member-produced social action in the context of one world from the perspective of another' (Agar, 1995: 127) is an important aspect of the researcher's role.

Researchers should aim to provide their audience with a comprehensive, detailed and understandable account of the findings of the research and the basis on which these findings were obtained. In doing so, however, a balance needs to be struck between organising the material so that it is understand-able to the audience and ensuring that it continues to provide a sympathetic reflection of the complexities of the social world(s) being researched.

13.7 CONCLUSION

This chapter has discussed the ways in which a range of methodological issues had an impact upon a qualitative study of police homicide investiga-tions and has shown how these issues can be resolved in practice. In drawing attention to the research process, I have considered the ways in which the focus of activity shifts over the course of a project. What is particularly interesting about the subject of detective work is the parallels with how social researchers perform their tasks. Thinking about issues of method-ology, evidence and case construction seems to be central to understanding all forms of investigation.

PART III

BACK HOME

CODING AND MANAGING DATA

14

JANE FIELDING

CONTENTS

After you have collected your research data, you will need to start the process of making sense of the material, whether it is a pile of completed questionnaires, a bulging notebook or a stack of interview tapes. The next step involves organising the information into a form that will facilitate your understanding of its meaning, using whatever modern technology is appropriate.

First, I will review the paths you could have taken to arrive at this point.

1. You designed a questionnaire, which may have been self-completion or interview-aided or even administered over the telephone (see Chapter 6). Hopefully, you gave some thought to how your respondents might answer your questions and you may have pre-coded the questionnaire so that they have already ticked appropriate boxes. If that is the case, then your next task, coding your questionnaire, is almost complete. However, you may have only just picked up this book, hoping to find a way out of a sea of completed questionnaires that have not been coded in any way. Or maybe you have something in between these two scenarios. In any case, if you have collected more than 20 questionnaires and have asked more than five questions, you should be using a computer to help analyse the results.

2. You conducted an in-depth, face-to-face interview and either recorded it on cassette tape or made notes (see Chapter 8).

3. You observed a social situation or setting and made covert or overt fieldnotes (see Chapter 9).

4. You collected administrative details from records (Chapter 12), possibly noting the information on a questionnaire.

5. You collected articles or newspaper cuttings about your research topic (as discussed in Chapter 12).

6. You decided to perform a content analysis on visual materials (Chapter 20).

7. You used a combination of these methods.

However you collected the data, whether the data is quantitative or qualitative, you will now be faced with a sorting task that, by its very nature, will impose a discipline on this stage of the research. As Silvey says: 'Research ultimately must be based on comparisons, whether it be comparisons between different groups of cases, between the same cases at different points in time, or even between what is and what might have been' (1975: 16).

In order to make comparisons you will have to access your data and organise it into categories or instances of occurrence. This is called coding the data. You will find that even a quantitative survey has qualitative elements and a qualitative transcript has quantitative aspects. For instance, many questions in a pre-coded survey will resort to a catch-all 'other, please specify' category as a safety net for those responses not anticipated in the original questionnaire design. Very often these responses are the most interesting, because they are exceptions to the rule and will need particularly careful consideration and coding. A common type of question is one that explores why a particular response was chosen for a previous question. For instance, respondents may be asked to pick one answer from a list and then the next question may be 'Why did you choose that answer?' This 'open response' will also have to be coded. With qualitative data such as an interview transcript, preliminary analysis may benefit from quantitative methods such as frequency counts of occurrences of certain phrases or words or the codes that you have assigned to your data.

The discussion that follows begins by considering the quantitative coding of a questionnaire with pre-coded questions, followed by a discussion of the coding of open questions. Coding of open questions may be seen as qualitative coding and many of the considerations for this activity apply equally to the coding of interview transcripts. The difference lies not in the activity of coding but in the treatment of the resulting categories or codes.

The primary purpose of coding a quantitative survey is to 'translate' your respondents' answers into numbers for subsequent statistical analysis. The result of coding a survey questionnaire is a data matrix stored in a separate computer file or within statistical software. In contrast, the coding process in qualitative research involves not only translation, but also analysis. Traditionally, the result of coding an interview transcript has been a stack of file cards each containing a segment of the text. The file cards are then sorted manually in various ways to generate and explore theoretical categories. However, computer programs for qualitative research are now becoming available to aid the coding and sorting processes and the chapter concludes with a discussion of qualitative coding using an example of this software.

14.1 QUANTITATIVE CODING

In order to put the coding process into perspective, let us consider the following survey question: 'Do you agree or disagree that nuclear power should be used to generate electricity?' Respondents are also to be asked how old they are, whether they are male or female, and if they are married or single. In the following sections we will explore what is involved in coding these questions, but first I will describe the result of such a quantitative coding exercise and then go through each step of the process. The steps are:

1. Developing the coding frame for both pre-coded and open questions.
2. Creating the code book and coding instructions.
3. Coding the questionnaires.
4. Transferring the values to a computer.
5. Checking and cleaning the data.

14.1.1 The result: the data matrix

A survey questionnaire is designed to gather information from a number of cases about various topics of investigation. By **cases**, we typically mean people, but a case could equally be a country or a school or even an observed incident. The information that we collect about each case, such as the sex and age of an individual, birth and death rates in a particular country, time of incident and number of people present, are the **variables**. The aim of coding is to assign a **value** to each piece of information. Each individual *case* will then consist of a complete set of *values* for each of the *variables*.

Variables (columns)

		Question 1	Question 2	Question 3	Question 4
Cases (rows)	Case 1	Age of person 1	Sex of person 1	Marital status of person 1	Attitude to nuclear power of person 1
	Case 2	Age of person 2	Sex of person 2	Marital status of person 2	Attitude to nuclear power of person 2
	Case 3	Age of person 3	Sex of person 3	Marital status of person 3	Attitude to nuclear power of person 3

The shaded part of the figure will form the **data file**.

Figure 14.1   *A data matrix*

The result of such a coding exercise will be the production of a **data file** that should consist of numbers (or sometimes letters and spaces) such that the rows correspond to each case and the columns correspond to each variable (see Figure 14.1). Notice how the shaded part of Figure 14.1 will form a block of numbers and/or letters once each variable has been assigned values. Even if the respondent has not replied to a particular question, or the question was 'not applicable' to the respondent, a value is still usually assigned to the variable for that case. This data matrix may be the 'spreadsheet view' you see of your coded data in your chosen statistical software package (e.g. SPSS) or it may be the contents of a data file. At this stage, it is worth considering the route by which your data is going to enter the computer. One route is by **direct data entry** into the statistical software chosen for analysis. A second route involves the creation of a data file which is then 'read' by the chosen statistical software. This second method would normally only be considered if you have a lot of data to enter (e.g. hundreds of questionnaires) and the resources or facilities for professional data entry. Figure 14.2 demonstrates these options. If you use the second route, you must make sure that the values for each variable for each case are in the same columns to create a **rectangular data matrix**. This sort of data file is known as a **fixed format** data file.

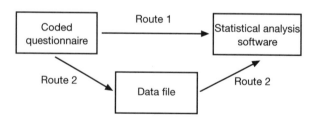

Figure 14.2   *From a survey questionnaire to statistical software: two alternative data routes*

Generally, this rectangular data matrix does not exceed 80 columns in width. This is so the whole data file can be seen on a computer monitor with no line 'wrapping round' to the next line. If you have many variables then you can use more than one line of data for each case.

The discussion that follows applies to *both* data entry routes.

14.1.2 Developing the coding frame

The coding frame for quantitative variables is a list of all possible responses to a question and their accompanying numeric codes, and, in some cases, the column location of the codes. As you develop the coding frame, you need to understand the different kinds of variable that you may come across. If you ask people how much they earn in a year you could compare someone earning £10,000 with someone earning £20,000, since this variable is measured on an **interval** or continuous scale. The former earns half as much as the latter.

If you ask the question, 'How well do you manage on your income?', allowing the respondent to tick one of a selection of answers ranging from 'not at all well' to 'very well', you would have some basis for comparing someone who said they were managing 'very well' with someone who said they were managing 'not at all well'. However, you would not know the difference between 'doing very well' and 'doing well'. And one person who thinks that they manage 'very well' may not mean the same as another who gives the same answer. This variable is being measured on an **ordinal** scale since the responses are ordered.

If you ask what religion someone belongs to, you would receive a response that merely nominates a particular religion (or no religion). There is no intrinsic ordering between religions. Religion is being measured on a **nominal** scale.

There is a special kind of nominal variable, called a **dummy** variable, where the measurement is either the presence of an attribute or its absence. For instance, instead of asking people what religion they belong to, creating a nominal variable, you could ask people if they are Protestant. All those who said they are Protestant could be coded with the value 1 and all the rest with the value 0. Similar dummy variables could be created if you asked people if they are Catholic, or if they are Jewish, and so on. The essential feature of a dummy variable is that it is a binary coded variable, having a value of either 0 or 1.

The sequence of levels of measurement is from nominal, the lowest, through ordinal, to interval. Each higher level possesses all the properties of the lower levels. With the increase in level of measurement comes greater flexibility and power in the statistical methods that can be employed in analysis.

In Figure 14.1 there are four questions corresponding to four variables that illustrate these levels of measurement. Age is measured at the interval level, Attitude to nuclear power is measured at the ordinal level, as we shall see in the next section, and Sex and Marital status are measured at the nominal level.

We will start by coding the pre-coded questions. This should ideally be carried out before the questionnaire is administered so that the anticipated responses and their codes can be printed on the questionnaire.

It is usual to assign a unique ID or case number to each questionnaire, so that, if necessary, you can refer back to the original once all the data is on the computer. This is very often the first variable, put into the first columns. So, you must make sure that you have reserved enough columns to allow space for the largest case number. For instance, if you expect no more than 99 filled-in questionnaires (99 cases), you only need to reserve columns 1 and 2 for the ID values. However, if you expect 100 or more completed questionnaires, but less than 1,000, you need to reserve columns 1, 2 and 3 for these ID values. These column assignments lead to variables being referred to as 'single column variables', 'two column variables', and so on.

If the questionnaire asked people how old they are, you could assign two columns, assuming there is no one older than 99, and code the actual age into those columns, thus creating Age as an interval variable. However, you may decide you do not need to retain all this information and are only interested in distinctions between age groupings. In other words, you could code Age as an ordinal variable with codes corresponding to young, middle-aged and old, for instance. Another reason why you might code Age as an ordinal variable is that people are often reticent about their age and feel happier if they just have to tick an age range on a questionnaire (see Chapter 6). So your coding frame for Age as an ordinal variable may resemble Figure 14.3.

Some people in your sample may have refused to answer this question and you need to decide what code to assign to these 'non-responses'. By convention, 9, 99 or 999 are reserved as **missing values** to be used to code non-responses. The code 9 would be used for single column variables and 99 for double column variables. If you code Age as a continuous variable, you should assign the value 99 to those people who did not respond. If there is a possibility of a respondent being 99 years of age, you could use the value

Age	Code
Under 20	1
21–35	2
36–50	3
51–65	4
66–80	5
Over 81	6

Figure 14.3   *Coding for the variable: Age*

999 for the missing value, or you could use 98 for all those who are 98 or older. If you decide to code Age into a smaller number of age groups, you could use the code 9 as the non-response code.

While on the subject of missing data, there are other possible reasons for data to be missing for a particular case. For instance, a respondent may not know the answer to a particular question and respond with a 'don't know'. Or a question or set of questions may be inapplicable. For instance, one would not ask for the salary of an unemployed person. Again, there are conventions to follow. 'Don't know' responses are often coded with an 8 or a 98 and 'not applicable' responses are often coded with a 0. If you have a large number of non-responses in your questionnaires, it is acceptable to leave blanks in the data file.

You might assign the value 1 for those who responded 'male' and a 2 for those who responded 'female' to a question about the respondent's sex. You could equally well have coded 'female' as 1 and 'male' as 2, but, whatever you decide, you must stick to it for the rest of your cases. You could have coded Sex with letters (e.g. 'm' and 'f'), but it is more usual to use numbers since the use of alphabetic coding sometimes imposes restriction on subsequent analysis.

A possible coding scheme for Marital status is shown in Figure 14.4. Marital status is a nominal variable. It is important that when the questionnaire is administered, it is made clear that this question refers to the current marital status of the respondent, and that 'married' means married at the moment, rather than 'ever been married'.

A common method of coding attitudinal questions is seen in Figure 14.5. Coded in this way, this variable is an ordinal variable. Note that the coding could have been reversed with 'Strongly disagree' coded 1 and 'Strongly agree' coded 5. For a fuller discussion of this kind of coding see Chapter 7.

After coding, the data file for three respondents might look like that in Figure 14.6. Here case 1 is a 23-year-old man who is living as married and agrees that nuclear power should be used to generate electricity. Once again the data file is shaded.

Marital status	Code
Married	1
Living as married	2
Separated/divorced	3
Widowed	4
Not married	5
No response	9

Figure 14.4 *Coding for the variable: Marital status*

Attitude to nuclear power	Code
Strongly agree	1
Agree	2
Neither agree nor disagree	3
Disagree	4
Strongly disagree	5

Figure 14.5 *Coding for the variable: Attitude to nuclear power*

		ID			Question 1 (age)		Question 2 (sex)	Question 3 (marital status)	Question 4 (Attitude to nuclear power)
	variable type				continuous		nominal	nominal	ordinal
	column number	*1*	*2*	*3*	*4*	*5*	*6*	*7*	*8*
Cases	Case 1	0	0	1	2	3	1	2	2
	Case 2	0	0	2	4	1	2	1	3
	Case 3	0	0	3	9	9	2	4	5

Variables

Figure 14.6 *The coded data matrix*

14.1.3 Rules for coding

There are some basic rules for coding.

1. Codes must be mutually exclusive. Any particular response must fit into one, and only one category. Someone cannot be both married and single at the same time.
2. Codes must be exhaustive. You must have covered all possible coding options and allowed for them in your scheme.
3. Codes must be applied consistently throughout.

You should be consistent within your questionnaire for the values you use for similar responses in different questions. For instance, if you decide to code a 'yes' responses with the value 1 and a 'no' responses with the value 2, use those values throughout the questionnaire for other yes/no questions. Similarly, code all non-response categories with a 9, 99, or 999, all 'don't know' responses with the values 8, 98, or 998, and all 'not applicable' categories with either a blank or a zero.

14.1.4 Comparability

When selecting categories for closed questions, it is a good idea to be consistent with the codes that have been used in other surveys. The *Standard Occupational Classification* (1990b) is a manual that indexes occupations according to qualifications, training, skills and industry and is widely used by labour market researchers. Other sources of coding for standard variables such as household composition, education, age, gender, race and leisure are described by Stacey (1969) and Burgess (1986). Using the same codes as other surveys makes it easier to compare results.

In recognition of the value of asking the same questions in the same way, in 1995 the UK government introduced a scheme to harmonise question wording for large-scale government surveys (and subsequently the coding of responses) in order to standardise the ways in which basic information is collected in government social surveys (see http://www.statistics.gov.uk/ harmony/harmonfp.asp. For further information about harmonised questions and question wording also see http://qb.soc.surrey.ac.uk/.).

So far, I have discussed the coding of closed questions in which codes have been assigned to each of the responses. It is often a good idea to type these codes on to the questionnaire so that respondents only have to tick boxes or circle numbers when filling out the form. This often leads to a better response because it is quicker for someone to tick a box than write out a response. Also, the next stage of transferring the data on to a computer is considerably quicker if as much pre-coding as possible has been done beforehand. In addition to the numerical codes assigned to each response, the column number is often also written on to the questionnaire, often under a heading such as 'For office use only'. The above set of questions could have been laid out as shown in Figure 14.7.

14.2   QUALITATIVE CODING

Often a pre-coded question in a survey questionnaire will offer the option of an 'other (please specify)' category to act as a 'safety net' to catch additional responses which may be encountered infrequently. There are also questions that qualify previous responses such as 'Why did you say that?', for which pre-coding is not possible. These represent qualitative elements in an otherwise quantitative analysis. Whether one is coding these kinds of question, open questions in which verbatim responses are recorded, or interview transcripts or fieldnotes, the initial process of coding is the same. The purpose of the first step is to reduce the data into analytic categories prior to analysis. However, while this 'code then analyse' sequence is unproblematically the case with the processing of open survey questions, it may not be such a rigidly sequential process while coding an interview transcript or fieldnote. Strauss (1987), in fact, identified three kinds of coding processes for qualitative data. The first pass through the data involves **open coding** the

Questionnaire

ID number: ☐☐☐ 1–3

Please can you provide the following details:

Q.1	Age:	☐☐	4–5
Q.2	Sex:		
Please tick one box:			
	Male ☐ 1	Female ☐ 2	6
Q.3	Marital status:		
	Married	☐ 1	7
	Living as married	☐ 2	
	Separated/divorced	☐ 3	
	Widowed	☐ 4	
	Not married	☐ 5	
Q.4	What is your opinion about using nuclear power to generate electricity?		
	Strongly agree	☐ 1	8
	Agree	☐ 2	
	Neither agree or disagree	☐ 3	
	Disagree	☐ 4	
	Strongly disagree	☐ 5	

Figure 14.7 *Sample questionnaire with pre-codes*

data into analytic themes in order to apply initial codes or labels to segments of the data. This step may be seen as comparable to coding open questions in a survey. However, the second and third passes through the qualitative data, also described as 'coding' by Strauss, should strictly be seen as part of the analysis. There will be more discussion about these stages of qualitative coding later in the chapter but the section that follows concerns itself with the first open coding stage.

The first set of categories into which the data will be coded is the equivalent to the coding frame for closed questions. The categories derived may come from theory or some other aspect of the literature, intuition or from the data themselves. If the research is designed to test a hypothesis, the categories should be derived from the theoretical framework and the data made to fit the categories. This is termed 'coding down'. However, if the aim is to describe data in order to generate theory, you can develop the categories from the data. This is called 'coding up'. The development of categories during coding up involves the following steps:

- Either take the first 20 or so questionnaires or the interview transcript or fieldnotes.
- Use filing cards to note down each response from the questionnaire or each significant feature or quote from the interview/fieldnote. Use a new filing card for each new response or concept.
- With survey questionnaires, code question by question (i.e. across all 20 questionnaires), not case by case. This leads to greater consistency in coding each variable. It also reduces the possibility of building up a preconceived picture of the respondent, which could lead to a bias in the coding of any ambiguous response.
- For an interview or transcript, it is important to code in semantically meaningful units. These may be words, phrases, sentences or paragraphs, depending on the analysis being developed.
- Sort the filing cards into related categories.
- Continue with another 20 questionnaires or another interview/fieldnote.
- Repeat the sorting exercise.
- Repeat the last two steps until no new categories are generated.
- Create coding instructions in order to define category membership.

14.2.1 An example of coding a fieldnote

Turner (1981) offers a clear example of coding up a fieldnote. In the example shown in Figure 14.8, the fieldnote describes an aspect of the queuing system at a cement factory. Turner generates a number of potential ways of coding the fieldnote through a 'brainstorming' session where as many plausible accounts of its meaning are listed as possible. These form possible codes that are then compared to other fieldnotes in the set. Some will be discarded because they do not resonate with the other data, while others will be seen to relate to each other and so will be combined. Thus, several codes are likely to end up being applicable to the fieldnote shown. For each code an attempt is made to 'define' it by writing it up in formal, abstract terms. Another important aspect of the procedure is that, once stated in formal terms, an effort should be made to identify parallel codes or processes in other, documented social phenomena. For example, if 'power' emerges as a code applicable to the data, you should try to think of other situations in which 'power' governs the course of interaction. This will help to identify elements of the operation of power which you can then look for in your own data. The competitive elements in the cement factory example may be related to the way tenants in a shared household work out who will get to use the bathroom first in the morning, and so on.

Coding strategies

Pfaffenberger (1988) has described coding strategies for qualitative data, some of which apply equally well to open questions in a survey or interview (see Figure 14.9). Note that 'strip' refers to a discrete segment of coded data.

A. First paragraph from a set of fieldnotes

Paragraph 1

A row of lorries varying between 30 and 50 queue up every morning in front of the factory to obtain cement. All lorry drivers and owners place great importance to be first in the queue as this means getting served first. This has added importance in times of cement shortages when the cement outflow from the factory to the private sector is rationed and when the prices of cement are high. In addition to cement customers, there is also a set of lorry owners stationed at H . . . who act as transport agents for other customers. Porcelli is one of these transport agents.

Source: Former factory manager who is embarking here upon a discussion of Porcelli's activities in the area.

B. Categories generated (to be placed on cards)

Cement shortage
Competitive behaviour among lorry drivers
Many agents transporting cement
Greater intensity of competition caused by cement shortage
Customers transporting their own cement
Role of factory
Significant of queue system as a means of distributing scarce resources
Economic context of scarcity
Porcelli's role
Significance of time in relation to the queue
Routinised pattern for the distribution of goods
Importance of priority position in queue

Source: Turner, 1981.

Figure 14.8   *Coding a fieldnote*

Prefer inclusive codes to exclusive codes
   The point of coding is to interlink units of data. The interlinkages thus created will play a major role in data analysis. To maximise the number of such interlinkages, use inclusive codes – codes that link at least two (and preferably many) strips together. The point is, that in any subsequent sifting of data, such codes will be more likely to include a relevant item than to leave it out. Try to code each strip, moreover, with two or more codes.

Let coding categories emerge from the data
   Mark off coherent stretches of the fieldnotes by the topical focus expressed in them. Question the a priori, exogenous categories developed before field research. If such categories obscure indigenous ones, and if the indigenous ones fit the data better, replace the exogenous categories with those recognised and used by the culture or organisation.

Develop abstract categories
   The exclusive use of indigenous categories makes it difficult to compare your data with cases derived from other contexts. While developing indigenous categories, therefore, strive also to find abstract categories that *do* fit the data, and apply them to all relevant instances.

Classify data and create typologies
   Using both indigenous and exogenous categories, subdivide and classify the data. Develop a framework that links the codes together typologically.

Change and refine the categories as understanding improves
   The achievement of a workable framework of codes, one that is sensitive to patterns in the data and does the best possible job of linking related data, is itself a form of theoretical discovery.

Source: Pfaffenberger, 1988.

Figure 14.9   *Some coding strategies*

14.2.2 Coding open questions in a survey questionnaire

Having created a workable coding frame for the closed questions in a survey, there are several points to consider before you can go ahead and code the rest of the questionnaires. For a survey questionnaire, you will be converting responses to numbers that are to be collated later by a statistical computer program. Each response category could be assigned a different value, the first category coded 1, the second coded 2, and so on. So if 15 categories were developed from the responses, the values will range from 1 to 15. However, before you decide on this scheme you need to consider how many answers to each question you will accept. For instance, to the question 'Why did you say that?', the respondent may offer one reason or many. You will need to decide whether to accept only the first-mentioned reason or several. For instance, you may decide to code the first three mentioned reasons. In this case, you will need to allow three variables, one for each reason. Of course, data from some respondents may be missing for one or more of these variables. Alternatively, you may decide that you want to code all responses, each one as a separate variable, in which case you would have as many variables as categories. Each variable would then be coded as either, 'yes, the reason is mentioned' and given the value 1, or 'no, not mentioned' and given the value 0. These points are considered in the example below.

In 1982, Social and Community Planning Research (SCPR) conducted a national survey of 1,195 members of the public about their attitudes to industrial, work-related and other risks. The respondents were asked the following, rather cumbersome question:

> Thinking of all the sorts of risks there are, at the present time what risks are you particularly worried or concerned about because they could happen to you or a member of your family?

The interviewers were instructed to 'probe and record fully' and therefore each individual might have mentioned more than one risk. With such an open question you cannot possibly anticipate all responses and therefore need to develop a coding scheme after the questionnaires have been filled out. In the original survey the answers to this question were left uncoded and unanalysed. The opportunity arose of carrying out a secondary analysis of this and other open questions from the survey (Brown et al., 1984). This involved designing a coding frame for the first 72 questionnaires and trying to define theoretically relevant distinctions between responses. A list of 23 different risks was elicited, although nearly 25 per cent of respondents did not proffer a risk at all. This list formed the basis of the coding frame used to code the rest of the questionnaires.

Because respondents could mention more than one risk, there was a problem in deciding how to code the answers. Figure 14.10 outlines three possible solutions.

Type of worry	Coding scheme 1: First-mentioned risk only coded in **ONE VARIABLE** called RISK	Coding scheme 2: Code the first three mentioned risks into three variables called RISK1, RISK2, RISK3			Coding scheme 3: Each risk mentioned is a variable and coded with a 1 if mentioned, otherwise 0. Therefore 24 variables are required.		
	Variable name	Variable names					
	RISK code	RISK1 code	RISK2 code	RISK3 code	Variable name	Code if mentioned	Code if not mentioned
None	1	1	1	1	RISK1	1	0
Car	2	2	2	2	RISK2	1	0
Crossing road	3	3	3	3	RISK3	1	0
Fire	4	4	4	4	RISK4	1	0
Other specific hazards	5	5	5	5	RISK5	1	0
Traffic	6	6	6	6	RISK6	1	0
Other health	7	7	7	7	RISK7	1	0
Falling	8	8	8	8	RISK8	1	0
Steam	9	9	9	9	RISK9	1	0
Work	10	10	10	10	RISK10	1	0
Electric current	11	11	11	11	RISK11	1	0
Children in traffic	12	12	12	12	RISK12	1	0
Military nuclear power	13	13	13	13	RISK13	1	0
Mugging	14	14	14	14	RISK14	1	0
Vandalism	15	15	15	15	RISK15	1	0
Other crime	16	16	16	16	RISK16	1	0
Unemployment	17	17	17	17	RISK17	1	0
Lightening	18	18	18	18	RISK18	1	0
Pollution	19	19	19	19	RISK19	1	0
Uneven pavements	20	20	20	20	RISK20	1	0
Civil nuclear war	21	21	21	21	RISK21	1	0
Smoking	22	22	22	22	RISK22	1	0
Stress at work	23	23	23	23	RISK23	1	0
Poor housing	24	24	24	24	RISK24	1	0

Figure 14.10   *Three coding schemes for risk responses*

We could have decided to code only the first-mentioned answer on the assumption that it would be the most important. (See coding scheme 1 in Figure 14.10.) However, we would have lost a lot of information from respondents who made multiple answers. Alternatively, we could have decided to code the first three responses from each respondent, each with the same coding scheme. (See coding scheme 2 in Figure 14.10.) However, this might still lead to a loss of information from those respondents offering more than three responses. The third coding scheme in Figure 14.10 involved creating 23 different variables, each one coded either 1 to indicate that it was mentioned or 0 to indicate that it was not. This scheme coded all the data, but the data may be more difficult to analyse.

The choice of which coding scheme to adopt should depend on the needs of the subsequent analysis. Schemes 1 and 2 lend themselves to a more descriptive account of people's responses. Scheme 3 would be more appropriate if the data were going to be analysed further. In fact, scheme 3 was employed in the study and the data were analysed using Smallest Space Analysis computer software. This provided a two-dimensional 'map' of people's responses such that those risks most frequently mentioned were located towards the centre of the 'map' and those risks mentioned together were located close to one another. From such a two-dimensional map, clusters of risks were identified as conceptually similar and given group names.

Another common method of dealing with multiple responses in open questions is to code only one that satisfies certain criteria. For instance, if you ask respondents what qualifications they have, perhaps offering them a list of pre-coded responses, they may tick more than one box. You may in this instance decide only to code the highest education qualification.

14.2.3 Storing verbatim responses

You may prefer to use the open responses as verbatim comments in your report to illustrate certain points, rather than reducing them to numerically coded categories. Obviously, if you have not quantified them, you will not be able to do any statistical analysis on these responses, but you will still have to read and sort them. You could just type a list of responses and then pick those that are useful for a particular point. Or you could use a database program to store the verbatim comments. For example, Access 2000 will allow you to store textual comments (not exceeding 65,535 characters each) as memo fields. Database programs have the advantage that you can save certain 'face-sheet' variables, such as the age and sex of the respondent, along with the verbatim comments. This would enable you to select, say, only those quotes for a particular question from all females over 65.

Some statistical packages, such as SPSS, can also store textual comments. However, many statistical programs limit the length of each comment. For example, with SPSS, quotes can be no more than 255 characters in length.

14.3   CREATION OF THE CODE BOOK

Having created your coding frame and written your coding instructions, you can now create the **code book**. This is best done before you carry out coding of the questionnaires. A code book is a form in which the following information is recorded for each variable:

- Question number and wording.
- Variable name for use by computer programs to refer to the variable (often restricted by the analysis software to eight characters).
- Column location of that variable (usually not necessary for direct data entry to a statistical software package).

● Values that the variable can take and what these values represent.
● Missing value(s).
● Range of valid values.

An example of a code book for a survey questionnaire is shown in Figure 14.11.

While a code book is mandatory with quantitative analysis, it is also good practice to create some form of code book in qualitative research. Here, the code book is important in providing a list of codes generated during **open coding.** The development of such a document is especially important for consistency if you are coding data over an extended period. These codes have several component parts which should be documented in the code book (Neuman, 2000):

1. A one to three word label.
2. A definition.
3. Any qualifications or exceptions.
4. An example.

Code books created during both the qualitative and quantitative coding processes are then used as the guide to the subsequent application of the codes to the data. This means that researchers could work in teams coding data for the same project guided by the code book instructions.

Question/ variable label	Variable name	Column location	Values	Value labels	Missing values	Range of valid values
Identification number	ID	1–3	–	–	–	1–450*
Age	AGE	4–5	–	–	99	18–91
Sex	SEX	6	1	Male	9	1, 2
			2	Female		
Marital status	MARSTAT	7	1	Married	9	1–5
			2	Living as married		
			3	Separated/divorced		
			4	Widowed		
			5	Not married		
			9	No response		
Attitude to nuclear power	ATTNUC	8	1	Strongly agree	9	1–5
			2	Agree		
			3	Neither agree nor disagree		
			4	Disagree		
			5	Strongly disagree		
			9	No response		

* Assuming there are no more than 450 completed questionnaires.

Figure 14.11 *The code book*

14.3.1 Coding the questionnaires

Having created the coding frame, written the coding instructions and created the code book, you are now ready to code the rest of the questionnaires. This means going through each questionnaire and writing on the ID number, if it is not already marked, checking for missed questions, marking the appropriate missing value, and marking the values for each open question.

At this stage, the importance of a pilot survey becomes apparent. Any unanticipated responses to your questionnaire may lead to the reorganisation of the coding frame. For instance, you may find during your pilot that you had not anticipated a frequent response that should be added to the pre-coded answers in the main questionnaire.

14.4 CODING THE DATA USING A COMPUTER

This section outlines how either quantitative or qualitative data can be directly entered into a computer analysis package. With quantitative data, the numeric codes themselves are entered into the software package while with qualitative data, the text file is imported or opened into the package for subsequent coding.

14.4.1 Coding quantitative data using SPSS

As mentioned in the introduction to this chapter, if you have more than about 20 questionnaires in which you asked more than five questions, it makes sense to use a computer to do the analysis. The analysis software that you use will often depend on what is available or within your budget.

There are many statistical programs for analysing survey data. The most popular and widespread is SPSS which is available in several different versions for mainframe and micro computers. There is also a cheap 'student-ware' version that only allows you to use 20 variables and has fewer statistical routines than the full version. The SocInfo Guide to IT Resources (available on the web) has a comprehensive list of software used in the social sciences (see http://www.stir.ac.uk/Departments/HumanSciences/SocInfo/).

Before you can analyse the data they must be transferred on to the computer. As mentioned previously, you have two options:

1. You can enter it yourself directly into the analysis software such as SPSS.
2. You can get a professional data entry service (possibly your computing services department) to enter the data for you into a data file that you can then read into the analysis software.

I am going to describe how you can enter the data yourself directly into one of the most popular statistical analysis software packages (SPSS) and then go on to consider the steps involved in data entry if you use a data entry service.

Whichever software you use, you will need to set up the program to recognise your variables. This usually involves giving a name to each variable, telling the program whether its values are numeric or alphanumeric and stating how many columns it occupies. In SPSS version 10, this preparatory work is carried out in the *Variable View* of the *Data Editor*. Figure 14.12 shows such a window after completing the definition of the five variables seen in Figure 14.11. The words in the *Values* column are called *Value Labels* and are labels that describe the codes that have been assigned to each response. For instance, the labels for the variable Sex are 'Male' for code 1 and 'Female' for code 2. They are added by clicking the appropriate gray square in the *Values* column to see the dialog box in Figure 14.13. Figure 14.14 is the *Missing Values* dialog box that appears when you click in the *Missing* column in Figure 14.12. Since all responses are usually assigned a code, even if the respondent refused to answer or if the question is not applicable, there has to be a way to indicate that you want these codes treated differently. Once a code has been flagged as a *Missing Value*, then that code is ignored in any subsequent analysis. For instance, you may assign the code 99 to all those people who refuse to tell you their age. You do not want this code treated as a valid code, age 99, and need to indicate that 99 is a *Missing Value*. The final column in Figure 14.12, headed

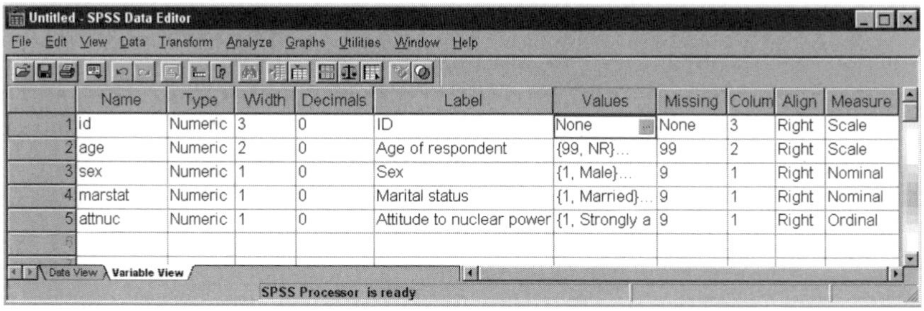

Figure 14.12   *The Variable View in SPSS 10*

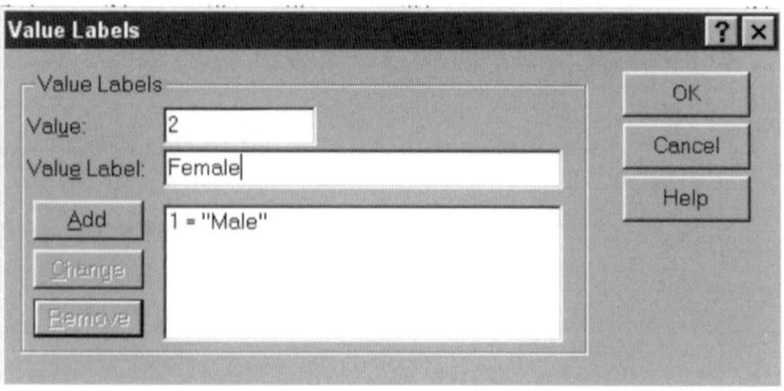

Figure 14.13   *The Value Labels dialog box in SPSS*

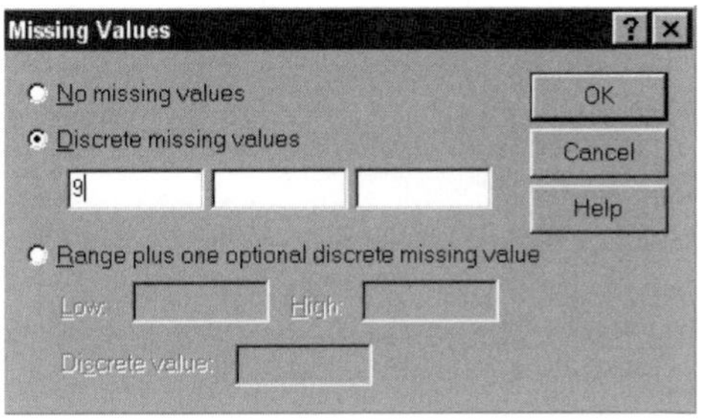

Figure 14.14   *The Missing Values dialog box in SPSS*

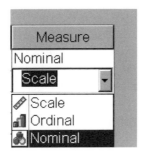

Figure 14.15   *Defining the level of measurement in SPSS*

Measure, is where you indicate the level of measurement of each variable (see Figure 14.15). Note that *Scale* measurement is the same as interval measurement.

Having set up the program with this initial information you can then enter the data by changing to the *Data View* screen. The codes are then entered in each cell of the data matrix. The final appearance of the *Data View* screen is shown in Figure 14.16. An alternative view of your data could be obtained by clicking on *View, Value Labels* (see Figure 14.17).

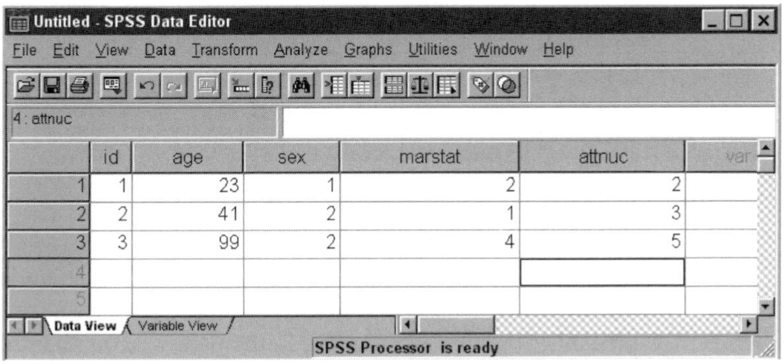

Figure 14.16   *The Data View in SPSS 10*

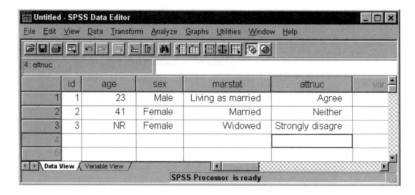

Figure 14.17   *The Data View in SPSS 10 showing Value Labels*

The second data entry route was to use a data entry service to create a data file for you which you then instruct your statistical software to read. You would normally only contemplate this route if you had a large number of questionnaires and a sizable budget. In addition, you would normally have prepared your paper questionnaire with this method of data entry in mind, anticipated the column locations of each variable and marked them on your questionnaires. The easiest way to get SPSS to read this fixed format data file would be to use the Text Import Wizard in SPSS versions 9.0 and above (see Norusis, 1999).

Once all the data is entered, but before serious analysis can begin, you must spend some time checking the data for obvious errors. This process is called data cleaning. The first step of cleaning is obtaining a frequency count for each variable. For instance, this will tell you for the variable Sex, how many men and how many women there are in your sample. The purpose of this frequency listing is to alert you to any 'wild codes' in your data. These are codes that may have been miscoded during the coding operation or have been wrongly entered at the data entry stage. For instance, you might find that there were some respondents coded with the value 3 for Sex. You should check the frequency listing for such inconsistencies and then identify the cases where these problems occur. Then you must return to the questionnaire to check the original coding. The next chapter discusses how to perform frequency analysis on your data.

14.4.2 Coding qualitative data using a computer

As mentioned previously, Strauss (1987) defined three stages of qualitative coding in which the data is reviewed using a different coding process in each of these passes. During the first stage, codes are developed and a code book is created. Applying these codes to the data – in qualitative research, usually text – is greatly facilitated by using Computer Assisted Qualitative Data AnalysiS software (CAQDAS). The way that they can be used for analysing

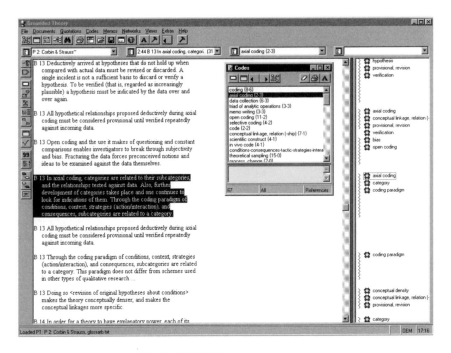

Figure 14.18   *Coding data in ATLAS.ti*

qualitative data is described in Chapter 18. Here, I will show how they are used to code qualitative data.

An example is seen in Figure 14.18 which demonstrates the **open coding** process in the program, ATLAS.ti. Text is imported into the program. Then, segments of text are highlighted by dragging the mouse over a phrase, sentence or paragraph and a pre-defined code is selected to apply to that segment.

The second pass through the data creates the **axial codes**. During axial coding the researcher concentrates on the codes created during the first (open coding) phase. In particular, the relationships between categories and sub-categories are considered, with tentative relationships being examined against data. The researcher looks for categories or codes that cluster together while thinking about such things as the causes or consequences relating to the processes to which the data refers and which may inform the analysis. Other questions the researcher may ask include: Can similar categories be grouped together into a more general category or do some categories need to be subdivided?; Can any categories be arranged into a sequential or time-ordered pattern?

While open coding can be seen as fragmenting the data, axial coding may be conceived of as bringing it back together in a web of relationships. Strauss and Corbin (1990) describe a useful paradigm to bear in mind while axial coding. They describe the questions you ask of the data in order to describe meaningful relationships between your initial open codes. These

Coding paradigm	Description	Example
Causal conditions	Events leading to the development of the phenomena	Breaking a leg
Phenomenon	What the action is about, the central idea	Pain
Context	Specific set of properties pertaining to the phenomenon	The break: • time since accident? • how did it occur? • number of fractures? Pain management: • duration • location • intensity
Intervening conditions	Broad conditions bearing on the action/interaction strategies	Time phenomenon occurred Location phenomenon occurred Age of person Past history of pain
Action/interaction	Action directed at managing, handling, carrying out, responding to phenomenon	Splint the leg Go for help Taking pills
Consequences	Outcomes or results of actions/ interactions	Pain relief

Figure 14.19 *The Paradigm Model (adapted from Strauss and Corbin, 1990)*

questions relate to the nature of the specific phenomenon, the conditions that relate to it, the strategy the people involved used to handle the phenomenon and any consequences of these strategies in relation to the phenomenon. This 'Paradigm Model' is outlined in Figure 14.19 and is illustrated by their example of someone breaking a leg and the subsequent process of pain management. Thus, while the central idea and research topic is concerned with pain, this open code in the data is linked to the code 'breaking a leg' through a causal or antecedent condition relationship. These codes are set in context and ultimately related to the strategies used to deal with the phenomenon and the consequences of such strategies. It is often an aid to conceptualisation if the researcher considers whether these relationships can be represented by a map or network view of the analysis. Figure 14.20 shows such a network view in the ATLAS.ti software. The example used, created by the developer of the software, is based on the Paradigm Model developed by Strauss and Corbin, once again illustrated by the pain example used above.

The final pass through the data occurs after the text has been coded and main themes and concepts have emerged from the text. This final coding phase, referred to by Strauss (1987) as **selective coding**, involves the researcher scanning both the codes and the data and then selecting cases to illustrate major themes uncovered during axial and open coding. This phase provides the researcher with quotable material for her or his final report.

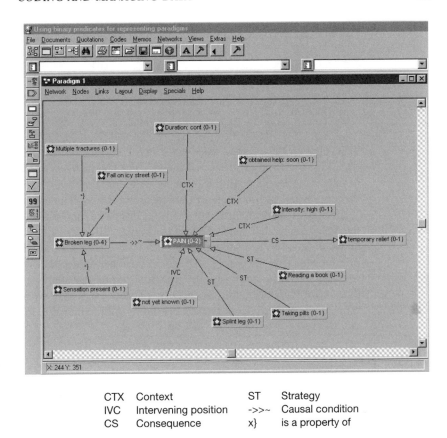

CTX	Context	ST	Strategy
IVC	Intervening position	->>~	Causal condition
CS	Consequence	x}	is a property of

Figure 14.20 *The Network view in ATLAS.ti showing relationships between open codes*

Finally, I will mention another important activity that researchers may carry out while coding data. **Analytic memos** are notes the researcher writes to him or herself about the coding phase. Their purpose is to help to develop new themes and to facilitate elaboration of the coding scheme. They show the development of thinking during any phase of the coding and analysis work and, in effect, provide an **audit trail** of the whole coding exercise. Many CAQDAS packages provide for the addition of memos to segments of text.

Although the methods used in quantitative surveys and qualitative field-work are often seen as fundamentally different, there are many areas of overlap, especially, as we have seen, in the process of coding. Of course, although the process of coding may be similar, the objectives of coding are different. With a quantitative survey, we try to allocate a value to each category which can then be manipulated statistically, even if only by a simple frequency count. However, categories obtained from interviews and fieldnotes are not normally allocated values but maintain their contextual position. Co-occurrences of categories are explored and themes are elicited. Chapter 18 reviews software specifically designed for the analysis of such data.

14.5 CONCLUSIONS

This chapter has shown the steps involved in coding data from survey questionnaires and unstructured interviews. The methods used for both types of data collection are similar in many ways and emphasis has been placed on the similarities at this stage of the research process. The differences between 'quantitative' and 'qualitative' methods are more marked in the treatment of the resulting coded data. The next chapter discusses in detail how to go about the analysis of quantitative data. The analysis of qualitative data has often been seen as being dependent on the approach of the individual researcher and is certainly not as formalised as the analysis of quantitative data. However, with the emergence of new computer software, even the process of qualitative analysis is becoming more amenable to formalisation.

14.6 PROJECT

You have been asked to investigate people's beliefs in the paranormal through administering a questionnaire in the street to the general public. From such a study you can begin to investigate people's understanding of scientific knowledge.

Decide whether you are going to administer a survey questionnaire or carry out a structured interview. Design your interview schedule or your interviewer-administered questionnaire to include the following questions. Try to pre-code the questions where possible and mark your questionnaire with response codes and column numbers in order to simplify data entry:

1. What kinds of thing come to mind when you think of the para-normal?
    This is an open question to which people may offer more than one answer. Allow several lines on the questionnaire in which to write the answers.

2. Do you think that any of the following are true?:
    (a) It is possible to make someone turn round just by looking at them.
    (b) Prayers can sometimes be answered.
    (c) It is possible to know what someone else is thinking or feeling even if they are hundreds of miles away and out of touch by ordinary means.
    (d) Some houses are haunted.

(e) The Earth has been visited by beings from outer space.
(f) Dreams can sometimes foretell the future.
(g) Some people can remember past lives (i.e. reincarnations they may have lived).
(h) It is possible to get messages from the dead.
You should expect people to respond with either a positive or negative answer, although it is likely that there will also need to be a 'Don't know' category.

3. Are you a religious person?
Decide whether to use a yes/no answer or an ordinal scale with responses ranging from very religious to not at all religious.

4. Age.
Decide whether to use age ranges or to ask people their actual age.

5. Sex.

6. Social class.

7. Ethnic group.

Remember to include columns for an identification number.

After designing your questionnaire, select a small sample to interview and administer it to them. Create a code book and then code the open question. Finally, you could create the data file.

14.7 FURTHER READING

For a discussion of coding survey questionnaires, Silvey (1975) is an early but comprehensive text. For a brief overview of using SPSS in statistics, see Chapter 2 in Fielding and Gilbert (2000). Chapter 3 includes a discussion about collecting and coding data for computer analysis.

Coding qualitative data is covered by Strauss and Corbin (1990), Pfaffenberger (1988) and Neuman (2000). Computer analysis and qualitative research is discussed by Fielding and Lee (1998). For a discussion about the classification of social class, see Rose (1995).

ANALYSING SURVEY DATA

15

MIKE PROCTER

Statistical analysis is seen as one of the more frightening and mysterious (some would even say 'mystifying') stages of the survey research process. This reputation is unfair to the other stages. At least as much intellectual effort is needed to conceptualise the problem, to design the sample, and to devise the interview schedule, not to mention the often enjoyable but always demanding task of writing the final report. Perhaps the reason for the special status of data analysis is that you *know* when you don't understand the technical details.

To try to take some of the fear away, this chapter goes through a small-scale example of a real-life analysis. 'Real-life' means real data, which in turn means more than you could hope to deal with equipped only with a pencil and paper and a calculator. It isn't sensible to try to analyse a survey of a reasonable size except with a computer and a suitable program. The most commonly used computer software for survey analysis is SPSS (see Chapter 14).

You can run SPSS on two main kinds of small computer: PCs running Windows and Apple Macintoshes. (You can run it on a UNIX workstation, or on a mainframe, too.) An minimal computer of this kind from a reputable mail order supplier costs as little as £500, though the SPSS software itself could cost a great deal more. However, most academic institutions in the UK, and in many other countries, subscribe to a *site licence* which allows them to distribute SPSS at very little cost to staff and students.

15.1 PROGRAMS FOR MANIPULATING DATA

A program like SPSS (comparable products include SAS, Minitab, P-Stat, Stata and BMD-P) has two main components: the statistical routines, which do the numerical calculations that produce tabulations and summary measures of various kinds, and the data management facilities. Perhaps surprisingly, it was the latter that really revolutionised quantitative social research. This is best clarified by a few examples.

Age is usually measured by asking respondents their date of birth because this is harder to misremember. Then 'age last birthday' is calculated from date of birth and the date of the interview using a special formula. This converts each date into the number of days since 15 October 1582 (the first day of the Gregorian calendar), and the difference is converted back into whole years. So far so good; but for many purposes you may want to use broader categories of age than whole years, for example the two categories 'up to 39' versus '40 or over'. All these manipulations count as simple kinds of data management.

The General Household Survey (GHS) is an annual survey carried out by a UK government agency, the Office of Population Censuses and Surveys (OPCS). The basic unit of analysis is the household: roughly, a group of people who live together and share catering arrangements. Variables that describe the household include the kind of housing tenure (private rented, public rented, owner-occupied, etc.) and whether it has central heating. Information is gathered about each individual in the household, too: his or her age, sex, health record, smoking habits, etc. Chapter 16 describes the GHS in more detail.

Looking at the relationship between central heating and housing tenure is fairly straightforward (presumably we would find that owner-occupiers are more likely to have the benefit of this feature than are public sector housing tenants) because both measures are household-level characteristics. It is just as easy to see whether smokers have more respiratory disease than non-smokers – this time both measures apply to individuals. But determining whether central heating is good for your lungs involves looking simultaneously at variables from different levels of analysis, household and individual. This would be done by copying the information about central heating down from the household to all its individual members. Even more complicated, the question whether you can suffer from the smoking of other people in the household involves first carrying each household member's smoking up to the household level and aggregating it, and then transferring household smoking back down to the individual and relating it to his or her health. All of this would be extremely difficult to do without the right kind of data management tools.

Having pointed out the importance of data management, there simply isn't space to say anything more about it here. You can start to acquire the necessary skills by reading Norusis (2000) or a corresponding guide to another data management program.

15.2 AN ANALYSIS

15.2.1 Frequency distributions

The first stage in the analysis of a new data set is almost always to get the 'marginal frequency distributions'. The origin of this term will be explained later; all that it means is that we count the number of respondents who answer each question in each of the possible ways. Actually, this isn't quite accurate: as Chapter 14 explains, sometimes answers will be processed before they are entered into the computer – for instance, a verbatim answer to a question about your job will be coded into one of a number of occupational categories – and it is the coded categories rather than the verbatim responses that will be tabulated.

Here, interspersed with a lot of commentary, are some printouts from SPSS, showing the frequency distributions for three variables. Other programs will produce similar tables. The data I have analysed is based on an American survey, the General Social Survey (GSS) carried out every year by the National Opinion Research Center (NORC).

The information reported in Figure 15.1 came from a sequence of four questions that asked the respondents whether they had graduated from high

RS HIGHEST DEGREE

		Frequency	Percent	Valid Percent	Cumulative Percent
Valid	0 LT HIGH SCHOOL	1072	35.0	35.2	35.2
	1 HIGH SCHOOL	1482	48.4	48.6	83.8
	2 JUNIOR COLLEGE	68	2.2	2.2	86.0
	3 BACHELOR	278	9.1	9.1	95.1
	4 GRADUATE	148	4.8	4.9	100.0
	Total	3048	99.6	100.0	
Missing	8 DK	4	.1		
	9 NA	8	.3		
	Total	12	.4		
Total		3060	100.0		

Figure 15.1 *Marginal frequency distribution for* DEGREE

school and, if so, what higher qualifications they had. The highest qualification mentioned was then coded, so that, for instance, someone with a first degree and a Master's would be put only in category 4. The original researchers have chosen to call this variable DEGREE, so that subsequent analysts will have a reasonable chance of remembering the name without having constantly to look it up in a manual. The other labels have been assigned in the same way: the program uses all of this information without 'knowing' what any of it means.

We can read from the figure that the value '0' occurs with a frequency of 1,072: these are all the people who didn't graduate from high school. (LT here means 'less than'.) A rather larger number, 1,482, did graduate from high school but got no further, and so on. Each of the 'Percent' figures is the corresponding 'Frequency' divided by the total, 3,060. Notice that twelve respondents are coded as 8, DK (don't know) and 9, NA (not applicable), which are grouped as missing. Data can be missing for a variety of reasons, and specific numerical codes are set aside to mark it (see section 14.1.2); then the program is told that cases with those values are not normally to be included in numerical calculations. For instance, the code for a missing income figure will not be used in the calculation of the average income. In the present example the total for percentaging should not include individuals for whom no data is available: hence the column headed 'Valid Percent', which is based on 3,048 not 3,060. Of course, it makes very little difference to the calculations here, but if there were more missing data it would be a different story.

Finally, the 'Cumulative Percent' (short for Cumulative Percentage) column gives partial sums of the previous one: $35.2 + 48.6 = 83.8, + 2.2 = 86.0$, and so on down the column. Thus we can see immediately that 95.1 per cent have a qualification up to and including a first degree. For this cumulation to make sense, the order of the categories must be meaningful: DEGREE is an example of an **ordinal scale** variable (see Chapter 14).

Marital status (see Figure 15.2), on the other hand, is said to be measured at the **nominal scale**, because there is no intrinsic order: it would be hard to argue that 'widowed' is intermediate between 'married' and 'divorced', for instance. Here the cumulative percentages are not meaningful, although SPSS calculates them regardless.

MARITAL STATUS

		Frequency	Percent	Valid Percent	Cumulative Percent
Valid	1 MARRIED	1950	63.7	63.7	63.7
	2 WIDOWED	330	10.8	10.8	74.5
	3 DIVORCED	206	6.7	6.7	81.2
	4 SEPARATED	124	4.1	4.1	85.3
	5 NEVER MARRIED	450	14.7	14.7	100.0
	Total	3060	100.0	100.0	

Figure 15.2 *Marginal frequency distribution of MARITAL STATUS*

Age has not only a meaningful order (from youngest to oldest or vice versa) but equal scale intervals: (as Gertrude Stein might have said) a year is a year is a year, and the difference between 27 and 28 is numerically identical to that between 33 and 34. This is not true of DEGREE: despite the numerical values (chosen for convenience) there is no reason to suppose that the difference between junior college and high school is in any sense equivalent to the difference between a doctorate and a bachelor's degree. AGE is referred to as an **interval scale** variable.

Age is also a **continuous** variable, whereas the others examined here have discrete categories. Age as recorded does in fact have a limited number of categories, since we content ourselves with 'age last birthday', but even this has so many categories that the form of frequency distribution table presented so far is rather cumbersome. As a special option SPSS displays a histogram, in which the almost continuous variable is split into a number of convenient groupings, and the relative frequency is represented by the length of a bar (see Figure 15.3). The class midpoint of 25, say, represents ages of 23, 24, 25, 26 and 27. Altogether this figure looks like one half of a population pyramid.

There are two main reasons for 'getting the marginals'. As mentioned in section 14.4, the first is to look for errors in the data. The second is that this is generally the best way of keeping tabs on the state of the data set, which necessarily gets modified during the process of analysis. This becomes especially necessary as research in general and data analysis in particular become cooperative enterprises: the costs of the fieldwork phase of a survey are so great that it makes sense to get the resulting data thoroughly analysed,

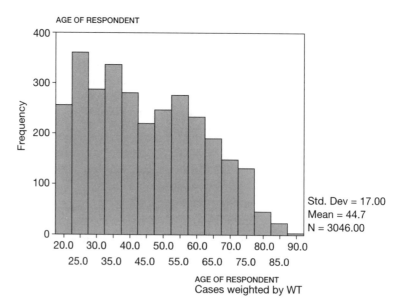

Figure 15.3 *Frequency distribution of* AGE

often by a whole team of social scientists. As was explained earlier, practically every data set will go through repeated modifications as the analysts conceptualise new variables and new analytical frameworks. Of course, it is essential that these modifications be carefully documented, especially if a derived variable is to be used by workers other than the one who has created it. One way to do this is to keep a logbook (either a physical volume or else in the form of a text file on the computer system being used). But in addition, it makes sense to generate a frequency table for every new variable and add it to the set you will have made at the beginning of the analysis process. Some programs will produce an alphabetical index to the marginals, and this makes it worthwhile from time to time to generate a complete new indexed set. Another useful feature is the ability to store general textual information in the data file itself, which can then serve as the logbook.

Finally, the most obvious reason to get a frequency distribution is because it gives you your first look at a new variable. It may be that the focus of your analysis is on the differences in health between smokers and non-smokers, but in your preliminary analysis you will certainly want to know simply what proportion of your sample smoke, and what proportion smoke less than ten a day, between ten and nineteen, and so on.

15.2.2 Cross-tabulation

The real analysis starts when you examine variables, not one at a time, but in pairs or more complex combinations. The point of this is to look at the relationship between variables, usually in order to explain differences on one variable in terms of differences on the other. As a simple example, if we find that workers with different jobs tend to have different health records, whereas workers with the same job are similar in their health, then we might say that differences in occupation at least partly explain differences in health or, more concisely, that occupation explains health. 'Explains' is here being used rather differently than in everyday language: it refers to a statistical relationship that may or may not lead to increased understanding.

What follows is the record of a run using SPSS. I make no attempt to define systematically what this requires; luckily, it is not difficult to acquire a reading knowledge of SPSS, so you should be able to follow what is going on. The main thing to understand is that the researcher types in commands that look like a version of English, and the program displays the results on the computer's screen or on a printer. The method of use and the output from other programs will differ, but the general principles of analysis are the same.

Most readers will be more accustomed to controlling a program by a point and click sequence – now practically universal in Windows applications, including SPSS. However, SPSS was originally written 30 years or so ago, and its internal architecture reflects this. This means that pointing and clicking actually generates a sequence of English-like instructions for the program to parse and obey. These instructions are displayed in the output window, and can be stored for later modification and recycling. Though most users never really notice the command language, the old-fashioned way of working can have certain advantages, one of which is that the logic of the procedure is easier to explain in a teaching situation like this chapter.

The question I have chosen to explore is: 'To what extent is a man's occupation determined by his father's?' This is perhaps one of the central questions in the study of social mobility. A legitimate preliminary question is: 'Why only men?' The simple answer is 'because our society is patriarchal, and the patriarchy pervades sociology just as it does other spheres of life, so that this survey doesn't ask about the respondent's mother's work'.

The first command to SPSS is to fetch the General Social Survey: thus

```
get file 'gss'.
```

A small subset of the data is provided as an example data set with the SPSS program, but I have chosen variables from the full list. In creating an SPSS-readable file, NORC provided standard variable names, and the two principal variables I used are called **occ** and **paocc16**. The first of these is formed by asking an elaborate series of questions designed to find out exactly what job the respondent does (or did, if they are retired), and then classifying every employed person into one of nearly 1,000 occupational categories defined by the US Bureau of the Census. The second is formed in the same way, except that the questions are asked about the respondent's father 'while you were growing up'; the mnemonic name suggests that this means 'when you were about sixteen'.

Social mobility usually means occupational mobility, which in turn means roughly 'having a job of a different status than your father'. A number of different status rankings have been suggested, but the simplest possible one, which I adopt here, simply differentiates between non-manual and manual occupations. Census codes 1 to 399 are non-manual occupations; 400 to 995 are manual. So in order to restrict the analysis to men (the variable **sex** is here coded 1, male and 2, female) and then divide the occupation variables into two groups, I typed in

```
select if (sex = 1).
recode occ, paocc16
  (0 thru 399 = 1)
  (400 thru 995 = 2)
into occ2 paocc162.
```

The mnemonic names used in SPSS are chosen arbitrarily – you could call the new variables **nigel** and **jane** if you wanted to. However, it is good practice to use meaningful names, and since the new variables are two-category versions of the old ones, I chose to simply add a '2' to the end of the name.

SPSS will print helpful labels on output tables, provided it 'knows' what labels to print. So I gave the program the necessary information by typing in

```
value labels occ2 paocc162
  1 'non-manual'
  2 'manual'.
```

Finally, I typed in the instruction that would actually generate the table of results:

```
crosstabs tables = occ2 by paocc162
  /cells = count, column.
```

The first line specifies the variables to be used in forming the table. The only thing that needs attention is the order of declaring the variables. The customary procedure is to ask if we can establish a causal order between the variables. Here it is straightforward: a father's job can influence his son's, but not vice versa (except, no doubt, in a few eccentric cases where, for instance, junior becomes a tennis star or rock singer and takes on Dad as manager). This being so, **occ2**, which is dependent on **paocc162**, is called the dependent variable, while **paocc162** is referred to as the independent variable. Then the order is conventionally **dependent** by **independent**, which SPSS interprets as instructions to lay out the table as it appears in Figure 15.4, that is, with the dependent variable as the rows and the independent as the columns. The second line, beginning with the '/' symbol (called 'slash' by computer users) is a subcommand: what it does will be explained in a moment.

Figure 15.4 is a typical cross-tabulation as produced by SPSS. To understand the table we must first name the parts. The total number of 'cases' (in this context, people) on which the table is based is printed at the bottom right: it's 1,210. Above this are the numbers in each of the categories of the variable that defines the rows of the table: there are 768 respondents with manual occupations and 442 with non-manual jobs. The relative numbers are given, too, in the form of percentages: 63.5% of respondents are manual workers. The column totals give the corresponding numbers for the respondents' fathers.

The first substantial point to notice is that the respondents (442) are more likely to be in a non-manual occupation than their fathers were (306). This is

OCC2 * PAOCC162 Crosstabulation

			PAOCC162 1.00 non-manual	2.00 manual	Total
OCC2	1.00 non-manual	Count	194	248	442
		% within PAOCC162	63.4%	27.4%	36.5%
	2.00 manual	Count	112	656	768
		% within PAOCC162	36.6%	72.6%	63.5%
Total		Count	306	904	1210
		% within PAOCC162	100.0%	100.0%	100.0%

Figure 15.4 *Respondent's occupation by father's occupation*

an example of **structural mobility**: the occupational structure has changed, so necessarily some sons must be in a different occupational group from their fathers. However, this could have been discovered by examining the simple frequency distributions, without arranging them in this sort of table. Here we see why those simple distributions are called marginals: they appear in the margins of a cross-tabulation.

The special interest of a table of this sort comes when we examine the conditional distributions: the distributions of one variable under particular conditions of the other. Here, we are interested in the distribution of respondents' occupations under different conditions of the fathers' occupations. The findings are clearest in terms of the percentages. Specifically, among the 306 respondents whose fathers had non-manual jobs, 112, or 36.6%, were in manual occupations and therefore the remainder, 63.4%, were in non-manual jobs. On the other hand, if the father was in a manual job there was a 72.6% chance that the respondent would be a manual worker, too, and only a 27.4% chance that he would be in a non-manual job.

The subcommand /**cells count, column** can now be explained: it means 'each cell is to contain a count of the number of respondents with that combination of characteristics, together with that number expressed as a percentage of the column total'.

This is already quite a lot to take in, so we can concentrate on just two numbers: for manual fathers 72.6% of their sons were in manual jobs; for non-manual fathers it was 36.6%. An even simpler summary might be: the chance of being in a manual job was 36% (i.e. 72.6 − 36.6) greater for sons of manual workers. Notice that it does not matter which row you choose: 63.4 − 27.4 = 36, just as before. In bigger tables (with more rows and columns) it's impossible to summarise the findings quite so simply, but in a 2 × 2 (two rows and two columns) table the standard procedure can be summed up as follows:

1. If possible, decide on the causal ordering of your variables.
2. Then tell your data analysis program to produce a table of the dependent variable against the independent variable.
3. Ask for column percentages.
4. Compare a pair of percentages in the same row.

More concisely, percentage down and compare across.

15.2.3 Interpreting the figures

What do these figures really mean? Simply that your father's occupation seems to have a substantial influence on your own, at least if you are an American man. One other reservation is necessary: we have only sample data, but we want to be able to make statements about the population as a whole. The justification for doing this – the general idea is called statistical inference – is a complicated one, and cannot be dealt with in less than a whole book, although some of the issues are introduced in section 15.5 and some suggestions for further reading are given at the end of this chapter. I will just say that it can be proved that, *provided we really have got a random sample*, our best guess for any percentage in the population is the corresponding sample percentage: in the USA as a whole, as in the table in Figure 15.4, about 63.5% of all men will be in manual jobs. Why 'about'? Because if we took another sample just as carefully we wouldn't be surprised to find a slightly different set of numbers, simply because of random sampling variability. The obvious consequence of this is that we shouldn't draw strong conclusions from small differences based on small samples. Here, though, we have a reasonably large sample (the public opinion polls whose results are discussed with such interest by politicians are typically based on a thousand interviews or so), and the difference is very large, so common sense suggests that the influence must be real, even if not necessarily of precisely the magnitude that we have found.

What about 'provided we really have got a random sample'? Almost certainly we haven't. NORC designs its sampling procedure to produce a random sample, but a problem with all survey research is non-response: people who were included in the sample design but not actually interviewed because they were never at home when the interviewer called, or because they thought the details of their life were no business of the survey organisation's (see section 5.8). These non-respondents are almost bound to be different in interesting but often unknowable ways from those who did take part. At best, then, we have a random sample of those adult male Americans who aren't always out and who aren't hostile to pollsters. This must introduce some distortion into the results, which is another reason for caution, and which is potentially more dangerous than the intrinsic sample-to-sample variability that the theory of statistical inference is all about.

I am in danger of being excessively pessimistic about survey methods. Half a century or more of experience by thousands of researchers suggest that we get more useful results than we are perhaps entitled to expect. So from now on, I shall interpret the results still to be presented without constantly worrying about what may have gone wrong.

15.2.4 Correlation and causation

Let me consider another interesting question. To what extent are we justified in making causal statements, such as that one's occupational status is influenced by one's father's, on the basis of statistical findings alone? The simple answer is that we aren't. For instance, there is no statistical reason why we should not consider **paocc162** as the dependent variable and **occ2** as the independent. The reason I haven't done this so far is that there is a good non-statistical reason against it: a father's occupation 'happens' before his son's, and it is universally accepted that (in this explanatory paradigm) an effect cannot precede its cause. So although **occ2** cannot (except exceptionally) influence **paocc162**, **paocc162** can influence **occ2**. 'Can', not 'must'. Another possibility is that both may be influenced by a third variable.

My favourite example of this is the discovery of a marked correlation between the price of rum in Barbados and the level of Methodist ministers' salaries: in any given year either both are high or both are low. There are two simple explanations of this, according to what you think the causal direction is. One says that ministers have a (secret) addiction to rum; when they get a pay rise they can afford to buy more liquor, and the price goes up in response to the increased demand, as can be predicted from elementary economics. The alternative version is even more conspiratorial: the Methodist Church is secretly financed by the distillers of rum (I haven't been able to work out why), and when the distillers' finances improve they can afford to give a bigger subvention.

You shouldn't read on without trying to find a more sensible explanation in terms of a third variable which could reasonably be expected to influence both salaries and rum prices. Yes, it's general price levels, or the result of inflation. Over time the value of money falls, so both the price of rum and ministers' salaries have to rise to compensate. Here general price level is referred to as the **antecedent** variable that accounts for the primary relationship between the price of rum and salary.

In other circumstances it's useful to introduce a third variable, not in order to explain away the primary relationship, but in order to explain how it works. This is what I shall do with the occupational mobility table. It would be quite legitimate to look for an antecedent variable, but I prefer for present purposes to think about an **intervening** variable. This time we start by assuming for the time being that a father's occupation really does influence the son's, and ask how it exerts that influence. The two possible general answers are, first, that the influence is direct (a nepotistic mechanism) or, second, that some third variable acts as a causal link.

Of course, nepotism does operate to some extent. A large proportion of 'company directors' get their start from Dad's position. The best way to get to be a farmer, or a doctor, or even a docker may still be to arrange to be born to a father in the same line of work. But these are special cases, which cover only a relatively small number of workers. So it may make more sense instead to look for a third factor which is influenced by a father's occupation and in turn influences the son's. An obvious candidate is education. A father in a higher status job is likely to improve his son's educational chances in a number of ways: by paying for private schooling, or by moving house to a good school district, or just by knowing the ropes and pushing hard. And, of course, on the whole, the better the son's education the higher the status of his eventual job. Figure 15.5 represents the causal model implied by this.

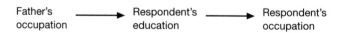

Figure 15.5 *Causal model to explain occupational mobility*

In an ideal world (ideal from the point of view of a power-crazy social scientist, that is) we would set up a randomised controlled trial to check this idea. A cohort of children would be assigned to schools at random, so that the causal flow would be interrupted: father's occupation would no longer influence education, so that this path would no longer be available for transmitting an effect from father's job to son's job. If this were indeed the only path through which father's occupation influenced son's, then the apparent effect of **paocc162** on **occ2** would disappear; if other paths were operating then the effect would persist.

Alas, such a research design is hardly practicable. However, we can simulate at least part of what it implies. Instead of artificially assigning children to schools at random, we can examine sub-groups in which there is *naturally* no variation in schooling. If there is no variation then, necessarily, there can be no co-variation, so the causal flow is interrupted. Then, if we find that within these sub-groups there is a reduced relationship (or even none at all) between father's and son's occupation, we can conclude that the relationship was at least partly a result of the path via differences in education.

To do this with existing survey data we tell SPSS to repeat the original tabulation within all education level groups – those who had one year of schooling separated from those with two years, three years, etc. (This seems to assume that everyone completes a whole number of years at school, which is no doubt not true, but the inaccuracy seems unlikely to be of crucial importance.) With any practicable sample size this will not quite work, because the sample will have to be divided across too many sub-groups, so we compromise by using broader education categories. In my example I compromise by using only three categories and, since this is US data, I divide my men into those who had at least some college education, those who have a high school diploma but no more, and those who didn't graduate from high school. Where to make that split will depend on what the investigator knows of important thresholds in the local education system.

First, then, I had to create my education variable. You have already seen the distribution of the variable, DEGREE (Figure 15.1). The three highest categories contained quite small numbers of men, so I decided to group them into a single one. The following SPSS commands did the grouping, labelled the variable, and requested the necessary tables:

```
recode degree
  (0 = 0)
  (1 = 1)
  (2 thru 4 = 2)
  into degree2.
value labels degree2
  0 '< high school'
  1 'high school'
  2 'college'.
crosstabs tables occ2 by paocc162 by degree2
  /cells = count column.
```

OCC2 * PAOCC162 * DEGREE2 Crosstabulation

DEGREE2				PAOCC162 1.00 non-manual	2.00 manual	Total
.00 < high school	OCC2	1.00 non-manual	Count	10	40	50
			% within PAOCC162	23.8%	10.7%	12.0%
		2.00 manual	Count	32	334	366
			% within PAOCC162	76.2%	89.3%	88.0%
	Total		Count	42	374	416
			% within PAOCC162	100.0%	100.0%	100.0%
1.00 high school	OCC2	1.00 non-manual	Count	64	104	168
			% within PAOCC162	50.0%	25.9%	31.7%
		2.00 manual	Count	64	298	362
			% within PAOCC162	50.0%	74.1%	68.3%
	Total		Count	128	402	530
			% within PAOCC162	100.0%	100.0%	100.0%
2.00 college	OCC2	1.00 non-manual	Count	120	104	224
			% within PAOCC162	88.2%	83.9%	86.2%
		2.00 manual	Count	16	20	36
			% within PAOCC162	11.8%	16.1%	13.8%
	Total		Count	136	124	260
			% within PAOCC162	100.0%	100.0%	100.0%

Figure 15.6   *Respondent's occupation by father's occupation controlling for education*

The 'crosstabs' command produces an **occ2** by **paocc162** table for every category of **degree**: three separate tables in each of which education is 'held constant'. It may help to think of this as a three-dimensional table: a stack of two-dimensional tables, in which the stacking axis is the third variable. What you actually get is Figure 15.6.

What are we to make of this? First, note a caveat: some of these conditional tables are rather short of cases, especially in certain sub-groups. In particular, there are only 42 non-manual fathers in the table of non-high-school graduates. This really means that we should be quite cautious about drawing firm conclusions. Having made this point, I shall put it on one side.

Next, some further points of terminology. The variable **degree2** is called the **control variable**, and we are investigating the relationship between occupation and father's occupation **controlling** for education. You will recall that the distribution of **occ2** on its own is called the marginal distribution, while the distributions of **occ2** within categories of **paocc162** are called the conditional distributions. By analogy, the original **occ2** by **paocc162** table is called a **marginal** table, and the three new tables are called **conditional** tables: they show the relationship between **occ2** and **paocc162** under specific conditions of **degree2**. Similarly, we sometimes speak of marginal and conditional relationships; and the process of **elaborating** a table, as it is classically called, consists in essence of comparing a marginal relationship with its conditional counterparts. Sometimes the several conditional associations are summarised into a single

partial association; in practice this is done by calculations based on the **correlation coefficients**, see section 7.2.1 (rather than by working on the conditional tables).

The marginal association here can best be summarised by the percentage difference already established: 36.6. In the marginal table it really didn't matter (apart, perhaps, from convenience in the wording of the verbal description of the findings) which row we chose to make the comparison. Now, however, it is important that we be consistent with that earlier decision: since we used the second row of the table and subtracted the first column from the second we must treat each conditional table in the same way; otherwise we might not notice if the sign of the difference (positive or negative) changes between marginal and conditional tables. In practice this will seldom happen, but it would not do to miss it.

So we find the same percentage difference in each conditional table, and get respectively

$$89.3 - 76.2 = 13.1$$
$$74.1 - 50.0 = 24.1$$
$$16.1 - 11.8 = \ \ 4.3.$$

The sign does, in fact, remain positive, so in every conditional table there is still a tendency for manual fathers to have manual sons. However, in every case the conditional association is weaker than the marginal 36.6. So the overall conclusion is that when education is held constant the relationship between father's and son's occupations is substantially weaker. A plausible causal interpretation is that, if non-manual fathers were not able to get a better education for their sons, there would be greater inter-generational mobility. But beware: there may be other variables involved whose inclusion in the analysis would lead to a quite different conclusion. For instance, IQ is quite highly correlated with education, and it is consistent with the results obtained here (though we have no direct evidence whatsoever) that non-manual fathers tend to have genetically brighter sons, who get better education through meritocratic selection rather than through father's efforts. (For an attempt to throw some light on this question, see Jencks (1973).)

Of course, almost as obvious as the difference between marginal and conditional associations is the variation *among* conditional associations, a phenomenon known in the traditional literature as **specification**, because education specifies the conditions that determine whether and to what extent the primary relationship holds. (In more recent literature, the term **interaction** is used in exactly the same sense.) In the present example, the association remains quite strong among those who have just graduated from high school (the second conditional table), but is considerably weaker in the other two, especially among those who have some college education. My interpretation of this would be along the following lines:

● Without a high school diploma, having a non-manual father doesn't help very much.

- Once you have a college education, a manual father is no longer an important handicap.
- If you are in the middle band of education, your father's occupation can have more influence.

It has to be recognised that all this is at best true only in terms of the rather crude educational and occupational classifications that I have used. These have been to an extent necessitated by the rate at which multidimensional tables can generate cells if they have too many categories per variable, but a measure of education which fails to take account of the *quality*, both real and perceived, of the school is hard to justify as a basis for 'holding constant'. Probably, if a better measure of education were available, the conditional associations would be even weaker – but the opposite is possible.

The problem of too many cells can sometimes be solved by using a different statistical method (multiple regression, for instance). The problem of measurement demands a constant alertness on the part of the researcher, so that measures can be developed that more closely approximate the often carefully explicated theoretical constructs. But the basic logic of causal analysis remains the same, however technically advanced the methods used to implement it.

15.3 A GENERAL APPROACH TO SURVEY ANALYSIS

In the words of Poul Anderson, the science fiction writer, 'there is no situation, however complex, which on careful examination does not become more complex'. The main application of this idea to the analysis of survey data is that the world is multivariate: every effect has not one but several causes. So to find a relationship between two variables is not the end but little more than the beginning of the analysis. It is the researcher's job to be sceptical about the causal interpretation that might be made from such a relationship, to think carefully, in a theoretically sensitive way, about what 'nuisance factors' might be involved in the system of variables, and to find ways of testing alternative explanatory hypotheses. The approach exemplified in this chapter has a long and distinguished history, and incorporates the logical principles – in particular the idea of holding constant the suspected nuisance factors – which underlie more statistically advanced methods, such as multiple regression and log-linear analysis.

15.4 STATISTICAL INFERENCE

Traditionally statistics textbooks are divided into two sections: **descriptive** and **inferential**: descriptive statistics is about the best way to describe or summarise the data on your desk; inferential methods explicitly recognise that the data on your desk are a finite **sample** (assumed to be representative) of a **universe** that the analyst is really interested in. The universe is often referred to as a **population**, whether or not it actually consists of everyone living in a particular country or other location.

You may remember that modes of reasoning are often divided into **deductive** and **inductive** argument. Deduction goes from the general to the particular (all men are mortal; Socrates was a man; therefore Socrates was mortal). Induction goes from the particular to the general (on every occasion (though only a finite number of occasions) that I (Isaac Newton) have observed an apple released in mid air, it has fallen to earth; from which I derive the Law of Universal Gravitation). You will see that statistical inference uses inductive reasoning.

Now statistical inference is in turn divided into two categories: **estimation** and **hypothesis testing**. To see the difference between, albeit in caricature, consider the work of a psephologist. In analysing a 'voting intentions' survey, she examines the responses to the simple question, if there were a general election tomorrow, would you vote for the Bigendian candidate (Swift, 1726) or for the Littlendian? She concentrates on the difference between the two percentages, $d = b - l$; where b is the percentage intending to vote Bigendian, etc. The difference could be negative if there is a majority for the Littlendians.

Estimation starts from the position that the psephologist has no idea what to expect, and wants to report the most likely result in the population, using only the sample difference. In fact the best **point estimate** in most situations is found by simply using the sample value to represent the population equivalent – the sample difference in percentages is the best estimate of the population difference. Best, but not perfect: almost certainly the sample difference will stray from the true population value, just because of sampling processes. So her next step will be to calculate an **interval estimate**: the range within which the true value is likely to fall, given the sample value. 'Likely' is usually taken to mean '95 per cent of the time'. In pre-election polling the point estimate is usually declared to have a margin of error of 5 or 6 per cent.

Hypothesis testing approaches the problem rather differently. Now the analyst has an advance expectation about the result, based on theory, or perhaps on last year's result. Often, for no very good reason, this expectation, or **hypothesis**, would be that the two parties get the same support, so that $d = 0$. Of course, even if it is exactly 0 in the population, it's unlikely to be exactly that in this sample. The statistician's job now is to decide whether the observed result could plausibly have been found if the hypothesis is true, or whether it casts too much doubt on the hypothesis for a rational person to continue to believe it. The scientist often sees her job as trying to reject the hypothesis – rather like Popper's ideas of falsification, though, many would argue, different in subtle but crucial ways (see Chapter 2).

15.5 PROJECT

If you have access to a computer with almost any version of SPSS, you will almost certainly be able to use the small subset of the General Social Survey which is included with the package. Ask your local SPSS coordinator how to do this, and how to get a frequency count for all the variables. Having got this far, browse through the variables until you find one that looks interesting as a dependent variable: you could start with **satjob**, **hapmar** or **life** (roughly satisfaction with job, marriage and life generally). Try to find out what sort of people are happiest with their lot. What marital status is most conducive to general life satisfaction? What truth is there in the assertion that men get more out of marriage than women? All these questions can be addressed by cross-tabulating a satisfaction variable by one or more background factor, possibly after recoding.

15.6 FURTHER READING

An excellent introduction to SPSS, which will also get you started in statistics, is Norusis (2000). There must be hundreds of books on statistical methods for social scientists, but relatively few of them deal adequately with cross-tabulation methods. By all means browse through the shelves of your library and bookshop; one of the best is Fielding and Gilbert (2000), which shows you how to perform a range of analyses in SPSS. More advanced is Agresti and Finlay (1997).

A very clear treatment of survey methods in general, from problem formulation to finished report, is to be found in De Vaus (1996).

Finally, when you get seriously interested in quantitative methods, Sage have a comprehensive series of short books called *Quantitative Applications in the Social Sciences* which is often an excellent starting point.

SECONDARY ANALYSIS OF SURVEY DATA

16

SARA ARBER

CONTENTS

Government and other large surveys, as well as the increasing number of panel/longitudinal studies, provide very rich sources of data for secondary analysis. Many of these are under-analysed, from both a statistical and a theoretical viewpoint. This chapter argues that secondary analysis requires sociological imagination and that the secondary analysis of large, primarily government, surveys has untapped potential as a source of sociological insights.

British students are usually encouraged to collect their own data for final year undergraduate projects, Masters dissertations and PhD theses. This contrasts with the USA, where most sociology students conduct secondary analysis of existing large-scale survey data, much of which has been collected by government. The lack of use of secondary analysis in Britain is surprising given that a large number of high-quality national surveys are readily available and that expertise in the analysis and data management of large surveys is in great demand by employers.

16.1   WHAT IS SECONDARY ANALYSIS?

Secondary analysis is the re-analysis of existing survey micro-data collected by another researcher or organisation for the analyst's own purposes. Survey **micro-data** are the original data available in an anonymised electronic datafile (Dale et al., 1988; Hakim, 1982).

The secondary analyst may be addressing quite distinct conceptual and theoretical issues from those of the original data collector. One of the challenges of secondary analysis for the researcher is to use sociological imagination to construct theoretically informed research questions that can be addressed by somebody else's data – data that may have been originally devised and collected for very different purposes.

The proliferation of survey research means that more and more data are available for secondary analysis. However, secondary analysis should only be conducted on survey data that the analyst considers meet appropriate criteria of reliability, validity and representativeness. A further issue relates to the conceptual assumptions embedded in surveys. These are often implicit, reflecting the underlying conceptual framework of the organisation or individuals who collected the original data, and need to be subjected to critical scrutiny. Only certain types of question will be asked, and whole areas that the analyst may be interested in may not be covered. For example, British government surveys contain detailed questions to measure income and poverty, but rarely collect data on wealth, for example the value of houses and other assets.

One of the creative aspects of secondary analysis is deciding how to measure concepts of theoretical interest. It is necessary to search through the questionnaires and codebooks of government and other surveys to identify variables of interest. It may be that the relevant data have been collected but not analysed or published previously, or analysed only in a certain way that reflects contested conceptual assumptions. For example, there may be sexist assumptions about the identity of the Head of Household or it may have been assumed that husband's occupation is an appropriate measure of married women's social class. Secondary analysts can apply alternative conceptual assumptions in their own analyses, for example classifying women by their own rather than their husband's occupation or characterising the household by the characteristics of the highest income earner rather than the Head of Household (Arber, 1989, 1997).

Secondary analysis is now easier than ever, since most students have their own personal computer and the average PC can hold a large survey containing upwards of 20,000 cases and several hundred variables. Statistical packages, such as SPSS, can usually be saved on to the student's PC as part of an educational licensing agreement with the student's higher education institution. Undertaking a project based on secondary analysis is facilitated if you have a statistical package and the dataset on your own PC. In addition, statistical packages have become more user friendly, capable of handling more complex survey data structures, and can produce high-quality graphical output.

16.2 TYPES OF SURVEY AVAILABLE FOR SECONDARY ANALYSIS

There is a vast range of survey data available for secondary analysis. It is likely that whatever your area of sociological interest, several survey datasets could be used to help answer your analytic questions. This section discusses some of the sources of data available in Britain. Survey data can also be obtained from other countries. Figure 16.1 provides an outline of the main types of British data available for secondary analysis.

16.2.1 Government surveys

Central government collects a wide range of survey data about the characteristics of the population that are of interest to sociologists. Some government surveys are annual, containing many of the same questions each year. Other government surveys are repeated every few years and some are one-off (or *ad hoc*) surveys conducted to provide representative data to address specific policy issues, for example the Women and Employment Survey (Martin and Roberts, 1984) and Disability Surveys (Martin et al., 1988). The Office for National Statistics website (http://www.statistics.gov.uk/nsbase/other_activities/socialsurveys.asp) provides comprehensive information about government statistical and survey data.

The General Household Survey (GHS) has interviewed all household members aged 16 and over in about 10,000 households every year since 1971, although there were no surveys in 1997 and 1999. Core data are

1. **Government Surveys**
   - **annual**
   General Household Survey (GHS)
   Family Expenditure Survey (FES)
   Labour Force Survey (LFS)
   Family Resources Survey (FRS)
   Health Survey for England (HSE)
   ONS Omnibus Survey
   - **repeated**
   British Crime Survey (BCS)
   - **ad hoc (one off)**
   Disability Surveys (Martin et al., 1988)
   Women and Employment Survey (Martin and Roberts, 1984)

2. **Other Large Surveys**
   - **annual**
   British Social Attitudes Survey (BSAS)
   - **repeated**
   British Election Surveys
   Fourth National Survey of Ethnic Minorities (Modood et al., 1997)
   - **ad hoc (one off)**
   National Survey of Sexual Attitudes and Lifestyles (Wellings et al., 1994)
   Social Change and Economic Life Initiative (SCELI) (Gallie, 1988)

3. **Population Census**
   Sample of Anonymised Records (SAR), for 1991 and 2001
   ONS Longitudinal Study (LS), from 1971 onwards
   Small Area and Local Base Statistics (SAS), from 1961 onwards

4. **Panel, Cohort and Longitudinal Studies**
   Birth Cohorts
   – 1946 National Survey of Health and Development (NSHD)
   – 1958 National Child Development Study (NCDS)
   – 1970 British Cohort Study (BCS)
   – 2001 Millennium Cohort
   Annual or regular follow-ups
   British Household Panel Survey (BHPS) – annual since 1991
   Irregular
   Retirement and Retirement Plans Surveys (1987 and 1994)
   Mixed panel and repeated
   Programme of Research into Low-Income Families (PRILIF) (Marsh, 2000)

Figure 16.1   *Types of British survey data available for secondary analysis*

collected each year, including housing characteristics, ownership of consumer goods, employment, educational qualifications, health, use of health services, income, marital status, and family history. Some topic areas are asked on alternate years, for example smoking and drinking, and others are asked less regularly, such as sections on leisure activities, informal care and older people. A list of the topics covered in each year can be found at the back of the GHS annual reports (Bennett et al., 1996; ONS, 2000).

The descriptive data collected in government surveys such as the GHS reflect the policy concerns of specific government departments. For example, during the late 1980s, Conservative government policy was to expand share ownership and increase the uptake of personal pensions and private medical insurance, and questions were asked in the GHS about these topics at this time.

Other government surveys of interest to secondary analysts (see Figure 16.1) include the Labour Force Survey (LFS), which collects data from all adults in 80,000 households per year. It focuses particularly on the social and demographic characteristics of the employed, self-employed and those seeking work. Although the LFS has a panel element (see section 16.2.4), in which members of the household are interviewed five times at three-monthly intervals, this panel element is rarely used by secondary analysts. The Health Survey for England (HSE) has been conducted annually on a sample of about 8,000 households since 1993 (Colhoune and Prescott-Clarke, 1996). It collects data from all adults and in recent years also from children. An unusual aspect is that respondents are examined by a nurse, who also takes a blood and urine sample. The results of these laboratory tests provide additional indicators of health status.

The British Crime Survey (BCS) is an example of a repeated survey, one which has surveyed a representative sample of adults every two to four years since 1982. There are both common features and differences between each of the British Crime Surveys.

16.2.2 Other large cross-sectional surveys

Large non-government surveys of value for secondary analysis can also be categorised as annual, repeated or one-off. A widely used dataset for secondary analysis is the British Social Attitudes Survey (BSAS), which interviews a representative sample of adults about a range of contemporary political, moral and environmental attitudes. Some topic areas are only asked about in certain years, for example attitudes towards women's roles and the household division of domestic labour. The BSAS has been conducted annually since 1983 by the National Centre for Social Research (NatCen, formerly called SCPR) (Jowell et al., 1998). It therefore provides a major time series that enables researchers to document changes in attitudes over the last 20 years.

There have been four national surveys of ethnic minorities in Britain conducted over a span of 30 years. The most recent is the 1994 Fourth National Survey of Ethnic Minorities (Modood et al., 1997). Each survey was designed to cover distinct topics, reflecting changes in the concerns and conceptual frameworks relating to the black and minority ethnic population in Britain. These surveys provide important data on the socio-economic characteristics and health of black and minority ethnic groups in Britain.

Surveys may be designed because of a perceived lack of information about an area of policy interest. The 1991 National Survey of Sexual Attitudes and Lifestyles (NATSAL) was conducted because of concerns about the spread of HIV/AIDs and the lack of knowledge about the sexual behaviour of adults. Nearly 19,000 men and women aged 16–59 were interviewed with funding provided by the Wellcome Trust (Wellings et al., 1994).

The high cost of conducting large and nationally representative surveys means that relatively few are conducted by academic social scientists. Notable exceptions are the surveys conducted in six areas of Britain as part of the ESRC (Economic and Social Research Council) Social Change and Economic Life Inititative (SCELI) in the late 1980s (Gallie, 1988; Gallie et al., 1994). Surveys conducted by government and other organisations are much more important sources of sociological data for secondary analysis than surveys carried out by academics. This is both because of the relative lack of 'tailor-made' sociological surveys, and because those that do exist have usually already been analysed to a greater depth and level of theoretical sophistication than is the case for government surveys.

16.2.3 The population census

The decennial population census provides bench-mark data about the social characteristics of the population, the extent of geographical migration and housing conditions in local areas (OPCS, 1993). A description of UK census materials can be found at http://www.census.ac.uk/datasets/descriptions.htm.

Secondary analysis can be conducted on 1991 population census data using the Samples of Anonymised Records (SARs), which comprise a 2 per cent sample of individuals and an independent 1 per cent sample of households (Marsh, 1993). The individual level SAR contains the census records of 1.1 million individuals living in both private households and institutional establishments. There are proposals to increase the SAR of 'individuals' to a 3 per cent sample for the 2001 census (Dale and Elliot, 2000). The SAR is particularly important for studying minority ethnic groups (Dale et al., 2000), since detailed analyses about members of different minority ethnic groups based on national sample surveys are often unreliable because of the relatively small numbers found even in large government surveys such as the GHS. Dale, Fieldhouse and Holdsworth (2000) provide a guide to analysing census microdata including exemplars of analyses using the SARs. For further information contact the Census Microdata Unit (CMU) at the University of Manchester (http://les.man.ac.uk/ccsr/).

In the USA, public-use microdata samples were made available following each census from 1960 onwards (Marsh et al., 1991), and have provided a major source of data for sociological research on issues such as occupational attainment and residential segregation according to ethnicity. They are available as 5 per cent and 1 per cent samples, depending on the level of geographical detail required. The US Census Bureau website shows the vast amount of census data available for secondary analysis (http://www.census.gov/). Past US censuses (since 1850) have also been made available as microdata that can be accessed via IPUMS (Integrated Public Use Microdata Series run from the University of Minnesota – http://www.ipums.org). However, there are no plans in Britain to produce samples of anonymised data from censuses prior to 1991.

The ONS Longitudinal Study (LS) contains microdata on 1 per cent of the population of England and Wales, with the sample based on all individuals with four birthdays spaced over the year. The LS links census records from 1971, 1981 and 1991 for the same individuals and other members of their household, as well as linking data about deaths, births and other vital events (Dale, 1993). For reasons of confidentiality, LS data are not available from the Data Archive at Essex, but can only be analysed in association with the Centre for Longitudinal Studies at the Institute of Education, London (http://www.cls.ioe.ac.uk/).

Aggregate census data for local areas, such as enumeration districts, electoral wards and local authority districts, are extensively used by geographers. These Small Area and Local Base Statistics (collectively called Area Statistics) consist of approximately 20,000 cross-tabulations based on all enumerated people in the 1991 and earlier censuses. The information contained includes age, sex, occupation, qualifications, ethnicity, social class, employment, family structure, amenities and housing tenure. The area statistics are aggregated to a hierarchy of geographical units and are available electronically via MIMAS at the University of Manchester (http://www.mimas.ac.uk/).

16.2.4 Panel, longitudinal and cohort studies

Panel, longitudinal and cohort studies are conducted by collecting data at a number of points in time from the same set of people, that is, **prospectively**. Time can be taken into account in cross-sectional surveys by asking respondents about their past work, family and migration histories. This is called **retrospective** data. However, accurate data on many issues of interest to sociologists cannot be obtained retrospectively, for example an individual's attitudes five years ago, their domestic division of labour prior to marriage, their income in the past, and their health or behaviour as a child. These issues can only be studied using a panel or longitudinal design, which collects information about the individuals' current attitudes or behaviour, and re-surveys them periodically.

Cross-sectional surveys can demonstrate associations but cannot reveal the causal ordering of variables. For example, unemployment is correlated with poor health, but the theoretical and policy implications of this association depend on the direction of causation: whether being unemployed causes poor health, or poor health leads a person to lose their job and have difficulty finding a new one (Blane et al., 1993; Fox et al., 1985). The direction of causation can only be resolved through panel or longitudinal studies, which measure health status prospectively at different points in time.

Britain is fortunate to have three birth cohort studies, based on births in one week in March 1946 (National Survey of Health and Development), in March 1958 (National Child Development Study, NCDS), and in March 1970 (the British Cohort Study, BCS, formerly Child Health and Education Study). In each case, survey data have been collected at intervals from the mother and the child, as well as from teachers and health professionals, and subsequently data collected during adulthood. The 1946 and 1958 studies have also surveyed the next generation, collecting data about the children of cohort members. The 1991 wave of the NCDS collected data from the partners of cohort members (Ferri, 1993). Further surveys collecting data for the NCDS and BCS were undertaken in 2000–01. The Millennium Cohort is a new cohort study of babies born during 2001, but no data will be available for analysis for several years. Secondary analysis of these birth cohort studies is a highly cost-effective method of answering a host of policy and theoretical research questions, many of which were never dreamt of by the data originators. For example, the three British birth cohort studies were not originally designed to clarify the direction of causation in relation to inequalities in health, but have been used extensively to address this and many other issues (Power et al., 1991; Wadsworth, 1986, 1991).

Another important longitudinal source of data for secondary analysis is the British Household Panel Study (BHPS), which began in 1991 and interviews all adults in about 5,000 households annually (Buck et al., 1994). One of the aims of the BHPS is to provide a 'basic resource for both strategic, fundamental research in the social sciences and for policy-relevant research' (Rose et al., 1992: 6). BHPS data are of high quality and are made available rapidly to users; comprehensive and user-friendly information about the BHPS is available at http://www.iser.ac.uk/bhps/.

Some surveys begin as one-off, and only later is it decided to add further waves of data collection from the same individuals. This occurred for the Retirement and Retirement Plans Survey which interviewed people aged 55–69 in 1988 about their retirement intentions and financial circumstances around the time of retirement (Bone et al., 1992). It was planned as a one-off survey, but later there was a follow-up interview, so it became a panel survey (Disney et al., 1997). The DSS/PSI Programme of Research into Low-income Families (PRILIF) has involved several separate inter-linked studies, beginning in 1991 with a postal survey of all parents (Ford et al., 1998; Marsh, 2000). All the lone parents were followed up each year until 1996. Alongside this were repeated cross-sectional surveys of parents in 1993 and in 1994. Thus, some surveys move from one category of Figure 16.1 to another if they develop from being a one-off survey to a repeated or panel study, and other studies represent a mixture of one-off, repeated and panel surveys.

16.2.5 Annual large surveys for quasi-cohort analysis

Secondary analysts can use annual and repeated cross-sectional surveys as quasi- or synthetic cohorts to address some of the policy issues which require an understanding of the impact of time, cohort and age (Harding, 1990; Waldfogel, 1993). Pseudo-cohorts can be constructed by using successive years of cross-sectional surveys such as the GHS to track a particular birth cohort through time. Although the same individuals are not surveyed each year, individuals from the same birth cohort are. Thus, the characteristics of one cohort can be compared with those of a group that represents them demographically five or ten years later. However, such an approach is limited in that it focuses on average group characteristics or behaviour, rather than those of individuals, and fails to capture the various changes in people's circumstances over time. It may be complemented by analysis of longitudinal data such as the NCDS (Waldfogel, 1993).

16.2.6 Surveys from other countries

There has been an explosion of data available for secondary analysis from other countries. Most of it is country-specific, but increasingly cross-national comparative data are available. The USA in particular has a vast number of high-quality datasets for secondary analysis. These include repeated cross-sectional surveys such as the General Social Survey (GSS), which has been conducted annually since 1972. By 2000 the combined GSS datafile contained over 40,000 individuals and over 3,500 variables. It is easily accessible and is used extensively in the USA for teaching (http://www.icpsr.umich.edu/GSS99/index.htm) (Davis and Smith, 1992). Many US government surveys can be used for secondary analysis. For example, the National Health Interview survey has public-use files available since 1969 (see http://www.cdc.gov/nchs/nhis.htm).

There are a number of important US panel studies, particularly the Panel Study of Income Dynamics (PSID) and the Health and Retirement Survey (HRS). HRS began in 1992 as a national survey of 12,000 people aged 51–61, interviewed biannually. Since 1998 it has been extended to cover a US nationally representative sample of 22,000 people aged 50 and over (see http://www.icpsr.umich.edu/~hrswww). Countries often develop a specific study because of the insights gleaned from a comparable study in another country. For example, elements of the BHPS were modelled on the PSID, and there are plans in the UK for an English Longitudinal Study of Ageing modelled on the HRS.

Some studies are designed for cross-national comparison and aim to ask equivalent questions in different countries. The British Social Attitudes Survey (BSAS) is linked to the International Social Survey Programme (ISSP), which began with four countries in 1984 (the USA, the UK, Germany and Australia) and now conducts annual surveys in 37 countries. Each year a different module of questions is asked simultaneously in each country, for example, on social inequality in 1999, the environment in 2000 and social support and social relations in 2001 (see http://www.issp.org/ and http://www.za.unikoeln.de/en/issp/). By combining cross-time and cross-nation research, this provides a powerful research design to study social processes (Jowell et al., 1989, 1998). There is now a European Community Household Panel Study, Europanel, which takes place annually in 13 European countries. Since 1999, collection of the British data for Europanel has been merged with that for the BHPS (see http://www.iser.essex.ac.uk/).

If you are planning cross-European research, you should contact the Resource Centre for Access to Data on Europe, r-cade, which is located at the University of Durham (see http://www-rcade.dur.ac.uk/).

16.3   THE VALUE OF SECONDARY ANALYSIS

Several types of research are only practicable using secondary analysis, because appropriate primary data would be too expensive to collect or cannot be obtained. Some examples will be discussed in this section.

16.3.1   Studying small or rare sub-groups

Many issues of sociological interest focus on proportionately small sub-groups of the population, for example a specific age group, ethnic minority group or type of family. It is usually impossible to identify a complete sampling frame for such groups in order to draw a representative sample, so research is often biased in significant ways (see Chapter 5). An alternative is to use large government surveys, if necessary combining data from consecutive years to increase the sample size of the sub-group of interest. For example, sociologists may be interested in the characteristics of people who cohabit or in comparing lone fathers with lone mothers. Three years of the GHS were combined to obtain a sufficiently large sample to analyse the health of children of lone parents and the health of children from minority ethnic groups (Cooper, Arber and Smaje, 1998a; Cooper, Smaje and Arber, 1998b).

Even for research that does not involve proportionately small population sub-groups, it is often beneficial to combine a number of years of survey data. For example, the research on pensions discussed in Chapter 17 used a combined dataset from two years of the GHS (1993 and 1994), allowing more robust analyses by marital status and examination of detailed age groups above 65.

16.3.2   Studying household relationships and social contexts

A key concern of many sociologists is to analyse how an individual's behaviour may be influenced by the characteristics of significant others and by the wider groupings of which they are a part. Many government datasets collect data on all adults in the household, allowing the researcher to analyse the interrelationships between the characteristics of different household members (Dale et al., 1988). For example, household surveys, such as the GHS, allow analysis of young people's unemployment and how this is related to whether their fathers and/or mothers are unemployed, and analysis of the effect of the smoking behaviour of parents on children's health.

16.3.3 Comparative analysis

Government surveys have grown in number in most industrialised countries. This opens up the possibility of cross-national analysis that addresses social policy or sociological issues. For example, Finland conducts a Level of Living Survey which is very similar to the British GHS. In Finland, women's employment rate is comparable to that of men, with nearly 90 per cent of women employed full-time during their child-bearing years; this contrasts with British women's high rate of part-time employment and lower overall employment participation rate. Arber and Lahelma (1993) compared the impact of employment participation on the nature of inequalities in women's health in these two societies. The ISSP is designed for cross-country analyses, as discussed in section 16.2.6.

16.3.4 Trends and historical analyses

Annual surveys allow the analysis of trends over time, for example, to monitor the impact of policy changes on poverty and attitudes towards welfare and moral issues. Many of the surveys discussed in section 16.2 have been running for several decades: the GHS since 1971, the Family Expenditure Survey (FES) since 1957 and the British Social Attitudes Survey (BSAS) since 1983, and can therefore be used in this way.

Researchers may collect their own survey data and use secondary analysis to examine changes between an earlier survey conducted by another researcher and their own surveys. The contemporary survey may be designed to include the same questions as earlier survey(s) to allow analysis of changes in attitudes or behaviour over time.

16.4 POTENTIAL PITFALLS OF SECONDARY ANALYSIS

Before undertaking secondary analysis, it is important to be aware of a number of potential pitfalls.

16.4.1 Assessing the validity of the data

When considering a potential survey for secondary analysis it is necessary to subject its methodology to critical scrutiny, including the quality of developmental and pilot work, interviewer training and fieldwork control, the method of sample selection, the nature of the sampling frame and the response rate. The secondary analyst needs to obtain as much documentation as possible about the collection of the survey data and be aware of any potential data limitations.

16.4.2 Measurement error

The conventional research paradigm in survey research is one of 'theory-testing', that is, the primary researcher designs a research instrument and collects data in order to test theoretical hypotheses. These are operationalised into empirical hypotheses and questions are developed to validly measure the theoretical concepts that constitute the various elements of the researcher's theory (see Chapter 2).

However, the secondary analyst has to work with someone else's survey questions and assess whether these questions adequately measure the theoretical concepts of the theory they wish to test. Unfortunately, it may not be possible to measure key theoretical concepts because appropriate questions have not been asked in the survey or the questions may not be valid indicators of the relevant concepts. Alternatively, appropriate questions may have been asked but the existing coding categories do not provide theoretically meaningful analytic distinctions. For example, the 1991 GHS asked a series of questions about childcare for children under 11, distinguishing between different sources of paid care. However, all forms of unpaid care were combined into a single category of 'family and friends', with childcare by partners or others living in the same household explicitly excluded. This coding meant a researcher could not assess how much childcare was provided by grandparents or other relatives while mothers were at work.

16.4.3 Timeliness of data

Government surveys are usually at least two years old before they are made available for secondary analysis, typically after the publication of the relevant government report. Only a few surveys are released more quickly. For example, the Labour Force Survey collects data on a quarterly basis and the datasets become available from the Data Archive 14 weeks after the end of each period of data collection.

Since most sociologists use secondary analysis to address analytic questions that are not highly time dependent, a lag in the release of data is not a major constraint. For example, the theoretical insights from analyses of class inequalities in health are likely to be the same irrespective of whether the survey data are one or four years old.

16.4.4 Size and number of variables

Many datasets are very large, which is valuable because analyses can be based on a sample large enough to produce robust (statistically significant) conclusions. However, this in itself is a danger, since all except the most modest associations will be statistically significant when analysing a dataset of several thousand cases. Analysts need to focus primarily on what is substantively important rather than what is statistically significant.

Surveys often contain a large number of derived variables, some of which may be similar and this may initially be confusing. For example, the GHS contains about 20 variables that describe the structure of the respondent's household. These exist because different government departments requested analyses using slightly different household structure definitions. The analyst needs to consider carefully the various derived variables that represent a given concept and perhaps select two or three for further exploratory analysis, before deciding which ones are most appropriate to analyse in detail.

16.4.5 Complexity of data structure

Household surveys generally interview all adults in the household, and so the amount of data collected from each household varies according to the number of adults interviewed. For each respondent, there may also be a hierarchical structure in which the amount of data varies depending on responses to certain questions. For example, the GHS asks for details about all doctor consultations in the last two weeks; most respondents have none but some will have six or more. The Data Archive at the University of Essex supplies the GHS as an SPSS file based on either individuals or households, which is straightforward to use but may not contain all the needed linkages between household members. The alternative is to obtain the GHS from the Data Archive as a hierarchical file in 'SIR format'. Secondary analysts who wish to examine the interrelationship between the characteristics of different household members may need to use a data management package such as SIR (Dale et al., 1988).

A longitudinal or panel survey inevitably has a more complex data structure than a cross-sectional survey. In particular, the analyst has to make decisions about how to handle cases where there is missing data in one or more waves of data collection, leading to a less representative sample and biases. A discussion of data handling using longitudinal data and the statistical analysis of event history and longitudinal data is beyond the scope of this chapter, and readers should consult texts such as Dale and Davies (1994).

It goes without saying that secondary analysts need sufficient knowledge of statistics, as well as the ability to use statistical analysis programs such as SPSS. This should no longer be a constraint as analysis programs have become more user friendly and the teaching of computing and basic statistics is widespread in undergraduate and postgraduate courses. However, most students lack knowledge of more advanced methods of multivariate analysis and the management of large and complex data structures.

16.5   How to obtain data for
secondary analysis

The Data Archive at the University of Essex (http://www.data-archive.ac.uk/) is a national archive where datasets are deposited and distributed to the academic community. This specialist resource contains the UK's largest collection of accessible computer-readable data in the social sciences. The Data Archive distributes almost all British government-funded surveys for secondary analysis. Datasets are supplied free of charge for unfunded research and educational uses. The only charge is for supplying printed documentation about the survey, such as interview schedules and code books, but these are often freely available electronically. The Data Archive also holds overseas datasets and provides a gateway to non-UK data for UK researchers and vice versa.

16.5.1   Choosing a dataset

If you are considering analysing a large dataset, a good place to start look-ing for more information is the Social Survey Question Bank. Question-naires for the main government surveys and other key surveys, such as the BHPS and BSAS, are available online through the Question Bank (http://qb.soc.surrey.ac.uk/). The Question Bank aims to increase the sharing of good practice on ways of designing questions to measure social scientific concepts, to document data collection instruments and to pro-vide insight into underlying conceptual and design issues. The full ques-tionnaires are online and can be easily downloaded for use by students and researchers.

The most comprehensive source of information about available data is the Data Archive's online catalogue and information retrieval system, BIRON (Bibliographic Information Retrieval Online: http://biron.essex.ac.uk/). Searches can be performed on study descriptions, keywords and geo-graphical locations relating to all the studies in the Archive's collection. Detailed information is available about each deposited study, including names of data collectors, details of the purposes of the research, the populations sampled, data collection methodologies and references to pub-lications and reports based on the data. BIRON also provides access to online user documentation for many of the datasets in the Archive, as well as searchable lists of variables, including variable labels and value labels (response codes) for the more popular datasets, such as most years of the large government surveys. Partly because it is comprehensive and detailed, students may not find BIRON very user-friendly. Within BIRON, the IDC (Integrated Data Catalogue) links to other European and worldwide data archive catalogues.

Once you have narrowed down your search for a suitable dataset, you should read as much as possible about the dataset before placing your order.

This includes reading thoroughly the online documentation (which can be downloaded), information about the sample design, response rates and data collection methodology, and reports and publications based on the dataset. You can review the lists of publications based on the dataset provided by BIRON, or you may be able to obtain further information about publications from the data orginators' web site or through direct contact. It is essential to do this background reading first, for otherwise you may find that another analyst has already used the dataset to answer the same research questions that you are planning to study. Of course, you may disagree with their results, analysis or interpretation of data, leading you to a closer refinement of your research questions.

16.5.2 Ordering data

Once a suitable dataset is identified from the Data Archive catalogue, the dataset can be ordered electronically by completing an order form online, or the order form can be downloaded from the Archive web site. The form requires information on the data and documentation requested, the format of the data, and how the data is to be supplied to the user, for example on a CD-Rom or a diskette. Since some datasets are very large and therefore may not be easy to analyse on a PC, it is sometimes desirable to select a subset. This may be a subset of variables, for example 200 variables from the over 2,000 variables in one year of GHS data, or may be a subset of cases, for example only people aged over 55. It is straightforward to select subsets of variables within BIRON, then e-mail the variable list to the Data Archive with your order. However, the analyst needs to make these selections very carefully, since it is extremely inconvenient and time-consuming for both the Data Archive and the analyst to have to go back to extract a further subset because a key variable was not requested.

Before a copy of a dataset is released by the Data Archive or permission is given to access the data online, the user must sign an undertaking on conditions of use. Most datasets are covered by a standard Undertaking Form, but government and some other surveys require further information, including the submission of a short proposal outlining the research purposes for which the data is to be used, as well as a special Undertaking Form which must be signed. Publications are not vetted in advance, so the secondary analyst's work is not controlled in any way. The only requirement of some depositors, for example government departments, is that two copies of any publications using the data must be submitted to the Data Archive, one of which is forwarded to the data depositor.

Many large datasets, such as the GHS, LFS and BHPS, can be accessed electronically via MIMAS (Manchester Information and Associated Surveys) at the University of Manchester. However, permission has to be first sought from the Data Archive in order to use the data online at MIMAS (see http://www.mimas.ac.uk/).

16.5.3 Obtaining data from originating organisations

Some datasets in the UK are not available from the Data Archive but can only be obtained from the orginating or an intermediary organisation. For example, the Samples of Anonymised Records from the census are supplied through the CMU at Manchester (see http://les.mac.ac.uk/ccsr/), see section 16.2.3. The ONS Longitudinal Study can only be analysed via the Centre for Longitudinal Studies at the Institute of Education, London.

16.5.4 Online Data Analysis Systems

Increasingly data is becoming available for online analysis. For example, MIMAS at the University of Manchester provides such a service for large national UK datasets. Online Data Analysis Systems (DAS) allow the user to generate frequencies and cross-tabulations and to perform exploratory analyses directly through the Internet. They are valuable either for conducting the whole of the researcher's analysis, or for helping the secondary analyst to decide if he or she wishes to obtain the survey as microdata and, if so, which variables to specify in requesting a data extract.

16.6   PROCESS OF ANALYSIS

The secondary analyst works in a much more iterative way, moving between existing survey questions and theory, than is suggested in the 'theory-testing' model of social research (see Chapter 2). The actual process of secondary analysis is in practice a combination of exploratory data analysis and theory-testing or confirmatory analysis (Erickson and Nosanchuk, 1992; Marsh, 1988).

The secondary analyst first needs to become familiar with the data by examining the frequencies of all variables of potential interest (see Chapter 15). It is particularly important to understand the questionnaire routing that determines who has been asked each question. Close attention should be paid to the various missing data categories and the numbers of missing cases. The analyst will also need to be fully informed about the range of derived variables available in the dataset. In some datasets, there will be detailed information about how each variable was derived, but this may not be available in all datasets. Information about the construction of derived variables will probably be in the form of syntax commands for SPSS, or whatever program was used to derive the variable.

Following a review of existing research literature, the analyst should be able to develop a theoretical model that he or she wishes to explore. It may be useful to draw this out as a conceptual model (or path diagram) which shows how each concept is related to the others and the expected causal direction of the relationships. The variables that can be used to measure each of the concepts within the conceptual model then need to be examined. This phase of exploratory data analysis is likely to involve the production of a range of cross-tabulations, graphical analyses and descriptive statistics. The analyst needs to try out different indicators of the concepts and alternative ways of constructing various new derived variables to measure the relevant concepts (see Dale et al., 1988). Only at this stage will the analyst finalise which variables and derived variables are most appropriate to use for their own analytic purposes. Finally, it will be necessary to decide which statistical techniques are most appropriate to use.

16.7 CONCLUSION

The challenge and opportunity of secondary analysis is to apply theoretical knowledge and conceptual skills to use existing survey datasets creatively to address sociological questions. In most cases, the term 'secondary analysis' is a misnomer, since the process of secondary analysis of large datasets is more akin to 'primary analysis'. The researcher may be analysing the dataset in new and novel ways both theoretically and statistically. A key value of secondary analysis for students is to develop their skills in data analysis and managing data, while at the same time creatively applying and developing theoretical ideas by translating survey questions into analytic concepts, and drawing conceptual conclusions from statistical analyses.

The rapid fall in the costs of computing power means that the cost advantage of secondary analysis over primary data collection is very great. This is occurring at the same time as the costs of primary data collection using interview surveys are increasing and survey organisations are increasingly finding it difficult to maintain acceptable levels of response. Another major change is the growth in the number of datasets that are easily and rapidly accessible via the Internet. Analysts can now quickly find out what is available, order datasets and even conduct analyses online.

16.8 PROJECT

1. Compare the advantages and disadvantages of conducting secondary analysis of a large government survey with carrying out primary research for a research study of the reasons for gender differences in earnings.
2. Think of a research problem that can be examined using secondary analysis. For example, how marital status and age of children influence the employment participation of women and men, or how gender differences in health-related behaviour vary throughout the life course. Then undertake the following:
   - Find out what surveys can be used to address your research problem by using the Data Archive online catalogue, BIRON.

- Having identified a relevant survey, select questions to measure the concepts needed to address your research problem. Provide a critical appraisal of the adequacy of these questions as measures of the concepts to be studied.
- Draw a conceptual model of the interrelationships between each of your concepts, including the direction of any expected causal relations.

3. Conduct secondary analysis using a subset of the 1995 General Household Survey, which can be downloaded from http://www.soc.surrey. ac.uk/uss/. For example, elaborate a two-variable relationship, by controlling for one or more theoretically relevant potentially intervening variables, and draw conclusions about the direction of relationship between these variables. Your analysis can be conducted using cross-tabulation or graphical techniques. Your analysis will be easier if you first recode all the variables to be analysed into either two or three categories.

16.9 FURTHER READING

Dale, Arber and Procter (1988) provides a comprehensive discussion of secondary analysis, including examples and practical guidance on how to conduct secondary analysis and derive variables using both SPSS and SIR. Dale, Fieldhouse and Holdsworth (2000) provides an excellent overview of analysing the Sample of Anonymised Records (SAR), including examples.

Fielding and Gilbert (2000) is a clearly written guide to the statistical analysis of social science data, which refers to the use of a web site containing datasets for secondary analysis, including a sample from the 1995 GHS. Hakim (1982) is now rather dated but provides an overview and discussion of sources of data for secondary analysis. Marsh (1988) is an excellent introduction to exploratory data analysis, which should be the first stage in any secondary analysis.

See also the various web sites mentioned in the chapter, in particular:

- The Social Survey Question Bank (http://qb.soc.surrey.ac.uk).
- The Data Archive at University of Essex (http://www.data-archive.ac.uk/) and (http://biron.essex.ac.uk/).
- The Institute for Social and Economic Research at University of Essex, which includes the British Household Panel Study (http://www.iser. ac.uk/).
- Government statistical surveys (http://www.statistics.gov.uk/).

EXEMPLAR: PRIVATISING PENSIONS – NEW OPTIONS AND NEW RISKS FOR WOMEN

17

JAY GINN

CONTENTS

This chapter will describe a practical example of secondary analysis using the General Household Surveys of 1987 and of 1993 and 1994 combined. The research is based on projects funded by the Economic and Social Research Council (ESRC) and the Leverhulme Trust. I show how the research question arose and consider the advantages and problems of using large government datasets to address it. The example illustrates the process of research using secondary analysis, including checking the data, operationalising concepts, preliminary analysis to guide the formulation of specific hypotheses and the use of cross-tabulation to test these.

17.1 THE RESEARCH QUESTION

Sociological theory and research on stratification have traditionally been predominantly concerned with work in the formal economy and with class as the main structural basis of inequality, while gender and the domestic economy have been relatively neglected. However, feminist sociologists have highlighted gender as an equally important basis of structured inequality, arguing that the concentration of women in jobs which are characterised by low pay, insecurity, lack of opportunities for promotion and poor working conditions (often referred to as the secondary labour market), is related to patriarchal power and the sexual division of domestic labour (Crompton and Mann, 1986; Walby, 1986). Motherhood, as well as being female, reduces women's employment and earnings in modern societies. The effects of gender and of motherhood on earnings over the lifetime can be quantified using computer modelling, distinguishing according to educational qualifications. Comparing those with middle-level skills, a childless woman can expect to earn on average 73 per cent of men's earnings and a mother of two only 57 per cent, over the working life (Rake et al., 2000). How do these earnings losses affect women's pension income?

The basic state pension is relatively women-friendly, in that the amount of pension is not affected by the individual's earnings. To receive the full amount, a woman must have paid National Insurance contributions for 39 years, although this requirement is relaxed for years covered by Home Responsibilities Protection, while caring for children or frail relatives. The State Earnings Related Pension (SERPS), however, depends on earnings level as well as years of contributions, its original women-friendly features having been removed by the 1986 Social Security Act. Occupational pension schemes, which are operated by most good employers, generally base the pension on years of membership and earnings in the final few years. Occupational pension scheme rules favour those with full-time continuous employment. Part-timers are less likely to be able to join a scheme and their lower earnings are reflected in a lower pension. Those who leave a scheme before retirement, for example to start a family or care for a frail relative, obtain poorer value for their contributions than those who remain members until normal retirement age. Nevertheless occupational pensions generally provide a more generous pension than SERPS, mainly because employers make a higher contribution.

Since 1988, employees have had the choice of contracting out of SERPS and out of occupational pension schemes into an Appropriate Personal Pension (APP). These are 'defined contribution' schemes, in which there is no pension formula (as in occupational Final Salary schemes or SERPS). Instead, the amount of income after retirement depends on the size of the fund built from the invested contributions and on the annuity (annual income) which can be bought with the fund. APPs therefore depend on lifetime earnings, as well as investment performance, annuity rates and charges made by the pension provider. Thus SERPS and private pensions (occupational and APPs), because they are linked to earnings, tend to disadvantage women, especially those who have raised children. Occupational pensions have played a major role in transmitting class and gender inequalities during the working life into later life (Ginn and Arber, 1991).

This aspect of gender inequality has received less attention than the earnings gap, although women on average spend 22 years as pensioners. Marital status, as well as class and gender, affect pension income; research showed that whereas single older women had higher pensions than single men, marriage or previous marriage reduced women's pension income drastically (Ginn and Arber, 1994, 1999). This indicated that older women's occupational pension disadvantage was due not only to sex segregation and discrimination in the labour market, but also to the effect of domestic responsibilities on women's employment histories and earnings. In the future, as more people retire with income from APPs, the gendered effects of these pensions will become apparent. It is expected that, because of high flat-rate charges, financial penalties for breaks in contributions and annuity rates which are sex-differentiated to reflect women's greater longevity, APPs will provide particularly poor value for women. Thus coverage by APPs may be a mixed blessing; no one can be sure that they will out-perform SERPS, or for which groups of people.

From 1988, those with access to an occupational pension scheme could reject it in favour of either an APP or remaining in SERPS. Those whose employers did not operate an occupational pension scheme, or who were ineligible to join, could choose only between an APP or SERPS. The Conservative government intended APPs mainly for younger employees on at least average earnings who had no access to an occupational pension. Because APPs are generally inadvisable for the low paid or for older workers, we wished to ascertain how far APPs had hit their target or had been taken up by other groups of workers. In particular we wished to understand how the widening pension choices would affect women, in view of their interrupted employment, periods of part-time work and lower earnings.

17.2 USING THE GENERAL HOUSEHOLD SURVEYS

The research problem required data from a large nationally representative probability sample of people about their domestic circumstances, age and employment. It was also necessary to be able to compare detailed data on pension scheme membership from surveys before and after the implementation (in 1988) of the relevant pensions legislation. A probability (or random) sample was needed in order to be able to infer, with a known degree of certainty, that the associations and mean values found in the sample apply generally in the population, and are not due to bias in the selection of the sample (see Chapter 5). A large sample was necessary in order to compare sub-groups (e.g. by age, sex, marital status and class) without the numbers in the sub-groups becoming so small that there might be distortion due to sampling error. When the research requires comparisons within statistically rare groups, such as ethnic minorities, women in the highest occupational positions, or divorced and separated people, a large sample is particularly important. Secondary analysis of the General Household Survey (GHS) is a suitable way of addressing the research question, since all these conditions are fulfilled.

The GHS, an annual survey carried out since 1971 by the UK government's Office for National Statistics (ONS) on a two-stage probability sample, has a response rate of over 80 per cent and provides high-quality information on over 25,000 people living in over 10,000 private households in Britain each year. All adults in a sampled household are interviewed and the responses are coded and stored on a computer in a way which preserves information about the household and family to which each individual belongs, and data on each individual may be analysed in relation to data on other family and household members (see section 15.1 and Dale et al., 1988: Chapter 4). For this research, two years of the GHS (1993 and 1994) were combined to increase the sample size to over 50,000, including over 15,000 employees aged 20–59. The number of cases is sufficient to allow comparison of the effect of several factors simultaneously, and to provide an accurate estimate of the rate of pension scheme membership for small population sub-groups. The data are of high quality and from a random sample, allowing inferences to be made of the whole population.

The GHS provides information that allows the effect of family circumstances and labour market position on women's and men's pension scheme membership to be explored. On the other hand, there is no information in the GHS as to the *amount* of pension entitlement, so that those who are likely to receive a substantial pension on retirement cannot be distinguished from those who expect a negligible amount.

A further limitation of the GHS for this research is that it is cross-sectional; the information has been collected at one point in time. Ideally, the process of gender differentiation in occupational pension entitlements through the working life would be traced using data on the same individuals as they grow older. This would also show whether gender differences in pension acquisition are diminishing with successive cohorts, reflecting more equality of opportunity for women since the 1970s. When comparing people of different ages it is difficult to separate the effect of age (or stage in the life course) from differences due to being in an earlier or later cohort. Large-scale longitudinal datasets on adults in Britain are available (e.g. the National Child Development Study and the OPCS Longitudinal Survey) but they do not include information on occupational pensions. The Retirement and Retirement Plans Surveys of 1988 and 1994 provide longitudinal data (with retrospective work and pension histories) but only on the cohort aged 55–69 in 1988. The 1994/95 Family and Working Lives Survey does include retrospective data on the employment, pension scheme membership and family circumstances of individuals aged 16–69, but the data was unavailable at the time of the project. Moreover, employment histories are subject to inaccurate recall, especially where a long time-span is covered and where the experience is fragmented into many short periods, as is often the case for women.

Although secondary analysis of the GHS has limitations compared with a specially designed survey, they are outweighed by the advantages of using an existing dataset that allows comparisons over time.

17.3 THE INITIAL STAGES OF RESEARCH

In order to analyse the GHS, permission must first be obtained from the Data Archive at Essex University and the ONS for each year of the survey which is required. The GHS, or more usually a subset of cases and selected variables, may be received from the Data Archive either in its original hierarchical format which links individuals to their family and household, or as a flat file (a case by variable matrix) at the household or the individual level (see section 16.4.6). If you request a flat file or files and need particular linkages between household and individual data, you need to check that these links have been preserved in the file(s). Data files and accompanying documentation, which lists both original and derived variables, can be transmitted to you in various electronic forms. Once system files have been mounted on your local mainframe computer or PC, they can be analysed using a software package such as SPSS.

17.3.1 Operationalising concepts and matching variables

Although secondary analysis may appear to short cut the task of operationalising concepts, since the questions have already been designed, it is important to understand the exact wording of the questions and how they could be interpreted by respondents, the sequence of questions, the definitions used in coding responses, and how each derived variable has been constructed from original ones. Documentation assists in this. For example, in distinguishing between employment in the public and private sectors, the ONS defines the 'public sector' as comprising nationalised industries, public corporations, central or local government and armed forces; universities are defined as 'private sector', a categorisation which is by no means obvious.

A crucial task when making comparisons across time (or when combining two or more years of data) is to check that the relevant variables in the different years of the survey match exactly. Is the question wording identical? Is the coding of responses the same? If not, can comparable variables be achieved by recoding? If a variable's meaning or categories change between years, this is usually indicated by a change in the variable name. For example, the household level variable **car** could have values 0, 1, 2, 3 and

Table 17.1   *Concepts and variables used as indicators*

	Concept	Indicators in GHS
Occupational welfare:	Occupational pension status	Scheme available Member of scheme
Domestic roles:	Marital role Parental role	Marital status Age of youngest child
Labour market position:	Occupation Extent of employment Level of job	Socio-economic group Hours of work per week Usual gross earnings per week
Life course stage:	Age Family responsibilities	Age group Age of youngest child

4+, while **car1** in a different year could have values 1, 2 and 3+, with a code of −9 where there is no **car**; both variables can be recoded to give values of 0, 1, 2 and 3+, enabling the two years to be combined in one dataset or compared.

Since your aim as a researcher is different from that of the originators of the survey, the questions asked and the respondents to whom they were applied may not be exactly as you would wish. Construction of additional derived variables may provide improved indicators and facilitate analysis. The questions in the GHS about membership of an occupational pension scheme or of an APP were only asked of employees, as the remainder (whether self-employed, unemployed or economically inactive) would have had no opportunity to join such schemes.

The major concepts of interest were the likelihood of benefiting from occupational welfare in the form of an occupational pension, position in the domestic economy, position in the labour market and life course stage. Table 17.1 summarises the concepts and indicators.

We carried out a preliminary analysis to assess the change in private pension arrangements since the introduction of APPs, before proceeding to analyse pension coverage in the mid-1990s.

17.3.2 Preliminary analysis to establish change in pension coverage over time

In order to analyse the rates of membership of occupational pension schemes and APPs, we constructed a new variable in the 1993–94 data which distinguished those belonging to an occupational pension (with or without additional voluntary contributions), those contributing to an APP (but not to an occupational pension) and those with no private pension cover. A simplified employment status variable was constructed by grouping into three categories: whether the person was an employee, self-employed or not employed. The pension variable was cross-tabulated by employment status and sex for all adults and then by sex alone for employees, for both the 1987

Table 17.2 *Private pension arrangements of men and women aged 20–59 in 1987 and 1993–94*

	1987	1993–94	1987	1993–94
(a) All adults:	Men		Women	
Member of occupational pension scheme	46	40	22	25
Contributing to an APP	–	13	–	9
Employee, no private pension	25	12	38	27
Self-employed	14	15	5	5
Not employed	15	20	35	34
Column (%)	100	100	100	100
N =	6,637	11,756	6,924	12,313
(b) Employees:				
Member of occupational pension scheme	64	62	36	41
Contributing to an APP	–	20	–	15
No private pension	36	18	64	44
Column (%)	100	100	100	100
N =	4,685	7,641	4,157	7,511

data and the 1993–94 data. Since few join pension schemes under age 20, the analysis was restricted to adults aged 20–59.

In 1987, over twice as many men as women were members of an occupational pension scheme, 46 per cent compared with 22 per cent (see Table 17.2(a)). By 1993–94, men's occupational pension coverage had declined to 40 per cent while women's had increased to 25 per cent. The introduction of APPs substantially increased private pension coverage, to 53 per cent among men and 34 per cent among women. Thus the gender gap in private pension coverage narrowed slightly over the time period, due to a fall in men's employment rate and occupational pension scheme membership, together with a rise in women's membership rate. APPs did not contribute to gender equality in private pension coverage since men were more likely than women to take up this new option. Among employees, private pension coverage rose from 64 to 82 per cent of men and from 36 to 56 per cent of women (Table 17.2(b)). The preliminary analysis of employees prompted several questions about the gender differences found, and more generally about what factors influenced employees to choose one pension arrangement over another. These questions were formulated as hypotheses, based on what seemed most likely given existing knowledge.

17.4 EXPLANATORY ANALYSIS

While it is well established that access to occupational pension scheme membership is associated with advantage in the labour market (higher socio-economic group, higher earnings, full-time employment, larger employer, longer tenure), with older age and with freedom from childcare responsibilities (Ginn and Arber, 1993), it was not known what characteristics would increase the likelihood of employees rejecting an occupational pension for an APP, or choosing an APP in preference to SERPS. However, we would expect that, since occupational pensions are not generally portable, perform relatively poorly for those who leave the scheme before retirement and require a certain level of contributions:

A. *Among those with access to an occupational pension, rejection was associated with younger age, lower socio-economic group, lower earnings, part-time employment and being female.*

We expect that, since APPs provide particularly poor value for the low paid, for those likely to experience gaps in employment and for older individuals:

B. *Among those rejecting an occupational pension (Rejectors), contributing to an APP rather than SERPS was associated with younger age, higher earnings, higher socio-economic group, full-time employment and being male.*

C. *Among those lacking access to an occupational pension (the Excluded), similar factors as for Hypothesis B favour contributing to an APP.*

17.4.1 Grouping of variables

At this stage of the analysis, cross-tabulation is the most appropriate way to examine relationships among variables. It enables the testing of bivariate relationships by the introduction of selected, theoretically relevant, control variables. Interpretation of the results is relatively straightforward provided the values of variables are suitably grouped. For the cross-tabulation we grouped variables as shown:

- **Age**. We used age groups 20–29, 30–39, 40–49 and 50–59.
- **Hours of employment**. Women employed 30 hours or less were categorised as part-time, 31 or more hours as full-time. Men were not divided according to hours of work since part-time employment is much less common.
- **Socio-economic category**. The 22 Socio-economic Groups (SEGs) assigned by ONS according to employees' occupations were grouped into six categories for employees, ranging from professionals and managers in large organisations (1) to unskilled manual (6), while those applying to the self-employed, armed forces and full-time students were excluded from the analysis.
- **Earnings**. We took the OPCS derived variable of usual gross weekly earnings, and calculated the mean value for each population sub-group. Ideally we would have obtained the median as this is less sensitive to extreme values, but the computation would have been far more lengthy.

17.4.2 Results

Rejecting an occupational pension

Nearly two-thirds of the employees (N = 9,457, 63 per cent) had access to an occupational pension, but only 52 per cent were members, while 11 per cent chose not to belong to their employer's scheme. These are referred to as **Rejectors**. When employees with access were selected, cross-tabulation confirmed that women, and especially part-timers, were more likely to be Rejectors (see Figure 17.1(a), bars labelled 'All'). However, when a third variable, age group, was used as control, an interesting interaction between age group and hours of work was evident (see Figure 17.1(a), bars labelled with age groups). For men and for women employed full-time, there was a near-linear relationship between age group and proportion of Rejectors, while among women part-timers, the proportion of Rejectors was high in all age groups at around 40 per cent, only falling below 30 per cent among those in their 50s. By controlling for age group, we have revealed that a quite different process operates for part-timers, compared with full-timers of either gender, probably reflecting their low pay irrespective of age group. Some confirmation of this was provided by controlling for socio-economic category (see Figure 17.1(b)). Among women part-timers in the highest-level occupations, the proportion of Rejectors was little higher than for women full-timers in this occupational group. This analysis also shows that even when we control for both hours of work and occupational group, women are still more likely to be Rejectors than men. Rejecting an occupational pension was also associated with lower earnings (not shown). Thus the first hypothesis, A, is supported.

The cross-tabulations also indicated that at least two variables (age and hours of work) interact. Moreover, it seems likely that the underlying reason for the high rate of rejection of an occupational pension by part-timers is their low earnings, these in turn being associated with the low occupational status of most part-timers. To test these suppositions, and to find out whether they are equally true for men and women required multivariate analysis (see Ginn and Arber, 2000), since cross-tabulation becomes unwieldy when more than three variables are analysed simultaneously.

Contributing to an APP

Employees rejecting membership of an occupational pension were selected (N = 1,690, 11 per cent of employees) and their take-up of APPs analysed. Figure 17.2 shows the proportion of Rejectors contributing to an APP by age group, hours of work and gender. Men were more likely to have an APP than women, and full-timers more likely than part-timers; 63 per cent of men, 42 per cent of women full-timers and 22 per cent of women part-timers (see Figure 17.2, 'All'). For men and women employed full-time, those in their 30s were most likely to have an APP, while part-timers showed a

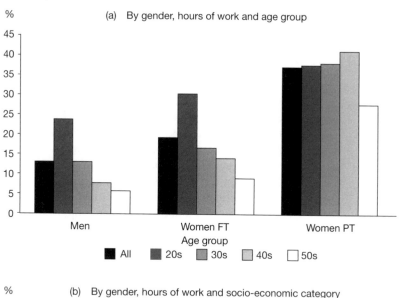

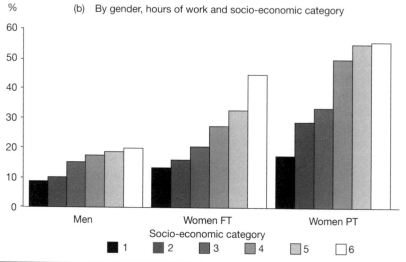

Socio-economic categories based on current occupation	Corresponding ONS socio-economic groups (SEGs)
1 Professionals/managers in organisations with 25+ employees	2, 6
2 Intermediate non-manual and managers, under 25 employees	4, 7, 8
3 Junior non-manual	9
4 Skilled manual, including supervisory	11, 12
5 Semi-skilled manual, personal service	10, 13, 18
6 Unskilled manual	14

Employers, self-employed, Armed Forces, full-time students and those who have never worked are not included.

Source: General Household Surveys, 1993–94 (author's analysis)

Figure 17.1   *Percentage rejecting an occupational pension scheme, among men and women employees with access*

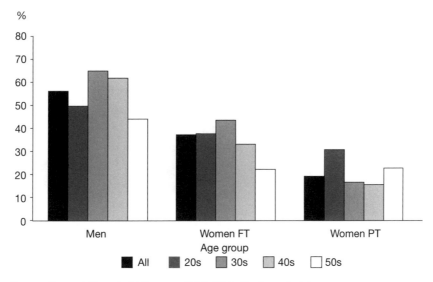

Source: General Household Surveys, 1993–94 (author's analysis)

Figure 17.2 *Percentage of Rejectors contributing to an APP, by age group and hours of work (men and women aged 20–59)*

different pattern, with those aged 30–49 least likely to contribute. Take-up of APPs was more common among those in higher socio-economic groups and with higher earnings (not shown). For example, 72 per cent of Rejectors earning over £400 per week had an APP compared with only 33 per cent of Rejectors earning £100–199 per week. Thus our second hypothesis, B, is mainly supported, although with some modification in respect of the age groups most likely to contribute to APPs, which vary with employment status and gender.

Employees may be **Excluded** from occupational pension scheme membership, either because their employers did not operate a scheme or because they were ineligible for their employers' scheme. These employees were selected (N = 5,612, 37 per cent of employees) and their rate of contribution to APPs analysed. Figure 17.3 shows the proportion of the Excluded who contributed to an APP, by age group, hours of work and gender.

The proportions of the Excluded who had taken up an APP were lower in each population sub-group than among Rejectors. Yet if Figures 17.2 and 17.3 are compared, it is evident that the pattern of APP membership is similar. Contributing is more likely for men than for women and for full-timers than for part-timers; 48 per cent of men, 34 per cent of women full-timers and 12 per cent of women part-timers. The pattern according to age group is also similar in the two groups (Rejectors and Excluded), although there is less variation with age group among Excluded part-timers. Thus our third hypothesis, C, is confirmed, except that take-up was not highest among the youngest but among those aged 30–49.

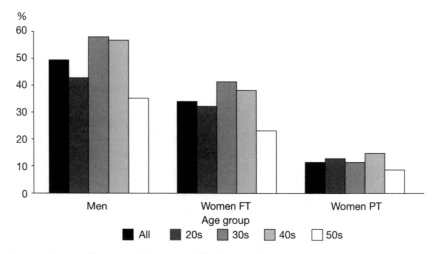

Source: General Household Surveys, 1993–94 (author's analysis)

Figure 17.3   *Percentage of Excluded contributing to an APP, by age group and hours of work (men and women aged 20–59)*

Multivariate analysis, in which a number of independent variables were included in logistic regression models (age group, socio-economic category, earnings, time with employer, size of organisation, hours of work and marital status) showed that all these had independent effects on the pension choices made by men and women (see Ginn and Arber, 2000).

The results confirmed that APPs had found their target among employees lacking access to an occupational pension, in that take-up among the Excluded was highest among the relatively young and well paid. However, APP take-up spread beyond these groups. The notorious mis-selling scandal, in which employees who would have been better off remaining in their occupational pension scheme were persuaded to switch to an APP by commission-driven sales techniques between 1988 and 1993, is well known. But for those less advantaged in the labour market, especially women, little was known about mis-selling to those who would have been better off in SERPS.

Mis-selling APPs to rejectors and excluded

An APP is expected to provide a better return on contributions than SERPS if, in the long run, the rate of interest exceeds the growth in national earnings. However, because of the disproportionate effect of charges on the contributions made by the lower paid, experts have estimated that opting out of SERPS into a personal pension would not be advantageous for those earning below £200 per week (in 1993) (Durham, 1994). Contributing to a personal pension when young and switching back into SERPS between ages 30 and 40 is considered the optimal strategy on average (Dilnot et al., 1994). Thus those who in 1993–94 were earning less than £200 per week or were

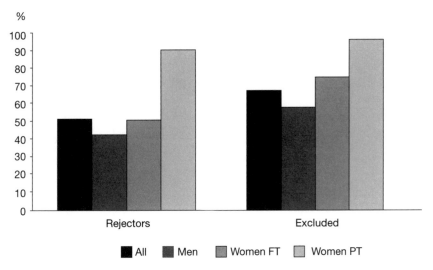

Source: General Household Surveys, 1993–94 (author's analysis)

Figure 17.4 *Percentage of APP contributors for whom this was likely to be an unsuitable decision due to age or low pay, among Rejectors and Excluded, by hours of work and gender*

aged over 40 were likely to have been better off contributing to SERPS than to an APP. Figure 17.4 shows the proportions of contributors to an APP who were probably ill-advised to do so, applying these criteria of age and earnings.

In all, half of Rejectors were apparently subject to mis-selling and 68 per cent of the Excluded. The proportions among women were much higher, 62 per cent and 83 per cent, but over 90 per cent among part-timers (see Figure 17.4). This estimate of mis-selling is inevitably crude, since the outcome will depend on the specific APP's charges and performance, the level and continuity of the individual's future earnings and on macro-economic developments far into the future. But the figures show that mis-selling to the Excluded is more extensive than to Rejectors. First, the Excluded are less advantaged on average than Rejectors. Secondly, they are more numerous. As a proportion of all employees, Rejectors who had been mis-sold an APP according to our criteria represent 2.7 per cent and the Excluded 8 per cent. Figure 17.5 summarises the pension choices made by employees.

17.4.3 Summary and discussion

Preliminary analysis established the change between 1987 and 1993–94 in pension arrangements of men and women, showing that although the introduction of APPs increased private pension coverage, they did not contribute to the increased gender equality in private pension coverage.

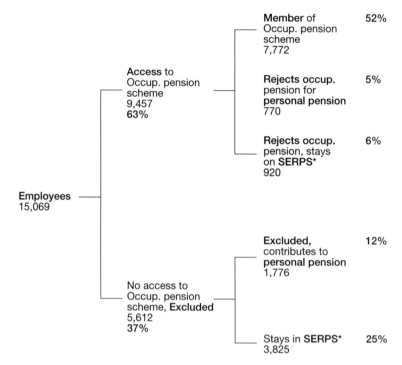

Member of Occup. pension scheme 7,772 — 52%

Rejects occup. pension for personal pension 770 — 5%

Rejects occup. pension, stays on SERPS* 920 — 6%

Access to Occup. pension scheme 9,457 63%

Excluded, contributes to personal pension 1,776 — 12%

Stays in SERPS* 3,825 — 25%

No access to Occup. pension scheme, Excluded 5,612 37%

Employees 15,069

*A minority currently paid no SERPS contributions because their earnings were too low.

Source: General Household Surveys, 1993 and 1994 (author's analysis)

Figure 17.5   *Pension arrangements of employees, 1993–94, Britain*

Cross-tabulation of pension arrangements in 1993–94 by a number of variables confirmed our hypotheses, A to C:

A.   Among those with access to an occupational pension, rejection was associated with younger age, lower socio-economic group, lower earnings, part-time employment (among women) and being female; but among women part-timers rejection was similarly high for age 20–49, only falling among those in their 50s.

B.   Among those rejecting an occupational pension, contributing to an APP rather than SERPS was associated with the prime years of 30–39 (except for women part-timers), with higher earnings, higher socio-economic group, full-time employment and being male.

C.   Among those lacking access to an occupational pension (the Excluded), similar factors as for hypothesis B favoured contributing to an APP, although the Excluded were less likely than Rejectors to contribute to an APP.

These results indicate that those targeted for APPs had disproportionately taken up the option. However, the analysis of APP contributors by earnings and age showed that this policy success was marred by extensive mis-selling, involving over 10 per cent of employees. Mis-selling was especially common to those lacking access to an occupational pension scheme, where over two-thirds of APP contributors had been mis-sold. The consequences for women are particularly serious, given that our analysis did not take account of future gaps in employment, which would further reduce the value of an APP.

Women's disadvantage in private pension income due to their role in marriage and childrearing will be an increasingly important issue as the value of the state pension relative to average incomes declines. The situation of the increasing number of elderly divorced women, who are likely to have lost the opportunity to build an adequate private pension of their own, yet will have no access to their ex-husband's, is particularly bleak. If older women in the future are not to suffer poverty as a result of their reproductive and nurturing roles, policies are needed which ensure an adequate income from the state for those who have undertaken unpaid caring responsibilities, as in other countries (Ginn et al., 2001).

Disseminating the research through academic journals and elsewhere (see Chapter 21), adds to the growing literature which demonstrates how women's financial disadvantage in later life is the result of socially struc-tured arrangements. Achieving policy change is more difficult, since it depends on the political and economic climate.

17.5 CONCLUSIONS: RESEARCH AS A PROCESS

This example has shown how secondary analysis can be used to contribute to understanding the effect of a particular policy instrument, which arose in the context of a political commitment to privatisation by a Conservative regime. It illustrates the strengths and limitations of secondary analysis of a large government dataset and traced the process of analysis through several stages.

My own interests and previous experience affected the choice of research problem, but each stage of the research affected my thinking and subsequent treatment of the data. Although earlier research and the work of other researchers had shaped my expectations in framing three hypotheses, the results were not wholly predictable. Moreover, the analysis prompted a further investigation, into the extent of mis-selling of APPs to two distinct groups of employees.

The research described here represents part of a project on 'The changing pensions mix in the 1990s: gender, pension acquisition and income', which has contributed to a further project on 'Gender, Employment and Pension Acquisition: Trends and International Comparisons' and a book (Ginn et al., 2001). As such it can be seen as a small piece in a jigsaw which can make a contribution to a wider body of research and theory about the policy challenges arising from ageing societies.

COMPUTER ASSISTED QUALITATIVE DATA ANALYSIS 18

ANN LEWINS

CONTENTS

Computer assistance in qualitative data analysis has become a respectable and accepted strategy for the management of qualitative data. This chapter refers to several categories of Computer Assisted Qualitative Data AnalysiS (CAQDAS) software. I will focus mainly, however, on a particular group of software packages, the 'code-based theory builders' (Weitzman and Miles, 1995), and some of the ways they seek to assist the researcher in working with large volumes of qualitative information and data. Theory building software programs will help you manage the data and to manage and interrogate your ideas. They have a dominant place in many academic and applied social research settings.

Transcripts of interviews, descriptions and narratives can produce a lot of text. Handling such data can be disorganised and *messy*. When interpreting and recording significance, commonality, exceptions, or tracking a story, it is difficult to keep in touch with all the ideas you may have about the data. You need to keep in touch with examples of the data that demonstrate those ideas and the connections between those ideas. Whether the data are in textual, audio, video, or graphic format, ideas about them nearly always relate to parts of them. In essence, software seeks to maintain an easy contact between the ideas and those parts, while allowing an overview of the whole.

This chapter shows how some of the tasks of analysis, mostly clerical, associated with the analysis of qualitative data can be assisted by a range of software programs. At the end of the chapter, there is a list of resources, from which comparative or software-specific information can be gathered. Many software packages offer similar tools, but the way in which they are provided varies.

One of the important aspects of software use is the ease with which software can be learnt or taught. This is not quite the same as 'user friendliness'. Researchers involved in substantive projects will have different needs and resources compared to students. The availability of support and the ease with which a software package can become useful are vital considerations. The package should not become an obstacle to getting on with 'real work' with data. It is also necessary to touch briefly on the different working styles of analysis, and the methodological debate surrounding them. Your way of working with qualitative data may spring from deeply held beliefs about the nature of knowledge and existence itself, or simply from project design. If you are going to be a user of software it is important to know and to understand your methodological standpoint first, and then to bring a methodology *to* the software, rather than see the software as being the architect of your method.

18.1 THE DEVELOPMENT OF CAQDAS
SOFTWARE

CAQDAS software developed largely from early work by academics who were involved in qualitative data analysis during the late 1980s (Fielding and Lee, 1991/1993). Early programs specifically developed to analyse qualitative (then, mainly textual) data were The Ethnograph (Seidel), Hyper-RESEARCH (Biber, Kinder) QSR NUD*IST (Richards and Richards) and a little later ATLAS.ti (Muhr). Some began as collaborative projects with universities but later became independently produced programs which were marketed and distributed by commercial software publishers. The influence of the 'user', too, has been an important factor. In a decade of software development, developers have been very responsive to critique and free upgrades to a package often reflect this. Developments in information technology have enabled an increase in the range of software packages and, similarly, the range and sophistication of tools within each software program.

As packages have been developed to handle textual data in various ways, typologies have been developed to categorise the software programs (Weitzman and Miles, 1995). Major groups of packages concerned with the analysis of textual or other qualitative data have been described as:

'Text retriever' and 'Text-based Managers' are mainly concerned with the quantitative 'content' of qualitative data and automatic generation of word/phrase indexes, statistical information on word frequency and the retrieval of text in context. They will often have internal dictionaries and thesaurus facilities. They fall into a wider category sometimes referred to as 'content analysis' packages. Examples include Sonar Professional, CISAID and SIMSTAT. Some content analysis programs, (e.g. Diction 4.0) set out to analyse the 'tone' of speech transcripts to produce, for example, a measure of confidence. (For more examples see http://www.content-analysis.de/quantitative.html)

'Code and Retrieve' and 'Code-based Theory Builders' have been more concerned with thematic analysis and interpretation of textual data. It is the functionality of the 'code and retrieve' and the 'code-based theory builders' which is used more widely in academic and applied social research settings. Examples include, QSR NUD*IST, ATLAS.ti, HyperRESEARCH, The Ethnograph, KWALITAN, WinMAX. (For more information see http://caqdas.soc.surrey.ac.uk)

The two code-based categories have tended to merge as enhancements to the 'code and retrieve' packages and have caught up with the range of tools available in the 'theory builders'. Packages in these last two categories use the database structure of the software to enable the assignment of 'codes' or labels to chunks of text, and the subsequent 'retrieval' of text segments according to selected code labels. Subsequent interrogation of codes, and their co-occurrence, proximity (or not) etc., in the data allows researchers to test relationships between identified themes and concepts. In the broad typology of software, this extra functionality allows the 'code-based theory building' label to be applied to an increasing range of software programs. The label 'theory builders' must not be misunderstood. No theory is built by the package itself and any theory or conclusions which are drawn are the result of the researcher's own thinking. The addition of networking and modelling tools (see Figure 18.6, p. 316) has added to the researcher's ability to visualise the connections between concepts, issues and themes, while work remains integrated with source data. The development of 'hyper-linking' functionality allows the user to jump instantly between points in the coding schema or text to other related points in the dataset. The incorporation of multimedia data into a working project is now possible in ATLAS.ti, HyperRESEARCH, NVivo, CISAID and CTanks. All make different use of hyperlinks to segments of audio or video files to enable different levels of multimedia integration with the project. Other software developers have resisted the move to multimedia tools (including WinMAX 99 Pro and The Ethnograph Version 5). Such packages have also been modernised and upgraded, but they tend to be smaller in size, easier to learn, and are therefore most useful for those with time constraints or those who can do without the more complex tools. Although the incorporation of multimedia data into projects has increased, the great majority of projects still consider text transcripts of interviews etc. as the best way to access large amounts of data quickly. This is the case even though the transcription of data is a very lengthy process (the use and development of Voice Recognition software has some way to go before it is widespread or fully efficient).

Increasingly, packages do not fit neatly into existing software typologies. ATLAS and KWALITAN both provide code-based theory building tools but also provide quantitative word frequency information, unusual in this category of program. CISAID has strong links with the 'text retrievers' and the family of programs which provide this type of 'content analysis'. It provides sophisticated statistical information about word and phrase content, but at the same time part of its functionality is code-based and this allows it into the 'code-based' category of programs. CTanks, does not fit into any existing category. It provides transcription function keys and early analysis

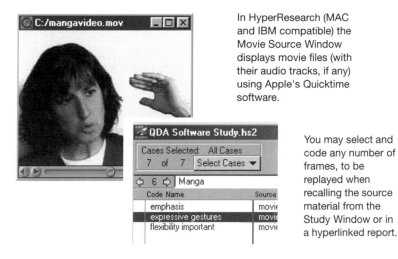

In HyperResearch (MAC and IBM compatible) the Movie Source Window displays movie files (with their audio tracks, if any) using Apple's Quicktime software.

You may select and code any number of frames, to be replayed when recalling the source material from the Study Window or in a hyperlinked report.

Figure 18.1 *Integrating multimedia files into a project*

tools, allowing the researcher to build hyperlinks from the transcript or commentary to points within the digital sound or video file. Linked multimedia documents remain synchronised with the text commentary; for example, when scrolling a section of the transcript or summarised commentary, the software will play back the relevant sound segment of the file. Multimedia support in HyperRESEARCH software is illustrated in Figure 18.1, where the Movie Source Window sits side by side with a coding window.

18.2 ANALYTIC PARADIGMS USING
QUALITATIVE DATA

Qualitative researchers approach projects, the analysis of data, and the use of software from a range of methodological and epistemological perspectives. Many specifically refer to 'Grounded Theory', a 'general method of constant comparative analysis' (Glaser and Strauss, 1967; Strauss and Corbin, 1994). Ideas are generated from what is seen after reading and re-reading the text. You may need to assign labels (**codes**) and annotations or memos to the data, based on your understanding of the data (see Chapters 9 and 14). This might be followed by the refinement of codes into concepts and categories in order *later* to generate theory that is thoroughly grounded in the data. Using similar methods, you may instead be using a less clearly defined descriptive, interpretative or comparative approach. You may start with questions you need to answer, but the theoretical or other framework of your findings will be what your analysis is working towards, not the starting point of the project.

In Layder's 'adaptive theory', he suggests that the process of coding can begin with sensitising concepts and ideas, as 'orienting devices' (Layder, 1998). These concepts are selectively plucked from existing theories to 'crank up' the theory building process, while always retaining 'theoretical openness' to new concepts arising from the data. He suggests that since there is a general acknowledgement that any observation and interpretation is **theory laden**, this means that starting the coding process from a 'clean slate' or *tabula rasa* is difficult. It is better therefore to be explicit about any theories that are contributing a priori to your ideas and knowledge about the subject that you are beginning to study.

Your project and its design may be completely pre-defined, or heavily influenced by theory. An example of this approach is included below (Speller, 2000). The coding framework is initially entirely built around the contributing theoretical concepts.

If you are involved in discourse analysis, you may be interested in language, conversation or discourse as social constructions or cultural expressions (see Chapter 19). Such an approach could be illustrated by taking a hypothetical approach to a recent e-mail exchange on 'qual-software' (the Internet discussion list created to enable debate and support the users of qualitative software). One subscriber used the word 'girls' in the context of a comment about people who do transcription. The use of the word 'girls' created an immediate and angry debate. If you used a constructionist, feminist approach to the analysis of this e-mail data, the use of the word *'girls'* within its context here, would be interesting. Thus, the annotations you make to the data may be more concerned with language, patterns and structures of the written word than with the concepts identified by someone analysing the outcomes of the more subject-specific debate concerning transcription *per se*, from the same data.

18.2.1 The suitability and limitations of software

Most programs are geared towards accessing large amounts of data and those smaller segments taken from the whole that represent examples of your thinking. The emphasis on large quantities of data places constraints on the flexible handling or marking up of individual data files. Although this is changing in some programs, you may have to work with 'Text only' formats (plain text – without word-processing characteristics, such as bold and underlining). Often data cannot be freely edited or annotated. The micro examination of a small dataset (for instance, for conversation analysis), is more likely to be hindered by the use of anything more complex than a word processor. The tracking of a sequence of events that is talked about in a disorderly way throughout a narrative, as in a life history, may not be handled with enough sensitivity with current 'theory building' software. Coffey, Holbrook and Atkinson (1996) consider the suitability of existing theory building packages for analysing narrative data, where reduction or fragmentation of the data can be unhelpful.

The **discourse analysis** of large volumes of news reportage might be better handled with a 'content analysis' or 'text retriever' package. This will depend on the researcher's individual needs and style of analysis. Sometimes what is required is a more quantitative analysis of content, together with the ability to retrieve text in context. Researchers often express a need for the early support of such quantitative analysis, followed by the later ability to assign codes based on identified themes as well. If this is the case, they need a software which contains elements of both the main categories of software described above (section 18.1), or they need two different packages.

Whatever approach you adopt, you should be clear about your needs before deciding to use a software package just because 'most people seem to use one' (see section 18.4). When thinking about making use of CAQDAS software it is useful to prioritise a list of requirements that suit the way you will prefer to work. If it is most important for you to be able to 'mark' the data as you analyse it, then make sure the package you chose will give you edit rights on your data files. If you are more concerned with quick navigation between points in the data than with data reduction in the text, make sure you can easily build hyperlinks between those points in the source data. Many of the tools are common to all theory building CAQDAS packages, but some functions exist only in a few or are exclusive to one.

18.3 HOW 'CODE-BASED THEORY BUILDING' SOFTWARE CAN HELP

Theory building CAQDAS software packages do not dictate the way or the order in which you might perform various tasks, but they might influence you in terms of the complexity of the tasks you undertake, and your readiness to perform them. Furthermore, they will encourage you to feel that you can change your mind about your analyses. Some of the tasks that they can assist with are listed in Table 18.1.

The main tasks and tools of CAQDAS software are explained in general and later the application of some of the tools will be illustrated and commented upon with three examples. The first is from applied research using a dataset of focus group transcripts. This was the qualitative phase of an assessment of the needs of elderly people commissioned by a local health authority. I was asked to use ATLAS.ti software to assist with my management of the data. The second example is a longitudinal, academic project, with a very large dataset, using QSR NUD*IST. The project, centred around the relocation of the entire mining community of Arkwright, examines notions of identity over five time phases (Speller, 2000). The third is a dataset created for use when teaching about qualitative software. It reports on a group of respondents' views of their community. The three examples each take quite different approaches to the development of coding frameworks and the role of theory. Generally, programs do not mind which

Table 18.1 *The main tasks of analysis, assisted by code-based theory building software*

1. Exploration and discovery by searching (for strings, words, phrases in verbatim content).
2. Coding during, after and leading to discovery (sorting, organising, categorising the data).
3. Theory-based coding.
4. Retrieval of coded segments.
5. Adding analytic memos.
6. Making visible indicators in the text.*
7. Linking to other parts of text and other files.*
8. Searching the database and the coding schema, testing ideas, interrogating subsets.
9. Mapping ideas, modelling processes and connections.*
10. Generating reports/output (print-outs or readable files in other applications).

* Not always available in all software programs.

approach you take. You can **open code** the text, as you work though it, or you can create codes in advance which focus your attention on theoretical issues and their occurrence in the data. You might work in a mix of both ways. Providing you are explicit about the way you have worked, and you can justify your choices, software will assist you to work in the way that suits you.

18.3.1 Sorting, organising, interpreting, identifying concepts – categorising

Even if you were working just with transcribed data on paper, you might want to annotate the data, write notes or scribble in the margin. You might highlight sections of the text in different colours to signify different themes or topics. If working on a word-processor with textual data, you might copy these sections of the text under different headings or into different files. Usually you will reduce the amount of text that you are dealing with and, to a certain extent, you will be lifting those **copied and pasted** sections of text out of their context.

Code-based retrieval packages will allow you to apply keywords/phrases (codes) to passages of text and put a label on the significance of a section or segment of the data. You can apply as many codes as you like to the same segments of text. The methodological approach being taken will affect how codes and themes are drawn out from the data. In other words, how the **coding schema** is to be established may be a vital outcome of project design. This in itself is not a software issue, although the flexibility with which you create, modify and refine the coding schema will be improved by the use of software. Codes might be created early on as part of a coding framework that arises from the objectives of the project and are then assigned to data where relevant (a 'top-down' method of coding). If your project is defined by theory, you may establish a coding schema which contains the main elements (e.g. sensitising concepts) from that theory before you begin to code the text. Or codes might emerge from, and be assigned to, segments of text during close work with the data (a 'bottom-up' approach to code creation). Subsequently, codes may encompass more abstract concepts from collections of issues and themes which seem to be related in some way.

The coding process will also allow you to **organise** the data if there are already significant known values that can be ascribed to the respondents – the sex and age of the respondents may be important, for instance. In Speller's example below, it was important to compare data across the five time phases of her longitudinal dataset. The five time phases were codes or values under the variable 'Time'. Each time phase code had to be assigned to the relevant data files. Such organisational coding can be a very important aspect of the coding process in any longitudinal project or where comparison across the source of data or type of respondent will be useful.

18.3.2 The coding schema

However codes are generated, and whatever methodological approach underpins this process, the 'coding schema' is the manifestation of the way they are listed or organised within the software program. Most theory building software programs encourage an inherently hierarchical organisation of the coding schema. In these packages, the hierarchy has a number of useful purposes later, when in retrieval or searching modes. For a few programs, such as ATLAS.ti and HyperRESEARCH, the default structure of the coding schema is not hierarchical. Hierarchies or the appearance of hierarchies can be imposed in some windows, but in the main 'code-lists' codes will be listed at the same level.

18.3.3 Retrieval

The software enables the **retrieval** of passages of text based on the presence of codes. You can then examine the retrieved segments, thus reducing the amount of data and stepping back from the dataset as a whole in order to focus on certain aspects. Retrieval can happen while in the software, in full contact with other functions, enabling, for example, the re-coding of segments or memoing. Or retrieval can be sent to output or report files which can be opened in other applications (word processor, spreadsheet applications, etc.).

18.3.4 Exploration and discovery by text searching

Discovery achieved by reading and re-reading is likely to be the most thorough method of exploring qualitative data. With large amounts of data, however, this may be impracticable without using the software to locate words and phrases that signal particular topics of interest. This tool is relevant only to textual data and varies slightly from one program to another. The differences, contexts and debate concerning the use of this tool are discussed at length by Fisher with reference to both code-based and text retriever categories of software (Fisher, 1997: 39–66). With most programs, you have the opportunity to search for several 'strings', words or phrases at the same time. The 'finds', or 'hits', can usually be saved, and then coded or autocoded. All textual references containing the finds will be stored where you choose to put them, in the coding schema.

In Figure 18.2, I searched the sample dataset I use when teaching about WinMAX software. I was interested in the words, strings or phrases that were used by the respondents when they were talking about wastage and decay in their community environment. The search retrieves segments containing these strings. I could reject the finds which are off-topic. Of course, this sort of search will not find where the speakers or respondents are talking *around* the subject without actually using any of the words put into

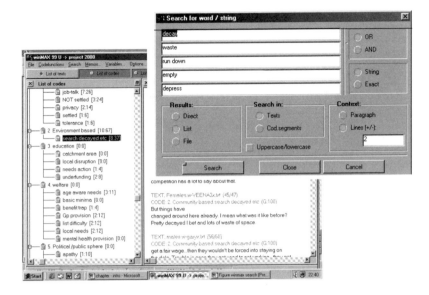

The search dialogue box, and the saved 'hits' at a code, showing the text segments found (across the whole dataset) in the bottom right-hand pane.

Figure 18.2   *The Text search tool in WinMAX 99 Pro*

the search dialogue box, so this tool is not a safe way to uncover everything said about an area of interest. It is, however, a fairly efficient way to look for buzz words or the use of jargon. The advantage of using CAQDAS software over searching files in a word-processing application is that in addition to finding the words, the CAQDAS software usually enables you to save those finds, together with some surrounding context, in a slot in a coding schema.

18.3.5 Making visible indicators in the text

Developments in a few software programs mean that the researcher can use Rich Text Format textual data, rather than plain, 'text only' formats. This means that you can integrate normal coding techniques (as above) with visibly 'marking' the text by colour coding or underlining, changing font size, etc., as you might if working in hard copy or with a word processor. This might be a suitable way to handle smaller datasets of narrative files.

18.3.6 Searching, making 'queries' – testing ideas and theories

The software can help you to ask questions about the relationships between codes as they occur in the text. Do the themes you have assigned to the text appear together? Do they appear close to each other? How do they compare

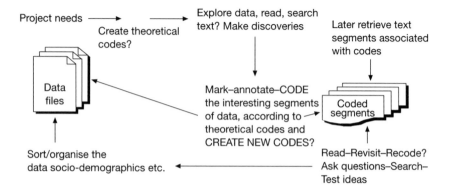

Figure 18.3 *Summarising the discovery/coding process*

across different sets of data and across the different groups of respondents? Before this type of searching and question asking can occur, you must have arrived at the point where you have achieved enough consistent coding to rely on the results of the queries you make. Figure 18.3 summarises the processes of discovery, coding and testing ideas.

18.3.7 Analytic memos

The ability to write analytical or procedural notes while working is provided in a number of ways. In some programs you can place annotations at points in the data. In others you are allowed to create one memo per data file. In most packages, you can also write comments or memos to explain codes and concepts – how they are defined and how they change. Memo-writing is an important aspect of the management and continuity of analysis.

18.4   EXAMPLES: HOW THE SOFTWARE HELPED

The working examples described below give some idea of some of the processes followed in two quite different projects. Both use theory building software, but they had different starting points and made use of different coding structures.

18.4.1 Example 1: the analysis of focus group interviews using ATLAS.ti

I had been given a relatively simple brief, to pull out the dominant themes from transcripts of focus groups generated in a health authority 'Needs

Assessment for the Elderly' exercise. At this stage, the client had no theoretical concerns and simply needed to be given a list of the themes as I saw them and the segments of data supporting them. Further analysis and writing-up would be based on the material I handed over. The client was also interested in having a measure of how frequently some words and expressions were used. Each group's discussion covered the main concerns that had been flagged up at the beginning (e.g. day care, health care, transport, personal safety). The client had requested that ATLAS.ti be used to assist in the process.

Analytic memoing

These concerns formed the starting point for a topic based group of memos where I wrote down absolutely everything worth noting as I read the data. In ATLAS.ti, drop-down lists of 'Files', 'Text segments', 'Codes' and 'Memos' provide interactive connections to source text during most analytic tasks. For example, I can be writing a memo while reviewing a code and the 'quotations' (text segments) to which it has been assigned. I also kept a central 'journal' memo, where I summarised my work each day, together with the questions and leads that I wanted to follow up at the next working session. As I began to develop other concepts while coding more data, I would begin a new memo in order to explain ideas about them as they occurred. Memo tools are available in all code-based theory building software programs and in some (including ATLAS.ti) you can locate a memo at a point in the text itself (though it will not be physically embedded in or cluttering up the text).

Word frequencies

Using the 'Word frequency' tool, I generated tables in which counts for every word in each data file were sorted both alphabetically and in frequency.

Coding

As I read the data I coded the flagged themes as they occurred in the data. This was straightforward. There were more subtle and interesting things in the data that seemed to cross the boundaries of all the major discussion themes. The issue of 'information', its accuracy, relevance and most importantly its source's respectability as perceived by elderly clients, was recurrently mentioned among the social service and care professionals. 'Resistance' to services was connected to the issue of information, but this was another concept that crossed all the main 'thematic' boundaries. So I proceeded with the coding of the data at several levels: obvious themes and more subtle observations. Figure 18.4 shows that in ATLAS.ti, once 'codes' have been assigned, the margin display approximates the way a file looks when marked up in hard copy.

In addition, the codes in the margin provide interactive connections to the sections of text to which the codes relate (in ATLAS.ti a text segment is

One way to assign codes to text: – *drag* the
code on to *selected* text

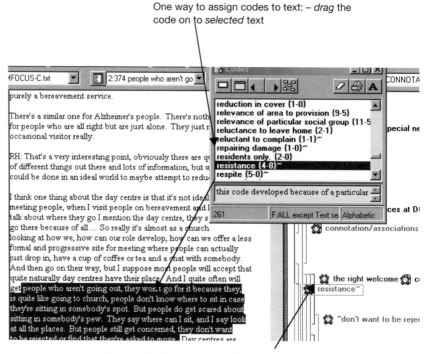

Once coding has been completed, *selecting* the assigned theme label
or code in the margin highlights the relevant segment of text

Figure 18.4   *Coding a data file in ATLAS.ti and reviewing a margin display
showing how the file has been coded so far*

described as a 'quotation'). Selecting the theme label or a code in the margin
highlights the relevant quotation. In the small section of text, about attendance
at day centres, one can see in the margin display that the codes, *connotations*,
Resistance (i.e. resistance to social services and help) '*the right welcome*' and
'*don't want to be rejected*' have been assigned separately but close together in
the text. I used quote marks around some codes to remind myself that some of
these began life as *In vivo* codes, that is codes which used the actual language
of the respondent. Short phrases and words can be dragged into the code list,
where they become codes, linked to the originating text.

Having coded the whole dataset in a first pass through the data, I could
now work in several ways.

Simple retrieval

I could examine particular themes in isolation by retrieving the data associated with them. In Figure 18.5, a partial report or output document can be
seen in which all examples of a selected code were collected together, from
across the whole dataset, lifting the text segments out of their original context.

8 quotation(s) for code: *Resistance*

P 1: FOCUS–B.txt – 1:139 (213:220) (Super)

... and I often usually ask do you go to the day centre sometimes. 'Oh no' and I find that one of the first signs of loneliness is resisting things of that kind and I'm sure it needs people being brought in by somebody, rather than, I don't know if that sort of person is going to come simply by having facilities here.

P 2: FOCUS–C.txt – 2:82 (242:245)

Day centres are fine for day centre people but there are quite a number of people who won't come to a place like this and therefore somewhere in the community we need to look for other places.

P 2: FOCUS–C.txt – 2:374 (237:242)

... people who aren't going out, they won't go for it because they, is quite like going to church, people don't know where to sit in case they're sitting in somebody's spot. But people do get scared about sitting in somebody's pew. They say where can I sit, and I say look at all the places. But people still get concerned, they don't want to be rejected or find they're asked to move.

P 3: FOCUS–A.txt – 3:389 (107:112)

I mean offering places at the day hospital I don't think will solve this underlying case because they will categorically refuse. They don't want to leave their home because they think that telling them to leave their home is taking their independence. They're attached to their home and you're trying to move them out, so I think there's very little care which goes into people's homes.

P 3: FOCUS–A.txt – 3:390 (116:119)

... particularly for professional people, they don't see it's for them and they won't even go and try because they've dismissed it as a bingo playing sing-along, it doesn't offer anything for them at all.

Figure 18.5   *Simple retrieval of text associated with the code,* Resistance

In ATLAS.ti, you can also remain linked directly to the whole context by choosing instead to double click on a code to 'List the quotations' in a small window. By clicking once on each quotation, you can see the quotation highlighted in the whole context of the file in the main window. A similar linkage between codes and text can be found in the network view (Figure 18.6), which helps with mapping ideas and concepts. When analysing focus group data, understanding the context is particularly important because of the collective and individual influences on the way that views are expressed.

Coding strategies and refining codes and concepts

In this project, I was unsure about the level of detail I needed to pick out from the data and represent in individual 'codes'. So at the first stage of my analysis, I was noticing and remarking and labelling everything I found interesting. To use a Grounded Theory term, I was **open coding**. Codes generated in this manner began as all having equal status. Initially, I was anxious that I might forget the detail I was seeing. I began to accumulate a lot of codes. As I began to refine the coding structure, I realised that *Resistance* was becoming a core concept, to which other themes could be related. Thinking more hierarchically, *Resistance* was a higher order concept within which other codes could be collected. The software could enable me

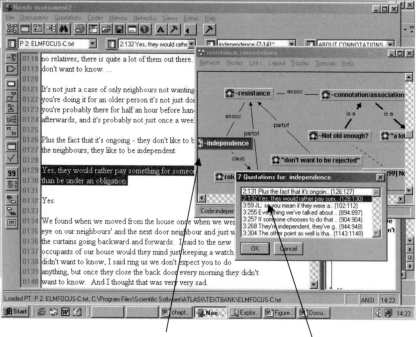

Working on a map or 'network' containing concepts generated from data, in ATLAS.ti.

Figure 18.6   *ATLAS.ti 'Network' (mapping) tool showing interactive links between network, codes and text*

to treat this new higher order concept in several ways. One method would be to 'link' the codes together in a Network, with the type of links signalling the nature of the relationship between the collection of codes and the higher concept. Another way would be to make structural changes to the coding schema by merging the detailed codes into *Resistance*. I eventually chose to create a *Resistance related* 'family' of codes, which could then be handled at the detailed sub-code level or at the broader macro-level of the collection or 'Code family'. Yet another similar option is to save a search expression using the 'Query' tool and the 'Supercode' tool, producing repeatable searches for a collection of codes in the data. Supercodes represent complex queries or combinations of codes, and are listed in the normal codes list. Selecting a supercode in the list re-runs the complex search. As part of the refining process, however, I also chose to merge several codes that represented much the same things but had been given different labels. All code-based theory building software will enable you to carry out such merging. Moving away from straightforward 'collections' of codes, I also mapped out some connections that began to express the nature of the relationship between codes (see Figure 18.6).

Mapping concepts and processes

Visualising connections between concepts and codes became part of the coding and 'note-taking' process. I had to be careful, because drawing a link, expressing, for example, a causal relationship, can be appropriate for one situation but not for another, and eventually these links needed to be broadly generalisable. I therefore made loosely associative connections to start with.

A mapping tool is also available in QSR NVivo, though with a different subset of tools. There are also packages, like Inspiration and Decision Explorer, that provide mapping facilities without direct integration with qualitative data. QSR NUD*IST 4.0, which does not have a mapping facility, has a direct interface with both Inspiration and Decision Explorer.

Hierarchical coding schemas

Some programs like WinMAX and QSR NUD*IST have inherently hier-archical coding schema that encourage the researcher to think in a structured way about coding frameworks. In ATLAS.ti, you have to arrange any hierarchical structure and subsequently you can only clearly visualise that hierarchy within specially arranged Network views. Thus the systematic, tidy support that a hierarchical coding schema gives you is lacking. On the other hand, many researchers feel constrained when it is not possible to move codes around freely to make visual connections that express more than just a hierarchical relationship.

To some extent, a hierarchical coding structure can make life within the software package simple. In WinMAX, the 'activated' hierarchy of codes provides very quick access to a set of related themes, and the text segments associated with them. The detailed smaller picture is thus displayed within the inclusive broad-brush picture, with just one click of a mouse button. Complex comparative qualitative cross-tabulations can be generated in QSR NUD*IST using coding hierarchies, as can be seen in the second example (section 18.4.2).

Searching and asking questions (queries) to test ideas

Whatever the inherent structure or lack of structure in a coding schema, the researcher is always able to test ideas, and relationships between themes and issues, by asking questions and performing searches of the database. Some examples of questions asked in this project were:

- Find where *Resistance* co-occurs with Independence.
- Find where *Resistance* is talked about – but only among 'Professional care givers' data.
- Find where the men talk about age relevance (when discussing day centres).

Every time you ask a question, the results can either be saved in a report file or, with some programs (NUD*IST, WinMAX and NVivo), the results can be coded and then integrated into an existing coding schema, as a secondary layer of coding and analysis. These new codes can then be used inside other questions. In ATLAS.ti, you can save the question itself as a 'supercode', as mentioned above.

18.4.2 Example 2: a longitudinal project, using QSR NUD*IST

In the second example, the shape of the coding schema was a key element in the way a very large dataset was managed. The hierarchical, structured nature of coding schema in QSR NUD*IST provided particularly powerful searching tools for Speller when analysing more than 100 interview files in her longitudinal study, 'The Relocation of Arkwright' (Speller, 2000). The project examined the relocation of an entire community of 177 householders to a new village (because of subsidence). The project involved the comparative study of 25 villagers during the relocation process, starting three years before the move and ending two years after the relocation. Interviews were carried out at five points in time. Speller's strategy of code creation was initially based entirely on concepts derived from a tranche of existing theory.

The role of theory in the project design and analysis

One of the main purposes of this study was to 'examine residents' place attachment in old and New Arkwright and to isolate aspects of the person–place transactions which may have affected their ability to detach from the old environment and attach to the new environment' (Speller, 2000: 81–3). The households were to receive a high level of compensation and had moved from a working-class environment to a middle-class one. Was the transition a positive or negative experience for residents? Was it seen as a facilitator or inhibitor to forming place attachments and identity? The project was underpinned by a theoretical framework, major elements of which were Place Attachment theory (Brown and Perkins, 1992) and Identity Process theory (Breakwell, 1986, 1992). There was little empirical work available on either theory, so Speller hoped that this study would add to the corpus of work in the area and ultimately refine current theories. Consequently, the principles of each theory were incorporated in a coding schema; a *top-down* approach was used to build the coding framework before coding of the text started. All theory building programs support this approach, but the size of the dataset, its longitudinal structure and the types of question Speller needed to ask made the structure of NUD*IST, its hierarchical coding schema and the nature of its search tools particularly useful.

Coding

Once theoretical concept codes had been created, Speller needed to read the text carefully and assign those codes to relevant chunks of text. She also remained open to new issues and therefore developed codes and concepts grounded in the data. The coding process took six to nine months, even with the help of the software. But when she had finished, she had ensured flexible access to a large body of coded data. She describes the next stage:

> The next stage in the analysis was to print out all the collected quotations within one category and to reread participants' responses in this concentrated form. This highlighted complexities within the category, including nuances of differences which frequently resulted in splitting the category or merging it with others. This process of searching for relationships between themes and emerging patterns also brought to the fore inconsistencies in participants' accounts. These often represented or were an indication of the process of adaptation to a new environment and were therefore considered an important element for inclusion in the analysis. (Speller, 2000: 147–8)

Organisational coding

QSR NUD*IST enables the factual/quantitative coding of a large corpus of data with an 'Import-table' tool. A spread sheet, consisting of a matrix of document names, variables and values not only builds that area of the coding schema, but assigns codes to documents based on that information. Using this facility, the time phase information, the respondents' names, how long they had lived in Arkwright, whether they rented or owned their homes, etc., were assigned to each document. Once the information had been imported, the researcher could (a) bring individual respondent's five time files together in order to see the respondent's data as a whole, and (b) evaluate change, perceptions of security, etc., across all time phases, either by an individual or sets of individuals, or across all or some individuals within a time phase.

Some sample questions and searches are:

How did talk about 'Previous rituals' feature, but just in Time 5 data for all respondents?

A simple *Intersect* search will produce this answer and can be similarly obtained in most theory building programs.

Using the longitudinal dimensions of the data:

How did talk about 'Previous rituals' feature, compare between Time 4 (6 months after the relocation) and Time 5 (2 years after) in data for all respondents?

In QSR NUD*IST, a 'vector' type Index search would produce this result in one step.

An example of a more complex question is:

Did Mary talk about her sense of 'security' in T1, T2 or T3 and also at T4 and T5? If Mary was positive about her sense of security in T1, 2 or 3, did she experience a sense of mastery at T4 and if so, was this sustained or not at T5?

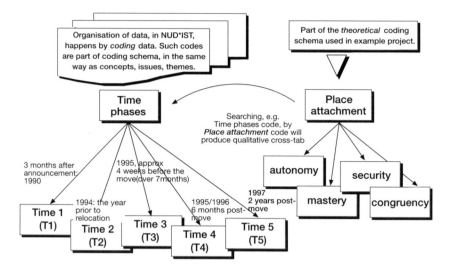

Making use of hierarchical structure of coding schema. Time phase codes have been applied to documents from each time phase, while the concepts found in files, have been coded to relevant segments of text across all files irrespective of time phase. (Graphic generated in Inspiration, a mapping tool with an interface with QSR NUD*IST.)

Figure 18.7   *Part of the longitudinal coding schema in QSR NUD*IST*

To assist in answering this question, QSR NUD*IST will produce a breakdown, or qualitative cross-tabulation by all time phases, of all the different elements of place attachment theory (including *sense of security* and *mastery*), built into one report. Such a level of output might require 20 or more separately performed searches in other programs (see Figure 18.7).

18.5   CONCLUSION

Not all analyses can or should happen within the program. This may be obvious, but it is important to make the point since so much of our lives revolve around the expectation that computers are part of the way we work. Alan Simpson commented in a recent e-mail discussion on his approach to qualitative analysis in a project on how community mental health nurses try to meet the needs of people with severe mental illness.

I am slowly beginning to make use of NVivo but most of my thinking and 'analysing' has been going on during interview and during transcription which I do myself. I find myself writing notes to myself, making vague or not so vague connections at the time or later as I am driving home, etc. – all long before I import into NVivo and start coding.

Michael Agar writes, in an essay that critiqued software in the light of his own needs,

> That critical way of seeing in my experience at least, comes out of numerous cycles through a little bit of data, massive amounts of thinking about that data, and slippery things like intuition and serendipity. An electronic ally doesn't have much of a role to play.
>
> I need to lay a couple of stretches of transcript on a table so I can look at it all at once. Then I need to mark different parts in different ways to find the pattern that holds the text together and ties it to whatever external frame I am developing. The software problem would be simple to solve. You'd need to be able to quickly insert different colored marks of different kinds at different points so you could see multi-threaded DNA laid on the text so you could look at the patterns that each thread revealed and then the patterns among the patterns. (Agar, 1993: 193)

Agar describes viewing data on paper, wanting more context and more data at a time. The use of software will probably never fix this particular problem. Agar's reservations were expressed in the context of the discourse analysis of one trial transcript. Analytic needs when working with many cases or files may be different. However, there is nothing to stop you working in a combination of ways, whatever the sources of data. Why not work with the software for certain tasks but have paper versions of the data on hand? Agar's essay was first published in 1991; much has changed since then, and at least two programs, ATLAS.ti and QSR NVivo, have added tools that seem to have been reactions to parts of Agar's critique (mapping tools and colour coding). So nothing remains the same for long.

In my day-to-day work, as a software teacher and advisor, I see that some of the problems of using computers are the result of a lack of resources – such as hardware, money and time to familiarise. The most common constraint is time, especially since many of the problems associated with effective use of software are linked to the problems of qualitative data analysis itself. In too many projects, the data collection and data preparation phases spread into the time allotted for analysis. Aggravating these difficulties is the lack of formally prescribed techniques for analysing qualitative data as a result of the variety of analytic paradigms and the personal nature of the relationship between data and the researcher. These issues, when added to the need to choose and become familiar with a program, combine to make the researcher's problems more complex.

What CAQDAS software can do now is to increase the efficiency of your access to data and your flexibility and your preparedness to re-think. It can be used at a very basic level and still be of benefit, and it can increase the number and complexity of tasks which can be performed. Always remember, though, that increasing your choices and tools in this way makes demands on your time.

18.6   CAQDAS RESOURCES

The CAQDAS Networking Project: Offers support to a worldwide research community. Provides platforms for debate, information and training concerning computer assistance in the analysis of qualitative data. Based at University of Surrey.	CAQDAS Networking Project Online Resources **Advisory help-lines** a.lewins@soc.surrey.ac.uk Tel: +44 (0) 1483 259455 **World Wide Web page** http://caqdas.soc.surrey.ac.uk Bibliography – Articles – Events – Courses – Seminars – Download demo versions of software. Links to software developer pages Links to other related resources Stop-press news, upgrades etc. **Internet Discussion List – qual-software** To join 'qual-software' Internet discussion group send a message to: jiscmail@jiscmail.ac.uk in the text enter: join qual-software Yourfirstname Yoursecondname see message archives below
Mailbase message archives	http://www.jiscmail.ac.uk/
Message archives for qual-software	http://www.jiscmail.ac.uk/lists/qual-software.htm/
Social Science Information Gateway	Multi-discipline information resource http://www.sosig.ac.uk/
Sociological Research Online	Electronic journal: Theoretical, empirical and methodological discussions, political, cultural topics and debates. Free Issues from March 1996–September 1998. http://www.socresonline.org.uk/
Free software	'CDC EZ-text' created by Centers for Disease Control and Protection http://www.cdc.gov/hiv/software/ez-text.htm 'AnSWR' created by Centers for Disease Control: Information Systems Support Services (CISSS) http://www.cdc.gov/hiv/software/answr.htm

18.7   FURTHER READING

Qualitative data analysis methodologies are systematically described in Miles and Huberman (1994), and an appendix in the same volume summarises a typology of software and a description of the tools supporting such methods of working. Weitzman and Miles (1995) reviews and describes practical processes which are served by a range of software programs. Similarly, Dey (1993) provides a readable, 'user friendly' assistance to qualitative data analysis with software use in mind. Books describing the practical processes of substantive project work, oriented to specific software use, can be very helpful. A good example of this is Bazeley and Richards (2000) who work systematically through a project using QSR NVivo.

Murphy et al. (1998) compiled a review of the literature concerning qualitative methodologies (294 pages), for the NHS R&D Health Technology Assessment Programme. The volume is available in hard copy and online at http://www.hta.nhsweb.nhs.uk/. This and other online papers concerning the use of CAQDAS software are accessible via links from the CAQDAS Networking Project web pages, at http://caqdas.soc.surrey.ac.uk/news.htm.

ANALYSING FACTUAL ACCOUNTS

19

ROBIN WOOFFITT

CONTENTS

Language use permeates and infuses all those aspects of society that are conventionally regarded as the core topics for sociological research. For example, everyday language is the medium through which society socialises young children; institutional norms and values are transmitted through a variety of forms of discourse; family life is rife with words, jokes and arguments; society's gender inequalities may resonate in patterns of conversation between women and men; the education of young people rests in part upon the verbal skills of teachers to interest, enthuse or cajole their students; and legal declarations are administered in courtroom trials which involve the verbal interrogation of witnesses and defendants for the benefit of an overhearing jury. Yet the sociological study of language use has not yet emerged as one of the central core topics of the discipline along with the study of class, gender, ethnicity, deviance, education, the family, and so on. Perhaps it is because 'people talking to each other' is so commonplace and taken for granted that for the majority of the twentieth century it was not treated as a central topic in social scientific research.

The analytic approach to be described and illustrated in this chapter seeks to rectify this deficiency by focusing primarily on language use. It shares many features of two other contemporary approaches to the study of language: conversation analysis in sociology and discourse analysis in social psychology.

19.1 LANGUAGE: DESCRIPTIONS AS ACTIONS

In the last 30 years sociological interest in the use of language has been influenced by the philosophy of Wittgenstein (1953) and Austin (1962), and the sociological research of Garfinkel (1967a; see also, Heritage, 1984) and Sacks (1992). In his early research, Wittgenstein examined language to explore how it represented objects and states of affairs in the world. In his later work, however, he rejected the theory that language is a medium which merely reflects or describes the world, and emphasised instead the importance of language use. He urged that we consider language as a tool box, and focus on the ways that people use these tools. His primary contribution was to propose that language is a central feature of the social and cultural milieu in which it was used, and not merely a logical system of symbols with which we can represent the world 'out there'.

Austin's (1962) work also emphasised the social and dynamic character of language, but his work focused on instances of specific types of sentence. He began by distinguishing between two types of utterance: constative utterances, which report some aspect of the world, and performative utterances, which perform a specific action. An example of a performative utterance is 'I suggest you do this', where saying these words is to perform the action of suggesting. Other examples are promises, warnings, declarations, and so on. He termed such utterances, speech acts. Austin subsequently rejected the distinction between performative and constative utterances: his investigations convinced him that all utterances could be treated as performative. He concluded that any use of language, regardless of what else it might be doing, was a series of actions.

A renewed interest in the sociological study of language was stimulated by the sociological approach that came to be known as ethnomethodology. Pioneered by Harold Garfinkel (1967a), the fundamental tenet of ethnomethodology is that the sense of social action is accomplished through the participants' use of tacit, practical reasoning skills and competencies. (These skills are referred to as 'tacit' and 'practical' because they are not the kinds of 'rules' or norms of behaviour which we could consciously articulate, or on which we would routinely reflect. Instead, they inhabit the very weave of social life, and thereby become invisible and unnoticeable.) As so much of social life is mediated through spoken and written communication, the study of language was placed at the very heart of ethnomethodology's sociological enterprise.

Harvey Sacks was a colleague of Garfinkel, and their work shares many concerns. However, Sacks's work was focused exclusively on the communicative competencies that informed ordinary, everyday conversation. Sacks and his colleagues conducted detailed and repeated analyses of tape-recordings of everyday telephone conversations, and produced transcripts which tried to capture the messiness and complexity of the exchanges. This research led to the discovery of systematic properties in the way that conversation is organised. The study of the structure of conversational organisation has come to be known as conversation analysis, or CA, and is one of the pre-eminent contemporary approaches to the study of language use.

Finally, discourse analysis (DA) is an analytic method which grew out of the sociological study of scientific knowledge (Gilbert and Mulkay, 1984), but which developed principally in social psychology (Potter and Wetherell, 1987). Unlike conversation analysts, discourse analysts examine all forms of verbal and textual materials: spoken and written accounts, letters, scientific journals, newspaper reports, and so on. The object is to describe the way that such texts are constructed, and to explore the functions served by specific constructions at both the interpersonal and societal level.

During the 1990s, discourse analysts working in social psychology pursued three main avenues of research. First, DA was used to explore how wider social and political concerns inform the use of language (e.g. Wetherell, 1998). Secondly, there has been an investigation of how aspects of mind – cognitions, personality, identity, memory, attitudes, attributions, and so on – are warrantably invoked and made relevant in the particulars of language use in a variety of discursive contexts. This branch of work has come to be known as discursive psychology (Edwards, 1997; Edwards and Potter, 1992). Finally, there were studies of factual discourse: how language may be used to provide accounts of events or opinions in such a way as to make them resistant to sceptical responses or alternative versions (Potter, 1996; Wooffitt, 1992). Conversation analytic methods and findings have proved to be a useful resource both in discursive psychology and the study of factual discourse.

As a consequence of these developments, it is now untenable to retain conceptions of language as a merely neutral medium for the transmission of information, values and beliefs about a world 'out there'. Instead, we can examine language use as a form of social action, the systematic properties of which can be described and rigorously analysed. To illustrate this, we shall examine part of an account, recorded during an informal conversational interview (see Chapter 8), of a series of events which followed a music concert. We will be focusing on the way in which the account is organised to establish that the speaker's version of events was robust and resistant to alternative versions of what happened on that night. First, however, we need to make some preliminary remarks about the source of data and the way the specific extract has been prepared for analysis.

19.2 DATA

The interview was conducted as part of a study of adolescent youth sub-cultures: punks, skinheads, rockers, gothics, hippies, and so on (Widdicombe and Wooffitt, 1995). The extract comes from a conversation between three punk rockers and a research colleague, recorded on the pavement in a back street of London's Camden Market area. In the interview from which the following extract has been taken, the speaker, a male punk, has been describing in general terms the police's hostile attitude to the concerts of punk rock bands. In this sequence he begins to describe what happened at the end of one specific concert.

(1)
And the police were all outside there at the concert. There wasn't a bit of trouble, apart from say one or two wee scraps, you know. But that happens ... every gig there's a scrap – there's always somebody that doesn't like somebody else. It doesn't matter what it is, it's always happening, you know you cannot stop that. And we go outside and there they are – fucking eight hundred Old Bill, just waiting for the chance – riot shields, truncheons, and you're not doing nothing – you're only trying to get down to the tube and go home. So what do they do? You're walking by and they're pushing you with their truncheons and they start hitting the odd punk here and there. And what happens? The punks rebel – they don't like getting hit in the face with a truncheon, nobody does. So what do you do? You push the copper back and what happens? Ten or twelve of them are beating the pure hell out of some poor bastard who's only trying to keep somebody off his back. Now that started a riot.

We will focus on two related issues. First, we will examine some of the descriptive resources used by the speaker to warrant the claim that the punks were not responsible for the violence. Then we will discuss the way that the speaker's account is organised to address the likelihood that negative stereotypical knowledge about punks may be drawn upon to inform a sceptical response to the factual status of his claims.

19.3 TRANSCRIPTION AND ANALYTIC
METHOD

The extract above was transcribed by a professional transcriber who was not asked to include all the 'uhms', 'errs' and complexities of speech production. In one sense, this is to our advantage: the transcript is relatively straightforward to read. It is important to realise, however, that many important details of the talk may have been lost in this transcription, and thus it is a good methodological practice always to produce as detailed a transcription as possible. Consequently, in conversation analysis, and, to a lesser extent, in discourse analysis, it is customary to produce a detailed transcription of the taped interview. (The 'Introduction' to Atkinson and Heritage's (1984) edited collection of conversation analytic studies argues persuasively for the importance of detailed transcriptions.)

Detailed transcription of any kind is an important part of the analytic process. Laborious as it may be, it forces the analyst to become intimately acquainted with the data. But be warned: it is unwise to transcribe those sections of the data which are anticipated to be the significant passages. At this preliminary stage it is sensible to be agnostic about what the data may reveal because, before getting to grips with the material, one simply does not know which passages will yield interesting phenomenon worthy of more detailed inspection. Any pre-analytic guesswork might only lead the analyst to overlook some detail which, although significant, does not fit in with intuitive speculation about 'what is really important'. Having said that, in the early stages of a research project, it is often useful to have 'rough and ready' basic transcription, such as the one shown in extract 1; then, after careful listening to the tape, while at the same time consulting the transcript, stretches of the data can be selected for more detailed transcription and analysis.

Let's reconsider the punk's account transcribed with the conventions used in conversation analysis. (The transcription symbols are explained in the appendix to this chapter.)

```
(2)
1    MR:   and the police were all outside there,
2          (.) (ehr) at the co:ncert,
3          there wasnae a bit of trouble 'part fro(m) 'nside
4          one or two wee scra:ps, you know? (0.2) But that
5          happens=ev'ry one– every gig ⌈there's a scrap?
6    FR:                                 ⌊°mm°
7    MR:   >(th)'s all's< somebody doesnae like somebody else.
8    FR:   Mm:
9    MR:   dunna mattah w:ha:t it is (0.4) i's always happenin',
10         °hh y' know you cannae sto:p that?
11         (0.6)
12   MR:   an' (.) we go outside. and there they are.
13         (0.8)
14   MR:   fucking eight hundred old b'll,(0.2) just wai:tin' for
15         the cha:nce, (0.3) riot shields truncheons (0.2) and
16         you're ↑not doin' nothin' you're only trying to get
17         doon to the tube and gae hame °hh so what do they
18         do?=you're walk(n) by 'en they're pushing you wi'tha'
19         (.) truncheons an' °h they star(t) hattin' the odd
20         punk here and there, (0.3) and what happens?=the
21         punks rebe-rebel, they don' wanna get hit in the face
22         with a truncheon ↑nobody does °hhh so what do you
23         do,=you push yer copper back and (>then<) wha'
24         happens? ten or twelve of 'em are beatin'
25         the ⌈pure hell out of some poor bastard
26   FR:       ⌊mm
```

```
27   MR:   who's only tried to keep somebody off his back,
28         (0.7)
29   MR:   Now: that started a ↑riot.
```

The revised transcript probably looks daunting and cluttered. This is a normal first reaction, but once you are used to the meaning of the symbols, transcripts do become easier to read.

The second transcript provides detailed information about speech delivery: stress, changes in pitch, breathing, the gaps between words, the ways in which sounds can be stretched, the relative loudness of words, and so on. From the careful representation of the features of speech delivery we can immediately get a sense of the richness lost by the more conventional transcription; at the very least, we become aware of the speaker's broad Scottish accent. The revised transcript also displays spates of overlapping talk, in which two or more parties speak at the same time. The precise onset of overlap is always carefully marked. It is also important that it includes non-lexical noises that people produce, such as the agreement marker, 'mm'. This can be quite crucial: in the revised version it is apparent that a co-participant is producing agreement markers in overlap with the main speaker. It would be interesting to study the precise placement of these markers in the ongoing narrative to see if we can begin to see how the account is a collaborative accomplishment by both speakers (and the interviewer, who is noticeably absent throughout this passage). Unfortunately, space prevents us from exploring this issue, but without a detailed transcription such empirical questions would not arise at all.

Before we examine the data extract, some warning notes need to be sounded. First, it is important to stress that analysis should not proceed solely by reference to the transcript, as it is simply a representation of the recording, Consequently, the analyst should work with both the recording and the subsequent transcription.

Secondly, the mode of analysis illustrated in this chapter is not conducted according to a set of hard-and-fast rules, and there are no pre-specified techniques to be used to manipulate data to furnish a set of results or findings. This analytic approach thus has little connection to the kinds of quantitative analysis described in some of the other chapters, but resembles most closely the ethnographic research tradition discussed in Chapter 9. In common with anthropologists and ethnographers, the study of language use advocated here requires the development of an 'analytic mentality': a repertoire of craft skills acquired through practical experience. This analytic approach gives rise to some difficult methodological problems. For example, how can an analyst warrant the validity or accuracy of specific empirical observations? However, we will not address such difficulties in this chapter.

Finally, it needs to be stressed that the analytic approach outlined in this chapter is informed by very different assumptions from those which underpin many other empirical methodologies employed in sociological research. Indeed, it will become clear that some of the arguments in this chapter will seem incompatible with assumptions which inform other research strategies described in this book. A plurality of competing and, at times, incompatible research approaches is to be expected in a discipline as theoretically diverse as sociology. In this chapter, however, there will be no attempt to track in detail the relationship between different research methods.

The empirical observations focus on three features of the data segment. First, we examine some properties of the varying ways in which the actions of the punks and the police are described. This allows us to focus on some broad organisational features of the account. Secondly, we focus on the ways in which specific descriptive sequences have been assembled. So, the description, 'one or two wee scra:ps' (line 4) will be analysed. Thirdly, we examine the statement 'every gig –there's a scrap? >(th)'s all's< somebody doesnae like somebody else.dunna mattah w:ha:t it is (0.4) i's always happenin', (lines 5 to 9). This allows us to emphasise that descriptive practices are not random or idiosyncratic events, but have systematic properties.

19.4 CONTRASTIVE STRUCTURES AND NORMALISING PRACTICES

Let us reconsider the punk's description of some incidents following a punk rock gig.

In lines 3 to 10 there is a short sequence in which the speaker describes some violent incidents which happened at the concert. (This part of the account is examined in a later section.) Then the speaker begins a series of descriptions of the actions of the punks, and the actions of the police. In lines 12 to 17 the speaker says 'an' (.) we go outside. and there they are. (0.8) fucking eight hundred old b'll, (0.2) just wai:tin' for the cha:nce, (0.3) riot shields truncheons (0.2) and you're ↑not doin' nothin' you're only trying to get doon to the tube and gae hame'. Note that the first reference to the punks' behaviour is a very minimal description of what they did after the concert: 'an' (.) we go outside'. The second reference provides a further characterisation of the unexceptional nature of their behaviour: 'doing nothing' and simply 'going home'. It is interesting to note that the speaker's reference to the punks changes in the course of the segment. He says, first, that 'we go outside' but then he reports their subsequent behaviour as *'you're* only trying to [go home]'. There is a sense in which 'we' clearly marks the speaker as a member of a specific group or collectivity. But the characterisation of their attempt to go home as *'you're* only trying . . .' does not invoke such a clear affiliation. Indeed, it appeals to 'what everybody does' or 'what anybody would do'. Initially, we might assume that this is simply an idiosyncratic and 'one-off' way of engendering a recipient's sympathy for the events that befell the punks on the night of the concert. As we progress through the rest of this account, however, we shall see that the character of this specific segment is tied to the broader organisation of the whole account of the incidents.

There is a contrast between the way that the behaviour of the punks is described, and the way in which the speaker reports the presence of the police. The speaker provides a numerical evaluation of the police officers in attendance after the concert which, regardless of its 'accuracy', portrays the police presence as 'excessive'. Furthermore, he reports that the officers came equipped for violent confrontation. So, he builds a contrast between the actions of the punks and the subsequent response by the police: the behaviour of the punks is portrayed as quite unexceptional and routine, whereas the response of the police is portrayed as extreme.

In lines 18 to 20 the speaker reports 'you're walk(n) by 'en they're pushing you wi'tha' (.) truncheons an' °h they star(t) hattin' the odd punk here and there,' As in the previous extract, there is first a description of the punks' behaviour and then a description of the actions of the police. And, like the previous segment, the behaviour of the punks is reported in minimal everyday terms: they are simply 'walking by'. By contrast, the police are portrayed as initiating violence in that they start 'hitting the odd punk'. Note also that the violence is portrayed as being indiscriminately inflicted, rather than directed at specific individuals, or as part of the police response to a particular contingency. This serves to undermine the warrant for such police behaviour. Furthermore, it portrays the police's actions as being propelled not by any 'rational' motives or plan of action, but as an irrational and prejudiced response. Thus, the speaker's description in this segment further emphasises the contrast between the behaviour of the punks and the police.

In lines 20 to 29 the speaker then recounts the events which culminated in what he describes as 'a riot', and provides a characterisation of the punks' contribution to the escalating violence. Note that this issue is raised via his posing the rhetorical question 'And what happens?' as a consequence of the police indiscriminately hitting the punks. Note also that the use of the verb 'rebel' portrays the punks' first active involvement in the violence as being responsive to, and a consequence of, police provocation, oppression, and so on. Furthermore, this response is warranted by an appeal to 'how any one would respond in these circumstances': '[the punks] don' wanna get hit in the face with a truncheon ↑nobody does'.

Finally, the speaker provides the first reference to violent actions actually perpetrated by the punks after the concert: 'you push yer copper back'. It is clear that he is not describing one specific event, or any number of specific incidents; rather, he describes a general response, which is again warranted by an appeal to what 'anyone would do in this situation'. There are two interesting features of the description of the punks as 'pushing back'. 'Pushing' is not a particularly aggressive act, and its use here portrays the punks' behaviour as being defensive, rather than offensive. Also, the characterisation of the punks as pushing back demonstrates that their actions are a form of resistance to an ongoing physical assault, rather than any attempt to initiate conflict.

Even from these preliminary observations, then, some interesting differences are emerging. So, for example, the behaviour of the punks is described as entirely mundane: they are characterised as simply doing what any 'ordinary' person might do. They are also portrayed as passive recipients of violence, rather than aggressive perpetrators; even when they are actively involved in violence the punks are portrayed as using physical force to effect the most minimal form of self-defence. The description of the behaviour of the police, however, is couched in terms of their orientation to, and pursuit of, aggressive confrontation: their presence is excessive and they engage in random physical assaults. Thus, the speaker portrays the ordinary and mundane activities of the punks, but formulates the behaviour of the police through a series of descriptions which emphasise the aggressive and extraordinary behaviour of the police. Studies by Sacks (1984 [1970]), Jefferson (1984) and Wooffitt (1992) also consider the ways that an individual's identity as an 'ordinary person' can be made relevant as an interactional resource.

We have noted that the speaker builds a series of contrasts between the behaviour of the punks and that of the police. In this, the speaker is using a rhetorical and interactional resource which occurs in a variety of occasions of natural language use. For example, they occur regularly in political speeches (Atkinson, 1984; Heritage and Greatbatch, 1986), in market pitchers' selling techniques (Pinch and Clark, 1986), and in an account of mental illness (Smith, 1978). These studies have shown that contrast structures are employed as a persuasive device. In political speeches, for example, it is found that these structures are regularly followed by audience applause. In this case the speaker uses contrastive organisation to emphasise the extreme nature of the police response. The inference that the presence of the police and their subsequent behaviour was unwarranted in part rests upon the juxtaposition of police action with the seemingly inconsequential and ordinary behaviour of the punks.

It is important to remember that we are not assessing this account to try to discover whether the speaker's description is accurate, or whether he is distorting 'what really happened'. Rather, we are interested in the descriptive resources that are used to construct this version, and to sketch what dynamic and functional properties this version has. Indeed, it is quite possible that the same linguistic resources could be used to achieve the opposite ends. It is not hard to imagine how the punks could be described to portray their extraordinary and potentially aggressive demeanour, thereby warranting the appropriateness of the police response.

19.5   ASSEMBLING DESCRIPTIONS

In this section we are going to attempt a more detailed consideration of a much smaller data segment: 'one or two wee scra:ps,' (line 4). A short utterance like this seems an unpromising target for detailed examination.

To indicate why even apparently minor statements such as this merit close attention, we need to discuss some salient features of the practice of 'describing'.

The first step in examining descriptive sequences is to ask why these specific words have been used in this specific combination. Initially, this might seem a trivial task with a self-evident answer: this description has been provided because it captures, represents or reflects the state of affairs in the world being described. But we have seen that there are a variety of philosophical and sociological arguments which suggest that descriptions are designed not merely to *represent* the world, but to do specific tasks *in* the world.

Similarly, it is important to keep in mind that any actual description, however sensible or accurate it may appear, has been assembled from a range of possible words and phrases. Schegloff (1972) has demonstrated the necessary selectivity of descriptions by illustrating the various ways that one state of affairs could be reported.

> Were I now to formulate where my notes are, it would be correct to say that they are: right in front of me, next to the telephone, on the desk, in my office, in the office, in Room 213, in Lewisohn Hall, on campus, at school, at Columbia, in Morningside Heights, on the upper West Side, in Manhatten, in New York City, in New York State, in the North East, on the Eastern seaboard, in the United States, etc. Each of these terms could in some sense be correct ... were its relevance provided for. (Schegloff, 1972: 81)

The point is that any description or reference is produced from a potentially inexhaustible list of possible utterances, each of which is 'logically' correct or true. So when we pose the analytic question 'Why this specific description?', we need also to ask 'What *tacit practical reasoning* informs the design of this description?' (see also the discussion in Heritage, 1978).

Let us consider the word 'scrap'. Of all the ways which could be used to describe two people hitting each other – 'fighting', 'violence', 'a punch up' – the word 'scrap' clearly minimises the seriousness of the incident. Indeed, 'scrap' evokes images of schoolboy tussles in playgrounds rather than incidents in which people may incur severe physical damage. The characterisation of the incidents as 'wee scraps' further portrays the relative insignificance of the incidents.

Consider also the numerical evaluation 'one or two wee scra:ps'. A first point is that 'one or two' clearly registers the 'occurring more than once' character of the incident being described. Referring to a *number* of violent incidents could easily be used by a sceptic to undermine the general thrust of the speaker's claim that the police presence after the concert was unwarranted. However, 'one or two' provides the most *minimal* characterisation of 'more than one'. Secondly, note that the speaker does not say 'one' or 'two', but 'one or two'. In one sense, this marks the speaker as 'not knowing' the precise number of incidents. More important, however, is that the display of 'not knowing' marks the precise number as not *requiring* clarification, and therefore as being relatively unimportant. Thirdly, in this sequence the speaker concedes that violent disturbances occurred at the gig. Thus the speaker makes an admission which could be damaging to his overriding claim that the punks were not to blame for the subsequent 'riot'. However, conceding such a potentially delicate point is one method by which the speaker can minimise the likelihood that his account will be seen as a biased version of events. This in turn augments his implicit claim to be an accurate reporter of 'what really happened'. So, although the speaker does reveal that indeed there were *some* violent incidents at the concert, he does so in such a way as to portray the 'more than one' number of incidents as minimally as possible, while at the same time registering the relative insignificance of these events, and portraying himself as an 'honest observer' (see also Potter, 1996: Chapter 5).

19.6 THE ORGANISATION OF DESCRIPTIVE SEQUENCES

In this section we will consider the main speaker's description in lines 4 to 9:

> But that happens=ev'ry one– every gig –there's a scrap? >(th)'s all's< somebody doesnae like somebody else. dunna mattah w:ha:t it is (0.4) i's always happenin',

A first preliminary observation: note the instances in which the speaker uses the words 'always' and 'every'. Pomerantz (1986) has studied the use of words like 'always' and 'never' in ordinary conversation. She provides a technical identification of this, referring to such words as **extreme case formulations**. Other examples are 'never', 'brand new', 'nobody', 'everybody', 'completely innocent' and 'forever'. Such formulations serve to portray the maximum (or minimum) character of the object, quality or state of affairs to which they refer.

A second preliminary observation: note that the speaker provides three discrete descriptions of some characteristics of violent incidents and, in each case, he uses an extreme case formulation.

These two aspects of the sequence in lines 4 to 9 warrant further inspection. We will begin by posing two (related) questions. How is this sequence organised? And what is it organised to do?

An initial answer to the first of these questions is, the sequence has been organised as a **list**: the speaker produces a series of three descriptions which focus on some underlying cause or feature of violent activities.

The study of everyday conversation has discovered that three-partedness in list construction is a common occurrence (Jefferson, 1990). For example:

(4)
while you've been talking tuh me,
I mended,
two nightshirts,   **1**
a pillowcase?   **2**
enna pair'v pants.   **3**

In ordinary conversation three-part lists can be used to indicate a general quality common to the items in the list. In (4) above, the speaker provides a summary of the items she has mended. By virtue of their placement in a list, the reference to these items is hearable as the speaker indicating 'look how much I've done'. Furthermore, listing these items displays to the recipient their **occasioned co-class membership**: that is, the way that they are used conveys the general class of objects to which the speaker's activity has been directed – mending household linen. This feature of listing is often employed as a resource in political speeches. For example:

(5) Tebbit, UK General Election, 1983.

1   Labour will
2   spend and spend   **1**
3   borrow and borrow   **2**
4   and tax and tax   **3**   (Atkinson, 1984: 60)

In the extract above the speaker is not concerned with spending, borrowing and taxing as separate features of the Labour Party's policies; rather, by listing these three features he is able to convey the *general* point that their economic policy is inherently flawed.

The sequence below is a three-part list of events that the speaker claims happen at rock concerts.

(6)
1   ev'ry one– every gig –there's a scrap?
2   (th)'s all's< somebody doesnae like somebody else.
3   dunna mattah w:ha:t it is (0.4) i's always happenin',

It is apparent that the speaker is using his own 'lay' knowledge of the practices of listing to furnish a description which is recognisably complete. Also, this reference is designed so that the characteristics he indexes will not be heard as specific particulars, but are hearable as pointing to general features of violent incidents.

Investigation of the **organisation** of the speaker's utterances in lines 4 to 9 only provides us with a partial understanding of what sort of pragmatic work is being addressed in this sequence. To obtain a more sophisticated understanding of the actions being accomplished here, it is necessary to examine in more detail the use of the extreme case formulations, 'always' and 'every'.

Initially these items might appear to be a case of simple exaggeration, with little indication that there is something systematic about their use. But let us return to Pomerantz's (1986) analysis of extreme case formulations in everyday conversation. She discovered that speakers use extreme case formulations to influence the judgement or conclusions of co-interactants, *especially in circumstances in which the speaker may anticipate that the account, story or claim being made will receive an unsympathetic hearing.*

This is illustrated in the following extract, which comes from a call to a suicide prevention centre in the USA.

```
(7)
 1   D   Do you have a gun at home?
 2       (.6)
 3   C   A forty fi:ve,
 4   D   You do have a forty fi:ve.
 5   C   Mm hm, it's loaded.
 6   D   What is it doing there, hh Whose is it.
 7   C   It's sitting there.
 8   D   Is it you:rs?
 9       (1.0)
10   C   It's Da:ve's.
11   D   It's your husband's hu:h?=
12   C   =I know how to shoot it,
13       (.4)
14   D   He isn't a police officer:r,
15   C   No:.
16   D   He just ha:s one.
17   C   Mm hm, It-u-Everyone doe:s don't they?
```

                                                            (Pomerantz, 1986: 225)

A gun is the type of possession for which an explanation may be sought. Indeed, the member of staff tries to find a reason for the caller's possession of a gun by asking whether her husband was a police officer. In this extract, C describes the practice of keeping a gun by using the extreme case formulation 'Everyone does', thereby proposing that this is a common practice and therefore something for which she does not have to offer a mitigating explanation.

Let us consider this example further. In the USA gun ownership is far more common than in Europe. So we might expect that the mere fact that the speaker possesses a gun is not the kind of thing that requires some special justification. But keep in mind that this is a call to a suicide prevention agency, and that the caller has just admitted that she has a gun. In this situation, ownership of a gun is a slightly more sensitive issue, simply because it presents one immediate method by which the caller can end her life. This casts light on the defensive character of the caller's statement that 'everyone' has a gun. She is displaying a sensitivity to what the recipient might infer about her ownership of a gun: that she will use it to kill herself. Her use of an extreme case formulation is thus designed to portray her specific possession of a weapon as a normal matter, and not related to her status as 'someone calling the suicide prevention agency', with all that that might imply. Thus we may say that by using 'everyone does' the caller attempts to circumscribe the range of inferences that the agent of the suicide prevention agency might arrive at. This is the inferential work that the statement 'Everyone doe:s don't they?' is designed to do.

To understand this extract, note that it was necessary to invoke a form of 'common-sense reasoning', or 'what everybody knows' about the category, 'potentially suicidal persons': that is, possession of a gun may be a very serious matter for someone who can be legitimately assigned to this category.

From our examination of the example of an extreme case formulation, we have three kinds of useful information which we can bear in mind when we return to the punk extract. First, extreme case formulations are, broadly, a device: a resource for doing things in spoken interaction. Secondly, we know that they are used in circumstances in which the recipient of the speaker's claim may attempt to undermine the accuracy or legitimacy of that claim. Thirdly, we have seen that it has been necessary as a methodological resource to draw upon stereotypical or common-sense knowledge which is, in principle, applicable to the kind of person who is speaking (in this case, the relevant category is a 'potentially suicidal person'), and the circumstances in which they are speaking (in this case, 'ringing a suicide prevention agency').

We can now return to the instances of extreme case formulations in the punk extract. (To allow us to focus on the extreme case formulations, in the extract below I've reverted to a standard transcription and italicised key sections.) Recall that the speaker has just revealed that there was a spate of violent activity at the concert he had attended. He then says:

(8)
every gig there's a scrap
there's *always* somebody that doesn't like somebody else.
It doesn't matter what it is, it's *always* happening,

Observe the work that the use of extreme case formulations does here. 'Every gig there's a scrap' portrays violence as being related to a general kind of social occasion, namely, rock concerts. Note that he does not say that these violent incidents occur at every *punk* rock gig. Rather it is the 'gigs' that are associated with the disturbance, and not the gigs of bands whose following comes from a specific youth sub-culture. The second extreme case formulation 'there's *always* somebody that doesn't like somebody else' characterises violence as arising inevitably from interpersonal conflict. Such conflicts are portrayed as having their roots in idiosyncratic clashes of personality, irrespective of the social groups to which individuals may belong. Finally, 'it's *always* happening' marks such conflicts as a recurrent and consistent feature of human existence, and not peculiar to specific sections of the community.

In reporting the violence which occurred at the concert, the speaker makes no reference to the fact that the combatants were punks. Indeed, he does considerable work to portray the incident as something which occurs routinely at rock gigs generally, or which arises from two people's dislike for each other, and which is endemic in human society. In so doing, he minimises the relevance of the social identity of the combatants as 'punk rockers', and thus implies that their sub-cultural membership is merely incidental to this violence and not the reason for it.

To develop our understanding of this sequence, it is necessary to consider the range of culturally available stereotypes about the category 'punks'. As punks and punk rock emerged in the mid-1970s, tabloid press coverage focused on and glorified the more extreme characteristics of their lifestyle and the music: rejection of societal convention, self-mutilation as decoration, violence, uncleanliness, rebellion, and so on. The sometimes violent exploits of bands like the Sex Pistols and some of their followers ensured that the punk sub-culture was ideally suited to be the subject of a media-initiated 'moral panic' (Cohen, 1972).

These stereotypical representations of the punk lifestyle permeate our culture, and constitute a powerful set of lay assumptions and common-sense knowledge. It is always possible that the behaviour of someone who seems to fit the category 'punk rocker' can be explained and interpreted by reference to this largely negative stock of knowledge.

Throughout the passage, the speaker is making the claim that the 'riot' which followed the concert was a consequence of the unwarranted presence of the police, and their subsequently provocative behaviour. However, the occurrence of a spate of violence at the concert could easily be interpreted in the light of negative stereotypical knowledge about punks: namely that their lifestyle and attitudes lead them to seek rebellion, confrontation with authority and violence. The mere fact that there was some disturbance could warrant the inference that the violence was another instance of 'typical punk behaviour'. Clearly, such a conclusion would severely undermine the validity of the speaker's (implied) claim that the problems after the concert were a consequence of the police presence. The design of the speaker's descriptions in lines 6 to 9 displays his sensitivity to precisely these kinds of alternative interpretations. He uses extreme case formulations as a rhetorical device to minimise the likelihood that his account of the violence following a punk rock concert may be called into question by reference to 'what everyone knows about punks'. Also, the speaker uses a three-part list, a form of conversational organisation which permits the speaker to portray further general characteristics of violent incidents, thereby augmenting his implicit claim that the disturbance was not a specific consequence of the presence of punk rockers. This sequence, then, has been designed to warrant the factual status of the account in the light of potentially sceptical responses.

19.7   CONCLUSION

This has been a brief examination of three features of the data extract: the asymmetrical description of the behaviour of the punks and the police; the speaker's description of some actual violent incidents; and the use of extreme case formulations. There are many further points which could be investigated in this extract. However, this exercise has been useful in that it has revealed some of the **design features** of the speaker's descriptive reports, and has indicated the kind of work his words are doing. In short, he is guarding against potentially sceptical responses to his account of the events following the punk rock concert, and warranting the authority and factual status of his own version of those events.

In the introduction to this chapter it was noted that the study of language use has not emerged as one of the central topics of sociological research. In part, this rests on a traditional commitment to the sociological study of specific social processes, rather than the investigation of talk about those processes, or the study of discourse which inextricably permeates social life. In this chapter, however, I have tried to illustrate that language use is a form of, and a vehicle for, social action. As such, it merits serious sociological attention.

However, there are additional methodological arguments which suggest the need for the systematic study of language use in sociology. To address these arguments, it is useful to discuss Gilbert and Mulkay's (1984) study of scientists' discourse.

Gilbert and Mulkay were interested in one dispute in an area of bio-chemistry about the correct way to understand the mechanisms by which chemical and other kinds of energy are stored within cell structures. To study this dispute, Gilbert and Mulkay collected taped interviews with the various biochemists involved in the dispute, read relevant research papers and obtained informal communications between the participants, such as letters and notes. However, these data presented them with a problem: within these accounts there were a variety of plausible and convincing versions of the dispute. Furthermore, they noted that any one feature of the debate, such as the significance of a series of experimental studies, could be described and accounted for in a number of different ways. Gilbert and Mulkay argued that it is imperative to attend directly to the variability in accounts, and not simply to employ techniques which purge it from the data. Consequently, they advocated the study of participants' discourse (or use of language) to reveal the interpretative practices, embodied in discourse, by which accounts of beliefs and actions are organised to portray events in a certain way. So, they did not examine their accounts to furnish definitive sociological state-ments about a specific state of affairs. Instead, they explicated the system-atic properties of language use through which scientists constructed their accounts.

Although Gilbert and Mulkay developed their discourse analytic approach to deal with variation in scientists' accounts, they realised that the variability they had observed was not peculiar to their project, but is a constituent feature of any sociological (and social psychological) research which relies on accounts of behaviour, events, mental states, attitudes, beliefs, and so on. Of course there are customary procedures by which sociologists can produce a single 'definitive' analytic version from the multiplicity of accounts which constitute their data. They can examine their data to look for broad similarities between the statements, and any similarities between accounts can be taken at 'face value', that is, as if they reflect accurately 'what really happened'. The analyst is then at liberty to construct a generalised version of participants' accounts and present these as analytic conclusions.

However, Gilbert and Mulkay question the role of the researcher when confronted by a variety of accounts of ostensibly the 'same' event or circumstances. In particular, they address the argument that, on account of sociological 'expertise', the analyst can recognise the difference between accurate accounts and inaccurate or irrelevant ones. They argue that this methodological strategy rests on the assumption that any social event has one 'true' meaning. They indicate, however, that social activities are the 'repositories' of multiple meanings, by which they mean that the 'same' circumstances can be described in a variety of ways to emphasise different features. (Indeed, earlier in this chapter we illustrated the way that the 'same thing' can be variously described by referring to Schegloff's illustrative formulation of where his notes were at one particular time.) So, Gilbert and Mulkay argue that there is no privilege for the analyst's decision as to what constitutes an 'objective' or 'accurate' version of the world, simply because any state of affairs can be described in a series of different ways.

For these reasons, Gilbert and Mulkay rejected the key methodological step in conventional sociological research, which is to attempt to reconstruct 'what actually happened' from accounts. They argue that

> Given that participants' use of language can never be taken as literally descriptive, it seems methodologically essential that we pay more attention . . . to the systematic ways in which our subjects fashion their discourse. Traditional questions . . . will continue to remain unanswered, and unanswerable, until we improve our understanding of how social actors construct the data which constitute the raw material for [sociologists'] interpretative efforts. (Gilbert and Mulkay, 1984: 15)

Instead, they began to examine the ways that accounts are organised through certain sets of interpretative practices to construct and warrant particular versions of 'what actually happened'. The implication of their argument, therefore, is that the study of discourse, and its dynamic, action-oriented properties, may be necessarily prior to, if not a replacement for, traditional forms of analysis.

19.8 PROJECT

Collect a video or tape-recording of a discussion between representatives of the major political parties, or an in-depth interview with one politician. Examine the ways in which specific positions and policies are described. What are the devices used to make specific policies seem reasonable and sensible? How do these devices work? (Atkinson's (1984) study of political rhetoric will be helpful for this project.) Alternatively, record interviews with friends who believe they have had a supernatural or paranormal experience. Ask them to describe what happened. Then transcribe their account, and try to identify how the account is organised to establish that the event actually happened, and wasn't, for example, an hallucination, dream or mis-identification. (Wooffitt (1992) describes some of the descriptive practices through which speakers build robust accounts of extraordinary experiences.)

19.9 FURTHER READING

Atkinson and Heritage (1984) is the best single collection of conversation analytic studies, and contains two chapters which are based on lectures given by Harvey Sacks. Introductions to CA can be found in Hutchby and Wooffitt (1998) and ten Have (1999).

Potter and Wetherell (1987) provide a clear introduction to discourse analysis, and its implications for social psychology. Potter (1996) provides a comprehensive overview of the interest in factual discourse across a range of social scientific approaches and subjects.

Edwards's (1997) critique of cognitivism in psychology is an extended argument for discursive psychology. It is, however, fairly complex in places, and a knowledge of psychology is required.

APPENDIX: TRANSCRIPTION CONVENTIONS

(.5)	The number in brackets indicates a time gap in tenths of a second.
(.)	A dot enclosed in a bracket indicates pause in the talk less then two tenths of a second.
˙hh	A dot before an 'h' indicates speaker in-breath. The more h's, the longer the in-breath.
hh	An 'h' indicates an out-breath. The more 'h's the longer the breath.
–	A dash indicates the sharp cut-off of the prior word or sound.
:	Colons indicate that the speaker has stretched the preceding sound or letter. The more colons the greater the extent of the stretching.
( )	Empty parentheses indicate the presence of an unclear fragment on the tape.
.	A full stop indicates a stopping fall in tone. It does not necessarily indicate the end of a sentence.
,	A comma indicates a continuing intonation.

?	A question mark indicates a rising inflection. It does not necessarily indicate a question.
↑↓	Pointed arrows indicate a marked rising or falling intonational shift. They are placed immediately before the onset of the shift.
<u>Under</u>	Underlined fragments indicate speaker emphasis.
CAPITALS	With the exception of proper nouns, capital letters indicate a section of speech noticeably louder than that surrounding it.
=	The 'equals' sign indicates contiguous utterances.
[ ]	Square brackets between adjacent lines of concurrent speech indicate the onset and end of a spate of overlapping talk.

A more detailed description of these transcription symbols can be found in Atkinson and Heritage (1984: ix–xvi).

Analysing Visual Materials

20

Victoria D. Alexander

Contents

Everywhere we look in the social world there are visual images. They are on television, in movies, on the World Wide Web, in our photo albums. Modern technology has helped them proliferate; indeed, some observers believe that the contemporary world is dominated by the visual (Gombrich, 1960; Johnson, 1997; Mirzoeff, 1999; Postman, 1986). Sociologists and other social researchers increasingly take advantage of this 'visuality'.

Early sociologists used photographs in their research. But the visual was set aside during most of the century (Becker, 1974). Though it has returned in recent years, it is still relatively uncommon and is considered by some to be marginal, unimportant, or unscientific. This will change in the coming years, as technologies such as digital scanning and printing, and the World Wide Web make it cheaper and easier to include visual results in essays and publications. Current research using visual methods is a vibrant, growing, and interdisciplinary endeavour (Prosser, 1998), with contributions from anthropologists (Banks, 2001), psychologists (McNiff, 1998), and art historians (Mirzoeff, 1999), as well as from sociologists (Ball and Smith, 1992; Chaplin, 1994; Evans and Hall, 1999; Wagner, 1979).

'Visual sociology' and 'visual research methods' are broad terms that embody many techniques and assumptions. Visual materials can come into play in distinct parts of the research process, creating four categories:

1. The analysis of **existing visual materials** (e.g. looking at the portrayal of gender or race on television).
2. The use of visual materials to **generate data** (e.g. showing photos to an individual during an interview or a film to a focus group).
3. **Creating** visual data to analyse (e.g. filming children on the playground to learn about their social interaction).
4. Using images to **present results**.

Cross-cutting these distinctions is the familiar divide in metatheory: Is sociology a systematic search for generalisable facts? Or is sociology an interpretative venture where one seeks local, historically-contingent meaning?

The goal of this chapter is to provide an overview of each of these uses of visual data, giving examples and highlighting some analytic techniques. It also points out some of the difficulties and debates in the analysis of visual data.

20.1   THE ANALYSIS OF EXISTING VISUAL
MATERIALS

A researcher can analyse existing visual texts – television shows, advertisements, paintings – to learn about the social world. This form of visual research, dominated by media studies, is well established in sociology. Existing visual materials are, in fact, **documents**. To analyse visual documents in this framework (see Chapter 12), you examine four aspects of each text – its authenticity, credibility, representativeness and meaning (Scott, 1990). Authenticity can be ignored for most analyses of media and art. An advertisement in *Cosmopolitan* doesn't pretend to be anything else, and museums have done the hard work of dating artworks and detecting forgeries for you. There are, however, occasional cases where the authenticity question is important. For instance, in studying a collection of old postcards portraying 'exotic' people, it is crucial to determine if the scenes depicted are natural or staged and when and where they were taken (Banks, 2001).

Credibility is a key issue in analysing visual materials. It is important to consider who made the image and why. Though pictures, especially photographs or videos, ask to be taken at face value, they cannot be. Photos are easily altered, retouched or cropped; one image is picked from many. These acts affect what you see, as does the original choice of framing. Most visual images, from photojournalism to advertisements and Hollywood movies, and even family photos, are highly constructed by their creators. Representativeness, which implies sampling, and meaning, the most difficult question, will be addressed below. As with written documents, triangulation of findings from visual materials is desirable.

Two other ways to study visual documents are content analysis and interpretative analysis. Content analysis is often based on reflection theory, and interpretative analysis on semiotics, though this is not always the case.

20.1.1 Reflection theory

Researchers who study visual documents, especially media texts, often rely implicitly on 'reflection theory'. They believe that visual documents mirror, or tell us something about, society. If television dramas portray ethnic minorities negatively, as criminals but not police officers, it might reasonably be assumed that the society producing the shows is itself racist. Reflection theory says that skinny models in today's advertisements reflect our society's belief that women should be slim but that Rubens's plump ladies show his society's preference for a little more flesh. It asserts that if we want to know what Dutch houses looked like in the seventeenth century, we need only look to old paintings of everyday life in Holland to see.

Reflection theory leaves a number of important questions unanswered (Albrecht, 1954). What, exactly, is reflected – reality, values, or fantasies? And whose ideas are reflected – those of the whole society, ruling elites, media executives, or sub-cultures? Indeed, social 'facts' might be present in media texts because they are commonplace, or precisely because they are not (Laslett, 1976), as the unusual captures your attention better than the mundane. Despite these problems, many researchers, especially in media studies, are interested in how visual materials indicate underlying social factors, especially around issues of race, ethnicity, gender, class and sexuality (e.g. Dines and Humez, 1995; Jewitt, 1997).

20.1.2 Semiotics

Alongside reflection theory, semiotic analysis is a key method of analysing visual texts (see especially Barthes, 1957 [1972]; Bignell, 1997; Hawkes, 1992; Kress and van Leeuwen, 1996). Semiotics is a method which draws inspiration from Saussure's (1915 [1959]) theory of language. The basic ideas are, first, **signs** are composed of a **signifier** (a word, say 'dog') that points to a **signified** (the object or concept the word refers to, in this case, a four legged thing that says woof). Secondly the relationship between words and concepts are arbitrary. We might just as well call the barking thing a '*chien*' or a '*perro*' or a 'woof-woof' – or for that matter, a 'cat' (so long as we then agree to call those meowing things something else). The point is that, as part of a language, we agree that certain signs match up with certain meanings. Furthermore, thirdly, signs do not stand alone. Instead, they become rich with meaning because they work in concert with other signs in the system. So, for instance, if I say 'hawk and dove' you will probably think 'belligerent and peaceful', noticing the contrast more than that they both fly. The idea is that meaning comes from binary opposites, and clear meanings come from sharp contrasts. It is less certain what I have in mind if I say 'hawk, tiger and jaguar', since three concepts cannot stand in opposition. Meaning is built up by adding opposites together.

Finally, there is a distinction between **langue** and **parole**. *Langue* refers to the language itself – its grammar, its system of binary oppositions, its meanings. *Parole* refers to speech, or 'utterances', and can mean either spoken words or written ones. The reason to make this distinction is that we can see language working only through *parole*. We have to infer how the utterances work together. We figure out the rules, the *langue*, by observing those utterances.

How do Saussure's ideas apply to visual materials? Metaphorically, visual systems are languages. The goal is to look at images – these are the utterances, so to speak, the *parole* – and from these deduce the *langue*, the grammar of the image system. Semiotics tells us to uncover signs and figure out how they work. Semioticians pay attention to a range of instances from one particular type (or genre) of visual images, to discover the relationship among signs and how they create meaning in the whole system.

There are some difficulties in applying semiotics to visual materials. Using Saussure's ideas by analogy can be fruitful, but they don't map neatly on to image systems. For instance, we can easily differentiate language systems – French versus English, for example. Finding different systems, or genres, is more difficult to do with images. Do Renaissance paintings use a different visual language from modern advertising images (Baxandall, 1988)? Certainly they do! But sometimes modern advertisers draw on codes from Renaissance art. Are advertisements used in women's magazines a different genre from those used in news magazines? Well, certainly adverts in *Cosmopolitan* look very different from those in *The Economist*, and they draw on knowledge from different sectors of society, but they also draw on ideas from the wider culture. Advertisers can expect that, to a great extent, readers of *Cosmopolitan* understand *The Economist* adverts and vice versa. In other words, genres of visual codes are multiple and overlapping. Members of a given society are familiar with a large number of them, from both past and present, while they might only know one spoken language fluently. This means that you cannot deduce a grammar for images in the same way that you can for a spoken language. And unlike linguistic signs, visual signs do not always relate to their signified in an arbitrary way. A picture of a dog somehow resembles real dogs. Pierce (1958) calls this kind of sign 'indexical'. As a result, images seem more direct than words. This can create problems when we forget that images are constructed.

20.1.3 Content analysis

A key way of analysing visual information sociologically is content analysis. In this, you choose a question that can be measured with variables and decide on a coding scheme to capture them. Chapter 14 describes how to choose codes and develop coding rules, and emphasises the importance of a code book. The usefulness of a pilot study is highlighted in Chapter 6. Books on general (textual) content analysis (Holsti, 1969; Weber, 1990) can also provide useful insights into coding visual data. You can code on sheets of paper. Alternatively, software programs can help you code visual or multimedia data, as described in Chapter 18 on Computer Assisted Qualitative Data AnalysiS, or CAQDAS.

Next, you make a sampling frame, choosing cases to analyse that are representative and unbiased (see Chapter 5). Most sampling procedures are designed to reduce the number of cases; you select a sample from a larger population of possibilities. Others, however, help you build up your sample from a limited number of possibilities; you search for relevant cases in contemporary or historical archives. Finally, you code all cases and analyse the resulting data. With a large number of cases you can produce semi-quantitative results using cross-tabulations, charts or graphs. With fewer cases, tables are useful. Content analyses are usually reported in a standard 'scientific' format.

I used this technique in a study of children in advertisements (Alexander, 1994). I wanted to know if the portrayal of children in American magazine advertisements had changed during the twentieth century; specifically how the relationship between parents and children might have shifted. I chose a sampling procedure that I hoped was representative and unbiased, and developed a coding scheme to record interactions between children and adults. I coded hundreds of advertisements picturing children and presented my results in a series of graphs. For instance, one graph showed that the proportion of American adverts picturing children is strongly related to the fertility rate in the USA, with one caveat: during times when child-rearing was strict there were fewer adverts showing youngsters than when child-rearing was permissive.

Macdonald's (1989) study of the headquarters of professional associations is a good example of a content analysis of a smaller number of cases. The study asked how these groups literally 'built' respectability. Macdonald carefully chose his cases to be representative and illustrative, and thoroughly researched each key variable. He examined six headquarters, three from accountancy organisations (his focus point) and three from comparable professional bodies in law and medicine. Each building was coded on 11 variables that measured its prestige. The codes ranged from -1 ('inappropriate or lacking') to $+3$ ('outstanding'), and were summed to give a single 'conspicuous consumption rating' to each case. Macdonald presents these findings in a table.

Content analysis has a number of advantages. It is formal and systematic, which lends structure to your research. It can give a good overview of your subject. If critics disagree with your interpretation of the data, they must still address the findings you presented. But there are some disadvantages as well. The main difficulty is that content analysis requires codes to be unambiguous and exclusive. It is designed to categorise variables in a precise manner, to see each case separately and to weight them equally. It strips down and fragments content in order to count it. But visual images are usually ambiguous and they often refer to other images. Content analysis ignores context and the potential for multiple meanings, and it often disguises, through the coding procedure, the investigator's input.

20.1.4 Interpretative analysis

Interpretative analysis, often based in semiotics, is used to capture hidden meaning, ambiguity, and intertextuality (the interrelationship among images) in visual objects. For instance, Barthel (1988) analysed American advertisements, specifically looking at gender. She was interested in such issues as how women can be portrayed as 'fair maidens' and also as 'dark ladies' – sometimes in the same advert. These signs reflect, but also construct, concepts of gender in the wider society. Williamson's (1978) study of British advertisements, also based on semiotics, shows how messages are **encoded** into advertisements by the interior logic and structure of individual advertisements and the system of advertisements as a whole. The overarching message of advertisements is, not surprisingly, to encourage consumerism. In individual adverts, advertisers use a variety of codes to this end. For instance, putting their products next to desirable people or places draws an analogy between the two and classes their product as desirable. Williamson also posits how people might **decode** these messages to get meaning out of them. She shows a variety of techniques used by advertisers to capture our attention and draw us in, such as visual and textual puns and puzzles, or the 'absent participant' into whose shoes viewers step. Often the meanings of adverts are not seen on their surface (the **manifest** content), but are hidden (the **latent** content).

Interpretative studies can also rely on other theoretical frameworks. A classic example of a structural study is Goffman's (1979) work on gender advertisements. He examined a huge number of adverts to demonstrate structural relationships between men and women. To uncover these 'gender displays', he analysed only the photos in the adverts, ignoring the text. While Barthel and Williamson are also interested in underlying, latent meanings, they specifically included the words. Semioticians posit that textual elements in advertisements are integral components of their meaning. Goffman, on the other hand, argues that the structural relationships in which he is interested are more easily seen if the manifest content of the advert, often conveyed in the words, is ignored. (Along these lines, Jhally (1990) argues that stripping music videos of their sound tracks makes it easier to discover important aspects of their meaning which are otherwise hidden.)

In sum, interpretative analysis can capture richness of meaning, and often deals with wholes rather than fragments. It can uncover latent meanings, rather than sticking to surface appearance only, and can give more weight to important cases. Yet research that is conducted using this framework is often accused of being unsystematic, unobjective, and 'just the researcher's opinion'. Unlike the examples presented here, interpretative analysis often rests – by necessity, justified choice or laziness – on only a few images. Even when the samples are large (Goffman presents about 500 images and must have looked at many more) the analysis usually proceeds without a stated sampling frame or coding scheme. These criticisms are the obverse of those of content analysis.

20.1.5 Combining content and interpretative analysis

Students often wish to combine a content analysis with an interpretative one. This is good if you can do it. Indeed, it seems daft to ignore interpretative information that comes along in a content analysis, and content analysis can provide empirical strength to a more interpretative frame. For instance, I did not code for the portrayal of gender or ethnicity in my content analysis of children in advertising. But being close to the data, I had observations on these issues.

It is not always possible to combine the two types of research, however, partly because doing so properly means completing two studies. Because the assumptions underlying content analysis and interpretative analysis are quite distinct, combining the two is not as easy as it sounds.

20.2 GENERATING DATA WITH VISUAL MATERIALS

Visual materials are evocative and can be quite useful stimuli in interviews and focus groups. This style of research is called 'photo elicitation' (Collier, 1967). Visual materials such as family or historical photos are shown to research subjects, in individual or group settings, to learn about a research question. Often researchers use existing visual information, but you can also create visual materials for this purpose, either yourself or, in a more complicated research design, you can ask your subjects to do this for you. I provide two examples of techniques using moving images.

Shively (1992) was interested in why American Indians enjoy western movies so much, given that cowboys are invariably the good guys and Indians the bad guys. She showed a classic western film to a focus group of Indians and to one of 'Anglos' (white Americans), and discovered that the meanings the two groups took from the film varied tremendously. The Anglos thought of the movie as part of their cultural heritage, as an authentic portrayal of the Historical West. Indians saw the stories as utter nonsense in terms of their historical value, but appreciated the depicted ideals of being one with your horse, the range and nature.

In a different type of research, Porter (1997) used 'video vignettes' to study respondents' views of interactions in work settings. Characters in the vignettes were played by trained actors and the resulting film was shown to respondents on a portable computer. This technique is similar to using text vignettes (Alexander and Becker, 1978; Finch, 1987), but allowed Porter to alter the race and/or gender of characters, as well as introduce differences in behaviour. For instance, he did not call attention to gender or race, as he would have done in a written vignette that begins, 'A white, female employee is talking to a black, male boss . . .'.

If you want to use visual materials to spur respondents, you need to be mindful of a few things. First, you must choose your visual materials carefully. Images convey information along a multitude of lines, so pictures that appear similar at a quick glance may differ markedly in important details. Consider what you wish the respondents to think about and be prepared to defend your choice of materials. Secondly, you need to develop your interview or focus group skills; Chapters 8 and 10 can help.

20.3 CREATING VISUAL DATA

Researchers often tape record interviews and focus groups. You may wish to videotape them instead. As with audio tapes, the resulting information can be coded or 'transcribed'. CAQDAS (see Chapter 18) can be extremely helpful, as the video can be clipped and quoted digitally, preserving the visual component of the data. You can reduce the visual information to text, through content analysis. Or you can document movement with complex transcription systems, for instance, those developed for dance (Heath, 1986: 20–1). These latter visual codes are difficult to master, however, and are not always adequate to the task.

Researchers can use photography or video to collect data on people or objects out there in the real world. For instance, Heath (1986) videotaped people in doctors' surgeries. He carefully analysed short clips in the close manner of conversation analysis (see Chapter 19). The minute details of motion of doctor and patient, which along with their talk teaches us about social interaction, would be missed by non-visual methods.

Macdonald (1989) took photographs of the buildings in his study of the architecture of professional associations. These photographs helped increase the validity and reliability of his codes through a process of triangulation: he showed his data (the look of the buildings) to a panel of experts, who confirmed his coding.

Corse and Robinson (1994) propose a method for studying cultural understandings through video interviewing of respondents from across cultures. They started with videotapes of American and Japanese preschools for three and four year-olds. From these, they chose clips that showed a child misbehaving and the reactions of other children and teachers. (These videos were made by another researcher for a different purpose, but you could also make your own videos to start the research.) Corse and Robinson showed the Japanese clips to a focus group of American respondents, and vice versa, and videoed the discussion. Then they showed the American discussion to the Japanese group and vice versa. (All tapes were dubbed in the appropriate language.) In this way they collected outsiders' reactions to a norm-breaking situation and the insiders' reactions to the outsiders' views. These steps uncovered differences in cultural understandings and values which are difficult to capture with survey instruments.

20.4 PRESENTING RESULTS WITH A VISUAL COMPONENT

One way to use visual information in reports and publications is to include images as decoration. This is the most common, and perhaps least interesting, mode of visual presentation. It occurs in undergraduate textbooks, especially introductory ones, where photographs of people, cartoons, advertisements, movie posters and the like are reproduced. They enliven the narrative and take up space so that reading seems less onerous. The illustrations, however, are often not tightly connected to the text and have a random feel to them.

More important is the use of visual materials for the illustration and elaboration of research findings. Halle (1993), for instance, studied pictures in people's homes. He looked at all the pictures – art works, religious iconography, family photos – displayed in houses in four neighbourhoods around New York City, varied by social class. The findings are brought to life in the book through photographs of the respondents, their rooms and the objects that they keep. Halle also included floor plans of their houses, to convey a sense of their spaces. The illustrations are closely connected to the research findings and enhance the written material.

Goffman (1979) used photographs of the advertisements he analysed to present his data. Indeed, his article is unusual in that it has relatively little text with a large number of images. He argues that the images are not just his raw data but, organised systematically, they are actually his findings – analogous to a table showing multiple regression results. His work literally lets you see his argument.

Berger's (1972) book on how we see, like Goffman's article, uses pictures as an integral part of a textual argument. Indeed, the book – a *mélange* of social theory and art historical analysis – would not really make sense without its pictures. It is no coincidence that Berger's book started as a television series and was later converted to print. Photo essays in Becker (1981) tell stories about society, as in ethnography. The photos and text, created by academics in several fields, are a mix of social research and art – some would say more art than research. In fact, the book is an exhibition catalogue, that is, a publication which accompanied a temporary exhibition in an art gallery. Becker (1998) would go further by claiming that a book made by an art photographer, Robert Frank (1959), was a beautiful example of social research. Photographs in *The Americans* have short captions telling where they were taken, but otherwise, there are no words in the book at all. While many sociologists might agree that it is beautiful, far fewer would say it is sociology.

This is because the best visual social science melds words and images. Because pictures are information-rich, worth at least a thousand words, they can save a lot of description. However, because they are information-rich, they are also ambiguous. Regardless of whether the goal of sociology is to study a phenomenon objectively, to make an argument, to posit a knowledge-claim in a discourse, or to tell a story, the researcher must put forward the scientific findings, argument, claim or story with clarity. Perhaps statistical tables speak for themselves (though this is arguable), but visual data clearly do not.

This is demonstrated in Berger's (1972) book, in which text and image are interwoven in odd-numbered chapters, but visual images with no text comprise the even-numbered ones. As Berger himself points out, the visual chapters raise questions, but it is not certain what, exactly, Berger had in mind when he chose the images. Similarly, although Becker (1998) argues that Frank's book makes its themes clear through repetition and careful choice of images, these themes might be unavailable to readers who do not have training in aesthetics and photography.

Some writers have theorised that writing is privileged over seeing in sociology. This is often asserted in the form of a complaint that visual images are not valued on their own. While I see great potential for visual sociology, I don't expect that sociology will give up writing any time soon. So the challenge for the researcher using visual materials is to incorporate the visual with the text to bolster its thrust, or to describe the visual data in words, not to use pictures without a supporting written analysis.

20.5   SOME PROBLEMS IN USING VISUAL MATERIALS

Using visual materials in research is not without its problems, practical, analytical and theoretical.

20.5.1   Practical concerns

Issues surrounding data collection include the standard problems of access, such as securing permission to videotape people, to photograph objects in private collections or to use personal images (such as family photographs) in the course of research. There is also the expense of collecting visual data, including photocopying fees, the price of film or video and the cost of equipment (cameras, digital scanners or playback devices).

More difficult are practical problems in getting images published (or reproduced in unpublished works). A common irony of much writing on visual sociology is that it is in words with no pictures, even as decoration! The trickiest issue involves copyright: images can be owned by an individual or organisation. You cannot, however, 'quote' a visual image under 'fair use' rules, as you can quote a passage from a book. To publish a proprietary image you must secure written permission, cover the cost of providing a transparency to the publisher and often pay a fee as well. Further, copyright holders have been known to refuse permission if they don't like the use to which you put their image, and they can even sue you, as Dubin (1995) discovered when he tried to portray two gay Ken dolls driving Barbie's pink convertible. Strict attention to copyright is not crucial for unpublished essays or dissertations, as most advertisers, artists, museums, television executives, movie studios and the like are not on the lookout for illegal photocopies, clips or stills taken from their adverts, paintings, sculptures, broadcasts, films or web pages when used for such purposes. Technically, though, permission is required for all uses of visual images that are not created by the researcher.

Even if you do create images yourself, there are important considerations, even for unpublished studies. The most important is the confidentiality of your subjects, as you cannot just change the names. You may wish to ask them to sign a release form giving permission to use pictures of them. You could digitally, or otherwise, blank out faces. Heath (1986) rendered his subjects anonymous by hiring an artist to draw the interactions he recorded in doctors' surgeries. Or, in promising confidentiality, you may simply agree never to release your visual data.

Harper's (1982) visual ethnography of American hobos brings up issues of safety and research ethics (Harper, 1979: 40–2; see Chapters 4 and 9). He took photographs, as a participant observer, of tramp life on the fringes of American society. Consent is required to photograph in private locations, for example corporate reception areas, shops and schools, and is customary in research settings. It is legal to photograph structures, objects and people in public settings, but people can object, sometimes violently. Don't put yourself at risk! In addition, taking photographs can be obtrusive, especially if you use a flash or stand near to your subjects.

Finally, including images in published or unpublished works involves some costs for photocopying or printing images. Colour costs much more than black and white, but can convey important information. Most publishers expect authors to bear the expense of providing illustrations, and are often unwilling to use large numbers of images due to the cost of printing them. Some publishers will print only black and white images, and others, especially print journals, refuse images altogether. Indeed, Macdonald's was the first article in the history of the journal *Sociology* to include photographs. Moving images are not possible to reproduce in print formats – unless your book or article is accompanied by a videotape or CD-ROM, which adds its own difficulties. Advances in electronic publishing and digital imaging will presumably make publishing and presenting visual information much easier.

Another practical concern is that visual research can produce a large amount of data. This is similar to the situation in qualitative or historical studies where you end up with large files of transcribed interviews, field notes or piles of government documents. You will need a research strategy to handle this. When you present results visually, use representative examples as you would use quotes in an interview study or ethnography. Editing is important. Not only are there issues of reproducing a large number of images, but you also must not overwhelm your reader.

Finally, while theoretical ideas about visual sociology may be clear, what, exactly, are you supposed to do when confronted with an image? Or when you have to decide what to study and how to study it? It is hard to get concrete answers to these questions from books. Some authors suggest you 'learn by doing', others that you take an apprenticeship (as you do when you write a dissertation or thesis under supervision). Becker (2000) proposes that photography courses should be included in sociology degree programmes. It is also useful to look up examples of the type of work you wish to do, and imagine yourself doing those studies.

20.5.2 Ambiguity and meaning

Visual images present problems to researchers because they are ambiguous. They can carry multiple meanings and are therefore called 'polysemic' or 'multivocal'. Furthermore, as Gombrich (1972) points out, pictures are better at conveying moods than specific arguments. If this is the case, how can the researcher possibly assert a single interpretation of an image? Does this mean that all research in visual sociology is, by definition, subjective?

To a great extent, these problems are not unique to visual data (Becker, 1974; Wagner, 1979: 20–1). Sociologists have always worried about how to measure their ideas validly and reliably and how to choose unbiased samples or representative cases. These problems are no less applicable to visual than other types of data, and can be solved for the visual with similar levels of success. Sociologists studying the reception of culture recognise that taking meaning from words is problematic, and that all texts allow some leeway for interpretation based on readers' own horizons of expectations. Further, post-modern sociologists have questioned the possibility of objective research, regardless of the source of data.

While every source of data implies problems with measurement and objectivity, these problems are more easily seen, so to speak, in visual images. This is because science, including social science, relies on a rational intelligence that is primarily verbal. Images draw on other forms of intelligence that do not set out to create clear, linear arguments. Whether your research draws inspiration from modernist or postmodernist thinking, it is worth constructing your argument about the images you use, clearly and bolstered with evidence; images must be accompanied by a text that reduces their possible meanings. If your writing is clear (as Becker (1986) argues), others may disagree with you, but you will make a stronger contribution than if you ramble, fudge, obfuscate and try to have it both ways.

20.5.3 Audiences and creators

People look at visual images. Looking creates meaning. In analysing existing visual materials, you cannot know how audiences actually receive and make meaning from them. One way to reduce this problem is to pay attention to the *intended* audience (e.g. readers of *The Economist* are, on average, more likely to be middle-aged, business and management-oriented, and male than readers of *Cosmopolitan*), and point this out in your research. But the only way to get at how people receive images is to ask them (as is done in photo elicitation). Nevertheless, there are situations where you wish to study just the images and not branch out into interviews (e.g. media representations of social groups), and those where interviews are impossible (e.g. studies of historical images, where the original viewers have long since died).

A similar difficulty is that the creators of visual documents always have reasons for making them, as was mentioned with respect to documents' 'credibility'. Some of these reasons are political or ideological, others commercial. There are also reasons relating to the conventions of the genre of representation. It can be useful to speculate about the motives of creators, though this is not always necessary. It is also useful to consider the original context of your images, not mixing examples from different 'frames' without good reason.

20.5.4 Reflexivity

'Reflexivity' denotes a style of research whereby one addresses how the research process affects the results. It requires precision about the analytical methods and data collection procedures used, and emphasises the researcher's own assumptions and beliefs through explicit statements of how the researcher's very presence affects what he or she is investigating. It is research that looks back at itself. At its best, it makes for better work (everything is stated, nothing, like the researcher's personal political beliefs, is left hidden), and it can create a useful humbleness in researchers. At its worst, especially when researchers spend the entire write-up talking about themselves rather than their subjects, it can lead to intellectually boring work.

Students are often quite aware of the fact that when they analyse a visual image they are starting from their own point of view. 'It's only my interpretation,' they worry. Here are three possible solutions:

1. You can add a 'disclaimer' that acknowledges the multivocality of your data, but leaves it aside for further research.
2. You can interview actual audiences about your material.
3. You can be reflexive in your empirical study (Banks, 2001).

At the end of the day, however, make an argument supported by your data, but don't apologise and look inward. Make your study a true one, but not the last word. As Becker says: 'The answer lies in distinguishing between the statement that *X* is true about something and the statement that *X* is all that is true about something' (1974: 15).

20.6 PROJECT

I hope that this chapter has helped you see social research in a different light. Now go out and take a *good look* at society!

1. **Media analysis**: Choose a research question, for instance, how a social group (either a broad one, like mothers or Gen-Xers, or a narrower one, like motorcyclists or police officers) is depicted. Choose a type of existing visual data – movies, newspaper photographs, advertisements, illustrations in children's books, television programmes, historical paintings or something else – which might portray your group. Analyse your data using one of the methodologies mentioned. In your write-up, defend your choice of method and sampling. Think about how to present the visual component in your essay.

2. **Photo elicitation**: Choose one of these projects or create your own.
   (a) Ask your grandparents, or a few elderly neighbours, to show you photographs from their youth. Interview them about consumption patterns (What did they buy, make, do without?) or social rituals (How did they celebrate birthdays? What did they do and where did they go with their friends?).
   (b) Pick a controversial topic, for instance, 'Fashion models encourage girls to be anorexic'. Gather a number of images (e.g. ten advertisements or pictures of famous people from newspapers, showing different body composition), or find a movie or TV show, on video, that captures the issue. Organise a focus group of your friends and lead a discussion using your visual material as prompts. Consider how best to convey the content of your images to your readers.

3. **Envision data**: Use your camera or camcorder to gather data.
   (a) Show how gravestones and cemeteries preserve memory, prestige, and power.
   (b) Study what the buildings that house different kinds of organisation say about their occupants.
   (c) Examine behaviour in shopping districts, asking how shoppers browse and circulate, or what people communicate by their dress and speed of walking.

In all of these, be scrupulous about research ethics. It is acceptable to photograph cemeteries and the outsides of buildings, but you will need permission to shoot inside offices and stores. You may find this permission difficult to obtain, but don't be tempted to cheat. You will be more unobtrusive, and safe, if you choose a busy high street in tourist areas. 'Quote' your data, or describe them, in your report.

20.7 FURTHER READING

Well worth reading are two overviews of visual methods in anthropology and sociology, Ball and Smith (1992) and Banks (2001), two edited collections, Prosser (1998) and Wagner (1979), and Becker's (1974) classic article. This chapter introduced a number of exemplars of research, incorporating the visual, in alphabetical order: Alexander (1994), Barthel (1988), Becker (1981), Berger (1972), Corse and Robinson (1994), Goffman (1979), Halle (1993), Heath (1986), Macdonald (1989), Porter (1997), Shively (1992), and Williamson (1978). These show the methods at work and, I hope, will provide inspiration. In addition, visual methods engage concerns in general sociology.

PART IV

ENDINGS

WRITING ABOUT SOCIAL RESEARCH

21

NIGEL GILBERT

CONTENTS

Until research has been published, available for all to read, it barely counts as social science at all. In science and social science, publication is an essential final step of the research process. There are good reasons for this. First, knowledge is itself a social creation. If you believe something, it remains a mere belief until you can persuade others that it is true; then it becomes knowledge that is shared. Secondly, as you will probably already have experienced yourself, it is not until you try to write down the results of your work in a way that is accessible to others that things become clear. Writing is a process of discovery as well as a process of clarification and of communication.

This last chapter is about writing and publishing social research. In the first section, we discuss some ways of thinking about the communication of research findings. The next section examines the origin and form of the research literature. This is followed by the dissection of a journal article published in the *American Sociological Review* to show how such articles are organised, with some hints about how you can create effective reports when writing research papers and dissertations.

21.1 TRUTH AND PERSUASION

There are several ways of thinking about sociological writing. At first sight, you might think that such writing merely records the facts for all to see. The ideal social scientific paper or book should be objective, setting out as clearly and precisely as possible what has been discovered. However, this view of scientific writing does not stand much scrutiny. It leaves un-examined several crucial questions: what do we mean by 'objective'?; what counts as a 'fact'?; why do research reports contain arguments as well as statements of fact?

A more sophisticated view of scientific writing recognises that writing is a form of rhetoric; that is, writing aims to persuade the reader of a position. It can be done well or badly. Over the years, writers have evolved stratagems for persuasion and have devised 'tricks of the trade'. Good writing is persuasive partly because of its use of these rhetorical devices, but also because it dares to go beyond them to invent new ways of putting arguments together.

A third view of scientific writing locates writing within the social structure of science. Sociological articles and books are written for and mainly read by other sociologists, who form a community with its own customs and beliefs. The shape of a journal article or the ways in which arguments are presented in sociological books are designed by writers for this community and in turn modify the community and its beliefs. Individually, sociologists write for the community because they prize the rewards it offers them, not financial rewards (often minimal or non-existent) but rewards of status, or 'recognition' of their labours and their abilities.

21.2 THE RESEARCH LITERATURE

One way to get a better understanding of the relationship of writing to the sociological community is to look at the history of the research paper in the natural sciences. The sociological literature has grown in much the same way as the scientific literature. This history has been well documented by Bazerman (1988).

21.2.1 The history of the scientific paper

The first scientific journal to be published in English, *The Philosophical Transactions*, was founded in 1665 by the Secretary of the Royal Society. It had its origins in the correspondence which members of the Royal Society wrote to each other to record their observations and ideas on topics of mutual interest, mainly about what today would be called natural science. Initially, the editor treated the journal much like a club newsletter, picking out interesting titbits from the correspondence and inviting the readers to send in further information. Gradually, however, the contributors were left to speak for themselves and, within a few years, the editor was reprinting letters verbatim, with only a few lines of editorial introduction.

The editor had to have a steady flow of correspondence coming to the journal to keep it afloat. Among the lures for authors were recognition of ideas, public acknowledgement of who was first to propose an idea or make a discovery, and the feeling that one was cooperating in a significant undertaking.

Over time, members began to write their letters, not as private correspondence to the editor which then happened to get published, but as public documents with an increasingly formal structure. Although many of the readers of the early *Transactions* were attracted by the tales of the curious and extraordinary which were reported there, there was a central circle of contributors who tended to be much more knowledgeable and much more sceptical, comparing what they read with what they believed and observed. As the journal also printed critical commentary, scientists for the first time had to defend themselves and their opinions in public.

According to Bazerman, this led to role conflict for the authors, who were torn between publicising their own work in the terms which would most appeal to the general reader, and defending their work from the criticisms of knowledgeable fellow scientists. A strategy for avoiding disputes with the other scientists was to present the work in the clearest possible way, anticipating possible objections. Gradually, standardised methods for presentation evolved.

Over the next century, several other scientific journals were started. These had to compete for readers and contributors. One way to get subscribers was to publish articles that were more carefully tuned to the particular interests of their readers. In addition to *The Philosophical Transactions*, which covered the whole of science, more specialised journals appeared for particular disciplines. In order to maintain its position in the face of this competition, there were increasing efforts to improve the articles in the *Transactions*, as first the editor excluded information only of interest to amateur scientists, and then kept out work judged to be of relatively low quality.

The use of the editor as a 'gatekeeper', who rejected some articles as unsuitable for the journal, imposed obvious strains on the post holder who had to fend off the disappointed contributors. After conflict erupted in the 1750s, an Editorial Board was created and later, the editor's decisions began to be made on the recommendation of 'referees', scientists chosen for their specialist knowledge who read and commented anonymously on papers.

Nowadays, when a paper is sent to an academic journal for publication, the editor first scans it to see whether the subject matter fits within the journal's scope. Then the editor sends it to two or three referees who write a commentary on it, indicating any weaknesses and recommending whether it should be published as it stands, revised to take account of the criticisms, or rejected as unsuitable for publication. The editor, acting on this advice, writes back to the author, usually enclosing the referees' comments. If the verdict is that changes need to be made, the author is invited to re-submit and, depending on the scale of the amendments required, may either have the revised paper accepted forthwith or sent to referees again for further consideration. In the social sciences, somewhere between 50 and 80 per cent of articles submitted are rejected, depending on the journal (although rejected articles may then be accepted by other journals which have less rigorous standards) (Hargens, 1988).

As the quality and prestige of the early scientific societies and their journals increased, so the advantages for the scientists of publishing in them increased also. Presenting work before the Royal Society and contributing to the *Transactions* identified one as a natural philosopher, as scientists were then called. The task of natural philosophers was to persuade the scientific community of the truth and originality of their discoveries. In the earliest days, this was a matter of showing other scientists what one had found, in a public demonstration before the assembled Royal Society; later it depended on persuasion through the written word. Various rhetorical devices for increasing the persuasive power of scientific writing were invented. These included de-emphasising the presence of the scientist by writing in the passive, so making it seem that the results could have been obtained by 'anyone', and using plain, rather than literary language, to emphasise the objectivity of the research.

One way of defending one's procedures and arguments against potential criticism was to make it clear that they were the same procedures and arguments which others, more illustrious than oneself, had themselves already used. As Newton once said, 'If I have seen further, it is by standing on the shoulders of giants'. (This famous quotation is the starting point for a fascinating book by the sociologist, Robert Merton (1965).) This is one of the functions of citations, references to previously published work, which gradually came to be a standard ingredient of scientific papers. Thus, by the late nineteenth century, the 'scientific paper', a social invention of enormous significance, had been born.

21.2.2 The modern sociological literature

The sociological literature is not as dominated by the research paper published in an academic journal as the natural scientific literature is, although journal articles are important as a method of communication. Sociologists also write books, reports and conference papers, as well as making occasional contributions to the mass media. It is harder to get books published as publishers merge and publishing is increasingly 'big business'. Academic books, such as you might find on a reading list, rarely sell more than 2,000 copies and specialised monographs often sell only a few hundred. The economics of publishing in such small quantities means that the books tend to be very expensive (reducing sales still further) and publishers are choosy about what they will take on. Thus considerations about the size of the potential market become much more important than the originality or quality of the research being reported.

The process of selection of books to be published is very different from that of the selection of articles to be printed in a journal. An author will approach a publishing house (or, often, several at once) with a brief proposal for a book. If the publisher likes the idea, they will usually ask for a sample chapter, to see whether the tone and style of the writing is to their liking. This may be sent out to 'readers', academics who are paid a small fee for commenting on the proposal and estimating the likely market for the book. If the publisher's editor is happy with the readers' advice, a contract will be issued which specifies when the complete manuscript is to be delivered, the length of the book in words and the percentage of the revenue which the author will receive (the 'royalties', usually between 7 and 10 per cent for an academic book). When the publisher receives the manuscript, it is copy edited by a professional who checks it for grammatical and spelling errors and it is then sent to the printer. Between six months and a year after the manuscript arrives at the publisher, the book is released to bookshops.

At the other end of the continuum in terms of time to publication is the conference paper. All professional societies, such as the British Sociological Association in the UK, organise conferences and there are many sub-groups which arrange meetings on specific topics. Researchers are invited to submit papers to these conferences and attend them to 'read' (or more usually, lecture on the general topic of) the paper. Sometimes the papers are collected together and published as a book, but more usually, they are only available as photocopied typescript by writing to the author. The time lag between writing and circulation is much shorter for such papers, but they are of course not so readily available as reports which have been more formally published.

21.3 Reporting research

We have seen that writing is an essential part of the research process, and that the object of writing is both communication and persuasion. This and the next section will offer some advice about how to organise writing about social research. Suppose that you were just embarking on a research project – it might be for a dissertation as part of a course, or a thesis for a postgraduate degree, or a full-time, large-scale funded project. What preparations are needed for reporting such work?

Getting down to writing is difficult for almost everyone, but particularly for researchers, because research is a mixture of very sociable activities (organising access, interviewing, and so on) and the very unsociable act of writing. Once one has got used to the sociable side of research it is sometimes hard to move to the writing-up stage, where one is often working alone, just you and a word processor. A consequence of the differences between these two kinds of activity is that many people put off writing until it is far too late.

You should be thinking about the organisation of your research report at the very beginning of the project. As the project continues, the shape of the report ought to become clearer. Some parts can even be written before any data is collected – accounts of the previous work on which your research is based and the theoretical grounding of your own work can both be drafted before data collection has been completed. One advantage of writing as you go along is that if you spend a long time not writing you can get 'rusty'. The act of writing, of trying to put down your thoughts as clearly as possible, can suggest new issues and new ideas and these can go back to influence data collection and analysis.

There are several steps you need to take before setting pen to paper. First, if you are working with colleagues, you need to decide who will be listed as the authors and the order of names. This may seem a trivial point, but some excellent research teams have come to grief because this issue was not settled before the writing began. Secondly, it helps if you can map out the reports, papers and other publications that you hope to write and where these will be published. If you think your work would best go into an academic journal, you will need to think about which journal is most appropriate and look through some back issues to see the style and type of article it publishes. If you are writing a thesis or dissertation, or to satisfy course requirements, it is worth looking at previous dissertations to see what length, style and format is expected.

Once you have decided on where to publish, there are further decisions to make about what to write. Usually, the temptation is to put too much in, so that the overall message gets confused. A single paper (or a chapter in a thesis or book) should only carry one message. It requires great skill to keep even two balls in the air at once and unless you are an expert, you should decide before you start what *the* one point you want to make will be, and then stick to it ruthlessly. Of course, to arrive at one specific conclusion, you will need to cover many supporting issues. But everything should be there because it is needed to argue the one basic message; if there is anything in the paper that cannot be justified in that way, it should be cast out (perhaps to become the seed of another publication).

A journal article in sociology is normally between 4,000 and 7,000 words in length and this is also the typical length of a book chapter (the chapters in this book average about 7,000 words). But no one other than undergraduate course tutors ever worries about a report being too short; it is much more likely that the complaint will be that it is too long. Perhaps this is because clarity and conciseness are harder to achieve than verbosity. Length also comes from the writer not having a clear plan of how the report will be organised before the writing starts, so making yourself an 'outline' of the structure of the report (as you may have been taught to do at school when writing essays) is an excellent way of preparing to start writing.

Even if you take this advice and begin writing drafts as early as you can, you may find it hard to get started. It is not necessary to write a chapter or article by starting at the beginning and working through to the end, although some people do that. Try beginning with whatever section seems easiest to get you started. The Introduction and Conclusion are best written last because they need to be composed with knowledge of what the rest of the piece is about, and this may change and develop as you write.

It often helps to have someone in mind to whom you can aim your writing. For an academic paper or dissertation, you should be writing for another researcher, but not one who is a specialist in your area. For more popular work, you will need to decide what kind of person is likely to read your report, what they are likely to be interested in and what they are likely to know already. No matter who you are writing for, however, keep your sentences short and straightforward and, whenever you can, use ordinary words in preference to technical terms. Convoluted sentences and complex constructions merely confuse the reader (and might lead to the suspicion that you, the writer, are not thinking clearly, either).

The first draft is often the hardest. After it is completed, you should put it away for a few days and then read it through critically, trying to look at it from the point of view of someone who is coming to it fresh. You will certainly find much that is wrong, from sentences that need phrasing more clearly to major omissions and repetitions. These problems should be put right in a second draft. This second draft can then be shown to colleagues with a request for comments. Their suggestions can be incorporated into the third draft. As this sequence suggests, writing about research always involves much re-writing and refinement, and you should plan for at least three rounds of comments and re-drafting.

21.3.1 The shape of a journal article

When writing a report, it helps to know how other people have organised their work, so that you can see what arrangements are clear and persuasive. In this section, we examine in some detail how one particular article, published in the *American Sociological Review*, was constructed. There is nothing special about the article we shall be looking at; it is typical of a particular style of quantitative sociology and there are many hundreds of similarly structured papers in the sociological literature. It does, however, have the merit of displaying its structure especially clearly. Other papers written in a more discursive style and those based on ethnographic data often do not reveal their structure so immediately, but you will usually find that more or less the same types of material are included in more or less the same order.

This section will therefore be about the standard, conventional structure for an article. Almost the same structure is typically used in project reports, Masters' and doctoral theses and in research reports written for sponsors and funders, rather than for publication. It is a structure that has been devised through much experience and it will usually serve you well. But it is just a convention. If, when you come to report on your research, you find that the conventional structure does not fit what you have to say, no one will stop you from breaking the convention (at least not in sociology; other disciplines are rather stricter. For example, it is almost impossible to get articles published in certain psychology journals unless they precisely follow the conventional structure.)

So what is this structure? The main sections of a research paper are:

- Title
- Author
- Abstract
- Introduction
- Theory
- Data and methods
- Results
- Conclusions
- References

Let us look at each of these sections in turn and see how the authors of the *American Sociological Review* article dealt with them.

The **Title** (in Figure 21.1, 'Sex segregation in voluntary associations') is the best advertisement that the article will get. Most readers will be attracted to the article by noticing the title on a journal's Contents page or in the list of references in another paper. The same applies to book titles: remember how often you have picked up a book in a bookshop just because the title made it seem interesting. The title needs to be short, snappy and above all, accurately descriptive of the content.

The **Abstract** ('We analyze the sex composition ... networks they generate') is expected to summarise the content of the paper. Abstracting journals (e.g. *Sociological Abstracts*) will reprint just the abstract, together with those from all the other articles which have been published that quarter, under a subject classification which makes it fairly easy to track down articles on a particular topic. The abstract therefore has a double function: it serves as an overview for people who are reading the article in a journal and as a self-standing summary for people who are reading an abstracting journal. Because for most readers the most interesting part of an article is the conclusion, it is wise to put this near the beginning of the abstract. Then specify the sample or setting to indicate the scope of the findings. Finish with a brief account of the method used to collect and analyse the data. Abstracts should never include citations to other work.

The **Acknowledgements** ('Work on this paper was supported ... for the interpretation of the data'): it is conventional to acknowledge the assistance of the people who funded the research, anyone who made a significant contribution to the research but is not an author, and colleagues who com-

SEX SEGREGATION IN VOLUNTARY ASSOCIATIONS*

J. Miller McPherson   Lynn Smith-Lovin

University of South Carolina

We analyze the sex composition of 815 face-to-face voluntary associations in 10 communities to determine the extent of sex integration produced by voluntary affiliation. The sex segregation in these groups is substantial; nearly one-half of the organizations are exclusively female, while one-fifth are all male. Instrumental organizations (business-related and political groups) are more likely to be sex heterogeneous, while expressive groups are likely to be exclusively male or female. From the point of view of the individual, the typical female membership generates face-to-face contact with about 29 other members, less than four of whom are men. Male memberships, on the other hand, produce contact with over 37 other members on the average, nearly eight of whom are female. Men's contacts are both more numerous and more heterogeneous. We conclude that there is little support for the sex integration hypothesis in these data, although the sex heterogeneity of instrumental groups (especially those which are job-related) indicates that this pattern may change as women move into the labour force in increasing numbers. The paper explores some consequences of segregation for the organizations and the social networks they generate.

The integration hypothesis has been a main theme of research on voluntary organizations since Toqueville (1969) first raised the issue in the nineteenth century. From Durkheim's (1902) and Kornhauser's (1959) notion of voluntary organizations as mediators between the mass and the elite, to Babchuk and Edwards' (1965) view of voluntary groups as multi-level integrators, researchers have argued that voluntary groups serve as a sort of interstitial glue. Yet the details of exactly what is integrated with what has remained remarkably unclear over the years. What emerges from the literature is a picture of voluntary groups which may represent the emergent interests of unspecified publics in the political domain, provide resources for useful contacts in the economic domain, allow the expression of altruistic impulses in the charitable domain, and provide a variety of peripheral and ephemeral services (Smith and Freedman, 1972). In contrast to this integrative view of voluntary groups, many of the early community studies emphasised that voluntary associations were sorting mechanisms (Hughes, 1943; Anderson, 1937). As Gans (1967: 61) noted, the groups "divided and segregated people by their interests and ultimately, of course, by socio-economic, educational, and religious differences". Of course, the integrating and sorting perspectives on voluntary associations are . . .

* Address all correspondence to J. Miller McPherson, Department of Sociology, University of South Carolina, Columbia, SC 29208. Work on this paper was supported by National Science Foundation grants SES-8120666 and SES-8319899, Miller McPherson, Principal Investigator. The authors would like to thank John McCarthy of Catholic University and the members of the structuralist group at the University of South Carolina for their helpful comments: Charles Brody, Michael Kennedy, Bruce H. Mayhew, Patrick Nolan, Jimmy Sanders, Eui-Hang Shin, and John V. Skvoretz. Data were collected through the facilities of the Bureau of Sociological Research of the University of Nebraska, Helen Moore, Director. The authors bear full responsibility for the interpretation of the data.

Figure 21.1   *The first page from McPherson and Smith-Lovin (1986)*

mented on drafts of the paper and helped to improve it. If you are student writing a thesis, it may be appropriate to acknowledge your supervisor.

The paper proper starts with an **Introduction** that should indicate the topic of the paper, demonstrate why this topic is interesting and important, and show how the approach taken in the paper is an advance on previous work. In brief, the purpose of the Introduction is to get the reader hooked. That means starting from the reader's present knowledge and leading him or her on to see that the topic is worth spending time investigating. Notice how McPherson and Smith-Lovin in their introduction locate their research immediately into 'classical' sociology, with references to Toqueville and Durkheim in the first sentence. Notice also how in the space of two paragraphs they introduce a potentially interesting controversy in the existing literature – is the function of voluntary groups that of integration or sorting? One of the objects of the paper is to offer evidence that might resolve this controversy. In these few lines of introduction, the authors have mapped out a domain of research, have suggested that there has been much sociological interest in the domain, have identified a gap in the research concerning the integrative versus sorting issue, and have implied that the paper will go some way towards filling that gap.

The hallmark of a good introduction is that it locates a 'hole' in the research literature that the rest of the paper will fill. This particular paper offers a very good example. But the same principle applies generally, not only to papers, but also to books and theses. A thesis or dissertation usually begins with a chapter intended to 'review the literature'. But in writing such a review, one needs to remember that the purpose is not to catalogue the available literature for its own sake, but rather, as with this introduction, to show that there is some research which has yet to be done – and here it is!

Notice also that, as a matter of convention, the text starts without any preceding sub-heading: there is no heading, 'Introduction'.

On the page after the one shown in Figure 21.1, the authors observe that the integrative and sorting mechanisms are not as opposed as they might seem, because both may operate simultaneously, producing homogeneity on some dimensions and heterogeneity on others. They argue that the question then becomes 'which social dimensions are integrated and which are sorted, and in what types of organisation?' (McPherson and Smith-Lovin, 1986: 62). They then move on to discuss sex segregation in voluntary organisations, which has previously been considered mainly in terms of the sorting view, and review the literature on this topic. This brings them to the second major section, headed 'Network Implications of Sex Segregation in Organizations', which is as close as this paper gets to a section devoted to 'theory'.

The **Theory** section is the place to introduce the concepts you will be using in your analysis. Although called the Theory section, it is not 'grand theory' that is needed here, but what Merton (1968: 39–72) called 'middle range theory': the specific concepts and ideas that you will use to explain your findings. In McPherson and Smith-Lovin's paper, this leads to the statement of a number of propositions which they then go on to test later in the article. For example, they write:

Based on our earlier discussion of the changing role of women, we would expect that working women, more highly educated women, and younger women would be less likely to participate in organizational environments which are single sex (all women's clubs) and more likely to participate in mixed sex groups (although they may often be in the minority there). (McPherson and Smith-Lovin, 1986: 63)

This is a proposition that they will compare with the data they have collected. But before we reach these results, there is a section on Data and methods.

The **Data and methods** section is often the most standardised and least interesting part of a research article, because it has to convey a lot of strictly factual information. The ideal is to provide just enough detail so that another researcher can find everything he or she needs to repeat the work. That means that you must specify here the decisions you made about matters such as how you selected the respondents, how you collected the data and any special methods you used. The important characteristics which you should consider mentioning in this section are listed below; include only those which are relevant to the research design you have chosen:

- Sample size
- Sample design
- Sampling frame
- Date of data collection
- How settings selected for observation were chosen
- Response rate achieved
- Limitations of and possible biases in the data
- Sources of secondary data (e.g. statistics from government surveys)
- Basic demographic characteristics of the sample
- Explanation of any special data analysis techniques used

In the McPherson and Smith-Lovin study, the design was complicated by the fact that they wished to sample not individuals, but voluntary organisations. This they did by asking a representative probability sample of adults from ten communities in Nebraska about the organisations to which they were affiliated. They write, in the section headed 'Data and methods':

In the first stage, a representative probability sample of 656 non-institutionalised adults was interviewed from the 10 communities. In the interviews, we obtained a list of all the organizations with which each individual was affiliated. We used a technique known as aided recall (Babchuk and Booth, 1969) to insure that all organizations were reported. Respondents were encouraged to report even small, relatively informal groups if these groups had an identifiable membership. A total of 2,091 organizational names were generated, representing an affiliation rate of about 3.2 (in smaller communities, of course, some names represented multiple reports of the same organization). Of the 2,091 organizations, 815 groups which met face-to-face in the local community constitute the sample for this analysis. (McPherson and Smith-Lovin, 1986: 64)

In this brief excerpt from a much longer description of their methods of sampling and data collection, note how the authors take pains to be precise about the way in which their sample was obtained and the criterion (face-to-face meetings) which they used to select those organisations chosen for further study. Note also how, rather than describe in detail the way that they maximised respondents' recall of all the organisations they belonged to, they just reference another article (Babchuk and Booth, 1969) where the technique is described.

After describing the methods used to collect data, the typical paper discusses the **Results**, which in the McPherson and Smith-Lovin article are described as the 'Analyses and Findings'. When writing this part of the paper, the problem is usually to know which of all the analyses you have done should be included and which should be left out. The primary rule is: be relevant. Remember that the Introduction has already stated what the paper is about and that the purpose of this Results section is to provide the findings on which your conclusions will be based. This means that data which may be very unexpected or significant, but which is not related to the point of the paper, should be excluded (it could form the basis of another paper). For a similar reason, this section needs to focus around your findings, not the way in which you came to reach the results. In particular, this is not the place for an account of the process of research, nor of all the dead-ends which all researchers encounter, nor the disasters and difficulties which you have overcome.

The Results section will probably contain summaries and analyses of the data you have collected, in the form of statistical tables (if your data are quantitative) or characteristic quotations or descriptions of observations (if your data are qualitative). McPherson and Smith-Lovin use the statistical technique called regression and present the results in tables which summarise the relative importance of marital status, employment status, education and age on being involved in voluntary organisations. They find overall that the voluntary groups they have studied are very segregated: almost half are all female and one-fifth are all male. Large organisations are less likely to be all female and those that recruit from the labour force are likely to be mixed, while those which are expressive in character are more likely to be segregated. Their Results section concludes:

At the individual level, single males are more likely to belong to sex-segregated groups, while widowed or separated women are more likely to be in all-female groups. The effects of work status are quite different for men and for women. Employed women are very much less likely to belong to all-female groups than employed men are to belong to all-male groups. (McPherson and Smith-Lovin, 1986: 75)

Notice that these results are closely tied to the data and are more or less devoid of theory. The above quotation consists of little more than the output of the statistical analysis put into words. In this article, the interpretation of these results is left to the next section. However, it is usual to link the results and their theoretical interpretation more closely together than they are here, with both data and interpretation included in the Results section.

Relating the results back to the issues raised in the Introduction and the Theory sections is the job of the **Conclusion**. In the McPherson and Smith-Lovin article, the Introduction posed the question of whether voluntary groups fulfil a sorting or integrative function. Now is the time for the authors to answer that question. In the previous section they reported that, overall, voluntary associations are very segregated. In this section they conclude that these organisations reaffirm sex distinctions rather than creating ties between the sexes. 'The sorting function, then, clearly dominates the integrative function with regard to sex' (McPherson and Smith-Lovin, 1986: 75). This is a good example of the way in which the Conclusion should relate back to the issues raised in the Introduction, thus closing the circle and tying up the article neatly. This is also the section in which you can speculate a little, going beyond the strict confines of the data, and where you can point to further issues that the research has raised.

The last paragraph of the Conclusion is one of the most difficult to write because it ought to summarise what the main findings of the research were, in a succinct and interesting way. This is because many readers will look first at the end of the article to see whether it has anything interesting to say, before they start at the beginning. And it is as well to anticipate this.

Lastly, there is the list of **References**. This is a list of the full bibliographical details of the books and articles cited in the text. ('References' are the list of details at the end of an article; 'citations' are the (Author, Year) pairs in the body of the text.) Citations are important in a sociological article for a number of reasons. First, they situate the article within existing research. We saw citations used in this way in the Introduction (Figure 21.1) where the particular topic of this paper is located within the sociological literature. Secondly, references act as a kind of shorthand. It was pointed out that in the Methods section, instead of describing the technique of 'aided recall', a citation to Babchuk and Booth (1969) was provided. This sort of citation saves space because the details of the technique need only be printed once in the original article, rather than being rolled out again and again in reports of every piece of research that uses it. Thirdly, citations to reports which have come to the same or similar results can help to give an article some authority, for the citations imply that the conclusions reproduce those found elsewhere by independent investigators.

For all these reasons, sociological books and papers are always sprinkled with citations. Each citation must be linked to a reference that provides the full details about where to find the work cited. There are several standard conventions for references. Sometimes the citation is a superscript number in the text, leading to a numbered reference at the end. More usually, as in this book, citations are given as the name of the author and the year of publication, and the references are listed alphabetically at the end. This is known as the Harvard convention and is probably the easiest for authors to use. Unless you are using a clever word processor which can do it for you, using numbered superscripts makes for difficulties if you change your mind and want to add or delete a citation; you then have to renumber all the citations following.

Ensuring that all the necessary details are correct and included in the References is part of intellectual good manners. It means that, for example, if you read a book that you might want to refer to later, you should take careful note of the author, the author's initials, the date of publication, the title, the city of publication and the publisher. With articles in journals, you should note the author, the author's initials, the date of publication, the title of the article, the name of the journal, the volume number of the journal in which the article is printed, and the starting and ending page numbers of the article. Keeping a record of these ought to become second nature. They are the standard data which librarians will want if you need to find the book or article again. One more item is needed if you copy out a direct quotation from a book or paper: the page number from which the quote is taken (how else will you be able to check that you've got the wording exactly right if you don't have the page number?).

21.3.2 Breaking the rules

So ends our tour of one sociological article. The general shape of this article is a good one to follow, not only for research papers, but also for more informal reports and for dissertations and theses. Often when research is funded by an agency or is commissioned, those sponsoring the research will demand a specially written report about the results. Such reports can keep to the conventional structure that we have seen in the previous section, but with some modifications to suit the audience for which it is intended. The Abstract is often replaced by a somewhat longer preliminary section headed 'Summary', in which the findings of the research are laid out as clearly as possible, perhaps as a list of the main conclusions. If the sponsors of the research are mainly interested in social policy, the summary might also indicate the policy implications of the research. Within the body of the report, it is usual to have less about the research design than is needed for an academic article, with further details relegated to an Appendix.

Dissertations written as part of a degree also often follow the standard structure, modified slightly. A doctoral thesis will typically have at least one chapter corresponding to each of the main sections listed on page 368. The Abstract will again be replaced by a Summary, usually about one page in length. The Introduction will probably include a rather more exhaustive literature review than would be appropriate for a published report.

McPherson and Smith-Lovin's paper was chosen for detailed examination because it follows the standard and conventional shape of a social research article very closely. It is a good example of following the 'rules'. But, of course, not all sociological articles do keep to the 'rules' and they are none the worse for that. Breaking the rules is fine, so long as the message you want to convey is nevertheless communicated effectively. There are some rules you should break only with the greatest of caution and others that should not give you a moment's worry. For example, it is almost always a bad idea to miss out either the Introduction or the Conclusion. These two sections tell the reader what to expect and what to take from the research. A rule that *can* be broken for many research reports is the one that says that you should divide the middle of the report into separate 'Theory', 'Methods' and 'Results' sections. Often, some other form of organisation will suit what you have to say much better. For example, it is possible to interweave theory and findings by telling a 'story' about your respondents (Richardson, 1990), or select themes which emerge from your data and devote one section to each theme. The best way of learning about these alternative structures is to look carefully at how the books and articles which you think communicate effectively have been constructed by their authors.

21.4 CONCLUSION

All through this chapter, I have emphasised that social research is only completed when its results have been published. Most research is published in the academic literature, in journals or in books aimed at the academic reader. However, social scientific knowledge is not only valuable for its own sake, to increase our understanding of the social world; much research is conducted in order to inform or to influence the making of public policy. Shouldn't research findings be made available ('disseminated' is the jargon) to the wider public as well?

Of course, the answer to this question must be, yes. But as we saw in Chapter 3, the process by which this dissemination generally occurs is much more complicated and less open to intervention by social researchers than one might imagine. When one thinks of the 'use' of research, the traditional view is that policy-makers ought to read and understand the research, consider its implications and then translate the findings into practice as soon as possible. In fact, policy-making is rarely done in this way and research findings, no matter how significant they may appear to be, rarely influence the policy-making process so directly (Weiss, 1980).

Social research does, however, have an indirect effect on policy. Individual research results add to a broad pool of work which accumulates over time and which raises new issues, provides new perspectives and asks new questions. There is a slow seepage of ideas from the academic literature into the policy process, working its way through indirect channels such as professional and trade journals, textbooks and university education as well as directly when policy-makers find themselves needing to obtain a broad understanding of a policy topic. And pressure groups and voluntary groups also use the research literature directly to press their case, often taking advantage of the authority which publication in the academic literature bestows on the research. This indirect influence can be very powerful, although sometimes in unexpected ways. For example, terms like deviance, ethnicity, institution, labour market, dependency and gender are now part of the common vocabulary of educated people, but were originally given their meaning by the social scientists who used them in reporting their research findings in the academic literature.

21.5 PROJECT

As was noted in section 21.2.1, every academic paper is reviewed before publication by at least two referees, chosen from among the academic community by journal editors for their knowledge of the paper's topic. Referees (who are rarely paid for their labours) receive a copy of the paper in typescript and a letter (or sometimes a form) from the editor that requests them to comment on the paper's suitability for publication in terms of its clarity, originality and the adequacy of its argument. The referee has between two and six weeks to respond with a verdict (one of: accept; accept with minor revisions such as spelling or stylistic errors; accept but require major revisions; or reject) and a report. The report, which will often be forwarded anonymously to the author, explains the referee's verdict, commenting on the overall strengths and weaknesses of the paper and making suggestions for improvements. Despite the care that many referees put into the task, editors often find that they get contradictory recommendations from referees and it is very common for two referees to make quite different suggestions for improvements.

The first step in this project is to identify a research area in which you have an interest (the sociology of health or deviance, for example). Look through the library 'current journals' shelves and find a recent issue of a journal publishing in your area. Choose one paper from that journal. If possible, make a photocopy of it.

You should imagine that you have received a typescript copy of this paper from a journal editor to referee. Examine the paper closely. Is it clear? Is it well organised? Can one quickly identify the main conclusions? Are the justifications for those conclusions soundly based? Are the data appropriate to the topic of the paper? Are the methods of data collection and analysis described in sufficient detail that someone else could repeat the study? Are there plausible alternative interpretations of the data or of the results that the author has not noticed? Does the abstract adequately describe the contents of the paper? Are there passages that could be rewritten to make them clearer? Has the author referenced all the relevant literature?

It is surprising how often even published papers will wilt under careful scrutiny of this kind. In about 300 words, write a report about the article. Your criticisms should be phrased so that they are constructive, polite and encouraging – the aim of a referee's report is to encourage the author towards a better article, not to damage the author's ego.

21.6 FURTHER READING

Becker (1986) is excellent on writing about social science. Mullins (1977) is also good, especially about the processes involved in getting published. Mulkay (1985) is a fascinating exploration of the textual forms that are, or could be, used by sociologists to report on the social world.

Richardson (1990) includes a reflective account of how she, as a sociologist, came to write a book intended for the lay person about her research, as well as offering wise words about writing. Wolcott (1990) concentrates on the particular problems of reporting on qualitative research.

If you are writing a dissertation for a research degree, Phillips and Pugh (1987) should be essential reading.

BIBLIOGRAPHY

Abbott, P. and Wallace, W. (1997) *An Introduction to Sociology: Feminist Perspectives* (2nd edition). London: Routledge.

Abrams, P. (1984) 'The uses of British sociology 1831–1981', in M. Bulmer (ed.), *Essays on the History of British Sociological Research*. Cambridge: Cambridge University Press, pp. 181–205.

Adler, P. (1985) *Wheeling and Dealing: an Ethnography of an Upper Level Dealing and Smuggling Community*. New York: Columbia University Press.

Adorno, T. and Goldmann, L. (1977) 'To describe, understand and explain', in L. Goldmann (ed.), *Cultural Creation*. Oxford: Blackwell.

Agar, M. (1986) *Speaking of Ethnography*. Beverly Hills, CA: Sage.

Agar, M. (1993) 'The right brain strikes back', in N. Fielding and R. Lee (eds), *Using Computers in Qualitative Research*. London: Sage, pp. 181–94.

Agar, M. (1995) 'Literary journalism as ethnography: exploring the excluded middle', in J. Van Maanen (ed.), *Representation in Ethnography*. Thousand Oaks, CA: Sage.

Agresti, A. and Finlay, B. (1997) *Statistical Methods for the Social Sciences*. Englewood Cliffs, NJ: Prentice-Hall.

Albrecht, M.C. (1954) 'The relationship between literature and society', *American Journal of Sociology*, 59: 425–36.

Alexander, C.S. and Becker, H.J. (1978) 'The use of vignettes in survey research', *Public Opinion Quarterly*, 42: 93–104.

Alexander, V.D. (1994) 'The image of children in magazine advertisements from 1905 to 1990', *Communication Research*, 21: 742–65.

Altheide, D. (1996) *Qualitative Media Analysis*. Thousand Oaks, CA: Sage.

Andersen, J. and Larsen, J.E. (1998) 'Gender, poverty and empowerment', *Critical Social Policy*, 18(2): 241–58.

Antal, F. (1962) *Hogarth and His Place in European Art*. London: Routledge and Kegan Paul.

Antal, F. (1987) *Florentine Painting and its Social Background*. Cambridge, MA: Harvard University Press.

Arber, S. (1989) 'Opening the "black" box: inequalities in women's health', in P. Abbott and G. Payne (eds), *New Directions in the Sociology of Health*. Brighton: Falmer Press.

Arber, S. (1997) 'Comparing inequalities in women's and men's health: Britain in the 1990s', *Social Science and Medicine*, 44(6): 773–87.

Arber, S. and Lahelma, E. (1993) 'Women, paid employment and ill-health in Britain and Finland', *Acta Sociologica*, 36: 121–38.

Arksey, H. and Knight, P. (1999) *Interviewing for Social Scientists: an Introductory Resource with Examples*. London: Sage.

Atkinson, J.M. (1978) *Discovering Suicide*. London: Macmillan.

Atkinson, J.M. (1984) *Our Master's Voices: the Language and Body Language of Politics*. London: Methuen.

Atkinson, J.M. and Heritage, J.C. (eds) (1984) *The Structures of Social Action: Studies in Conversation Analysis*. Cambridge: Cambridge University Press.

Atkinson, R. (1998) *The Life Story Interview*. London: Sage.

Austin, J.L. (1962) *How To Do Things With Words*. Oxford: Oxford University Press.

Babbie, E. (1995) *The Practice of Social Research* (7th edition). Belmont, CA: Wadsworth.

Babchuck, N. and Booth, A. (1969) 'Voluntary association memberships: a longitudinal analysis', *American Sociological Review*, 34: 1–45.

Bachelard, G. (1984) *The New Scientific Spirit* (trans. A. Goldhammer). Boston, MA: Beacon Press.

Ball, M.S. and Smith, G.W.H. (1992) *Analyzing Visual Data*. London: Sage.

Banks, M. (2001) *Visual Methods in Social Research*. London: Sage.

Barbour, R.S. and Kitzenger, J. (eds) (1999) *Developing Focus Group Research: Politics, Theory and Practice*. London: Sage.

Barnes, B., Bloor, D. and Henry, J. (1996) *Scientific Knowledge: a Sociological Analysis*. London: Athlone Press.

Barnes, J.A. (1979) *Who Should Know What? Social Science, Privacy and Ethics*. Cambridge: Cambridge University Press.

Barthel, D. (1988) *Putting on Appearances*. Philadelphia, PA: Temple University Press.

Barthes, R. ([1957] 1972) *Mythologies*. London: Vintage.

Barthes, R. (1967) *Elements of Semiology* (trans. Annette Lavers and Colin Smith). London: Jonathan Cape.

Bartley, M. (1996) ' "Probably, Minister . . .": the "strong programme" approach to the relationship between research and policy', in C. Samson and N. South (eds), *The Social Construction of Social Policy: Methodologies, Racism, Citizenship and the Environment*. London: Macmillan, pp. 17–33.

Bauman, Z. (1990) *Thinking Sociologically*. Oxford: Blackwell.

Baxandall, M. (1988) *Painting and Experience in Fifteenth-century Italy* (2nd edition). Oxford: Oxford University Press.

Bazeley, P. and Richards, L. (2000) *The Nvivo Project Book*, London: Sage.

Bazerman, C. (1988) *Shaping Written Knowledge*. Madison, WI: University of Wisconsin Press.

Beauchamp, T.L., Faden, R.R., Wallace, R.J. and Walters, L. (eds) (1982) *Ethical Issues in Social Science Research*. Baltimore, MD: Johns Hopkins University Press.

Becker, H.S. (1971) *Sociological Work*. London: Allen Lane.

Becker, H.S. (1974) 'Photography and sociology', *Studies in the Anthropology of Visual Communication*, 1(1): 3–26.

Becker, H.S. (1979) 'Do photographs tell the truth?', in T. Cook and C. Reichardt (eds), *Qualitative and Quantitative Methods in Evaluation Research*. London: Sage.

Becker, H.S. (1981) *Exploring Society Photographically*. Chicago: University of Chicago Press.

Becker, H.S. (1986) *Writing for Social Scientists*. Chicago: University of Chicago Press.

Becker, H.S. (1998) 'Visual sociology, documentary photography, and photojournalism: it's (almost) all a matter of context', in J. Prosser (ed.), *Image-Based Research*. London: Routledge/Falmer, pp. 84–96.

Becker, H.S. (2000) 'What should sociology look like in the (near) future?', *Contemporary Sociology*, 29(2): 333–6.

Bellenger, D.N., Bernhardt, K.L. and Goldstucker, J.L. (1976) 'Qualitative research techniques: focus group interviews', in D.N. Bellenger, K.L. Bernhardt and J.L. Goldstucker (eds), *Qualitative Research in Marketing*. Chicago: American Marketing Association.

Bennett, H.S. (1922) *The Pastons and their England*. Cambridge: Cambridge University Press.

Bennett, N., Jarvis, L., Rowlands, O., Singleton, N. and Haselden, W. (1996) *Living in Britain: Results from the 1994 General Household Survey*. London: OPCS/HMSO.

Berger, J. (1972) *Ways of Seeing*. London: Penguin Books.

Bertrand, J.T., Brown, J.E. and Ward, V.M. (1992) 'Techniques for analysing focus group data', *Evaluation Review*, 16(2): 198–209.

Bettelheim, B. (1943) 'Individual and mass behaviour under extreme situations', *Journal of Abnormal and Social Psychology*, 38: 417–52. (Reprinted in B. Bettleheim (1979) *Surviving and Other Essays*. London: Thames and Hudson, pp. 48–73.)

Bignell, J. (1997) *Media Semiotics*. Manchester: Manchester University Press.

Blalock, H.M. (1969) *Theory Construction*. Englewood Cliffs, NJ: Prentice-Hall.

Blane, D., Smith, G.D. and Bartley, M. (1993) 'Social selection: what does it contribute to social class differences in health?', *Sociology of Health and Illness*, 15(1): 1–15.

Blau, P.M. (1964) *Exchange and Power in Social Life*. New York: Wiley.

Bloomfield, D., Collins, K., Fry, C. and Munton, R. (1998) 'Deliberative and inclusionary processes: their contribution to environmental governance'. Paper given at the ESRC conference 'Environmental Governance: Responding to the Challenge of Deliberative Democracy', University of London, 17 September 1998, available from http://www.geog.ucl.ac.uk/esru/dip/

Blowers, A. and Leroy, P. (1994) 'Power, politics and environmental inequality: a theoretical and empirical analysis of the process of "peripheralisation"', *Environmental Politics*, 3(2): 197–228.

Blume, S.S. (1979) 'Policy studies and social policy in Britain', *Journal of Social Policy*, 8: 311–34.

Blumer, H. (1969) *Symbolic Interactionism*. Berkeley, CA: University of California Press.

Boardman, B. (1991) *Fuel Poverty: From Cold Homes to Affordable Warmth*. London: Belhaven/Wiley.

Bok, S. (1979) *Lying: Moral Choice in Public and Private Life*. Hassocks: Harvester.

Bone, M., Gregory, J., Gill, B. and Lader, D. (1992) *Retirement and Retirement Plans*. London: OPCS/HMSO.

Booth, T. (1988) *Developing Policy Research*. Aldershot: Avebury.

Boruch, R.F. and Cecil, J.S. (1979) *Assuring the Confidentiality of Social Research Data*. Philadelphia, PA: University of Pennsylvania Press.

Bourdieu, P. (1990) *In Other Words: Essays towards a Reflexive Sociology*. Cambridge: Polity Press.

Bourdieu, P. (with J.-C. Passeron and J.-C. Chamboredon) (1991) *The Craft of Sociology: Epistemological Preliminaries*. New York: Aldine.

Braithwaite, J. (1981) 'The myth of social class and criminality reconsidered', *American Sociological Review*, 46: 36–57.

Brannen, J. and Moss, P. (1988) *New Mothers at Work: Employment and Childcare.* London: Unwin Hyman.

Breakwell, G.M. (1986) *Coping with Threatened Identities.* London: Methuen.

Breakwell, G.M. (ed.) (1992) *Social Psychology of Identity and the Self Concept.* Guildford: Surrey University Press in association with Academic Press.

Brettell, C. (ed.) (1993) *When They Read What We Write: the Politics of Ethnography.* New York: Bergin Garvey.

Bridgwood, A., Lilly, R., Thomas, M., Bacon, J., Sykes, W. and Morris, S. (2000) *Living in Britain: Results from the 1998 General Household Survey.* London: The Stationery Office.

Brown, B.B. and Perkins, D.D. (1992) 'Disruption in place attachment', in I. Alman and S.M. Low (eds), *Place Attachment.* New York: Blenheim Press.

Brown, J., Fielding, J. and Lee, T. (1984) *Perception of Risk – a Secondary Analysis of Data Collected by the Social and Community Planning Research.* Report for the Health and Safety Executive. University of Surrey.

Brown, P. (1991) 'The popular epidemiology approach to toxic waste contamination', in S.R. Couch and J. Kroll-Smith (eds), *Communities at Risk: Collective Responses to Technological Hazards.* New York: Peter Lang, pp. 133–55.

Brown, P. (1993) 'When the public knows better: popular epidemiology', *Environment*, 35(8): 17–41.

Bruyn, S.T. (1966) *The Human Perspective in Sociology.* Englewood Cliffs, NJ: Prentice-Hall.

Buck, N., Gershuny, J., Rose, D. and Scott, J. (1994) *Changing Households: the British Household Panel Survey 1990–1992.* Colchester: ESRC Research Centre on Micro-social Change.

Bullard, R. (ed.) (1993) *Confronting Environmental Racism: Voices from the Grassroots.* Boston, MA: Southend Press.

Bullock, R., Little, M. and Millham, S. (1995) 'The relationships between quantitative and qualitative approaches in social policy research', in J. Brannen (ed.), *Mixing Methods: Qualitative and Quantitative Research.* Aldershot: Avebury, pp. 81–99.

Bulmer, M. (1982a) *The Uses of Social Research: Social Investigation in Public Policy-making.* London: Allen and Unwin.

Bulmer, M. (ed.) (1982b) *Social Research Ethics: an Examination of the Merits of Covert Participant Observation.* London: Macmillan.

Bulmer, M. (ed.) (1986) *Social Science and Social Policy.* London: Allen and Unwin.

Bulmer, M. (1993) 'Successful applications of sociology: can Britain learn from America?', in G. Payne and M. Cross (eds), *Sociology in Action: Applications and Opportunities for the 1990s.* London: Macmillan, pp. 22–39.

Bulmer, M., Sykes, W. and Moorhouse, J. (1999) *Directory of Social Research Organisations in the UK* (2nd edition). London: Continuum.

Burgess, R.G. (1982) *Field Research.* London: Allen and Unwin.

Burgess, R.G. (1984) *In the Field: an Introduction to Field Research.* London: George Allen and Unwin.

Burgess, R.G. (ed.) (1986) *Key Variables in Social Investigation.* London: Routledge.

Burrows, R. and Rhodes, D. (1998) *Unpopular Places? Area Disadvantage and the Geography of Misery.* York: Policy Press/Joseph Rowntree Foundation.

Butcher, B. and Dodd, P. (1983) 'The Electoral Register – two surveys', *Population Trends*, 31: 15–19.

Campbell, D.T. and Fiske, D.W. (1955) 'Convergent and discriminant validation by the multitrait-multimethod matrix', *Psychological Bulletin*, 56: 81–105. (Reprinted in Gene F. Summers (ed.) (1970) *Attitude Measurement*. Chicago: Rand McNally.)

Caudill, W. et al. (1952) 'Social structure and interaction processes on a psychiatric ward', *American Journal of Orthopsychiatry*, 22: 314–34.

Chamberlayne, P., Bornat, J. and Wengraf, T. (eds) (2000) *The Turn to Biographical Methods in Social Science*. London: Routledge, pp. 33–52.

Chaplin, E. (1994) *Sociology and Visual Representation*. London: Routledge.

Cicourel, A. (1964) *Method and Measurement in Sociology*. New York: The Free Press.

Clarke, A. (1999) *Evaluation Research: an Introduction to Principles, Methods and Practice*. London: Sage.

Cloke, P., Goodwin, M., Milbourne, P. and Thomas, C. (1995) 'Deprivation, poverty and marginalization in rural lifestyles in England and Wales', *Journal of Rural Studies*, 11(4): 351–65.

Cloward, R.A. and Ohlin, L. (1960) *Delinquency and Opportunity*. New York: The Free Press.

Coffey, A. and Atkinson, P. (1996) *Making Sense of Qualitative Data*. Farnborough: Avebury.

Coffey, A., Holbrook, B. and Atkinson, P. (1996) 'Qualitative data analysis: technologies and representations', *Sociological Research On-line*, 1(1).

Cohen, S. (1972) *Folk Devils and Moral Panics*. Oxford: Oxford University Press.

Cohen, W. (1989) 'Symbols of power: statues in nineteenth-century France', *Comparative Studies in Society and History*, 31(3): 491–513.

Colhoune, H. and Prescott-Clarke, P. (eds) (1996) *Health Survey for England 1994*. London: HMSO.

Collier, J., Jr (1967) *Visual Anthropology*. New York: Holt, Rinehart and Winston.

Cooper, H., Arber, S. and Smaje, C. (1998a) 'Social class or deprivation? Structural factors and children's limiting longstanding illness in the 1990s', *Sociology of Health and Illness*, 20(3): 289–311.

Cooper, H., Smaje, C. and Arber, S. (1998b) 'Use of health services by children and young people according to ethnicity and social class: secondary analysis of a national survey', *British Medical Journal*, 317: 1047–51.

Corse, S.M. and Robinson, M.A. (1994) 'Cross-cultural measurement and new conceptions of culture: measuring cultural capacities in Japanese and American preschools', *Poetics*, 22: 313–25.

Cresswell, J. (1998) *Qualitative Inquiry and Research Design*. London: Sage.

Crompton, R. and Mann, M. (1986) *Gender and Stratification*. Cambridge: Polity Press.

Cronbach, L.J. (1951) 'Coefficient alpha and the internal consistency of tests', *Psychometrika*, 16: 297–334.

Cronbach, L.J. and Meehl, P.E. (1955) 'Construct validity in psychological tests', *Psychological Bulletin*, 52: 281–302.

Cuff, E., Sharrock, W. and Francis, D. (1998) *Perspectives in Sociology* (4th edition). London: Routledge.

Culler, J. (1987) 'Criticism and institutions: the American university', in D. Attridge and R. Young (eds), *Post-Structuralism and the Question of History*. Cambridge: Cambridge University Press.

Dale, A. (1993) 'The OPCS longitudinal study', in A. Dale and C. Marsh (eds), *The 1991 Census User's Guide*. London: HMSO.

Dale, A. and Davies, R. (eds) (1994) *Analyzing Social and Political Change: a Codebook of Methods*. London: Sage.

Dale, A. and Elliot, M. (2000) 'Confidentiality work to support the specification for an individual SAR from the 2001 census', *SARS Newsletter*, 14: 4–9.

Dale, A., Arber, S. and Procter, M. (1988) *Doing Secondary Analysis*. London: Allen and Unwin.

Dale, A., Fieldhouse, E., and Holdsworth, C. (2000) *Analysing Census Microdata*. London: Arnold.

Daniels, A.K. (1975) 'Feminist perspectives in sociological research', in M. Millman and R. Kanter (eds), *Another Voice*. Garden City. New York: Doubleday.

Davis, J.A. and Smith, T. (1992) *The NORC General Social Survey: a User's Guide*. Newbury Park, CA: Sage.

De Vaus, D.A. (1996) *Surveys in Social Research* (3rd edition). London: Unwin Hyman.

Denzin, N.K. (1970) *The Research Act in Sociology*. London: Butterworths.

Denzin, N.K. (1978) *Sociological Methods: a Sourcebook* (2nd edition). New York: McGraw-Hill.

Denzin, N.K. (1981) *The Research Act: a Theoretical Introduction to Sociological Methods*. New York: McGraw-Hill.

Denzin, N.K. and Lincoln, Y. (eds) (2000) *Handbook of Qualitative Research* (2nd edition). London: Sage.

Deutscher, I. (1973) *What We Say/What We Do*. Glenview, IL: Scott Foresman.

Devault, M. (1990) 'Talking and listening from women's standpoint: feminist strategies for interviewing and analysis', *Social Problems*, 37(1): 96–116.

Devine, F. and Heath, S. (1999) 'Health: Wellings and colleagues' Sexual Behaviour in Britain', *Sociological Research Methods in Context*. Basingstoke: Macmillan, Chapter 6.

Dey, I. (1993) *Qualitative Data Analysis: a User-friendly Guide*. London: Routledge.

Dillman, D.A. (1978) *Mail and Telephone Surveys: the Total Design Method*. New York: John Wiley & Sons.

Dilnot, A., Disney, R., Johnson, P. and Whitehouse, E. (1994) *Pensions Policy in the UK: an Economic Analysis*. London: Institute of Fiscal Studies.

Dines, G. and Humez, J.M. (eds) (1995) *Gender, Race and Class in Media*. London: Sage.

Disney, R., Grundy, E. and Johnson, P. (1997) *The Dynamics of Retirement: Analysis of the Retirement Survey*. London: Department of Social Security/HMSO.

Dohrenwend, B. (1964) 'A use for leading questions in research interviewing', *Human Organization*, 23: 76–7.

Dohrenwend, B. and Richardson, S. (1956) 'Analysis of the interviewer's behaviour', *Human Organization*, 15(2): 29–32.

Doig, B. and Littlewood, J. (eds) (1992) *Policy Evaluation: the Role of Social Research*. London: Department of the Environment/HMSO.

Donkin, A., Dowler, E., Stevenson, S. and Turner, S. (1999) 'Mapping access to food at a local level', *British Food Journal*, 101(7): 554–64.

Douglas, J.D. (1971) *American Social Order*. New York: The Free Press.

Douglas, J.D. (1976) *Investigative Social Research: Individual and Team Field Research*. Beverly Hills, CA and London: Sage.

Dubin, S.C. (1995) 'How I got screwed by Barbie: a cautionary tale', *New Art Examiner*, November: 20–3.

Durham, P. (1994) 'Millions will lose money on private pensions', *The Independent*, 28 March.

Durkheim, E. ([1897] 1952) *Le suicide: étude de sociologie* (trans. J.A. Spaulding and G. Simpson). London: Routledge and Kegan Paul.

Durkheim, E. (1951) *Suicide*. Glencoe, IL: The Free Press.

Eco, U. (1988) *Foucault's Pendulum*. London: Pan Books.

Edwards, D. (1997) *Discourse and Cognition*. London: Sage.

Edwards, D. and Potter, J. (1992) *Discursive Psychology*. London: Sage.

Ellen, R.F. (ed.) (1984) *Ethnographic Research: a Guide to General Conduct*. London: Academic Press.

Emerson, R., Fretz, R. and Shaw, L. (1995) *Writing Ethnographic Fieldnotes*. Chicago: University of Chicago Press.

Empey, L. and Erickson, M. (1966) 'Hidden delinquency and social status', *Social Forces*, 44: 546–54.

Erben, M. (1993) 'The problem of other lives: social perspectives on written biography', *Sociology*, 27: 15–26.

Erickson, B.H. and Nosanchuk, T.A. (1992) *Understanding Data* (2nd edition). Milton Keynes: Open University Press.

Ericson, R. (1993) *Making Crime* (2nd edition). Toronto: University of Toronto Press.

Ericson, R., Bareaneck, P. and Chan, J. (1991) *Representing Order: Crime, Law and Justice in the News Media*. Milton Keynes: Open University Press.

Erikson, K. (1967) 'A comment on disguised observation in sociology', *Social Problems*, 14: 366–73.

Evans, J. and Hall, S. (eds) (1999) *Visual Culture*. London: Sage.

Evans, M. (1993) 'Reading lives: how the personal might be social', *Sociology*, 27: 5–14.

Farrell, J.G. (1973) *The Siege of Krishnapur*. London: Fontana.

Farrell, J.G. (1978) *The Singapore Grip*. London: Fontana.

Ferri, E. (ed.) (1993) *Britain's 33 Year Olds*. London: National Children's Bureau and ESRC.

Festinger, L. (1964) *When Prophecy Fails*. New York: Harper & Row.

Fetterman, D. (1989) *Ethnography: Step by Step*. London: Sage.

Fichter, J. (1973) *One-Man Research: Reminiscences of a Catholic Sociologist*. New York: Wiley.

Fielding, J. and Gilbert, N. (2000) *Understanding Social Statistics*. London: Sage.

Fielding, N. (1981) *The National Front*. London: Routledge and Kegan Paul.

Fielding, N. (1982) 'Observational research on the National Front', in M. Bulmer, (ed.), *Social Research Ethics: an Examination of the Merits of Covert Participant Observation*. London: Macmillan, pp. 80–104.

Fielding, N. (1988) *Joining Forces*. London, Routledge.

Fielding, N. (1990) 'Mediating the message: affinity and hostility in research on sensitive topics', *American Behavioral Scientist*, 33(5): 608–20.

Fielding, N. and Lee R. (eds) (1991) *Using Computers in Qualitative Research* (2nd edition, 1993). London: Sage.

Fielding, N. and Lee, R. (1998) *Computer Analysis and Qualitative Research*. London: Sage.

Filmer, P. (1998) 'Analysing literary texts', in C. Seale (ed.), *Researching Society and Culture*. London: Sage.

Filstead, W.J. (ed.) (1970) *Qualitative Methodology: First-hand Involvement with the Social World*. Chicago: Markham.

Finch, J. (1986) *Research and Policy: the Uses of Qualitative Methods in Social and Educational Research*. London: Falmer Press.

Finch, J. (1987) 'The vignette technique in survey research', *Sociology*, 21(1): 105–14.

Finch, J. (1993) 'Applied sociology in the contemporary British context', in G. Payne and M. Cross (eds), *Sociology in Action: Applications and Opportunities for the 1990s*. London: Macmillan, pp. 138–54.

Finch, J. and Mason, J. (1992) *Negotiating Family Responsibilities*. London: Routledge.

Fishbein, M. and Ajzen, I. (1975) *Belief, Attitude, Intention and Behavior: an Introduction to Theory and Research*. Reading, MA: Addison-Wesley.

Fisher, M. (1997) 'Qualitative computing: using software for qualitative data analysis', *Cardiff Papers in Qualitative Research*. Aldershot: Ashgate.

Foddy, W. (1992) *Constructing Questions for Interviews and Questionnaires*. Cambridge: Cambridge University Press.

Ford, R., Marsh, A. and Finlayson, L. (1998) *What Happens to Lone Parents: a Cohort Study 1991–1995*. London: HMSO.

Foster, K. (1994) 'The coverage of the Postcode Address File as a sampling frame', *Survey Methodology Bulletin*, 34: 9–18.

Foucault, M. (1977) *Discipline and Punish: the Birth of the Prison*. Harmondsworth: Allen Lane.

Fox, A.J., Goldblatt, P.O. and Jones, D.R. (1985) 'Social class mortality differentials: artefact, selection or life circumstances', *Journal of Epidemiology and Community Health*, 39: 1–8.

Frank, R. (1959) *The Americans*. New York: Aperture.

Frankland, J. and Bloor, M. (1999) 'Some issues arising in the systematic analysis of focus group materials', in R.S. Barbour and J. Kitzenger (eds), *Developing Focus Group Research: Politics, Theory and Practice*. London: Sage.

Freeman, D (1998) *The Fateful Hoaxing of Margaret Mead*. New York: Westview.

Fussell, P. (1975) *The Great War and Modern Memory*. London: Oxford University Press.

Fussell, P. (1989) *Wartime: Understanding and Behavior in the Second World War*. Oxford: Oxford University Press.

Gallie, D. (1988) *The Social Change and Economic Life Initiative: an Overview*. SCELI Working Paper 1. Oxford: Nuffield College.

Gallie, D., Marsh, C. and Vogler, C. (eds) (1994) *The Social Consequences of Unemployment*. Oxford: Oxford University Press.

Garfinkel, H. (1967a) *Studies in Ethnomethodology*. Englewood Cliffs, NJ: Prentice-Hall.

Garfinkel, H. (1967b), ' "Good" organizational reasons for "bad" clinical records', in Harold Garfinkel, *Studies in Ethnomethodology*. Englewood Cliffs, NJ: Prentice-Hall, pp. 186–207 (Reprinted in R. Turner (ed.) (1974) *Ethnomethodology*. Harmondsworth: Penguin.)

Geertz, C. (1973) *The Interpretation of Cultures*. New York: Basic Books.

Gellner, E. (1988) *Plough, Sword and Book*. London: Collins-Harvill.

Giddens, A. (1976) *New Rules of the Sociological Method*. London: Hutchinson.

Gilbert, G.N. and Mulkay, M.J. (1984) *Opening Pandora's Box: a Sociological Analysis of Scientists' Discourse*. Cambridge: Cambridge University Press.

Ginn, J. and Arber, S. (1991) 'Gender, class and income inequalities in later life', *British Journal of Sociology*, 42(3): 369–96.

Ginn, J. and Arber, S. (1993) 'Pension penalties: the gendered division of occupational welfare', *Work, Employment and Society*, 7(1): 47–70.

Ginn, J. and Arber, S. (1994) 'Heading for hardship: how the British pension system has failed women', in S. Baldwin and J. Falkingham (eds), *Social Security and Social Change: New Challenges to the Beveridge Model.* Hemel Hempstead: Harvester Wheatsheaf, Chapter 13. pp. 216–34.

Ginn, J. and Arber, S. (1999) 'Changing patterns of pension inequality: the shift from state to private sources', *Ageing and Society*, 19(3): 319–42.

Ginn, J. and Arber, S. (2000) 'Personal pension take-up in the 1990s in relation to position in the labour market', *Journal of Social Policy*, 29(2): 205–28.

Ginn, J., Street, D. and Arber, S. (2001) *Women, Work and Pensions: International Issues and Prospects.* Buckingham: Open University Press.

Glaser, B.G. and Strauss, A.L. (1965) *Awareness of Dying.* New York: Aldine.

Glaser, B.G. and Strauss, A.L. (1967) *The Discovery of Grounded Theory.* Chicago: Aldine.

Goffman, E. (1959) *The Presentation of Self in Everyday Life.* London: Penguin.

Goffman, E. (1961) *Asylums.* London: Penguin.

Goffman, E. (1971) *Relations in Public: Microstudies of the Public Order.* New York: Basic Books.

Goffman, E. (1979) *Gender Advertisements.* London: Macmillan.

Gombrich, E.H. (1960) *Art and Illusion.* Oxford: Phaidon.

Gombrich, E.H. (1972) 'The visual image', in Scientific American (ed.), *Communication.* San Francisco: W.H. Freeman and Company, pp. 46–60.

Goodale, J. (1996) *Experiencing Fieldwork.* New York: Rowman and Littlefield.

Gorden, R. (1975) *Interviewing: Strategy, Techniques and Tactics.* Homewood, IL: Dorsey.

Graves, R. ([1927] 1954) *Goodbye to All That.* Harmandsworth: Penguin.

Gray, J.N., Lyons, P.M., Jr and Melton, G.B. (1995) *Ethical and Legal Issues in AIDS Research.* Baltimore, MD: Johns Hopkins University Press.

Green, J. and Hart, L. (1999) 'The impact of context on data', in R.S. Barbour and J. Kitzenger (eds), *Developing Focus Group Research: Politics, Theory and Practice.* London: Sage.

Greenbaum, A. (1995) 'Taking stock of two decades of research on the social bases of environmental concern', in M. Mehta and E. Ouellet (eds), *Environmental Sociology: Theory and Practice.* North York, Ontario: Captus Press, pp. 125–52.

Grene, D. (ed.) (1959) *Thucydides' History of the Peloponnesian War.* New York: Cape.

Gumilev, L.N. ([1970 in Russian] 1987) *Searches for an Imaginary Kingdom: the Legend of the Kingdom of Prester John.* Cambridge: Cambridge University Press.

Guttman, Louis (1944). 'A basis for scaling qualitative data', *American Sociological Review*, 9: 139–50. (Reprinted in Gene F. Summers (ed.) (1970) *Attitude Measurement.* Chicago: Rand McNally.)

Hakim, C. (1982) *Secondary Analysis in Social Research.* London: Allen and Unwin.

Halle, D. (1993) *Inside Culture.* London: University of Chicago Press.

Hammersley, M. and Atkinson, P. (1994) *Ethnography: Principles in Practice* (2nd edition). London: Tavistock.

Harding, A. (1990) 'Dynamic micro-simulation models: problems and prospects'. Welfare State Programme Discussion Paper No. 48. London: London School of Economics.

Hargens, L.L. (1988) 'Scholarly consensus and journal rejection rates', *American Sociological Review*, 53: 139–51.

Harper, D. (1979) 'Life on the road', in D. Wagner (ed.), *Images of Information: Still Photography in the Social Sciences*. London: Sage, pp. 25–42.

Harper, D. (1982) *Good Company*. Chicago: University of Chicago Press.

Haslam, C. and Bryman, A. (eds) (1994) *Social Scientists Meet the Media*. London: Routledge.

Hawe, P., Degeling, D. and Hall, J. (1990) *Evaluating Health Promotion: a Health Worker's Guide*. Artarmon, NSW: MacLennan & Petty.

Hawkes, T. (1992) *Structuralism and Semiotics*. London: Routledge.

Heath, C. (1986) *Body Movement and Speech in Medical Interaction*. Cambridge: Cambridge University Press.

Herbert, A. and Kempson, E. (1995) *Water Debt and Disconnection*. London: Policy Studies Institute.

Herbert, A.P. (1977) *Misleading Cases in the Common Law*. London: Eyre Methuen.

Heritage, J. (1978) 'Aspects of the flexibilities of language use', *Sociology*, 12(1): 79–104.

Heritage, J. (1984) *Garfinkel and Ethnomethodology*. Cambridge: Polity Press.

Heritage, J. and Greatbatch, D. (1986) 'Generating applause: a study of rhetoric and response at party political conferences', *American Journal of Sociology*, 92(1): 110–57.

Hindess, B. (1973) *The Use of Official Statistics in Sociology*. London: Macmillan.

Hobbs, D. (1988) *Doing the Business*. Oxford: Oxford University Press.

Hochschild, A. (1983) *The Managed Heart: the Commercialization of Human Feeling*. Berkeley, CA: University of California Press.

Holland, J., Ramazanoglu, C., Sharpe, S. and Thomson, R. (1998) *The Male in the Head: Young People, Heterosexuality and Power*. London: The Tufnell Press.

Holsti, O.R. (1969) *Content Analysis for the Social Sciences and Humanities*. Reading, MA: Addison-Wesley.

Homan, R. (1991) *The Ethics of Social Research*. London: Pearson Education.

Hughes, J.A. (1976) *Sociological Analysis: Methods of Discovery*. London: Nelson.

Humphrey, C. (1983) *Karl Marx Collective: Economy, Society and Religion in a Siberian Collective Farm*. Cambridge: Cambridge University Press.

Humphreys, L. (1970) *Tearoom Trade*. Chicago: Aldine.

Hutchby, I. and Wooffitt, R. (1998) *Conversation Analysis: Principles, Practices and Applications*. Oxford: Polity Press.

Hyman, H. (1954) *Interviewing in Social Research*. Chicago: University of Chicago Press.

Insalaco, F. (2000) 'Choosing stratifiers for the General Household Survey', *Survey Methodology Bulletin*, 46: 6–14.

Irving, B. and McKenzie, I. (1988) *Regulating Custodial Interviews*. London: Police Foundation.

Irwin, A. (1995) *Citizen Science: a Study of People, Expertise and Sustainable Development*. London: Routledge.

Jacoby, William G. (1991) *Data Theory and Dimensional Analysis*, Sage University Paper series on *Quantitative Applications in the Social Sciences No. 78*. Beverly Hills, CA and London: Sage.

Janis, I.L. (1982) *Groupthink* (2nd edition). Boston, MA: Houghton-Mifflin.

Janowitz, M. (1970) *Political Conflict*. Chicago: Quadrangle.

Jefferson, G. (1984) ' "At first I thought": a normalizing device for extraordinary events'. Unpublished manuscript, Katholieke Hogeschool, Tilburg, The Netherlands.

Jefferson, G. (1990) 'List construction as a task and resource', in G. Psathas (ed.), *Interactional Competence*. Washington, DC: University Press of America.

Jencks, C. (1973) *Inequality*. London: Allen Lane.

Jenks, C. (1998) *Core Sociological Dichotomies*. London: Sage.

Jewitt, C. (1997) 'Images of men: male sexuality in sexual health leaflets and posters for young people', *Sociological Research Online*, 2(2): http://www.socresonline.org.uk/socresonline/2/2/6.html

Jhally, S. (1990) *Dreamworlds* (video). Amherst, MA: University of Massachusetts at Amherst.

Johnson, S. (1997) *Interface Culture*. New York: HarperEdge.

Jowell, R., Witherspoon, S. and Brook, L. (eds) (1989) *British Social Attitudes: Special International Report*. Aldershot: Gower.

Jowell, R., Curtice, J., Park, A., Brook, L., Thomson, K. and Bryson, C. (eds) (1998) *British – and European – Social Attitudes: the 15th Report*. Aldershot: Gower.

Jowell, R., Curtice, J., Park, A. and Thomson, K. (1999) *British Social Attitudes: the 16th Report. Who Shares New Labour Values?* Aldershot: Ashgate.

Kalton, G. (1983) *Introduction to Survey Sampling*, Sage University Paper series on Quantitative Applications in the Social Sciences No. 35. London: Sage.

Karapin, R.S. (1986) 'What's the use of social science? A review of the literature', in F. Heller (ed.), *The Use and Abuse of Social Science*. London: Sage, pp. 236–65.

Kasemir, B., Dahinden, U., Gerger, Å., Schüle, R., Tabara, D. and Jaeger, C. (1999) 'Fear hope and ambiguity: citizen's perspectives on climate change and energy use'. ULYSSES Working Paper available at: http://www.zit.tudarmstadt.de/ulysses/docmain.htm

Katz, J., with the assistance of Alexander Morgan Cafron and Eleanor Swift Glass (1972) *Experimentation with Human Beings: the Authority of the Investigator, Subject, Professions and State in the Human Experimentation Process*. New York: Russell Sage Foundation.

Kish, L. (1965) *Survey Sampling*. New York: Wiley.

Kitsuse, J.I. and Cicourel, A.V. (1963) 'A note on the uses of official statistics', *Social Problems*, 11: 131–9.

Knoedel, J. (1993) 'The design and analysis of focus group studies: a practical approach', in D. Morgan (ed.), *Successful Focus Groups. Advancing the State of the Art*. Newbury Park, CA: Sage.

Kress, G. and van Leeuwen, T. (1996) *Reading Images*. London: Routledge.

Krueger, R.A. (1994) *Focus Groups: a Practical Guide for Applied Research*. Newbury Park, CA: Sage.

Kuhn, T.S. (1962) *The Structure of Scientific Revolutions*. Chicago: University of Chicago Press.

Kuhn, T.S. (1970) *The Structure of Scientific Revolutions* (2nd edition). Chicago: University of Chicago Press.

LaPiere, R.T. (1934). 'Attitudes vs actions', *Social Forces*, 13: 230–7.

Laslett, P. (1976) 'The wrong way through the telescope: a note on literary evidence in sociology and in historical sociology, *British Journal of Sociology*, 27(3): 319–42.

Latané, B., Williams, K. and Harkins, S.G. (1979) 'Many hands make light work: the causes and consequences of social loafing', *Journal of Experimental Social Psychology*, 37: 822–32.

Layder, D. (1998) *Sociological Practice*, London: Sage.

Lee, R.M. (1993) *Doing Research on Sensitive Topics*. London: Sage.

Lees, S. (1993) *Sugar and Spice: Sexuality and Adolescent Girls*. London: Penguin.

Lemert, C. (1997) *Social Things: an Introduction to the Sociological Life*. Oxford: Rowman and Littlefield.

Ley, D. (1996) *The New Middle Class and the Remaking of the Central City*. Oxford: Oxford University Press.

Likert, Rensis (1932) 'A technique for the measurement of attitudes', *Archives of Psychology*, 140. (Reprinted in Gene F. Summers (ed.) (1970) *Attitude Measurement*. Chicago: Rand McNally.)

Lindblom, C. (1968) *The Policy-making Process*. Englewood Cliffs, NJ: Prentice-Hall.

Lindblom, C. (1979) 'Still muddling, not yet through', *Public Administration Review*, 39: 517–26.

Lodge, M. (1981) *Magnitude Estimation*. Sage University Paper series on Quantitative Applications in the Social Sciences, Series No. 07–025. Beverly Hills, CA and London: Sage.

Lofland, J. (1971) *Analyzing Social Settings*. Belmont, CA: Wadsworth.

Lofland, J. and Lofland, L. (1994) *Analyzing Social Settings*, Belmont, CA: Wadsworth.

Lohr, S.L. (1999) *Sampling: Design and Analysis*. Pacific Grove, CA: Duxbury Press.

Lurie, A. (1967) *Imaginary Friends*. London: Heinemann.

Lynn, P. and Lievesley, D. (1991) *Drawing General Population Samples in Great Britain*. London: Social and Community Planning Research.

Macdonald, K.M. (1989) 'Building respectability', *Sociology*, 23(1): 55–88.

Macfarlane Smith, J. (1972) *Interviewing in Market and Social Research*. London: Routledge and Kegan Paul.

Macnaghten, P., Grove-White, R., Jacobs, M. and Wynne, B. (1995) *Public Perceptions and Sustainability in Lancashire: Indicators, Institutions, Participation*. A report by the Centre for the Study of Environmental Change commissioned by Lancashire County Council.

Mann, C. and Stewart, F. (2000) *Internet Communication and Qualitative Research: a Handbook for Researching Online*. London: Sage.

Mansfield, P. and Collard, J. (1988) *The Beginning of the Rest of Your Life? A Portrait of Newly-wed Marriage*. London: Macmillan.

Marsh, A. (2000) 'The DSS/PSI programme of research into lone-income families (PRILIF)', *Data Archive Bulletin*, 73: 5–9.

Marsh, C. (1988) *Exploring Data: an Introduction to Data Analysis for Social Scientists*. Cambridge: Polity Press.

Marsh, C. (1993) 'The sample of anonymised records', in A. Dale and C. Marsh (eds), *The 1991 Census User's Guide*. London: HMSO.

Marsh, C. and Scarborough, E. (1990) 'Testing nine hypotheses about quota sampling', *Journal of the Market Research Society*, 32(4): 485–506.

Marsh, C., Skinner, C., Arber, S., Penhale, B., Openshaw, S., Hobcraft, J., Lievesley, D. and Walford, N. (1991) 'The case for a sample of anonymised records from the 1991 census', *Journal of the Royal Statistical Society*, Series A, 154(2): 305–40.

Martin, J. and Roberts, C. (1984) *Women and Employment: a Lifetime Perspective*. London: Department of Employment/Office of Population Censuses and Surveys/ HMSO.

Martin, J., Meltzer, H. and Elliot, D. (1988) *The Prevalence of Disability among Adults*. OPCS Surveys of Disability in Great Britain, Report 1. London: HMSO.

McCall, G. and Simmons, J. (1969) *Issues in Participant Observation*. New York: Addison-Wesley.

McCann, K., Clark, D., Taylor, R. and Morrice, K. (1984) 'Telephone screening as a research technique', *Sociology*, 18(3): 393–402.

McConville, M., Sanders, A. and Leng, R. (1991) *The Case for the Prosecution*. London: Routledge.

McCormick, J. (1995) *The Global Environmental Movement*. Chichester: John Wiley and Sons.

McLaren, D., Cottray, O., Taylor, M., Pipes, S. and Bullock, S. (1999) *Pollution Injustice: the Geographic Relation between Household Income and Polluting Factories*. A Report for Friends of the Earth: http://www.foe.org.uk/pollutioninjustice/ poll-inj.html

McNally, R. and Mabey, N. (1999) 'The distributional effects of ecological tax reform'. World Wildlife Fund Unpublished Draft Discussion Paper (contact Richard McNally at rmcnally@wwfnet.org or Nick Mabey at nmabey@wwfnet.org for copies) Godalming: WWF.

McNiff, S. (1998) *Art-Based Research*. London: Jessica Kingsley Publishers.

McPherson, J.M. and Smith-Lovin, L. (1986) 'Sex segregation in voluntary associations', *American Sociological Review*, 51: 61–79.

McRobbie, A. (1978) *Jackie: an Ideology of Adolescent Femininity*. Birmingham: Centre for Contemporary Cultural Studies.

McRobbie, A. (1991) *Feminism and Youth Culture: From Jackie to Just Seventeen*. London: Macmillan.

Merton, R.K. (1965) *On the Shoulders of Giants: a Shandean Postscript*. New York: Harcourt Brace Jovanovich.

Merton, R.K. (1967) *On Theoretical Sociology*. New York: The Free Press.

Merton, R.K. (1968) *Social Theory and Social Structure* (revised and enlarged edition). New York: The Free Press.

Merton, R.K. (1973) 'Technical and moral dimensions of policy research', in R.K. Merton, *The Sociology of Science: Theoretical and Empirical Investigations*. Chicago: Chicago University Press.

Merton, R.K. and Kendall, P.L. (1946) 'The focused interview', *American Journal of Sociology*, 51(6): 541–57.

Merton, R.K., Fiske, M. and Kendall, P.L. (1956) *The Focused Interview*. Glencoe, IL: The Free Press.

Middlebrook, M. (1978) *The Kaiser's Battle*. Harmondsworth: Penguin.

Middlebrook, M. (1983) *The Schweinfurt–Regensburg Mission*. Harmondsworth: Penguin.

Miles, M. and Huberman, A. (1984) *Qualitative Data Analysis*. London: Sage.

Miles, M. and Huberman, A. (1994, 2nd edn) *Qualitative Data Analysis: an Expanded Sourcebook*. London: Sage.

Mirzoeff, N. (1999) *An Introduction to Visual Culture*. London: Routledge.

Mishler, E. (1986) *Research Interviewing*. Cambridge, MA: Harvard University Press.

Modood, T., Berthoud, R., Lakey, J. (1997) *Ethnic Minorities in Britain: Diversity and Disadvantage*. London: Policy Studies Institute.

Moran-Ellis, J. and Fielding, N.G. (1996) 'A national survey of the investigation of child sexual abuse', *British Journal of Social Work*, 26: 337–56.

Morgan, D.L. (1988) *Focus Groups as Qualitative Research*. London: Sage.

Morgan, D.L. (ed.) (1993) *Successful Focus Groups. Advancing the State of the Art*. Newbury Park, CA: Sage.

Moser, C.A. and Kalton, G. (1971) *Survey Methods in Social Investigation* (2nd edition). London: Heinemann.

Mulkay, M. (1985) *The Word and the World*. London: Allen and Unwin.

Mullins, C.J. (1977) *A Guide to Writing and Publishing in the Social and Behavioural Sciences*. New York: Wiley.

Munck, R. and Rolston, W. (1987) *Belfast in the '30s: an Oral History*. Belfast: Blackstaff Press.

Murphy, E., Dingwall, R., Greatbatch, D., Parker, S. and Watson, P. (1998) 'Qualitative research methods in health technology assessment: a review of the literature', *Health Technology Assessment*, 2(16): 1–294.

Myers, G. and Macnaghten, P. (1999) 'Can focus groups be analysed as talk?', in R.S. Barbour and J. Kitzinger (eds), *Developing Focus Group Research: Politics, Theory and Practice*. London: Sage.

Nas, P.J.M., Prins, W.J.M. and Shadid, W.A. (1987) 'A plea for praxeology', in G.C. Wenger (ed.), *The Research Relationship: Practice and Politics in Social Policy Research*. London: Allen and Unwin, pp. 18–42.

Neuman, W.L. (2000) *Social Research Methods: Qualitative and Quantitative Approaches* (4th edition). Boston, MA: Allyn and Bacon.

Norris, M. (1983) *A Beginner's Guide to Repertory Grid*. Guildford: University of Surrey Department of Sociology.

Norusis, M. (1993) *SPSS for Windows: Advanced Statistics, Release 6.0*. Chicago: SPSS.

Norusis, M. (1999) *SPSS 9.0 Guide to Data Analysis*. Englewood Cliffs, NJ: Prentice-Hall.

Norusis, M. (2000) *SPSS 10.0 Guide to Data Analysis*. Chicago: SPSS Inc.

Oakley, A. (1974) *The Sociology of Housework*. Oxford: Martin Robertson.

O'Brian, P. (1970) *Master and Commander*. London: HarperCollins.

O'Brian, P. (1997) *The Yellow Admiral*. London: HarperCollins.

ONS (2000) *Living in Britain: Results from the 1998 General Household Survey*. London: HMSO.

OPCS (1993) *1991 Census: Age, Sex and Marital Status, Great Britain*. London: HMSO.

Oppenheim, A.N. (1992), *Questionnaire Design, Interviewing and Attitude Measurement* (2nd edition). London and Washington, DC: Pinter.

Patton, M.Q. (1987) *How to Use Qualitative Methods in Evaluation*. London: Sage.

Patton, M. (1990) *Qualitative Evaluation and Research Methods*. London: Sage.

Pawson, R. (1989) 'Methodology', in M. Haralambos (ed.), *Developments in Sociology* (vol. 5). Ormskirk: Causeway.

Pearson, G. (1983) *Hooligan*. London: Macmillan.

Pfaffenberger, B. (1988) *Microcomputers in Applications in Qualitative Research*. Qualitative Research Methods Series No. 14. Newbury Park, CA: Sage.

Phillimore, P. and Moffatt, S. (2000) ' "Industry causes lung cancer": would you be happy with that headline?', in S. Allan, B. Adam and C. Carter (eds), *Environmental Risks and the Media*. London: Routledge.

Phillips, M. and Pugh, D.S. (1987) *How To Get a PhD*. Milton Keynes: Open University Press.

Pierce, C.S. (1958) *Selected Writings* (ed. P. Wiener). New York: Dover Press.

Pinch, T.J. and Clark, C. (1986) 'The hard sell: "patter merchanting" and the strategic (re)production and local management of economic reasoning in the sales routines of market pitchers', *Sociology*, 20(2): 169–91.

Platt, J. (1981) 'Evidence and proof in documentary research', *Sociological Review*, 29(1): 31–66.

Plummer, K. (1983) *Documents of Life: an Introduction to the Problems and Literature of a Humanistic Method*. London: Allen and Unwin.

Polsky, N. (1971) *Hustlers, Beats and Others*. New York: Anchor Books.

Pomerantz, A.M. (1986) 'Extreme case formulations: a way of legitimizing claims', in G. Button, P. Drew and J. Heritage (eds), *Human Studies*, 9 (special issue on Interaction and Language Use): 219–29.

Porter, D.M., Jr (1997) 'The eye of the beholder: the impact of race and gender on managers' attributions and conceptions of commitment to the organization'. PhD Thesis, Harvard University, Cambridge, MA.

Postman, N. (1986) *Amusing Ourselves to Death*. New York: Penguin Books.

Potter, J. (1996) *Representing Reality: Discourse, Rhetoric and Social Construction*. London: Sage.

Potter, J. and Wetherell, M. (1987) *Discourse and Social Psychology: Beyond Attitudes and Behaviour*. London: Sage.

Power, C., Manor, O. and Fox, J. (1991) *Health and Class: the Early Years*. London: Chapman and Hall.

Prosser, J. (ed.) (1998) *Image-based Research*. London: Routledge/Falmer Press.

Punch, M. (1986) *The Politics and Ethics of Fieldwork*. London: Sage.

Quigly, I. (1984) *The Heirs of Tom Brown: the English School Story*. Oxford: Oxford University Press.

Quinney, R. and Wilderman, J. (1977) *The Problem of Crime* (2nd edition). New York: Harper & Row.

Qureshi, H. (1995) 'Integrating methods in applied research in social policy: a case study of carers', in J. Brannen (ed.), *Mixing Methods: Qualitative and Quantitative Research*. Aldershot: Avebury, pp. 101–25.

Rake, K., Davies, H., Joshi, H. and Alami, R. (2000) *Women's Incomes over the Lifetime*. London: HMSO.

Rein, M. (1983) *From Policy to Practice*. London: Macmillan.

Richardson, L. (1990) *Writing Strategies*. Newbury Park, CA: Sage.

Rickman, H.P. (1961) *Meaning in History: William Dilthey's Thought on Society and History*. London: Allen and Unwin.

Robb, J. (1954) *Working Class AntiSemite*. London: Tavistock.

Rock, P. (1979) *The Making of Symbolic Interactionism*. London: Macmillan.

Rorty, R. (2000) *Philosophy and Social Hope*. Harmondsworth: Penguin.

Rose, D. (1995) *Official Social Classifications in the UK*. Social Research Update 9, University of Surrey: http://www.soc.surrey.ac.uk/sru/SRU9.html

Rose, D. et al. (1992) 'Micro-social change in Britain: current and future research using the British Household Panel Survey'. *Working Papers of the ESRC Research Centre on Micro-Social Change* No. 21. Colchester: University of Essex.

Rosenhan, D.L. (1973) 'On being sane in insane places', *Science* 179 (19 January): 250–8. (Reprinted in M. Bulmer (ed.) (1982) *Social Research Ethics: an Examination of the Merits of Covert Participant Observation*. London: Macmillan, pp. 15–37.)

Rossi, P.H. and Freeman, H.E. (1993) *Evaluation: a Systematic Approach* (5th edition). Newbury Park, CA: Sage.

Rossi, P.H. and Whyte, W.F. (1983) 'The applied side of sociology', in H.E. Freeman, R.R. Dynes, P.H. Rossi and W.F. Whyte (eds), *Applied Sociology*. San Francisco: Jossey-Bass, pp. 5–31.

Rossi, P., Wright, J.D. and Wright, S.R. (1978) 'The theory and practice of applied social research', *Evaluation Quarterly*, 2: 171–91.

Royal Commission on Environmental Pollution (1998) *Setting Environmental Standards*. Twenty-First Report. London: HMSO.

Rubin, H. and Rubin, I. (1995) *Qualitative Interviewing*. London: Sage.

Rustin, M. (2000) 'Reflections on the biographical turn in social science', in P. Chamberlayne, J. Bornat and T. Wengraf (eds), *The Turn to Biographical Methods in Social Science*. London: Routledge, pp. 33–52.

Sacks, H. (1963) 'Sociological description', *Berkeley Journal of Sociology*, 8: 1–16.

Sacks, H. (1984) 'On doing "Being Ordinary" ', in J.M. Atkinson and J. Heritage (eds), *Structures of Social Action: Studies in Conversation Analysis* (ed. G. Jefferson from unpublished lectures, Spring 1970: lecture 1). Cambridge: Cambridge University Press, pp. 413–29.

Sacks, H. (1992) *Lectures on Conversation* (ed. G. Jefferson with an introduction by E.A. Schegloff). Oxford and Cambridge, MA: Basil Blackwell.

Sapsford, R. (1999) *Survey Research*. London: Sage.

Sassoon, S. (1937) *The Complete Memoirs of George Sherston: Memoirs of a Foxhunting Man; Memoirs of an Infantry Officer; Sherston's Progress*. London: Faber and Faber.

Saussure, F. de ([1915] 1959) *Course in General Linguistics*. New York: Philosophical Library.

Schegloff, E.A. (1972) 'Notes on a conversational practice: formulating place', in D. Sudnow (ed.), *Studies in Social Interaction*. New York: The Free Press, pp. 75–119.

Schur, E.M. (1971) *Labeling Deviant Behaviour*. New York: Harper & Row.

Scott, J. (1990) *A Matter of Record*. Cambridge: Polity Press.

Scott, P. (1966) *The Jewel in the Crown*. London: Granada.

Scott, P. (1968) *The Day of the Scorpion*. London: Granada.

Scott, P. (1971) *The Towers of Silence*. London: Granada.

Scott, P. (1975) *A Division of Spoils*. London: Granada.

Seale, C. (1999) *The Quality of Qualitative Research*. London: Sage.

Seale, C. and Filmer, P. (1998) 'Doing social surveys', in C. Seale (ed.), *Researching Society and Culture*. London: Sage.

Sellin, T. and Wolfgang, M.E. (1964) *The Measurement of Delinquency*. New York: John Wiley and Sons.

Selltiz, C. and Jahoda, M. (1962) *Research Methods in Social Relations*. New York: Methuen.

Seymour-Smith, M. (1990) *Rudyard Kipling*. London: Papermac.

Shapiro, S. and Eberhart, J. (1947) 'Interviewer differences in an intensive survey', *International Journal of Opinion and Attitude Research*, 1(2): 1–17.

Shively, J. (1992) 'Cowboys and Indians: perceptions of western films among American Indians and Anglos', *American Sociological Review*, 57: 725–34.

Short, J., Jr and Nye, F.I. (1958) 'The extent of unrecorded juvenile delinquency: tentative conclusions', *Journal of Criminal Law and Criminology*, 49: 296–302.

Sica, A. (ed.) (1998) *What is Social Theory? The Philosophical Debates*. Oxford: Blackwell.

Silverman, D. (1985) *Qualitative Methodology and Sociology*. Farnborough: Gower.

Silverman, D. (1993) *Interpreting Qualitative Data*. London: Sage.

Silvey, J. (1975) *Deciphering Data: the Analysis of Social Surveys*. London: Longman.

Simmel, G. (1950) *The Sociology of George Simmel* (ed. K. Wolff). Glencoe, IL: The Free Press.

Singer, E., Frankel, M. and Glassman, M. (1983) 'The effect of interviewer characteristics and expectations on response', *Public Opinion Quarterly*, 47(1): 68–83.

Slater, D. (1998) 'Analysing cultural objects: content analysis and semiotics', in C. Seale (ed.), *Researching Society and Culture*. London: Sage.

Smelser, N.J. (1994) *Sociology*. Oxford: Blackwell.

Smith, D.E. (1978) ' "K is mentally ill": the anatomy of a factual account', *Sociology*, 12: 23–53.

Smith, N. and Williams, P. (1986) *Gentrification of the City*. Boston, MA: Allen and Unwin.

Smythe, A.P. (1995) *King Alfred the Great*. Oxford: Oxford University Press.

Social Exclusion Unit (1998) *Bringing Britain Together: a National Strategy for Neighbourhood Renewal*. London: Cabinet Office.

SocInfo Guide to IT Resources: http://www.stir.ac.uk/Departments/HumanSciences/SocInfo/

Spector, M. and Kitsuse, J.I. (1977) *Constructing Social Problems*. Menlo Park, CA: Cummings.

Spector, P.E. (1992) *Summated Rating Scale Construction*. Sage University Paper series on *Quantitative Applications in the Social Sciences No. 82*. Beverly Hills, CA and London: Sage.

Speller, G.M. (2000) 'A community in transition: a longitudinal study of place attachment and identity processes in the context of an enforced relocation'. Unpublished Thesis, University of Surrey, Guildford.

Spiegelberg, S. (1980) 'Phenomenology and observation', in B. Glassner (ed.), *Essential Interactionism*. London: Routledge and Kegan Paul.

Stacey, M. (1969) *Comparability in Social Research*. London: Heinemann.

Stacey, M. (1982) *Methods of Social Research*. Oxford: Pergamon Press.

Standard Occupational Classification (1990a) *Structure and Definition of Major, Minor and Unit Groups* (Vol. 1). London: HMSO.

Standard Occupational Classification (1990b) *Coding Index* (Vol. 2). London: HMSO.

Stinchcombe, A.L. (1968) *Constructing Social Theories*. Chicago: University of Chicago Press.

Stones, R. (ed.) (1998) *Key Sociological Thinkers*. London: Macmillan.

Strauss, A. (1987) *Qualitative Analysis for Social Scientists*. New York: Cambridge University Press.

Strauss, A. (1993) *Continual Permutations of Action*. Thousand Oaks, CA: Sage.

Strauss, A. and Corbin, J. (1990) *Basics of Qualitative Research*. Newbury Park, CA: Sage.

Strauss, A. and Corbin, J. (1994) 'Grounded theory methodology: an overview', in N.K. Denzin and Y.S. Lincoln (eds), *Handbook of Qualitative Research*. Thousand Oaks, CA: Sage.

Sudman, S. and Bradburn, N.M. (1974) *Response Effects in Surveys*. Chicago: Aldine.

Sudman, S. and Bradburn, N.M. (1983) *Asking Questions*. San Francisco: Jossey-Bass.

Summers, Gene F. (ed.) (1970) *Attitude Measurement*. Chicago: Rand McNally.

Swift, D. (1726) *Travels into Several Remote Regions of the World*. London: Benj. Motte.

Tamanaha, B. (1997) *Realistic Socio-Legal Theory*. Oxford: Clarendon Press.

Taylor, D. (1993) 'Minority environmental activism in Britain: from Brixton to the Lake District', *Qualitative Sociology*, 16(3): 263–95.

ten Have, P. (1999) *Doing Conversation Analysis: a Practical Guide*. London and Thousand Oaks, CA: Sage.

Thomas, P. (1987) 'The use of social research: myths and models', in M. Bulmer (ed.), *Social Science Research and Government: Comparative Essays on Britain and the United States*. Cambridge: Cambridge University Press, pp. 51–60.

Thomas, W.I. and Znaniecki, F. ([1918–20] 1958) *The Polish Peasant in Europe and America*. New York: Dover Publications.

Thompson, K. (1985) *Readings from Emile Durkheim*. Chichester: Ellis Horwood.

Thurstone, L.L. (1928) 'Attitudes can be measured', *American Journal of Sociology*, 33: 529–54. (Reprinted in Gene F. Summers (ed.) (1970) *Attitude Measurement*. Chicago: Rand McNally.)

Tizard, B. (1990) 'Research and policy: is there a link?', *The Psychologist*, 10: 435–40.

Tonkiss, F. (1998) 'Analysing discourse', in C. Seale (ed.), *Researching Society and Culture*. London: Sage.

Turner, B. (1981) 'Some practical aspects of qualitative data analysis: one way of organising the cognitive processes associated with the generation of grounded theory', *Quality and Quantity*, 15: 225–47.

Turner, R. (ed.) (1974) *Ethnomethodology*. Harmondsworth: Penguin.

Twigg, J. and Atkin, K. (1994) *Carers Perceived: Policy and Practice in Informal Care*. Buckingham: Open University Press.

Van Maanen, J. (1982) *Varieties of Qualitative Research*. Beverly Hills, CA: Sage.

Van Maanen, J. (1988) *Tales of the Field*. Chicago: University of Chicago Press.

Wadsworth, M.E.J. (1986) 'Serious illness in childhood and its association with later-life achievement', in R.G. Wilkinson (ed.), *Class and Health: Research and Longitudinal Data*. London: Tavistock.

Wadsworth, M.E.J. (1991) *The Imprint of Time: Childhood, History and Adult Life*. Oxford: Clarendon Press.

Wagner, J. (ed.) (1979) *Images of Information*. Ann Arbor, MI: UMI Books on Demand [London: Sage].

Walby, S. (1986) *Patriarchy at Work*. Cambridge: Polity Press.

Waldfogel, J. (1993) *Women Working for Less: a Longitudinal Analysis of the Family Gap*. Welfare State Programme Discussion Paper No. 93. London: London School of Economics.

Walker, G., Simmons, P., Wynne, B. and Irwin, A. (1998) *Public Perception of Risks Associated with Major Accident Hazards*. Sudbury, Suffolk: HSE Books.

Warwick, D.P. (1982) 'Types of harm in social research', in T.L. Beauchamp, R.R. Faden, R.J. Wallace and L. Walters (eds), *Ethical Issues in Social Science Research*. Baltimore, MD: Johns Hopkins University Press, pp. 101–24.

Weaver, T. (ed.) (1973) *To See Ourselves: Anthropology and Modern Social Issues*. Glenview, IL: Scott Foresman.

Weber, R. (1990) *Basic Content Analysis* (2nd edition). London: Sage.

Weick, K. (1995) *Sense-making in Organizations*. Thousand Oaks, CA: Sage.

Weiss, C. (1980) 'Knowledge creep and decision accretion', *Knowledge: Creation, Diffusion, Utilisation*, 1: 381–404.

Weiss, C. (1982) 'Policy research in the context of diffuse decision making', in D. Kallen, G. Kosse, H. Wagenaar, J. Klopkogge and M. Vorbeck (eds), *Social Science Research and Public Policy-Making: a Reappraisal*. Windsor: NFER/Nelson.

Weiss, C. (1986) 'The many meanings of research utilization', in M. Bulmer (ed.), *Social Science and Social Policy*. London: Allen and Unwin, pp. 31–40.

Weitzman, E. and Miles, M. (1995) *Computer Programs for Qualitative Data Analysis: a Software Source Book*. Thousand Oaks, CA: Sage.

Wellings, K., Field, J., Wadsworth, J., Johnson, A., Anderson, R. and Bradshaw, S. (1994) *The National Survey of Sexual Attitudes and Lifestyles*. Harmondsworth: Penguin.

Wetherell, M. (1998) 'Positioning and interpretative repertoires: conversation analysis and post-structuralism in dialogue', *Discourse and Society*, 9(3): 387–412.

Widdicombe, S. and Wooffitt, R. (1995) *The Language of Youth Subcultures: Social Identity in Action*. Hemel Hempstead: Harvester Wheatsheaf.

Williams, M. (2000) 'Social research – the emergence of a discipline?', *International Journal of Research Methodology*, 3(2): 157–66.

Williamson, J. (1978) *Decoding Advertisements*. London: Marion Boyars.

Wilson, P. and Elliot, D. (1987) 'An evaluation of the Postcode Address File and its use within OPCS', *Journal of the Royal Statistical Society*, Series A, 150(3): 230–40.

Witherspoon, S. and Martin, J. (1992) 'What do we mean by green?', in R. Jowell, L. Brook, G. Prior and B. Taylor (eds), *British Social Attitudes: the 9th Report*. Aldershot: Dartmouth.

Wittgenstein, L. (1953) *Philosophical Investigations* (ed. G. Anscombe). Oxford: Basil Blackwell.

Wolcott, H.F. (1990) *Writing-up Qualitative Research*. Newbury Park, CA: Sage.

Wooffitt, R. (1992) *Telling Tales of the Unexpected: the Organisation of Factual Discourse*. Hemel Hempstead: Harvester Wheatsheaf.

Wright, M. (1998) 'Do you have to be white to be green?', *Green Futures*, November/December: 24–8.

Wright Mills, C. (1959) *The Sociological Imagination*. Oxford: Oxford University Press.

Yin, R. (1984) *Case Study Research*. Beverly Hills, CA: Sage.

Zimmerman, D. and Pollner, M. (1973) 'The everyday world as a phenomenon', in J. Douglas (ed.), *Understanding Everyday Life: Towards the Reconstruction of Sociological Knowledge*. London: Routledge.

INDEX